JULIA
2010
The caretaker election

JULIA
2010
The caretaker election

Edited by Marian Simms and John Wanna

Australian
National
University

E PRESS

ANU
E PRESS

Published by ANU E Press
The Australian National University
Canberra ACT 0200, Australia
Email: anuepress@anu.edu.au
This title is also available online at http://epress.anu.edu.au

National Library of Australia Cataloguing-in-Publication entry

Title:	Julia 2010 : the caretaker election / edited by Marian Simms and John Wanna.
ISBN:	9781921862632 (pbk.) 9781921862649 (eBook)
Series:	ANZSOG series
Notes:	Includes bibliographical references.
Subjects:	Gillard, Julia. Elections--Australia--2010. Political campaigns--Australia--21st century. Australia--Politics and government--21st century.

Other Authors/Contributors:
      Simms, Marian.
      Wanna, John.

Dewey Number: 324.70994

Cover design and layout by ANU E Press

Printed by Griffin Press

This edition © 2012 ANU E Press

ACADEMY OF THE SOCIAL SCIENCES IN AUSTRALIA

Contents

Part 3. The Parties' Perspectives

Part 4. The States and Regions

Part 5. Policies and Issues

Part 6. Election Results

Acknowledgments

This project is the latest in a series of post-election workshops and books that emerged from the (then) Political Science Department in the Faculty of Arts at The Australian National University (ANU), commencing with the 1996 election workshop. The Academy of the Social Sciences in Australia has been a partner in this series since the 1998 election. The previous workshops have all resulted in publications: *The Politics of Retribution: The 1996 federal election* (Clive Bean, Scott Bennett, Marian Simms and John Warhurst [eds], Allen & Unwin, 1997); *Howard's Agenda: The 1998 Australian election* (Marian Simms and John Warhurst [eds], University of Queensland Press, 2000); *2001: The centenary election* (John Warhurst and Marian Simms [eds], University of Queensland Press, 2002); *Mortgage Nation: The 2004 Australian election* (Marian Simms and John Warhurst [eds], Australian Public Intellectuals Network, 2005); and a two-part special issue of *Australian Cultural History* (Marian Simms [ed.], 2009), *Kevin07: The 2007 Australian election*. The publications have been well reviewed by academics and well received by the general community. Influential writers such as Paul Kelly utilise the books as valuable sources for their interpretative histories of Australia.

The purpose of these projects is to bring together a team of about 22 to 25 comprising academics and practitioners to present and debate their points of view about the national election. The unique value of the Canberra location is that it provides useful synergies between town and gown, and facilitates practitioners providing important data—for example, their own quantitative and qualitative survey research—and receiving feedback from academics about the relevance of party research in terms of intellectual agendas. Equally, academics benefit from learning about the internal decision-making processes of election campaigning, and from accessing some of the internal party research findings, which provide useful insights that are often beyond the scope of more cash-strapped academic research. Normally, workshops have been held six to eight weeks after the national election when memories are still fresh and some data are available from empirical surveys.

The workshop and the book both include academics who are experts on the politics of their States; others who are leading experts on key interest groups and social movements, especially unions, business, migrants and women; writers on political leadership, political culture, campaigning, media—print, electronic and 'new'; and opinion polls, and the Australian Election Study group. The team includes leading specialists—for example, Marian Sawer (ANU), James Jupp (ANU), Clive Bean (Queensland University of Technology), Ian McAllister (ANU), Murray Goot (Macquarie University), John Wanna (ANU) and

Malcolm Mackerras (Australian Catholic University), as well as emerging scholars such as Peter Chen (University of Sydney). Party directors or their nominees from all parties with parliamentary representation were invited. Their workshop session has previously been reported in the media.

The two-day workshop to discuss the 2010 federal election was held at University House on 9 and 10 October 2010. Much of the lively discussion related to the role of the Labor Party's new leadership team, Julia Gillard and Wayne Swan, reasons for the failure of the Rudd team to retain its previous popularity, and the remarkable leadership transition of 24 June, which saw Rudd deposed as leader and Prime Minister. The first afternoon session featured presentations by the Labor Party's Elias Hallaj and by the Australian Greens Campaign Director, Ebony Green, and high-profile candidate (and former Australian Democrats Senator) Andrew Bartlett. Apologies were received from the Liberal Party Director and the Labor Party's Secretary, Karl Bitar. A paper was received from the Liberals for inclusion in the edited volume.

We are grateful to the practitioners for their continuing interest in this project and for the Academy of the Social Sciences in Australia Workshop Program for their recognition of the importance of this work. Valuable assistance was also provided by Deakin University's Areti Tsemelis, the Australia New Zealand School of Government's Sam Vincent, and Kirsty McLaren of the Australian National University.

This volume is dedicated to our friend and colleague Dr Dennis Woodward who passed away in May 2011 and whose knowledgeable and gentle presence will be sadly missed.

Marian Simms, Deakin University
John Wanna, ANU

Contributors

Editors

Marian Simms, Professor of Australian Studies, Deakin University

John Wanna, Sir John Bunting Chair of Public Administration, Australian National University (ANU)

Contributors

Andrew Bartlett, Greens candidate and former Australian Democrats Senator

Clive Bean, Professor of Political Science, Queensland University of Technology

Rodney Cavalier, political commentator and former NSW Minister

Peter John Chen, Lecturer in Politics, University of Sydney

Brian Costar, Professor of Victorian Parliamentary Democracy, Swinburne University of Technology

Geoffrey Craig, Associate Professor in Media, Film and Communication Studies, University of Otago

Jennifer Curtin, Senior Lecturer in Political Studies, University of Auckland

Nick Economou, Senior Lecturer in Politics, Monash University

Murray Goot, Australian Research Council Australian Professorial Fellow and Distinguished Professor, Department of Modern History, Politics and International Relations, Macquarie University

Geordan Graetz, Lecturer in Politics, Flinders University

Dean Jaensch, Emeritus Professor of Politics, Flinders University

Carol Johnson, Professor of Politics, University of Adelaide

James Jupp, Director, Centre for Immigration and Multicultural Studies, ANU

Elias Hallaj, ACT Branch Secretary, Australian Labor Party

Brian Loughnane, Federal Director, Liberal Party

Ian McAllister, Distinguished Professor of Political Science, ANU

Tony McCall, Senior Lecturer, School of Government, University of Tasmania

Malcolm Mackerras, Visiting Fellow in the Public Policy Institute, Australian Catholic University, Canberra Campus

Haydon Manning, Associate Professor of Politics, Flinders University

Narelle Miragliotta, Lecturer in Politics, Monash University

Robert Phiddian, Associate Professor in English, Flinders University

Geoffrey Robinson, Senior Lecturer in Australian Studies/Politics, Deakin University

Marian Sawer, Emeritus Professor, School of Politics and International Relations, ANU

Campbell Sharman, Adjunct Professor in Political Science, University of British Columbia (Canada)

Elaine Thompson, independent scholar, formerly Associate Professor in Politics, UNSW

Ian Ward, Reader in Politics, University of Queensland

John Warhurst, Emeritus Professor, School of Politics and International Relations, ANU

Abbreviations

AAP	Australian Associated Press
ABCC	Australian Building and Construction Commission
ABC	Australian Broadcasting Corporation
ACCI	Australian Chamber of Commerce and Industry
ACF	Australian Conservation Foundation
ACL	Australian Christian Lobby
ACT	Australian Capital Territory
ACTU	Australian Council of Trade Unions
ADFA	Australian Defence Force Academy
AEC	Australian Electoral Commission
AES	Australian Election Survey
AIG	Australian Industry Group
ALP	Australian Labor Party
AMEC	Association of Mining and Exploration
ANU	Australian National University
ASIO	Australian Security Intelligence Organisation
AWA	Australian Workplace Agreement
BCA	Business Council of Australia
BER	Building the Education Revolution
CDP	Christian Democratic Party
CFMEU	Construction, Forestry, Mining & Engineering Union
CLP	Country Liberal Party
COAG	Council of Australian Governments
CPRS	Carbon Pollution Reduction Scheme
DIAC	Department of Immigration and Citizenship
DLP	Democratic Labor Party
ERA	Equality Rights Alliance
ETS	Emissions Trading Scheme
ETU	Electricity Trades Union
FP	First Preference
FOI	Freedom of Information
GDP	Gross domestic product
GFC	Global Financial Crisis
GST	Goods and Services Tax

GTV	Group Ticket Vote
HECS	Higher Education Contribution Scheme
ILO	International labour Organisation
IND	Independent
IT	Information Technology
IPU	Inter-Parliamentary Union
LGAQ	Local Government Association of Queensland
LNP	Liberal National Party
MCA	Mining Council of Australia
MDBA	Murray Darling Basin Authority
MRRT	Minerals Resource Rent Tax
NBN	National Broadband Network
NESB	Non-English speaking background
NFF	National Farmers' Federation
NGO	Non-governmental organisation
NP	National Party
NT	Northern Territory
NSW	New South Wales
QRC	Queensland Resources Council
RAAF	Royal Australian Air Force
RSL	Returned Services League
SNS	Social Networking Services
SA	South Australia
SDA	Shop, Distributive and Allied Employees Association
TPP	Two party preferred
UN	United Nations
UNSW	University of New South Wales
VIC	Victoria
WA	Western Australia
WEL	Women's Electoral Lobby

1. The Caretaker Election of 2010: 'Julia 10' versus 'Tony 10' and the onset of minority government

Marian Simms and John Wanna

Labor emerged from the 2007 federal election with an overwhelming victory in the House of Representatives—commanding a substantial majority of some 16 seats over and above the Coalition plus the two Independents. Labor had captured an additional 23 seats across the land and secured swings towards it across all States (although in Western Australia Labor still managed to lose a seat). Prime Minister John Howard's stunning loss to Labor's Maxine McKew in Bennelong was a fascinating microcosm of the election, but the result was actually predicted by very few (and turned only on Greens preferences). The 'battle for Bennelong' subsequently became the leitmotiv of the election especially as it was only the second time since Federation that a prime minister had lost his seat. At the time, it was widely believed that the 2007 election campaign had become 'a testing ground for the Liberal leadership team of John Howard and Peter Costello and a proving ground for the new Opposition leadership team of Kevin Rudd and Julia Gillard' (Simms 2009a, 2009b). And the Liberals were found wanting by an electorate eager for a change of government.

Labor's gains in the Senate were more modest, with an additional four seats captured to bring Labor up to 32 seats but still needing the support of the Greens (with five seats) as well as Family First and the Independent Nick Xenophon. New South Wales, Queensland and Victoria divided their six seats between the major parties. In Queensland, Ron Boswell was re-elected on a separate Nationals ticket. The Australian Labor Party (ALP) was weaker in South Australia and Western Australia; and the Liberals were weaker in South Australia and Tasmania. Overall, the major-party vote in the Senate was higher than at any time in the preceding decade. In South Australia, an Independent, Nick Xenophon, and a Green, Sarah Hanson-Young, were elected to fill the fifth and sixth quotas. In Tasmania, Greens leader Bob Brown was re-elected, and in the west a Green was also elected as the sixth senator. The Australian Democrats—first formed in 1977 and, at the height of their influence, controlling nine Senate seats—had entirely disappeared.

In office, Labor had attempted an ambitious political and policy agenda (see Aulich 2010; Wanna 2010) driven largely by the somewhat mercurial interests of the Prime Minister and exacerbated by his renowned short attention span when dealing with fluctuating priorities. Rudd was accused of not providing a coherent strategy or 'guiding thread' to his government (Burchell 2008) and of repeatedly initiating new agendas but then not completing them; he was famously portrayed as a 'home handyman in a house full of half-finished jobs, while still eager to begin more' (Phillip Coorey, cited in Marr 2010, 73). Arguably, all first-term governments take time to settle, but not all deliberately crank up the policy expectations as high as did the Rudd Government over its short, two-and-a-half-year lifespan. Rudd made governing a highwire act, with all the risks associated with such performances.

After being commissioned in December 2007, Labor's unique challenge once it settled into office was to manage its escalating policy commitments whilst facing the sudden onset of the global financial crisis (GFC) of 2008–09. Two timely stimulus packages injecting about $60 billion in three successive tranches were critical in maintaining effective demand and reassuring business and consumer confidence. But once the eye of the crisis passed, Labor found itself with substantial deficits (almost $85 billion over two years, meaning no new money for programs) and mounting debt levels of up to $365 billion. Some stimulus injection programs with a 'long tail' were compromised in implementation, including the $2.7 billion home insulation program, the green loans program, and the $16 billion Building the Education Revolution (BER) school infrastructural projects (where value for money was widely questioned). Suddenly, Rudd was being accused of being profligate and irresponsible and of spending for the sake of it by a resurgent Opposition now under its third leader, Tony Abbott. Rudd was also facing political difficulties in getting his carbon pollution reduction scheme (CPRS) into law, being twice rejected by the Senate (at the time it was seen as a 'manageable stuff up'; Penberthy 2010).

The Prime Minister opted not to call a double dissolution but instead chose to jettison the initiative entirely. By April, Newspoll data indicated that New South Wales and Queensland were 'turning to the Liberals' and Labor's support was 'fractured' in Queensland (Shanahan 2010, 1). Labor's primary vote had fallen to 40 per cent. As Kevin Rudd began the election year of 2010, writing and launching a children's picture book about *Jasper and Abby*, the poll ratings for 'Kevin 07' began to decline dramatically, never to recover. In contrast, in the first three months after Abbott's election as Liberal leader in December 2010, the Coalition had 'picked up support in every mainland State and every age group' (Shanahan 2010, 1).

When some of Labor's factional leaders moved against Kevin Rudd in June 2010, an early election was suddenly on the agenda—supposedly to give the new Prime Minister, Julia Gillard, a mandate in her own right; she wanted to be an 'elected prime minister'. The subsequent election turned into an odd affair, showing that the historic decision (or rash gamble) to replace a first-term prime minister with his loyal deputy leader was not the circuit-breaker predicted by Labor strategists and some media pundits. Under Gillard, Labor's primary vote at the election sank to 37.99 per cent—a substantial swing away from the party of 5.4 per cent. This compared with a primary vote of 43.62 per cent for the Coalition even though the conservatives managed only a small positive swing of 1.5 per cent. In two-party preferred terms, Labor nosed in front with just 50.1 per cent to the Coalition's 49.9 per cent. It was an electoral mauling for both sides of politics, with perhaps only the Greens (recording 11.76 per cent and a 4 per cent swing) and a few Independents emerging as the unlikely winners (and 'king-makers').

How well the major protagonists managed the unique combination of events will be answered in the six parts of this book, which draw upon a range of perspectives from a diverse array of experts including some of the actual players in the fray of the battle. There are many questions that inform the in-depth analysis and help explain the unusual outcome. Some of the more thematic and recurring questions are the following.

- Was leadership the pivotal issue in the campaign? (And how did the electorate warm to the first-ever female Prime Minister?)

- How did the change of leadership on both sides of politics (from Malcolm Turnbull to Tony Abbott in the Liberal camp, and from Kevin Rudd to Julia Gillard in Labor's) influence the campaign and the eventual outcome? (And were the abrupt changes of leadership on both sides unsettling to the electoral nerve?)

- How did the parties gear up for the election and pitch their appeal to voters (especially given that they were seemingly unprepared and without much room to manoeuvre)?

- How did the alleged 'spoiler tactics' of Kevin Rudd and his supporters affect the election? (The Coalition maintained a fairly disciplined campaign, in contrast with Labor, which appeared desperate and divided.)

- How did the various States and regions of Australia respond to the political messages of the electoral protagonists (especially given the two-speed economy, changing State political complexions and regional sentiments of neglect)?

- How did the various media, cartoonists and commentators represent the campaign and what was the influence of opinion polls, the diagnoses of focus groups and the hastily organised town-hall meetings on the protagonists and on the sizeable proportion of undecided voters throughout the campaign?

- What happened to the battle over policy ideas in the campaign? (Was the election fought about nothing in particular except for differences over a couple of policy proposals?)

- How did various social movements and sectional interest groups respond to the electoral contest fought out between two inexperienced but determined leaders?

These questions will be approached in a range of complementary ways by various authors in each section, as outlined below. Sources will include interviews and observations; published material, including televised interviews, transcripts of speeches and published opinion polls, internal party research, the Australian Election Survey (AES) and aggregate data, including previous results and census data.

In Part 1, Marian Simms, Rodney Cavalier and Carol Johnson present their overview assessments of the campaign, including a diary of events, important time lines and campaign highlights, the perception of a leadership vacuum or flawed governmental performance, and the ideological contest. They quickly cut to the essential explanations of why we ended with a 'caretaker election' and why a hung parliament resulted from the contest.

In Part 2, focusing on the media coverage, public events and polling, Peter Chen traces the influence of new social media in reinforcing voting preferences. Murray Goot tries to explain the incredible accuracy of the opinion polls and the fact that almost all the reputable polls converged within a very narrow band of prediction. Geoff Craig records one of the more noteworthy aspects of the campaign: the resort to impromptu town-hall meetings with non-aligned voters held in sporting clubs and halls. Haydon Manning and Robert Phiddian present their selection of the best or most evocative cartoons covering the poll.

Part 3 brings to the fore the perspectives of the campaign directors from the major parties. Brian Loughnane traces the Liberal strategy, which he considers stuck to plan and was relatively successful. It managed to harness the strengths of Tony Abbott while effectively containing his weaknesses, and at the same time kept the focus on the negative aspects of Gillard's incumbency. Elias Hallaj from the ALP recalls how Labor was knocked off its strategy while other distractions occupied centre stage and were hard to budge. These distractions included the early phoney campaigning that was seen as too dull and stage-managed (leading to the release of the 'Real Julia'), the damage of the 'leaks' to Labor's message, the distraction of having the former Prime Minister gain considerable media attention, and the final 'end run', which descended into meaningless gimmicks. Andrew Bartlett explains the Greens' campaign strategy as focussed on the Senate and on developing a strong base vote across a number of seats, notably Brisbane, not just a Senate plus Melbourne approach.

Nine chapters in Part 4 discuss the detailed campaigns and results in the six States and two Territories, plus a special examination of the rural and regional dimensions of the campaign. Labor managed to attract swings towards itself in Victoria, South Australia and Tasmania; the Coalition received significant swings towards it in Queensland, New South Wales, Western Australia, the Northern Territory and a small increment in the Australian Capital Territory. In the important measure of changing seats, the Liberals won 11 from Labor but lost one in Western Australia to the Nationals. Seven of the Liberal wins were in Queensland seats, two in New South Wales and one each in Western Australia and the Northern Territory. Labor lost 13 seats (11 seats net), 11 of which were lost to the Liberals, and one each to an Independent (Andrew Wilkie in Dennison, Tasmania) and the Greens (Adam Bandt in Melbourne, Victoria). Labor also won three seats, all from the Liberals: two in Victoria and one in New South Wales. The Nationals won one seat from Labor and one from the Liberals (O'Connor in Western Australia), but lost one to the Independent Robert Oakeshott (a former NSW Independent and National Party MP) who had captured Lyne at the by-election of September 2008. Four seats were retaken by former members who recontested (Ross Vasta, Teresa Gambaro and Warren Entsch in Queensland and Louise Markus in New South Wales). Interestingly, the swing against Labor was greater in the metropolitan seats than in the non-metropolitan ones, while the Liberals and Nationals largely held their own.

In Part 5, we examine a selection of important policy areas and issues, including: gender issues, immigration and ethnic influences, the economy through the eyes of business and the unions, the environment, and finally the significance of religion in the campaign. Overall in the 2010 election, gender was a factor in the debates due to Julia Gillard being Australia's first woman Prime Minister, and because Tony Abbott was often perceived as having a 'problem with women voters' (Shanahan 2010, 1). Immigration and refugees featured in the discourses and in the Coalition's advertising, and Gillard was forced to commit to getting tougher on boat people if not stopping the boats entirely. The 'boats' issue was one that Labor was perceived as having difficulty managing. The unions and business groups played a lesser role in the 2010 election than in the 2007 'WorkChoices' election, and religion and the environment were more muted than they had previously been.

The final section, Part 6, commences with an assessment of the electoral results in historical perspective, comparing the close result in 2010 with the similar outcome in 1961. Malcolm Mackerras traces the detailed results according to the seats won and lost, commenting on the pattern of seats to change hands in both directions that has generally applied since 1972. He analyses the representational patterns in the Senate where the larger parties are over-represented. Clive Bean and Ian McAllister's chapter presents the findings of the 2010 AES, and the key features were that Labor's support had dropped off with the old and the young, and that the economy was the most significant issue across the board. Traditionally, Labor had scored well with young voters but in 2010 it was losing them to the Greens. Finally, Brian Costar describes the 17 days it took to form a minority government, between 21 August and 7 September. He recounts the pork-barrelling, the deals and negotiations, and the limited reforms proposed to parliamentary procedure. He also briefly canvasses the stability and likely longevity of the minority Gillard second government.

Julia Gillard had wanted to be an 'elected prime minister', yet she led Labor into minority government—interestingly, with one seat less than the Coalition parties. The primary vote of Labor, as incumbents, collapsed to 37.99 per cent, sinking back to the poor results it had achieved in Opposition in 2001 and 2004. Yet, as Paul Kelly (2010, 1) reminded his readers immediately after the election and while the final results were still unclear, the critical issue in determining government was seats, not votes. In this respect, Gillard's achievements in cobbling together a disparate group of one Green, two rural 'mavericks' and the enigmatic Andrew Wilkie cannot be underestimated. The Greens victory in Lindsay Tanner's vacated seat of Melbourne was a historic win as no minor party had previously achieved a breakthrough into the House of Representatives at a general election in the post–World War II era.

The Gillard Government has been in office for just over a year and, despite media reports of backbenchers—on both sides—feeling left out and apparently envious of the ready access accorded to the Independents and the Greens, the governing arrangements appear stable. One of the reasons Tony Windsor and Rob Oakeshott gave in supporting a Gillard government was that in their opinion it was more likely to deliver stability and integrity. But there are difficult days ahead for Prime Minister Gillard, not least in terms of securing budgets, getting contentious policies adopted by the legislature (such as a carbon reduction tax, the Murray–Darling Basin plan, flood levies, the new resource tax and tax reform more generally), and all the while managing Labor's nervous caucus. Her forays into international relations might assist her to develop a more rounded image as a national leader, but she will have to deliver on the domestic front to win plaudits and keep her opponents at bay. Her principal opponent, Tony Abbott, remains trapped in the politics of adversarial campaigning, looking to oppose the government on almost every issue. Even though the next election is not due until 2013, it is beginning to look likely that the next election will be a rerun of 2010, even if the results next time around might play out differently.

References

Aulich, Chris. 2010. 'It was the best of times; it was the worst of times'. In Chris Aulich and Mark Evans (eds). *The Rudd Government*. Canberra: ANU E Press.

Burchell, David. 2008. 'A thousand days'. *The Weekend Australian*, 22–23 March.

Kelly, Paul. 2010. 'Seats, not votes, the critical measure'. *The Australian*, 23 August, 1.

Marr, David. 2010. *Power Trip: The political journey of Kevin Rudd*. Quarterly Essays No. 38. Melbourne: Black Inc.

Penberthy, David. 2010. 'Why Kevin Rudd will still win the election'. *The Punch*, viewed 21 April 2011, <http:www.the punch.com.au/articles/why-kevin-rudd-will-still-win-the-election/>

Shanahan, Dennis. 2010. 'Rudd faces struggle in key states: NSW, Queensland turning to Liberals'. *The Australian*, 5 April, 1.

Simms, Marian. 2009a. 'Preface: Kevin 07—the 2007 Australian election, part 1'. *Australian Cultural History* 27(2): 79–83.

Simms, Marian. 2009b. 'The campaigns'. *Australian Cultural History* 27(2): 87–96.

Wanna, John. 2010. 'Issues and agendas for the term'. In Chris Aulich and Mark Evans (eds). *The Rudd Government*. Canberra: ANU E Press.

Part 1. Leaders, Ideologies and the Campaign

2. Diary of an Election

Marian Simms

That the 2010 election was unusual is not in dispute. The 'sacking' of a prime minister during an election year, the decision to go to the polls only 22 days after the leadership change, a controversial campaign marred by serial leaks from within the government, a change in the campaign slogan and strategy by the government, a low-key campaign launch, and a series of ad-hoc decisions regarding debates and community forums—these were some of its defining features. Moreover, the election result was so close as to create a further 17 days of indecision and a total of 24 days before the formal creation of a minority government under Julia Gillard's leadership.

This chapter argues that drawing upon New Zealand's experience, the term 'interregnum' captures the nature of the period. Interregnum refers to the time in the lead-up to the election, the campaign itself, the declaration of the result and the swearing in of the government (see Simms 2011). It incorporates a caretaker period and assumes that there could be a delay in forming government. The interregnum idea also includes the immediate pre-election period. It de-emphasises the incumbency factor, and includes the suggestion of tentativeness and searching for new rules.

In Australian federal politics, discussions about the 'caretaker' issues normally refer to the campaign period itself, and the brief period between the announcement of the election and the dissolution of the Parliament. The idea of the interregnum moves away from the traditional idea of the campaign 'map' where the Prime Minister calls an election, based on a well-developed strategy, and implements this via a well-choreographed sequence of events. Since 1993, Australian prime ministers have announced their intention to call an election outside the Parliament, and while the Parliament is not in session. The writs are issued and the nation moves into campaign mode. The map includes a leaders' debate and well-timed policy launches, culminating—usually in week three—with the formal party launches. In the final week, the Leader of the Opposition and the Prime Minister separately address the National Press Club.

This caretaker election commenced with the Prime Minister deliberately positioning herself in caretaker mode, by refusing to move into the Lodge and by indicating at the outset that an election would need to be held to vindicate her position, and to provide a mandate (see Table 2.1).

Table 2.1 Labor's Early Interregnum, June–July 2010

24 June 2010	Julia Gillard replaces Kevin Rudd as ALP leader	Government 'losing its way under Rudd', cancels mining tax ads and reviewspolicies on asylum-seekers and climate change Gillard indicates she will not move into the Lodge unless elected
6 July	Julia Gillard announces the 'Timor solution' of an offshore processing centre in the region in response to questions about 'boat people' in Penrith	See *The Age* [Insight], 10 July 2010
7 July	Julia Gillard visits border-patrol vessels in Darwin accompanied by David Bradbury, ALP MP for Lindsay in Sydney's west	See *The Age* [Insight], 10 July 2010
15 July 2010	Julia Gillard at the Press Club challenged by Laurie Oakes' question regarding the Rudd deal to step down	Leak No. 1

The interregnum can be divided into four stages: the first, before the election was called (24 June – 16 July); the second, the initial part of the campaign after the election was called—dominated by crises, leaks and the drop in the opinion polls (17 July – 28–31 July); the third, marked by the emergence of the 'real' Julia and ending with the election (1 August – 21 August); and the fourth and final stage, where the crafting of a majority occurred (22 August – 14 September). The middle, second and third periods—the campaign—are potentially divisible in a number of ways. The sharp drop in the ALP's opinion poll results (31 July) and the emergence of the so-called 'new' or 'real' Julia are defining events that occurred at about the same time. Julia Gillard's well-crafted response to Leak No. 4 (see Table 2.2) was on 28 July. Hence, stage two is from 17 to 31 July; and stage three is 1 August – 21 August.

The focus here is on the second and third stages of the interregnum; and the first and fourth stages are briefly outlined in Tables 2.1 and 2.3, and are dealt with by other chapters in this volume (Chapters 3 and 28). This chapter relies on close analysis of New Limited's *Sky TV News* (Foxtel and Austar) programs, including its interactive news features and blogs; *ABC News, 7.30 Report* and *Lateline*; and the Sydney and Melbourne newspapers.[1] As in 2007, in 2010, the role of *Sky News* provided an attractive tool for campaigning, a tool for commentators and a challenge for campaigners. Whilst the audience size was limited, *Sky 24-Hour News* provided a greater immediacy and allowed a dialogue between the campaigners that could be picked up by other players and media outlets, and thus set the agenda. For example, Julia Gillard's interview with David Speers on the first day of the campaign tackled climate change, and, while

---

1 *Sky News* transcripts are available for *The Nation, Australian Agenda* and Sky Business Channel's *The Perrett Report*.

Gillard indicated broad support or even commitment to a price on carbon, she expressed concern about the lack of community-based consensus on the issue, and suggested that it would be essential in order to forge a workable policy (*Sky News*, 17 July 2010). Later in the campaign, Kerry O'Brien quoted from George Brandis's interview on *Sky News* (we 'cannot be certain when the budget will be back in surplus') to ask Tony Abbott for 'clarification' on the Coalition's fiscal policies (*7.30 Report*, ABC TV, 17 August 2010).

Stage Two

On Saturday, 17 July, Julia Gillard flew to Canberra to seek the dissolution of the Parliament, and then gave a press conference, announcing the election date of 21 August and outlining her rationale (see Table 2.1). This speech (Gillard 2010d) built upon the economic reform agenda and 'moving forward' theme of the 15 July Press Club speech (Gillard 2010c); the 'refugees' and 'sustainability' concerns of the Lowy Institute speech of 6 July (Gillard 2010b); and the political legitimacy or 'mandate' theme of her press conference of 24 June (Gillard 2010a).

Tony Abbott's response was immediate, stating that, if elected, he would: 'stand up for Australia', 'stop new taxes', 'stop the boats' and 'stop the waste'. He also announced a three-year moratorium on industrial relations and that he would not be changing the current law; yet he remained a 'conviction politician'.

The first fumble of the campaign occurred in a *Sky News* interview with Eric Abetz on 17 July, with him saying that industrial relations could be 'tweaked' through ministerial regulations, without recourse to amending the legislation.

From the outset, the electronic and print media commentary focused on the geography of the campaign, and the precise mapping of the leaders' movements became a feature of the commentary. A favourite metaphor was 'battleground'— applied to the States (John Roskam, Sky TV, 17 July 2010) and 'seats' (Bruce Hawker, Sky TV, 17 July 2010). This early focus on the local, regional and State levels was significant, for it marked a shift away from the overarching sense of a presidential-style generic national campaign. Both leaders spent time in Queensland in the first few days, and then in the western suburbs of Sydney.

Table 2.2 Key Dates in the 2010 Election Campaign

Date	Event	Comments	Media coverage highlights
17 July	Election called for 21 August		
19 July	Writs issued for the election		
19 July	Rolls close for new electors		
19 July	Tony Abbott's comment: WorkChoices is 'dead, buried and cremated'		
22 July	Rolls close for electors updating details		
22 July	Campaigning suspended for digger's funeral		
23 July	Kevin Rudd denies ignoring security concerns by sending chief of staff to National Security meetings	Leak No. 2 via the ABC	
23 July	Julia Gillard announces policy of citizens' assembly on climate change		
24 July	Gillard announces second-hand car trade-in discount		
24 July	GetUp!'s High Court challenge to early roll closure		
25 July	The leaders' debate	The 'worm' supports Gillard, but most commentators on Sky and Nine see Abbott as the better performer	News Limited press focus on Gillard's 'ear lobes'
26 July	Abbott's first 7.30 Report interview		
27 July	Cabinet leak story by Laurie Oakes (Nine News) and Peter Hartcher (*Sydney Morning Herald*)	That Gillard opposed pension increases and the introduction of paid parental leave in Cabinet discussions Leak No. 3	*The Australian* promotes Newspoll results: 'Labor's core intact'
28 July	Gillard's rebuttal of the claim, suggesting people should examine her record	Previously, Gillard had cited Cabinet confidentiality in neither confirming nor denying the claim	Peter Hartcher's comment: 'prime ministerial image is cracking and peeling' David Speers: Gillard was 'impressive'

Date	Event	Comments	Media coverage highlights
29 July	Belinda Neal ends speculation she will contest Robertson as an Independent	Preselection won by Deborah O'Neill in March 2010	
29 July	Kevin Rudd admitted to hospital		
30 July	Spokesperson announces Kevin Rudd will resume campaigning next week		
31 July	Another leak: that Gillard sent former security guard to National Security meetings	Leak No. 4 via *The Australian*	*The Australian* headline: 'Bodyguard deputising for Gillard' Dennis Shanahan notes that the 'leaks are working for Abbott'
31 July	Labor loses lead in Nielsen poll for two-party preferred vote		
1 August	Greens policy launch		
2 August	The 'real Julia' appears		
3 August	No interest rate rise		
4 August	Labor loses 6 % in two-party preferred vote in one week, and 7 % in prime ministerial approval rating according to Newspoll		*The Australian* promotes Newspoll results (Qld, NSW voters turn on Labor) *The Age* criticises Abbott's parental-leave plans *Herald Sun* praises Abbott's 'gold-collar workers' scheme' to employ older workers
6 August	High Court decision to support GetUp! challenge to Howard electoral law		
6 August	Release of Orgill (Interim) Report on BER scheme	Finds programs meeting overall objectives	Negative media in *The Australian, Sydney Morning Herald* around Julia's 'pork pies'
7 August	Gillard and Rudd 'meeting' in Brisbane		
8 August	Coalition launch in Brisbane		'He's [Abbott] tough and targeted but has no new message', Paul Kelly (*The Australian*, 9 August 2010)
11 August	Gillard/Keneally announce Epping–Parramatta rail link		
11 August	Community forum in western Sydney		

Date	Event	Comments	Media coverage highlights
12 August	Gillard launches Tasmanian broadband		
15 August	'Huge swing to Abbott'	Galaxy poll in 20 marginal seats	*Sunday Herald Sun* (15 August)
16 August	Labor launch in Brisbane	Jobs, economy and health Thirtieth day of campaign	
17 August	Gillard's comment about the republic		
17 August	Abbott at the Press Club	The monarchy 'ongoing' (response to Gillard)	
18 August	Second community forum, Brisbane		
19 August	Gillard at the Press Club		
19–20 August	Abbott's non-stop campaign	3AM talkback radio	
21 August	Polling day		

For the first few days, the main policy and political issues attracting comment were whether a Coalition government would reintroduce WorkChoices—as in Abbott's famous 'dead, buried and cremated' comment on Melbourne radio 3AW; and the relations between the ALP and the Greens regarding preferencing arrangements. Gillard's first of three interviews on the *7.30 Report* covered climate change, and the relations with the Greens. Bob Brown made his first major intervention by rather curiously suggesting (on *Lateline*) that he had no advice and that people were free to preference as they wish. It was Tony Abbott's interview with Neil Mitchell on Melbourne radio on 19 August declaring the end of WorkChoices (featuring a signed contract to that effect) that was to replay throughout the election campaign and into the 'politics' of the new Gillard Government (see, for example, *The Age* 2010c). The radio interview was photographed for the print and electronic media.[2]

The debate about debating—which would be a feature of the campaign—started, however, by focusing on the clash with a particularly popular commercial television show, *MasterChef*, and the debate time was shifted to 6.30 pm to avoid a clash.

---

2   According to *The Age* (2010c): 'WorkChoices is the Coalition's zombie policy. It won't go away despite Opposition Leader Tony Abbott repeatedly declaring it "dead, buried and cremated" before August's federal election.'

While the print media focused on the two major-party leaders, the other media utilised a range of party spokespeople. Notable were the ALP's Chris Bowen (Finance and Superannuation Minister and campaign spokesman), Bruce Hawker (ALP political consultant) and Paul Howes (Australian Workers' Union: AWU); and on the other side, Coalition spokesman Andrew Robb, Senators Eric Abetz and George Brandis and former Victorian Liberal Party President Michael Kroger. Paul Howes' colourful reference to Abbott's radio contract as reflective of 'a Newt Gingrich contract style campaign' was a case in point of his attacking style (*Lateline*, ABC TV, 20 July 2010). Chris Bowen's (in AFL terms: the 'smiling assassin') reference to Abbott as a 'WorkChoices addict' was equally biting (*Lateline*, ABC TV, 20 July 2010). From the other side of politics, Andrew Robb's comments were more measured if equally critical as he spoke of the need for cuts of $1.2 billion from the Commonwealth bureaucracy. His comments were in tune with the first Liberal advertisement that under Labor there would be 'more waste, more debt, more taxes'; whereas the first advertisement from the Labor side (AWU) was colourful: an *Addams Family* spoof on the Coalition reintroducing WorkChoices.

Victoria became an issue a few days into the campaign; while Abbott had visited Melbourne twice in the first three to four days of the campaign, the Coalition had not established its campaign headquarters (normally in Melbourne) by 21 July. Andrew Robb was forced to defend this delay and to explain why candidates had not been preselected in a number of seats.

The media interest in State and regional questions firmed early with the focus on key marginal seats.[3] Sky had started its analysis on day one of the campaign with an overview of the raft of key seats in New South Wales and particularly Queensland and the impact of the redistribution. The ABC picked up on key marginal seats with a detailed case-study approach, commencing in the ultra-marginal Victorian seat of McEwen, with the retirement of the Liberal's Fran Bailey.

Back in Sydney, Julia Gillard's carefully crafted style moved into attack mode when, speaking at an education conference, she said 'Abbott can't be trusted' and launched National Trade Cadetships (*Sky National News*, 21 July 2010). That day, immigration was on the agenda for Gillard in a radio interview on 2UE, in which she was quizzed over the details of her immigration policy.

---

3   *Lateline* on 'marginal seats' (ABC TV, 20 July 2010). In McEwen (Vic.): MP Fran Bailey was retiring, and the seat was being contested by Rob Mitchell (Labor) and Cam Caine (Liberals); bushfires were a major concern, as well as the fact that 10 000 people had moved to the area since 2007. There was a 32-vote margin in 2007—the narrowest in the country, with five recounts and a High Court challenge. In Dawson (Qld): the ALP MP was retiring, and Mike Barker, Mayor of Whitsundays, was standing for the ALP; the LNP candidate was Mackay councillor George Christensen.

In Brisbane, Tony Abbott announced a school initiative tax rebate, in conjunction with Christopher Pyne, who presented himself as a father of four. Questions were subsequently raised by the media about the Coalition's focus upon the marital status of their leadership group—as implying some lack on Gillard's side.

Yet to appear on the *7.30 Report*, Abbott, on 21 July, made an appearance on the popular live Melbourne TV show *Hey Hey It's Saturday* with Kylie Minogue— an opportunity Julia Gillard had declined (Shepherd 2010).

Then on 22 July the campaign was suspended for a digger's funeral. Yet the involvement by Australia in the Afghan war attracted little discussion, apart from the Greens' wish to call a parliamentary debate on the subject.

Labor resumed its campaign on 23 July, in Brisbane, with the announcement of the new climate change policy of a citizens' assembly; the policy was pre-released for that day's media. It seemed a sign that Labor was grasping the nettle and producing a coordinated media campaign around an important policy—one that Gillard had indicated (on 24 June) was one of her priority issues.

Abbott meanwhile had travelled to Perth to keep an appointment at the Liberals' State Conference, and to proselytise about the evils of the mining tax. Having emphasised his credentials as a parent earlier in the campaign, he now chose to speak of the 'women in his life'. Deputy leader, Julie Bishop, followed up on this theme.

Perhaps this discussion of gender was in response to the morning's Nielsen poll showing a 54–46 gender gap among women favouring Gillard? These polls are normally previewed on the Friday-night edition of *Lateline*. Friday's Morgan Poll (*Sky News* 23 July 2010) also showed a gender gap. A Westpoll based on four marginal seats showed strong movement to the ALP; *Sky News* referred to the 'female vote', especially in Canning, with former State MP Alannah MacTiernan ahead and the sitting MHR, Sharyn Jackson, in Hasluck on 54:46 two-party preferred. The *Today* show (Channel Nine 2010) decided that Abbott might have a problem with women.

Whilst the gender gap was working in Gillard's favour at this stage of the campaign (see Stewart 2010), her new policy initiatives were, however, poorly received, and to commentators such as Michelle Grattan (2010) suggested a lack of policy capacity. The ill-fated climate change assembly policy was followed quickly (on 24 July in Brisbane) by another policy initiative: a $2000 rebate for second-hand cars traded in for new cars—criticised almost immediately as a copy of the 'cash for clunkers' policy of US President Barack Obama.

In the lead-up to the National Press Club debate scheduled for Sunday, 25 July, activist group GetUp!'s High Court challenge to the early roll closure—based on Howard legislation that had not been amended by the ALP due to the numbers in the Senate—was launched.[4] It had to await an actual challenge by late enrolees. The Press Club debate is the subject of another chapter in this volume (Chapter 7), so will be outlined only briefly (see also Gilbert 2010a). The Liberals won the coin toss and decided Julia Gillard would speak first (announced 24 July). There was little of substance in the debate. Julia Gillard announced $6.8 billion to support retrenched workers. Tony Abbott announced his 'Action Contract' with the Australian people; mentioning gender, he argued that the Prime Minister is elected on 'ability, not gender'.

The Sky TV forum noted Julia Gillard arrived at between 3 and 4 pm and Tony Abbott at 4 pm. In its backgrounder, presenter Ashleigh Gillon commented on the stage-managed nature of Julia Gillard's campaign, with only one street walk (in Leichhardt in Sydney), conceding, however, that 'a lot of women' were going up to Julia. The Sky studio panel split, predictably on partisan lines. John Hewson said 'the debate was hers [Gillard's] to lose', and Bruce Hawker spoke of the good momentum achieved over the past five days.

The Sky panel gave the debate to Abbott; a lone dissenter from *The Daily Telegraph* said that Julia Gillard 'engaged and responded' and was the victor by a narrow margin. Gillon commented that it was stage-managed and dull. Tony Abbott was 'not convincing' on industrial relations, and his 'human side' was not on display.

The classic comment—that there was 'no knockout blow'—came from the Sky compere, Kieran Gilbert, and overall the panel thought Gillard should have been more attacking especially over Abbott's record as Health Minister. David Speers, who had hosted the actual debate, saw Julia Gillard as 'very polished' and 'more confident' than Abbott, who read his speech.

Over on Channel Nine's *60 Minutes*, of the panel of Laurie Oakes, Helen McCabe (Editor, *Australian Women's Weekly*) and the famous worm, Oakes thought Abbott performed better. McCabe noted the gender gap of the worm: overall, the worm scored Julia Gillard 63 per cent and Tony Abbott 37 per cent. Sixty per cent of women preferred Julia Gillard and 61 per cent of men, and 39 per cent of men preferred Tony Abbott and 34 per cent of women.

The gender theme continued, but not in a positive way, when the next day (Monday, 26 July) Julia Gillard was in Tasmania (Bass) where questions regarding her spouse ('where was Tim?') overshadowed her health announcements of $96 million for emergency doctors and nurses.

---

4   Closed Monday 8 pm, and change of address Thursday, 8 pm; writs issued on Monday, 19 July.

Tony Abbott was in Brisbane (Petrie) with his wife, who runs an early childhood centre, and stated that the best way of boosting the population was children.

One new announcement was the restoration of tax indexation to the childcare rebate, and Abbott referred to the previous week's announcement of tax rebates for all educational expenses, noting the 'cost of living pressures' for 'struggling families'. He appeared on the *7.30 Report* to be examined over his immigration policy, and could 'not specify exact cuts'. Host Kerry O'Brien said that the figures were trending down after the high levels of the Howard years. Abbott looked uncomfortable.

Questioning of Gillard about her marital status continued in Brisbane the next day when she announced a 'male-friendly' policy of more investment in suicide prevention, saying: 'We want to reach out to men.' Asked whether she was getting married, she replied: 'personal decisions are for personal reasons.' On the *7.30 Report* (ABC TV, 27 July 2010) that evening, Bob Brown expressed 'disgust' at the personal attacks on Gillard, and the ABC's political reporter Heather Ewart claimed that voters were turned off by personal attacks and negative campaigning.

Tony Abbott, also in Queensland, campaigning in Dawson, returned to policy and announced suspension of marine protection legislation to 'open up jobs'.

The big news on 27 July was the 'leak story' by Laurie Oakes (Nine Network) and Peter Hartcher (*Sydney Morning Herald*) that Gillard opposed pension increases and the introduction of paid parental leave (see also Gilbert 2010b). Her initial response that day was to declare that Cabinet discussions were confidential. The next day in her home town of Adelaide, she called a press conference to deal with allegations of her opposing parental leave and pension increases in the Rudd Cabinet. She denied having opposed them: 'I'm denying that.' The claim was 'not credible', based on everything about her, in terms of '[w]ho I am, and what I have done'; she said her interest was in 'the cost'. The subsequent headlines and front pages in the tabloids were extraordinarily critical of Gillard, and *The Daily Telegraph* (29 July 2010) digitally altered her image to age it 25 years. In a subsequent *Sky Agenda* interview with Peter Hartcher, who broke the Gillard Cabinet story in the *Sydney Morning Herald*, David Speers, conducting the interview, said her response was 'impressive'.

Meanwhile, Tony Abbott had commenced his action-hero phase of the campaign and was interviewed discussing tax policy reform (that is, personal tax cuts and family cuts and indexation) while travelling on the Manly ferry in Sydney.

In an attempt to provide a balanced analysis of Cabinet and shadow Cabinet issues, Barnaby Joyce was interviewed on Sky over the original parental-leave policy announcement not being discussed in shadow Cabinet.

There followed a few quiet days with 'low-key', 'low-cost' announcements on both sides (*Lateline*, ABC TV, 29 July 2010).[5] Julia Gillard travelled to Perth and made a broadband announcement with Stephen Conroy. She was pictured—in television clips and in the print media—handpassing a football at Coolbinia Bombers junior Australian football club. The *Today* show (Channel Nine, 29 July 2010) picked up on 'Abbott's woman problem' as reflected in the gender gap in the polls, the perceptions of commentators and voices in the street.

Tony Abbott travelled to Adelaide (Sturt—Christopher Pyne's seat). There were front-page photos of Christopher Pyne and his family, including disabled children. There was an announcement on $134 million for school students with a disability, and education vouchers. Bronwyn Bishop also attended. The weekend of 31 July and 1 August was disastrous for Labor and a triumph for the Coalition. The Nielsen poll, published in the weekend *Sydney Morning Herald* and *The Age*, was headlined as follows: 'Abbott takes the lead' (*Sydney Morning Herald* 2010) and 'Blow to Labor as Abbott surges' (*The Age* 2010).[6]

Both leaders campaigned across the country: Gillard was at home in Melbourne watching the Western Bulldogs (AFL) at Etihad Stadium; and Tony Abbott was in Darwin on board the *HMAS Maitland* remaining disciplined and announcing caring social policies including additional nursing-home beds, pet therapy in nursing homes, and free medical care to families of defence personnel. Then on Saturday night's *ABC News* came the headline: 'Deputy PM sent former security guard to national security meetings when she was acting PM.' This was followed by mention of Kevin Rudd's illness and an interview with Thérèse Rein.

Stage Three

By August, the Labor campaign was in dire straits and attempts to gain media space for policy announcements were overshadowed by the number of embarrassing leaks and leak stories (Gilbert 2010b). For example, Gillard's attempt to launch Peter Garrett's campaign in Maroubra and hand over government coastal land to the community was overshadowed by an incredibly bizarre interview with Alexander Downer that dominated the Sunday tabloids. Witness *The Sunday Telegraph*'s front-page story (1 August 2010)—'Libs: we used Rudd as a leaking double agent'—and the interview with Downer providing details. The Greens' launch that day was also overshadowed.

---

5   29 July: Julia Gillard in Melbourne, where she announced disability measures; Tony Abbott in Melbourne. 30 July: Julia Gillard in Perth, photographed handballing a football at Coolbinia Bombers junior football club while Tony Abbot was in Adelaide.

6   Nielsen poll: two-party preferred—Coalition 52 to ALP 48; and preferred prime minister, 49:41, with Gillard down 5 per cent and Abbott up 6 per cent.

Monday's Newspoll showed Labor holding on better than in the Nielsen poll in terms of the two-party preferred vote, and Gillard redoubled her campaigning and her policy announcements.[7] Her symbolic reaching out to the conservative Christian community was replayed on the evening news; when visiting a western Sydney school, she clearly was shown saying 'amen' at the school prayer. She also announced a greater role for principals and additional tax benefits for sixteen to eighteen-year-olds in school.

That evening—evidently based on the slipping polls—she offered Abbott a second debate (on the economy) the following Sunday (the day of the Coalition launch). Abbott declined. While Gillard's invitation was on Network Seven's *Today Tonight*, Abbott's decline was on *Sky News*. Jenny Macklin also appeared on Sky (*Agenda*) referring to herself as 'a mother, as well as an MP'.

The Coalition—having one theme of stopping waste, and so on, and another of no more WorkChoices—developed a third: the ALP's 'faceless men'.[8]

The next day, 2 August, saw the appearance of the 'real Julia'. This was based on an interview with the *Herald Sun* aboard her jet: 'I think it's time for me to make sure that the real Julia is well and truly on display…So I am going to step up and take personal charge of what we do in the campaign from this point' (Hudson 2010). Gillard and Swan subsequently travelled on the media bus from Sydney to Newcastle. She was the first leader since Paul Keating in 1996 to do this and it showed in the words of her *Herald Sun* interview she was 'go[ing] for it'.

Gillard's statement concerning a second debate was made on the press bus: 'I'd be happy to debate him [Abbott] on the economy on Sunday night…[I] would be happy to debate him on any night.' Abbott quickly responded to the debate challenge: 'The time for changing the rules has passed.' And infamously: 'No doesn't mean no when you are speaking to Julia; she said no repeatedly.'

The unfortunate choice of words was seized upon by female MPs—for example, Senator Sarah Hanson-Young (Greens)—and Tony replied: 'I'm not going to cop this vicious smear from the Labor Party.'

Tony Abbott was back in Brisbane—with daughter Louise—re-announcing paid parental leave (first introduced in March), with modifications that included starting in mid-2012 and a lower levy on business: 26 weeks at full pay up to $150 000 and the paperwork handled by government. According to Abbott, his was a better scheme than the government's of 18 weeks paid for by taxpayers.

---

7   Newspoll: two-party preferred, 50:50.
8   Tony Abbott in Cairns and Townsville offering more money for tourism, and referring to the ALP's 'faceless men'.

The next day (4 August) Julia Gillard was also in Brisbane (and Cairns), where she announced more generous baby bonuses, including a $500 cash bonus. Gillard continued to focus on jobs and families, renewed the challenge to Abbott to debate economic matters and reminded the nation that '[w]hen the GFC hit we had the better plan to support jobs'.

The Labor team's attempt to focus on its economic strengths was derailed again with Gillard's second interview on the *7.30 Report* (3 August); host Kerry O'Brien had invited both leaders to appear three times and that night was Julia's second interview. O'Brien said: 'Last week was a very bad week', then followed up with: 'Why didn't you call Kevin Rudd in hospital?' (Rudd was just home after three days in hospital for minor gall-bladder surgery.) The first part of the interview was on Labor's economic strengths, and the second part concerned the price of carbon.

Tony Abbott continued to campaign in Brisbane (Dickson). His message was directed towards retirees and he promised changes to the Commonwealth Seniors Health Card, incentives for business to hire older workers (aged fifty to sixty-five) to be paid after six months, and that he would remove the age bar on accessing superannuation. He was drawn to comment on the WA burqa case:[9] 'It is a confronting type of attire.' Overall, he remained on message: 'End the waste, debt repaid, big taxes and boats [would be] stopped.'

This was the week that saw Labor lose 6 per cent in the Newspoll, and the *7.30 Report* (ABC TV, 4 August 2010) interviewed electoral expert Antony Green on the likely electoral result. It was agreed that different swings would occur in different States and that pro-Labor swings likely in Victoria and South Australia might 'save the day' for the ALP. Green foresaw different swings within States and regions and cast doubt on there being a uniform swing. Kerry O'Brien commented that the 'Liberals have less money for direct mail'. Newspoll had more pronounced State swings than Nielsen.

Julia Gillard campaigned in Townsville (Leichhardt) on 5 August and then travelled to Sydney for a 'Mary McKillop' fundraising dinner, while Kevin Rudd announced at his first post-hospital press conference that he would campaign vigorously to '[s]top Abbott sliding into office'.

The *7.30 Report* (ABC TV, 5 August 2010) invited Liberal Shadow Health Minister, Peter Dutton, to debate health policy; he refused and Health Minister, Nicola Roxon, outlined Labor's policy. That evening, Transport and Infrastructure

---

9   A woman in WA asked to wear a burqa in order to give evidence in a trial; this provoked community debate and was criticised by Tony Abbott and the WA Premier Colin Barnett. The judge subsequently ordered her to remove the burqa.

Minister, Anthony Albanese, announced the eastern seaboard highway—'a commitment now to be built in the future'. Tony Abbott, in Sydney, said that the Coalition's health policy would spend 'more on doctors, less on bureaucrats'.

The next day (6 August) former party leaders entered the fray. John Howard was on the campaign trail in Sydney while in Melbourne Malcolm Fraser said the Coalition was 'not ready for government'. Former Labor leader Mark Latham entered the campaign as a journalist for Channel Nine's *60 Minutes*.

Julia Gillard campaigned in Melbourne and lost her shoe on a building site (*Herald Sun* 2010). In response to questions from journalists regarding Kevin Rudd, she replied: 'we are chronic texters.' Tony Abbott was in Sydney attending a black-tie fundraising dinner with John Howard and would be at 'a mystery location tomorrow'.

On 6 August the High Court handed down its decision to support the GetUp! challenge to Howard legislation that closed the electoral rolls at 8 pm on the day the writs were issued. The case was first heard on 4 August.

On 7 August, Julia Gillard was in Brisbane and 'appeared' at a face-to-face meeting with Kevin Rudd at the Brisbane Commonwealth Offices (Maher 2010). A strangely choreographed affair, the meeting was captured with no sound. Campaigning at the Brisbane Show (the EKKA), she was interviewed by Mark Latham and photos show his aggressive body language (see AAP 2010). Gillard announced a 'pensioner pledge' where pensioners could earn up to $6500 without affecting their pension. Tony Abbott was also in Brisbane and met with the President of Nauru (returning from the South Pacific Forum in Fiji); this was arranged by the Shadow Immigration Minister, Scott Morrison, and Deputy Opposition Leader, Julie Bishop.

The Nielsen poll was a front-page feature in the Fairfax broadsheets: 'Labor trailing Coalition 2PP 48:52' (*The Age* 2010b; *Sydney Morning Herald* 2010b). The articles made mention of the Coalition winning in 1998 with 49 per cent of the two-party preferred vote. (For a detailed analysis of the polls, see Chapter 6 in this volume.) The Orgill Report on the Building the Education Revolution (BER) scheme was released, and was not entirely negative, with some positives mentioned.

On 8 August, Julia Gillard was in Darwin speaking about her School Chaplains' Scheme, and Kevin Rudd was campaigning in Brisbane where he held a press conference that was captured on the evening TV news programs. Jenny Macklin promised to recognise Indigenous people in the Constitution (*ABC National News*, 8 August 2010); Channel Nine apologised to Gillard over Mark Latham (AAP 2010).

This day also saw the Coalition launch in Brisbane. Tony Abbott promised a debt-reduction committee, and the main themes were continued: pay back the debt, cut the waste, secure the borders. He spoke of a contract with Australia and provided a detailed time line—for example, day one: phone the President of Nauru. Julie Bishop focused on Labor's 'soap opera' with leadership issues. The Nationals' Warren Truss—picking up on Julia Gillard's recent comment that she texted Kevin Rudd—mentioned Julia had to 'text her ex' to have someone to dance with (see *Australian Agenda*, Sky TV, 8 August 2010).

On Monday, 9 August, Julia Gillard was in Perth—calling for performance pay for school principals, moves towards a standard national curriculum and the baccalaureate. She agreed to a Wednesday-night forum in Sydney. She was well received on the ABC's *Q&A* program.

Tony Abbott remained in Brisbane. He visited the Brisbane Show and a home with faulty insulation. The *7.30 Report* announced that Tony Abbott was to have his second interview on Wednesday, 11 August.

Wayne Swan and Joe Hockey debated the economy at the National Press Club. Hockey was questioned about the Coalition's costings, which were to be submitted that day. Peter Costello hit back at the use of his anti-Abbott comment in an ALP advertisement.

Julia Gillard travelled back to the east from Perth for events in Adelaide and Geelong on 10 August. In Adelaide, she announced the findings of the *Murray–Darling Report*, which recommended funding extra water for the river system, and extra funds for professionals to undergo teacher training. She visited her old school in Adelaide. In Geelong (Corangamite), she announced the Geelong–Winchelsea duplication (with Anthony Albanese) and Belmont super clinic (with Darren Cheeseman).

Tony Abbott travelled south to Sydney for his second *7.30 Report* interview. He appeared to muff his answer on information technology (IT) and then referred to himself as not a 'tech head' and regrouped to define the Coalition's IT policy as a 'national, not nationalised system'; it was to be based on wireless technology. In general, he left the broadband debate to his communications and finance shadow ministers. Kevin Rudd was appointed to the UN Secretary-General's Panel on Sustainability.

On Wednesday, 11 August, Abbott and Gillard swapped places. Gillard was in Sydney, where, beside NSW Premier, Kristina Keneally, and Infrastructure Minister, Anthony Albanese, she announced the Parramatta to Epping rail link, with the money to flow from 2018.

Tony Abbott was at the mouth of the River Murray, with Barnaby Joyce, announcing a government water buy-back scheme to enable the river to flow again. He also provided a welfare update with the family allowance contingent upon compulsory health checks for four-year-olds, and $6000 for workers relocating to rural and regional Australia.

Wednesday evening saw the Rooty Hill RSL Club civic debate. Julia Gillard spoke first and encountered a number of 'hostile' questions, especially regarding Kevin Rudd's dispatch. This was according to *The Daily Telegraph*'s Malcolm Farr, who was part of the Sky studio panel. Tony Abbott then spoke and stayed on the floor rather than sitting on a stool on the stage as Gillard had done. He introduced himself as a 'fellow Sydneysider'. Farr referred to Gillard's 'headmistressy high chair' but also noted a 'hubris' moment for Abbott's comment 'when I'm Prime Minister'.

Earlier in the day, the National Press Club hosted a 'health policy' debate between Nicola Roxon and Peter Dutton. Key policy differences emerged: the ALP promised hospital takeovers by the Commonwealth (negotiated by Rudd before the election), with local boards, GP super clinics, and block funding for diabetes; and the Coalition promised $36 billion for community-controlled hospitals, mental health funding and after-hours rebates under the rubric of 'cutting the bureaucrats'. Aged care and Indigenous housing were, however, omitted.

On 12 August, Julia Gillard was in northern Tasmania to launch the Tasmanian broadband rollout, with Communications Minister, Stephen Conroy. Tony Abbott remained in western Sydney. At the Penrith RSL Club, he promised a welfare boost for veterans and an 'office of due diligence', and critiqued the ALP's broadband scheme as a 'technological rabbit out of the hat'. Mark Latham dropped in on Tony Abbott at the RSL.

The evening news noted that the Coalition's expenditure was not yet in for Treasury costing. This set the scene for the Wayne Swan and Joe Hockey interview on the *7.30 Report*. On 13 August, Julia Gillard was in Sydney to make education announcements regarding $350 million for individual bonuses for trades training and $5500 per apprentice. She referred to the Coalition's 'dog ate my homework excuse' to avoid costings.

Tony Abbott was in Melbourne with Christopher Pyne for education policy announcements and visited a Christian college in the seat of Deakin and schools in Colac and Geelong (Corangamite). He announced the Coalition's 'new technology fund' and awards for high-achieving teachers; he promised to axe the Government's computers in schools program. No prior details were released of Abbott's Victorian trip.

On 14 August, Julia Gillard campaigned on the NSW North Coast (Page) near Ballina. She announced a carbon-credit scheme for farmers and for traditional landowners, to be sold to polluters. She was wearing riding boots (*ABC News Victoria*, 15 August 2010; *The Age*, 15 August 2010). She headed back to Melbourne for campaigning that evening and the next day. Both Nielsen and Newspoll showed Labor 'on the nose' in Queensland and New South Wales.

Tony Abbott was in Perth where he flipped the coin at a football match and spoke at the head office of Barmino, a mining contractor. The *ABC News Victoria* headline was Abbott '[p]ledges more help for miners'.

On Sunday, 15 August, Julia Gillard was in the northern suburbs of Melbourne (Diamond Creek) calling on Tony Abbott to debate the economy. She was flying to Brisbane that evening for the ALP policy launch. Tony Abbott was on the NSW Central Coast.

That evening *Sky News*'s *Agenda* featured an interview with Nick Xenophon regarding a possible hung parliament. It also discussed the three Independents— Rob Oakeshott, Tony Windsor and Bob Katter—who were all ex-Nationals, stating that the Coalition was campaigning against Windsor.

On Monday, 16 August, Julia Gillard was in Brisbane for the official ALP launch, in the early afternoon. It was a low-key 'bread and butter' launch. Health, jobs and the economy were major themes. *Sky News* referred to the 'display of unity'. Tony Abbott toured five marginal seats in western Sydney and also the Australian Defence Force Academy (ADFA) in Canberra. In Sydney's west, he campaigned on an anti-mining tax platform, and against gangs.

There was also the final *7.30 Report* interview with Julia Gillard; Kerry O'Brien referred to the 'last-minute launch…on the thirtieth day of the campaign'. He questioned Gillard over why there were no Cabinet discussions over the Epping– Parramatta rail link; she replied that 'there are no formal Cabinet meetings during election campaigns. We are in caretaker mode.' Tony Abbott agreed to debate the economy (*PM*, Sky TV, 16 August 2010).

On 17 August, Julia Gillard campaigned in north and central Queensland, visiting Townsville, Mackay and Emerald, and agreed to another town-hall-style forum to be held in Brisbane on Wednesday, 18 August. She was flying to Perth that evening so was unable to debate the economy 'then and there'. She made a brief reference to a republic 'when we see the monarch change'. Tony Abbott spoke at the Press Club later that day and responded to Gillard's comment by referring to the monarchy as 'on-going'.

Joe Hockey was interviewed by David Speers on Sky regarding when the economy would be back in surplus, and he apparently contradicted comments by Queensland Senator George Brandis who had earlier stated that the budget would not be back in surplus for 10 years.

On community forum day—18 August—Julia Gillard commenced by campaigning in Perth (Hasluck), and then travelled back to Brisbane for the forum at the Brisbane Broncos Rugby League Club. She would be flying out again only half an hour after the forum.

Tony Abbott spoke first and received a cooler reception than he had in Sydney. (Abbott had earlier been in Gladstone—Flynn.) Julia Gillard appeared more relaxed and comfortable; she received questions about same-sex marriage.

On 19 August, Julia Gillard spoke at the National Press Club and announced paternity leave for 'new dads'.[10] She would be travelling to the NSW Central Coast (Patterson) that evening.

Earlier that morning (19 August), Tony Abbott had started out at the Brisbane markets at dawn, was interviewed for the *Today* show, and promised an all-night 'campaigning marathon'. He visited four Brisbane marginal seats and then travelled to Sydney (Bennelong). He was not planning to sleep before polling day (36 hours).

Channel Seven News noted Labor was ahead on national polling, 52 to 48, but 'at risk', and showed a copy of Labor's 'secret polling' in which it was in 'danger of losing seats in Queensland and New South Wales'. The news also showed the 'polligraph' 2:1 in favour of Julia Gillard (audience watching the Brisbane forum in Melbourne). It noted that Gillard received support from women and Abbott from men. Voters were unhappy at the dumping of Rudd.

The *7.30 Report* had Hugh McKay referring to the 'ratification poll'. Antony Green noted that the polling only 'made sense' by States. While all polls were showing Labor ahead nationally, it was barely ahead in New South Wales and Queensland.

Queensland was vulnerable as there were 10 Labor seats with margins of 5 per cent or less. The Liberal National Party (LNP) was a new party. In New South Wales, there was a 'complicated' redistribution. According to Kerry O'Brien, there were also likely to be different patterns within States: Victoria and South Australia 'may save Labor'. Possible gains were Sturt and Boothby

---

10   *A Current Affair* reported on the Press Club speech.

(South Australia) and McEwen and Corangamite (Victoria). The prospect of a hung parliament was raised: 'Greens have said they would support a Labor Government', noted Antony Green.

Lateline's Tony Jones interrogated Labor's Chris Bowen: 'Why has Labor leaked its polling?' Bowen sidestepped, saying it would be the closest result since 1961. Andrew Robb claimed Labor was 'rolling out the leak' to condition expectations. It was, however, 'not far off the Liberal internal polling and the other published polls'.

The Newspoll of 50:50 (Tuesday and Wednesday) suggested a momentum shift and that 'every day is critical' (Tony Jones, *Lateline* 19 August 2010). The discussion shifted to the 'Charter of Budget Honesty', introduced in 1998: this was the first time the Coalition had not followed procedures. The aim was to allow the Opposition to have costings advice provided free.

By 20 August, there had been 35 days of non-stop campaigning. Julia Gillard campaigned on the NSW Central Coast and finished up in Sydney in Bennelong with Maxine McKew where she opened the Top Ryde shopping centre. She warned of the 'risks' of WorkChoices and that 'every vote is about the choice of Prime Minister'. In her interview with David Speers, she stated that the '[c]hoice is between me and Mr Abbott. We are investing, building, training.'

Tony Abbott's 'campaign blitz' commenced at the early morning markets, and, in his interview on *A Current Affair*, he said the 'real risk' was a 'really bad government'; and he denied that he would reintroduce WorkChoices. The polls showed the Coalition expecting to pick up six to 10 seats and Labor expecting it to be 'a lot closer than that'.

The final TV interviews on the ABC and commercial stations saw the distillation of the main themes by the two leaders: Gillard (ABC) saw 'a real choice, a tough contest...I do have a positive plan for jobs, health, hospitals, broadband'. Abbott (ABC) argued Australia would '[f]ix problems by changing the government'. In his final Channel Nine interview (20 August), he was more low key, commenting on how 'hard' he had campaigned in his efforts to hold the government to account and to present a 'clear alternative'. Table 2.3 outlines the post-election saga.

Table 2.3 Post-Election Events

Date	Event	Comment
23 August	'Adam Bandt to back ALP'	Media commentary that Bandt had previously agreed to support the ALP; see Tally Room, 23 August 2010
1 September	Greens back ALP	Climate change committee at Cabinet level, dental care, high-speed rail, parliamentary debate on Afghanistan and political donation laws
2 September	Andrew Wilkie to support ALP	
3 September	Bob Katter's 20-point plan	
7 September	Katter supports Coalition	
7 September	Tony Windsor and Rob Oakeshott support ALP	
7 September	Julia Gillard meets the Governor-General	
11 September	Gillard announces ministerial reshuffle	
14 September	Gillard, followed by the ministry, is sworn in	

Conclusion

Opposition Leader, Tony Abbott, referred to the experience as the 'longest election'; commentator Hugh McKay spoke of the campaign as a process of 'ratification' (*7.30 Report*, ABC TV, 19 August); SBS's Karen Middleton framed the campaign as a 'referendum on Julia Gillard' (*SBS News*, 20 August 2010); still others raised serious questions as to the competency of the ALP's strategy and tactics. The subsequent experience of minority government has left the leading media commentators somewhat puzzled and searching for a script. A few commentators—mainly in the tabloid media (for example, Simon Kearney from the *Herald Sun* and *the Sun-Herald*'s Mia Freedman)—latched on to gender as a defining feature; whereas the broadsheets, as typified by *The Age* (see Michelle Grattan's work), had decided Australia was in a post-gender paradigm, and gender was no longer relevant.

Other longer-term and deeper explanations provide important context. As in 2007, David Marr's (2010) perceptive and biting analysis of the personality and style of the incumbent Prime Minister (John Howard in 2007 and Kevin Rudd in 2010) was picked up by political commentators. The economy, while featured in Julia Gillard's early speeches, did not gain sustained coverage, although Andrew Scott (2010) reminds us that the GFC saw governments tumble internationally, replaced with hung parliaments and minority governments.

References

Australian Associated Press (AAP). 2010. 'Nine boss apologises after Mark Latham's Julia Gillard interview "lacked proper respect"'. *AAP*, 8 August, viewed 20 January 2011, <http://www.news.com.au/features/federal-election/nine-boss-apologies-after-mark-lathams-interview-lacked proper-respect/>

Channel Nine. 2010. 'Do women hate Tony Abbott?'. *Today*, 29 July, <http://video.au.msn.com/watch/video/do-women-hate-tony-abbott/xik81jz>

Gilbert, Kieran. 2010a. 'The debate'. Kieran Gilbert Blog, viewed 21 January 2011, <http://www.skynews.com.au/blogs/blog.aspx?Blog=2&Post=1115>

Gilbert, Kieran. 2010b. 'The Coalition wins week two'. Kieran Gilbert Blog, viewed 21 January 2011, <http://www.skynews.com.au/blogs/blog.aspx?Blog=2&Post=1125>

Gillard, Julia. 2010a. Edited transcript of Julia Gillard's acceptance speech, 24 June, <http://www.theaustralian.com.au.news/edited-transcript-of-julia-gillards-acceptance-speech/story-e6frg6nb-122588-3840584>

Gillard, Julia. 2010b. Speech to the Lowy Institute, 6 July, Sydney.

Gillard, Julia. 2010c. Full transcript of Prime Minister Julia Gillard's address to the National Press Club, 15 July, Canberra, <tonyserve.wcanberraorddpress.com/2010.../full-transcript-of-prime-ministerjulia-gillards-adress-to-the-national-press-club-canberra/>

Gillard, Julia. 2010d. Opening statement at press conference, 17 July, Parliament House, Canberra, <http://www.alp.org/federal-government/news/speech-julia-gillard-opening-statement-at-press/>

Grattan, Michelle. 2010. 'PM rocked by Labor leaks amid bitter divisions'. *The Age*, 28 July, 1.

Herald Sun. 2010. 'Gillard loses her footing'. *Herald Sun*, 6 August, viewed 24 February 2011, <http://video.dailytelegraph.com.au/1560359121/Gillard-loses-her-footing>

Hudson, Philip. 2010. 'Julia Gillard vows to take control of her election campaign'. *Herald Sun*, 2 August, viewed 20 January 2011, <http://www.heraldsun.com.au/news/special-reports/julia-gillard-vows-to-take-control-of-her-election-campaign>

Kelly, Paul. 2010. 'He's tough and targeted but has no new message'. *The Australian*, 9 August, 1.

Maher, Sid. 2010. 'Julia Gillard and Kevin Rudd meet, but won't campaign together'. *The Australian*, 7 August, viewed 24 February 2011, <http://www.theaustralian.com.au/national-affairs/julia-gillard-meets-kevin-rudd-but-won't-campaign-together/>

Marr, David. 2010. *Power Trip: The political journey of Kevin Rudd*. Quarterly Essay 38 (June). Melbourne: Black Inc.

Scott, Andrew. 2010. Paper presented to Deakin University Workshop on the Politics of Economic Crisis, 12 November, Melbourne.

Shepherd, Tony. 2010. 'Hey Hey Saturday crowd boos Tony Abbott'. *The Daily Telegraph*, 22 July.

Simms, Marian. 2011. 'Westminster norms and caretaker conventions: Australian and New Zealand transition debates'. In Paul t'Hart and John Uhr (eds), *How Power Changes Hands: Transition and succession in government*. Basingstoke, UK: Palgrave Macmillan.

Stewart, Cameron. 2010. 'Julia Gillard hot but women cool on Tony Abbott'. *The Australian*, 22 July.

Sydney Morning Herald. 2010a. 'Abbott takes the lead'. *Sydney Morning Herald*, 31 July – 1 August.

Sydney Morning Herald. 2010b. 'Labor trailing Coalition 2PP 48:52'. *Sydney Morning Herald*, 7 August.

The Age. 2010a. 'Blow to Labor as Abbott surges'. *The Age*, 31 July – 1 August.

The Age. 2010b. 'Labor trailing Coalition 2PP 48:52'. *The Age*, 7 August.

The Age. 2010c. 'Coalition must redefine itself on IR' [Editorial]. *The Age*, 7 October.

The Sunday Telegraph. 2010. 'Libs: we used Rudd as a leaking double agent'. *The Sunday Telegraph*, 1 August.

3. Bad Governments Lose: Surely there is no mystery there

Rodney Cavalier

In every choice between courage and safety, Labor chose safety. Across the full spectrum of supposed virtues, Labor chose the alternative. We witnessed a Labor campaign without courage, flair, imagination or principle. Technically, it was predictable, flat and no better than fair– average quality. The essence of the strategy was doing whatever it takes. Labor began by being as reckless as necessary to win—hence the matching of the tax cuts. Labor's recklessness was calculated. The absence of responsibility was based on the template of John Howard [in] 1996 and the three outings following. If politics is about winning—and it is hard to conjure any other purpose—the Labor campaign of 2007 was genius unparalleled.

— (Cavalier 2009, 201).

Humane but tough. Three words came to define the character of the Rudd Government. Words in a torrent became the response whenever the position to be taken was not safely predictable; a beguiling entrapment of self-contradiction of which the author seemed unaware. Australians became accustomed to full-blown bursts from a prime minister who had an opinion on everything, oft preceded by the non-apology 'I make no apology for'. We knew Kevin Rudd was opposed to Bill Henson taking photos of pre-pubescent girls, he was appalled at an assault on a female MP, and he regarded the response to climate change as the 'great moral challenge' of our times.

Outside such matters of moment, what exactly the Rudd Government stood for was not clear. Such concern was, to be sure, a boutique concern of political commentators and the dwindling band of ALP stalwarts who were wondering aloud what the new government had altered, bar the symbolics. Certainly, there had been the grand theatre of the Apology; there was the ratification. After which, there was?

In no time, 2007 became 2008 and politics meandered. The Coalition parties formed the scene of troubles. Brendan Nelson was an unlikely leader always. It did not assist that Peter Costello remained in the frame and in the Parliament, the obvious alternative, though by neither word nor deed did he encourage that possibility. Malcolm Turnbull—less circumspect, certainly less patient—did not conceal his intentions.

Divisions in the other side were the most reportable show in town. The ALP at every level was four square behind its leader, the Prime Minister and election winner. Dissent and criticism had disappeared. The ordinary processes of Cabinet government broke down; caucus was neither bellwether nor monitor; the ALP National Secretariat regarded its role as discovering the wishes of the leader and delivering them. The ALP National Conference was a week in which democratic discourse went into exile. The party had become the captive of the political class—that narrow funnel of operatives on splendid salaries who work for the ALP machine, affiliated unions, the staffs of ministers and MPs. This was their government. This was their government untrammelled. The Rudd Government was going to provide a textbook on how a new model of Labor governance worked. In that it certainly succeeded. The model did not end with the demise of its author.

This chapter is about the government that fell on 21 August 2010. The election was in play after just one term of government because the incumbents lost the support of the Australian people. When the last vote was counted, it transpired that some 62 per cent of Australian electors had voted against the ALP; only in 1931 has the primary vote for Labor been worse.

A Ship Moored in Indonesia

The moment when private concerns about the Rudd Government became widespread public doubt was the response (or non-response) to the presence of the *Oceanic Viking* moored in Indonesian waters, holding seekers of asylum in Australia unwilling to disembark in Indonesia. The Indonesians were disinclined to compel the seekers to get off the ship. Australia's defence forces could not intervene. Vessels without a lawful right of entry had been seeking entry to Australia in numbers uncomfortable for the government. The cumulative impact of these arrivals occasioned grievous harm to the perception the government preferred of itself. With the *Viking* anchored and going nowhere, the rhetoric employed by Rudd was directed at one side of this debate. The government was determined not to allow a perception it was led by a bleeding heart. Humane, nonetheless, the government remained. We knew it was humane because we were told that so often.

The nerve refugees need to touch is reached by acts of commission and omission sufficient to cause embarrassment to an Australian government. That way, Australia's authorities will offer to have applications considered with expedition. Those on board the *Viking* jumped ahead of the orderly process that was considering pre-existing applications. Not that those who disembarked chose to disembark because there was a special deal for them. We know that the circumstance of their disembarkation was non-extraordinary—a lexical first—because the Prime Minister said so. The electorate was being asked to believe: 1) no special deal was offered the asylum-seekers on board the *Oceanic Viking* in order to induce them to disembark; but, if there was, then 2) the Prime Minister did not know the terms of any special deal offered to those asylum-seekers.

The then Leader of the Opposition, Malcolm Turnbull, was constrained in his criticism of the statements of his opposite. A highly vulnerable Prime Minister, having talked himself into a sea of troubles, was not eviscerated because the Opposition Leader dared not utter the accusation that the Prime Minister had misled the Parliament. In the absence of a direct accusation by the Opposition, the headlines were missing. Turnbull had disabled himself some months earlier by making the most extreme demand on the Prime Minister without building his scale of demands in lockstep with emerging evidence. Turnbull relied on the evidence of a public servant—evidence later revealed as tainted. Turnbull did not recover from that error. Turnbull was effectively dead in the water. He was holding on for the reason that no alternative Liberal leader wanted to lead the Coalition to defeat. The situation was similar to federal Labor in 2005–06 when the Beazley leadership was treading water.

While it might have suited the alternative Liberal leaders to allow Turnbull to take the Coalition to an overwhelming defeat, the Opposition Leader brought about his own ruin by attempting to compel the doubters in his party to back Rudd on the government's emissions trading scheme (ETS). Such zealotry by an Opposition leader in support of a government he is supposed to be opposing and against the opposition of a sizeable segment of the party he is leading is unique in the history of federation. What then followed was revealing of something quite shocking in modern politics: evidence of a critical mass of MPs and senators who believe in something other than their own careers. Believing in what they believe, these Liberals and Nationals advanced their cause by argument and memo, intrigue, dirty tricks, leaks, false rumour, challenges, resignations, text messages and statements on the record.

A novelty for modern times. A party divided on policy. A party divided by a debate on what should constitute its core beliefs. A party whose members hold their beliefs so dearly they placed those beliefs ahead of the unity of the party. A party whose differences could not be managed. The absence of any and all of those qualities in the modern Australian Labor Party is its greatest strength, so we are told. Labor knew what it believed about climate change because the leadership had promulgated an ETS as the way to proceed. In lockstep, no dissent audible, Labor followed its leadership. Twice legislation passed the House; twice it was rejected by the Senate. Yet the government—riding so high in the polls—chose not to take the issue to a double dissolution.

Some of the reason for this caution were fear and uncertainty; some was the sheer pleasure of toying with the other side. Modern government seeks to make its Opposition the issue. For all of 2008, going into late 2009, it mattered not that many who actually believe in the need for action against climate change—such as the Greens and respected scientists—attested the government's scheme was not worth a thimble of ice water. What mattered in terms of the politics was whether the government was prepared to risk all on implementing an ETS by making it the issue in a double dissolution. Malcolm Turnbull risked all in an attempt to deny the government the pleasures of this squeeze play. He duly lost all. He and the nation shortly discovered the Rudd Government was not prepared to risk anything.

As 2009 became 2010, a powerful question emerged: what exactly does this government intend to do about climate change? These were powerful, unsettling questions that Labor stalwarts were asking of their elected representatives. If polling picked up a sharp fall in support for the rhetoric coming from Rudd and his Climate Change Minister, Penny Wong, did anyone believe that the ALP federal leadership would commit itself to persuading the nation to accept what the pollsters were saying a majority did not believe in? Would the Labor leadership argue against the tides of popular opinion? There was a winning hand going into the 2007 election, a winning hand through 2007, 2008 and 2009. It helped Labor mightily that the Liberals were split and The Nationals opposed. Legislation did not come to pass; objective, favourable circumstance moved against the government. So much goodwill was lost by pursuing a phoney deadline ahead of the Copenhagen climate conference; not even the most enthusiastic believer in the dangers of climate change asserted that legislative action by Australia mattered a damn. By the end of 2009, ahead of Copenhagen, much more than goodwill was lost.

Failing to Go Early

Labor was to pay a heavy price—one seat short of the ultimate price—for the failure to go early. Through 2009 the possibilities of an early poll were under constant watch. With the Turnbull leadership floundering and the polls high for Labor wherever you looked—primary, two-party preferred, approval for Rudd, State-by-State federal voting intentions—the arguments against going early were not strong. Since the Second World War, prime ministers in their first term have taken an early election. The Menzies victory of 1949 was followed by a double dissolution in 1951. The great victory of 1972 was followed by a double dissolution in 1974. Changes of government since have followed that pattern: 1975 followed by 1977; 1983 by 1984; 1996 by 1998.

A decision not to take the plunge was not taken at a single meeting. The party leader has to be an enthusiast for the enterprise. The then Prime Minister was not. The party denied itself a certain five years in government and a probable eight in exchange for a wholly different atmosphere going into 2010; hardheads feared (and wrote at the time) that the winning of another three years was not going to be a lay-down misère. Failing to go early characterised the caution that beset the former government.

Street smarts did not countenance any possibility of a Labor defeat. (Street smarts being defined as a conventional wisdom not yet demolished by a real-world event.) Drilling into the reasons for a Labor victory was not all that flattering. Two factors were considered insurmountable obstacles to an Opposition in the first term of a government. One was the ancient truth that the punters do not want to admit they got it wrong last time. The second was that those who have known Tony Abbott for decades were counting on him to blow up—to say something or do something when the cameras were rolling that was going to take him out of contention. The certainty Abbott was going to blow up became an article of faith, the last refuge even into the last week of the campaign itself. Underestimating Abbott began with those who had known him at university: they declared that the student of then was the real, unchanged man of now and was, therefore, of no account. It was a fatal miscalculation.

You do not have to be a good government to gain re-election. You need only be better than the other side. Any prospect of a good government emerging under Kevin Rudd was sunk by the intellectual tenets of the 2007 election campaign. Rudd succeeded in convincing those who wanted a policy continuum minus Howard that they would score such a continuum while, simultaneously, he convinced those who wanted a change of direction with Howard blessedly gone they would get that change. The achievement was nought less than genius and warrants acknowledging. The problem is that there comes a time in the life of a government when consequence rules.

A Government of Limited Possibility

The ALP campaign of 2007 guaranteed a government of limited possibility was going to emerge. The Rudd Government was cruelled from the outset when it promised to match irresponsible tax cuts in the sum of $31 billion and, having been elected, failed to renege on the promise as new circumstance and knowledge surely dictated. In his memoirs, Peter Costello has acknowledged that the succession of tax cuts not once delivered the electoral rewards the Howard Government hoped for. Joe Hockey, on becoming Treasury spokesman, spoke aloud about abandoning the 2007 tax cuts as unnecessary and unhelpful. Wayne

Swan made his own editorial contribution on the absence of value (economic or political) in the 2007 cuts by omitting all reference to the final tranche in his 2009 budget speech.

What could have been an age of wonders after 2007 became another round of the customary pieties about fiscal rectitude. Notwithstanding that rhetoric, the government unhesitatingly tolerated record levels of public debt in order to combat the global financial crisis. While spending big on infrastructure, it was demanding of the Public Service and the military that they effect economies and cutbacks. Only insolence and sleight of hand made the delivery of public services possible. The failure of the roof-insulation scheme was a failure in public service practice. Good government depends on time and careful thinking, minuted decisions with a course for action. Good government requires the involvement of a competent public service, properly encouraged, working reasonable hours. A viable program for roof insulation required the involvement of public servants, working to a reasonable timetable, who would be expected to draft regulations that set out standards that were enforceable at law. Behind the regulations there needed to be a supervisory force which ensured the standards were met—basic nineteenth-century tenets of government. Good government is secondary when the big effort—the principal ministerial involvement—is devoted to the announcement of the scheme, the when and the where and the visuals. Roof insulation was a scandal. Inadequate resources have a consequence.

The great injection into universities and training did not come to pass. The arts—the whole notion of creative expression—was simply not a part of the government's thinking, not even when thousands of millions of dollars were being splurged on make-work schemes. A consultant's report into the Attorney-General's Department revealed that the principal source of legal advice to the Executive Government on the lawfulness of its proposed actions was not providing that advice. The overworked staff was not providing that advice because funding pressures caused them to concentrate on serving the needs of paying customers.

Their decision was rational in the exact fashion intended by the economic rationalists.

Successive governments have failed to harness the benefits of past productivity improvements. The colossal revenue potential of our present prosperity—untouched by the zephyr that reached Australia from the North Atlantic crisis—continues to be squandered. Governments have handed back the bounty by way of constant revisions downwards of the marginal rates of tax and the proportion to be extracted as taxation. Governments have squandered Australia's prosperity. The competence and capacity of the public sector suffer from the craven failure of successive governments to build a tax system that sustains the revenue requirements of Australia's social needs. The challenges will only get harder as the population ages. You cannot have good government unless the government has an adequate and reliable revenue base. The absence of revenue that is adequate and reliable is why each State government is in difficulty. The Commonwealth has a tax base from multiple sources that is adequate and reliable but prefers to squander it in tax cuts and splashy short-term programs while taking the shortfall out of the hide of public servants. The easy solutions of assets sales are gone now the great public enterprises went for a song.

Winning power by blue smoke and mirrors (against a master of that same game) brings an obvious consequence once you take power. Appearance might be contrived for a good while, task forces and inquiries can stall hard decisions. The day, however, cometh when a government must take decisions or, in not taking them, reveals itself. The punters became aware during 2009 of what was happening before the commentators dared to articulate a gathering impression of the man who then led the government. He says a lot but I am not sure that he means it. Can you work out what this bloke believes in? He says what his audience wants to hear. Does he believe in anything? He talks a lot but nothing happens.

The punters' awakening to disturbing truths came at different moments. The phrase about 'a fair shake of the sauce bottle' came from one who is unconnected with the way Australians speak. No Australian has ever used that phrase in ordinary discourse and no-one ever will. It was very interesting to hear the reactions to the phrase. It proved to be the moment when the penny dropped.

The North Atlantic Crisis

After the votes were cast, there were those who lamented that the former government failed to claim credit for avoiding what became known as the global financial crisis. We suffered least of all developed countries because Australia alone of the countries in the G20 has a debt ratio as a proportion of gross domestic product (GDP) below 10 per cent. We are also alone below 20 per cent. If you were not exposed to shares and financial services, you likely remained employed, and it was a crisis you did not notice. The Australian Government did not have to nationalise banks and insurance companies, it did not have to prop up motor vehicle manufacturing (any more than it already was, that is), it did not become the owner of much of the nation's housing stock.

That is why its borrowings could go directly into stimulus spending. Ours was a light affair, a setback for Australia not to be compared with 1982–83 or 1990–91, or even the collapse of developers and financiers during 1974–75.

Being in power and coming through the other side, the government is entitled to take the credit for avoiding recession. Credit for this escape should be shared more generously and belongs to: 1) Chifley's banking reforms in the 1940s; 2) prudential safeguards implemented in the Menzies era; 3) the near-death experience of Westpac in North America in the 1990s, which gave all our banks an aversion to that continent; 4) the mining boom; 5) the decisions of Hawke and Keating to expose the Australian economy to world market forces; and 6) the decision of Howard and Costello to repay all sovereign debt.

The economy did not play big in the campaign. Sound economic management was a given. The assertions of the government, though valid, were met with a ho-hum. The government ruined the chequerboard all by itself because of its decision on an ETS. With remarkable prescience, Paul Kelly (2010) nailed the government's desperation as follows after the debacle at Copenhagen:

> The Rudd government is stranded without any apparent game plan on its most important first-term policy (outside its response to the global financial crisis). It is rare for a national government to face this predicament in its first term. Labor seems unable to abandon its ETS yet unable to champion its ETS; it cannot tolerate the ignominy of policy retreat yet cannot declare it will take its beliefs to a double-dissolution election; it remains pledged to its ETS yet cannot fathom how to make its ETS the law of the land. Such uncertainties are understandable, yet they are dangerously debilitating for any government. In such a rapidly shifting policy and political climate, even fallback positions risk being rendered obsolete.

What Kelly was discovering was that the political class in absolute control of Australian Labor is without values. Focus groups will not point a finger in the way of the Promised Land. Only the values of the people making up a government and the party behind those people can provide those values. After the Copenhagen fiasco, the politics of climate change turned on its head. The politics moved from election winner to a matter of no positive electoral consequence unto the single most powerful reason for customary Labor voters to withdraw their first preference from Labor.

A Government of and for Insiders

A government of the political class is a government of and for insiders. The decision to grant rebates on licensing fees to free-to-air television was symptomatic of a government in its degenerative phase except this was a government not 30 months old. The $250 million as a rebate on licences for free-to-air television revealed a government that believed public life and statecraft were the preserve of insiders. The Rudd Government was the first to be built on and out of the political class. The political class—being men and women of process—find their way forward by way of focus groups, qualitative polling and talking to each other.

Once upon a time, the intellectual depths of the parliamentary party provided policy sustenance. Not now. Once the decisions of the ALP National Conference provided a program for action. The National Conference is now of no policy consequence. It said much that the 2020 summit took priority as an ideas forum over and above the party notionally in government. It says even more that the outcomes of the summit have disappeared without trace.

Polling Turns South

Throughout the heady days of 2008 and 2009, becoming nauseated at the flakery that was going down a treat, this writer predicted and wrote that, when the Rudd bubble burst, his descent in the polls would be the most rapid in the history of polling. Newspoll captured what was an ebbing of support for Rudd poll upon poll, gradual to begin, so that in February 2010—many fortnights after Turnbull had departed—Rudd's approval was down 16 points. I predicted a geometric decline in which the ground opened up. The first February poll placed the Coalition's primary vote ahead of Labor for the first time since Howard was riding well. The Coalition lead of 42–41 meant little given the two-party preferred vote had Labor comfortable on 52–48. Rudd, however, had slipped in approval to fifty. The second Newspoll of February maintained all three trends: Rudd down, Labor down, two-party preferred up to 53–47. The first poll of March found the three indicators were broadly steady. The ALP was moving deep into Beazley territory in which the party is travelling well but the leader is the problem.

Was there any mystery in these poll findings? None at all. The drop in support for the party leader was translating into a drop in the ALP vote. Where the support was going tells you much of the rest of the story. When Labor mismanaged the *Oceanic Viking*, its primary vote drop went directly to the Liberals. The February 2010 drop sprayed—principal beneficiary, the Greens—before returning through gritted teeth as preferences. Greens and 'Other' were sitting on a massive 21 per cent. If such numbers were concentrated in the inner cities, Labor was in trouble in seats such as Sydney, Grayndler, Melbourne, Batman, Cunningham and Newcastle.

The sense of drift was coming back to the Labor machine in strong terms from the focus groups. The groups were reporting a consistent thread of promises unfulfilled, expectations raised, expectations dashed. Something had to be done. Fatefully, the government decided to bring inquiries into hospital 'reform' and tax reform to the front of the agenda. A package on hospitals was all but unavoidable as so many voters were expecting a takeover and/or massive injection of Commonwealth dollars into the hospital systems of several States.

The failure with hospitals necessarily begins at the National Press Club in March at which Rudd—then possessed by unbridled hubris—declared war on the States. Only a palooka would so gratuitously insult the very people he was going to need in order to pull off his reforms. Rudd was counting on the financial shortcomings of the States to be matched by a moral deficit in their political leaderships. Rudd was reacting to and mouthing grabs from focus groups that said the States were on the nose. Advice was: there is no downside to attacking the States. Under serious questioning that day, the spectacle was saddening. Briefed in a hurry after squandering two years, pretending that this announcement had a long provenance, he could only bluster when hit with questions outside his briefing. Rudd blustered when he was ignorant.

Hospitals established the template of a Rudd policy announcement

- 12 hours of pyrotechnics
- 48 hours of bluster
- a slow unravelling as the details become known and the explanations do not stack up.

The corker in the hospitals debate was when Rudd behaved totally in character at a meeting with the Premier of New South Wales, Kristina Keneally. Television footage showed a premier trying so hard to be conciliatory but met by a stone-faced Prime Minister, no eye contact, looking vaguely downwards to the table. When Keneally was done, without a comment on her effort, he asked to get down to business. It was a most revealing rudeness.

The health reforms ended in game, set and match to the States. By not agreeing to the proposals announced at the National Press Club, the premiers of New South Wales and Victoria gave up nothing and gained much. Between the first announcement and the meeting of the Council of Australian Governments (COAG), this ever elastic package added extra funds for aged care, training specialists, money for junior doctors, GP training places, emergency departments and the bottomless hole of elective surgery. Some of these announcements were foreshadowed; all measures would have emerged as worthy initiatives in the course of the near future as part of the unending rounds of Commonwealth–State health agreements. In early 2011, Julia Gillard announced the abandoning of much of what was agreed to.

The polls were capturing how deeply unimpressed the voters were by the lack of substance that finally emerged from each big announcement. The Newspoll published on 4 May 2010 reported that Rudd's approval rating had collapsed to 39 from 51—the greatest single fall in the history of polling. Labor's primary vote fell a massive eight points to thirty-five.

ETS Abandoned, Mining Tax Announced

With just two days of April remaining, the about-face occurred on the ETS. For Rudd, the abandonment was the end game. Against a backdrop of falling personal ratings in the published polls, a slide in Labor's primary vote and the asking aloud of questions about personal judgment, Rudd announced the government's response to the Henry Review of taxation. The response concentrated on a new tax on mining companies—said to raise a bonanza in tax receipts that would enable the whole nation to reap the windfall accruing to the miners because of ever-growing demand from China, India and elsewhere for what is won from the ground in Australia. The revenues so won would not go to a sovereign wealth fund. No, it would be spent as reaped—or squandered—on a reduction in company tax rates, a topping up of superannuation to mums and dads (though no tax dollars would actually find their way to such funds), additional infrastructure spending and a budget back in deficit ahead of forecasts.

The problem began with the pyrotechnics of the announcement. The prospects of carrying public opinion were effectively forfeited within a few days. Everyone inside the industry accepted that miners had to pay more tax. The increase might have come about by any of several possibilities—most obviously, extra royalty payments and/or the application of a resources rent tax. Something like this was not far from what the emissaries of Ken Henry had been canvassing, not at all far from the discussions with Martin Ferguson. None of the miners had cause to suspect hostile intent from Wayne Swan or Treasury. They expected the new arrangements would come to pass after the usual consultations, perhaps harsh words along the way but all inside the bounds of customary political discourse. Australia has been there before with petroleum. The Henry Review had been somewhere inside the government for five months; announcements would surely be based on broad expectations raised after which details would go into the maw of a negotiated settlement. It required a special kind of political genius to unite the mining companies against a tax they were expecting. To lose the ensuing debate—a debate in favour of an unanswerable good—required ineptitude beyond any contemporary precedent. The government lost the debate for one reason: Rudd inserted himself.

The then Prime Minister used a press conference on the Henry Review to provide distractions from another week of horrors that his own behaviour, his absence of a compass, had inflicted on the government he led. Front and centre of the policy announcement was daring Abbott to block the tax bills. The gambit was intended to position Abbott as being for the miners, against extra superannuation payments to mums and dads and against a reduction in company tax. Laura Tingle used her column the Friday following to describe the preparations for the media announcement. Briefings to tame reporters favoured by the Rudd court concentrated on the coming pleasure of wedging Abbott. The baiters thought they would position Abbott somewhere uncomfortable. That was all there was.

After several months of Abbott's leadership, Rudd's court still did not understand that Abbott will take any dare. Labor's political class did not grasp Abbott is fearless. His greatest strength is his greatest weakness: he believes so strongly in what he believes in that he will do anything in pursuit of those beliefs.

Breakdown in Cabinet Government

A situation is not helped when so little that matters goes to Cabinet. When it came to adopting the Henry Review, Cabinet gave a tick to the broad outlines. The ministers were as astonished as the mining companies at how Rudd chose to play it. They started to ask of themselves and confidants whether there was any end to the harm this Prime Minister might do.

Any chance of consensus or general acceptance was dashed by the template of announcement first, scorch the opposition, wallow in hyperbole, maximise opposition; insult then consult. Under pressure, in days following, Rudd assaulted BHP and Rio Tinto for reason that their share registers had large numbers of foreigners. It was a xenophobia not seen since Jack Lang was in full cry.

The media conference had no paper to back it up. Rudd could not explain the detail. His knowledge base had been acquired very recently. Definitions shifted day by day of what was the threshold when the tax cut in. The polls were showing a tidal movement away from the major parties. The Newspoll on the first day of June revealed that Labor was going to lose the election. The approval rating for Rudd was down to 35 per cent. When he touched 33, his caucus colleagues were not going to be able to avoid discussing a leader who enjoyed the active hostility of two out of every three Australian voters. Hardheads had decided Rudd was not going to recover. Voters were not embracing the Liberals or Nationals. They turned to the Greens. The 2010 election was going to turn on what proportion of Labor's disillusioned—a critical mass of perhaps the most intelligent voters in the land—were going to return via preferences. Could enough of them really go all the way and put the Coalition ahead of Labor?

People who cared about the future of Labor made a calculation as follows: barring an act of suicide by the Opposition—which seemed determined to find a cliff to jump off—and barring a decision by the caucus to act on the leadership, the government would go down at the next election. The lack of quality in the Liberal Party was not going to matter.

In mid-May, the polling companies were beginning to report a separate horror about the trouble for Labor in marginal seats in Western Australia and Queensland. The Morgan poll and private polling confirmed difficulties in Leichhardt, Flynn, Dawson and Herbert in Queensland; and in Swan, Hasluck, Stirling and Cowan in Western Australia.

Civil society took a battering when an objective, discoverable number such as actual taxes paid by the miners was a subject for vicious, partisan contest. Australia's national institutions are part of the thin thread that preserves our civilisation. While ever the basic institutions of Treasury, the Reserve Bank, the Australian Taxation Office, the Bureau of Statistics, the Electoral Commission and the armed forces are in the hands of people of integrity, Australia can survive any government.

A Final, Fatal About-Face

Beaten hollow in the debate, the government decided to spend tax dollars on government advertising in support of the mining tax. The weakness of Rudd determined this desperation. Unable to afford another about-face when, this time, an about-face was good policy, Rudd authorised an about-face of spectacular proportions to spend tax dollars in defence of his lost cause. Rudd had been crystal clear ahead of the 2007 election that party-political government advertising would come to an end. Government advertising in support of the political programs of a government, any government, was (said Rudd in 2007 over and over) 'a long-term cancer on democracy'. So it was. This about-face proved to be the final straw. Labor operatives not usually concerned with high standards of governance did understand what this betrayal meant. They spoke to each other and select others. One sentence sums up volumes of self-searching: 'If the caucus does not act, the nation will.'

When it came, the end was swift. The end was always going to be swift. Rudd lacked a friend or ally. His only factional base was high ratings in Newspoll. An alliance of convenience had become inconvenient. The fall was always going to be sudden—a surprise when it was finally launched, obvious and inevitable in retrospect.

For months the caucus had avoided addressing the certainty of defeat. Slowly but surely, all the rationalisations perished—first-term governments do not lose, people will not want to admit they were wrong—until all that remained was the codswallop that the punters will not vote for Abbott. As June was ending, the emptiness of that hope was shot. People were not prepared to vote for Abbott so much as they were determined not to vote for the government. Abbott was in a sweet spot and keeping low. Move then to the Victorian ALP right. One salient move directly to Julia Gillard—a foray sufficient to know her refusal was not a final word; a second foray to the NSW right where they discovered an enthusiasm equal to their own. It was not a lot of effort to establish pretty well all the right across Australia was united and ready to strike.

Perfect Strike

A story was planted in the *Sydney Morning Herald* that a staffer for the Prime Minister was canvassing support. In the cause of that canvass, he had reflected on the loyalty of the deputy. The story could not be planted in Melbourne. It did not matter that the story was not true. The substance of the story belies its truth; if it was true that a staffer was canvassing, the canvassing would have revealed itself to Gillard and others even as the canvass was taking place. Activity of that magnitude does not a secret remain.

Truth was not a critical factor; impact was. Gillard was prepared to believe that her leader was capable of such behaviour. Her colleagues and circle were hearing and seeing the shift in the electorate. Loyalty counted for only so much. Her defenders are entitled to observe she had offered more loyalty than was rational. Was the Deputy Prime Minister expected to sit on her hands so as to allow the government to proceed to certain defeat? Anyone who knows how politics works knew that the position for the government was irrecoverable. The leader had lost respect across the spectrum.

On the Tuesday going into Wednesday as June was ending, the arithmetic in caucus worked like this: the national right plus Gillard's support base plus those recognising the need for change equals 100-plus MPs and senators in a caucus of one hundred and twelve. Or you can write the same numbers in a different way: deep personal loathing (an absolute majority in its own right) plus terror of losing plus doing the right thing by the party equals 100-plus. However you counted, a spill was certain. Loyalty was not a card anyone was prepared to play. The caucus felt not a shard of loyalty was owing. A leadership contest would come to pass in which the leader would be struggling to poll two handfuls.

Sentiment, not reality, changed in 2010. The reality was constant; the reality was unpleasant. Sentiment changed when caucus members apprehended the one win they thought was in the bag was not going to happen. The certainty of defeat concentrates a mind powerfully. The leadership group in the government— all those in regular contact with the then leader—knew that the problem was personal. The mining tax had become a killer, an unnecessary war that the government was losing. The inner circle was as heartily sick as the punters at hearing the same words recited in defence of the tax as if repetition replaced the need for argument. The net effect of a government becalmed was an exponential shift in votes away. One-quarter of the Australian electorate had taken refuge with the Greens and 'don't know'.

In An Election in Which Neither Side Deserved to Win, Neither Side Won

Surely, there was no mystery about what happened on election day. Bad governments are treated harshly by the electorate. The government that fell without a shred of glory on 21 August was a very bad government. Without a record to vaunt and no program for the future, the leadership of the government and the ALP machine offered a campaign that was devoid of sparkle, ideas and conviction. The absence of intellectual depth to Labor's campaign came as a surprise to outsiders. Acres of newspapers and hours of broadcast time were devoted to 'discovering' that belief had departed Australian Labor. Believe in something, you attract and repel support. Believe powerfully, advocate rationally, get out and about driving ideas, you will also win respect. In elected office, beliefs are supposed to be the driving force to implement what you promised. If the electorate is unimpressed, you set about persuading the electorate of the correctness of your course. You do not retreat because of poll numbers. If the numbers are adverse, engage in an art you grew up understanding was intrinsic to Labor: the art of persuasion.

The Greens are backed by idealism and all the energy of youth. Now they are sanctified by a formal alliance with a minority Labor government. The alliance confers legitimacy on a political force whose central strategic purpose is the elimination of Labor as the alternative to mainstream conservatism—a mission made easier by Labor's redefining of itself as a party to the right of centre. It is remarkable that Labor is referred to without challenge by friend and foe alike as a 'brand'. Not a project, not a mission. 'If we are not a crusade we are nothing,' once declared Harold Wilson of UK Labour. Australian Labor is not a crusade; Labor is what it is: the rhetoric of the hour, words for the moment when only words will do.

Labor's model of governance is discredited. Caucus members have become abject servants of the will of the leader. Servitude will last as long as the poll numbers remain high. During it, there is no discussion, debate or discourse. The leader enunciates by diktat: his or her authority is accepted without question, usually with toadying. When the numbers fall, the phase ends. The end is swift. Total surrender is followed by assassination without an intervening period of soul searching. The electorate took a harsh view of the swiftness of assassination, as necessary as it was in June 2010. You cannot run a government this way.

For the moment and for maybe three years more, Labor can rely on the army of salaried staffers and taxpayer-funded postage, printing, telephones and electronic mail to offer the impression that the party is something more than a few hundred insiders. Without a party membership out there, the trickery and puffs of Labor's parliamentary leadership will have to be dead right. Labor has proven it can win elections without a party membership. Now it has no choice.

References

Cavalier, Rodney. 2009. 'Realigning the Planets: When Kevin took a walk down the corridor for a quiet talk with Kim, the next federal election was decided'. *Australian Cultural History* 27(2): 195–204.

Kelly, Paul. 2010. 'Labor in denial as ETS fairyland fractures'. *The Australian*, 24 February.

4. The Ideological Contest

Carol Johnson

The year before Kevin Rudd won office, Julia Gillard (2006, 106–7) discussed how to defeat the Howard Government. She argued that Labor needed to 'unshackle' itself from the factional system. Ideological differences between the factions were no longer important given that members of Labor's left factions were often amongst the keenest supporters of market-oriented policies. She also argued that moving to the left to oppose Howard's so-called Culture Wars would not work. Rather, one needed to combat Howard by building 'a broader vision of Australia which is inclusive of those who rightly worry about jobs, health, education, roads, border security and the like' (Gillard 2003, 107).

Gillard's comments are instructive. First, they explain how Gillard, as a member of a left faction, gained the support of right factional leaders to topple Rudd. Second, despite her avowedly 'post-ideological' position, they explain some of her own ideological influences in the 2010 campaign, including why the ideological differentiation with the Liberals was not as explicit as it could have been on economic issues such as market failure. Third, her arguments about the need to address mainstream voters' concerns (as she conceived them) help to explain why Labor had such a small-target strategy on social issues and the steps taken to reassure socially conservative voters on issues from asylum-seekers to immigration. In other words, Gillard's views influenced the 2010 campaign; key features cannot be explained just in terms of the influence of Labor figures such as Mark Arbib and Karl Bitar.

On the eve of his removal as leader, Rudd (2010) suggested that supporting Gillard would involve a move to the right on issues such as asylum-seekers and climate change. Rudd had a point and it was not just because Gillard was electorally pragmatic or trying to downplay her left credentials in order to get right-wing support. Gillard's position on climate change and asylum-seekers will be discussed later. Her views on markets, however, also suggest a degree of difference with Rudd. For Rudd was not the only ghost of leaders past who haunted Gillard. The other was Mark Latham—a campaign distraction in 2007, but also a leader to whom Gillard had once been close. When reflecting on Labor's 2004 election defeat, Gillard had argued that Labor should ditch any old ideological allegiances to the public as opposed to the private sector:

> People rightly expect a government that will strive to meet [their] expectations, free of the ideological public/private divides…We have not yet extended that same flexibility (as in past economic reforms)—and

in some cases market forces—to expanding the opportunity, delivering more effective public services and protecting our environment. (Cited in Schubert 2004)

Gillard went on to praise Latham's performance as Labor leader—and her comments reflect his influence. Latham (2003a; see further Johnson 2004) saw markets as a cleansing force that would utilise market competition to undermine the position of overly powerful elite capitalists. His arguments help to explain the appeal of neo-liberalism to some social democrats (Johnson 2007, 180). Latham, however, went further than most social democrats, including Gillard, by arguing that the struggle between labour and capital had now been replaced with aspirational voters and an information economy (Johnson 2004, 537). Significantly, as we will see later in terms of Gillard's 2010 position, Latham (2003b) had also argued for a focus on hard work and responsibility, and for downplaying 'symbolic' social issues, to win key suburban seats.

Rudd also frequently supported markets but identified major areas of market failure. Indeed, recognition of market failure underlay Rudd's arguments in the 2007 election campaign for the need for government to regulate fair working conditions (as opposed to the market commodification of people he believed underlay WorkChoices); the need for major government expenditure and involvement to provide high-speed broadband; and the need to tackle climate change, including putting a price on carbon (see Rudd 2006a, 2006b, 2007). These deep reservations about markets subsequently reinforced Rudd's (2009) support for a substantial stimulus package during the global financial crisis (GFC).

In contrast, Gillard (2010c) only occasionally criticised the market, although she noted the need to engage in 'market design' to 'unblock' market failures. Yet her comments on 'market design' said much less about market failure than some of the writings by the Per Capita Think Tank that had influenced her use of that term (Hetherington 2010). Consequently, there was no overarching narrative into which to fit Gillard's support for measures such as a carbon price. The market failures of the GFC were not outlined during the election campaign but alluded to only indirectly through her argument that the Government's stimulus package had supported jobs. There was no detailed attempt to explain a Keynesian argument that government deficits were necessary and justifiable in times of cyclical capitalist downturn to keep up employment and consumption. While Rudd's critiques of the downside of free-market capitalism were prominent, one was left with little idea of what Gillard (2010c) thought had caused the GFC.

Indeed, the Gillard Government's (and the public's) focus on returning the budget to surplus so quickly and tackling government debt (despite the low level of net public-sector debt as a proportion of GDP compared with other Organisation for Economic Cooperation and Development countries such as Britain) reflected an ongoing neo-liberal influence that had also been present under Rudd (but had been partially balanced by his critique of extreme neo-liberalism). Gillard's education revolution also reflected Latham's neo-liberal influences, including implementing market competitiveness via parental choice in the MySchool web site and an emphasis on individual capability (Gillard 2010b).

Gillard did claim to be still committed to a carbon price but her electoral cautiousness, and desire to get the budget back into surplus quickly, had apparently led her and Wayne Swan to argue initially that an emissions trading scheme (ETS) should be dumped—a move reportedly fiercely resisted by Climate Change Minister Penny Wong and Finance Minister Lindsay Tanner (Franklin 2010b, 4; Taylor 2010). The end result was an argument for the long-term delay of an ETS until 'consensus' had been achieved (Oakes 2010), partly via the utilisation of a (much derided) citizens' assembly. Labor's support for the Mining Super Profits Tax (that sparked a major campaign against it by the miners before Gillard's concessions bought off some of the biggest opponents) was also based not only on addressing the issues of a two-speed economy but also on finding a revenue source for infrastructural and other expenses that would avoid a further blowout of the bottom line.

Gillard did make some key distinctions between Labor and the Liberals. For example, she claimed that she had felt obliged to become leader because 'I love this country and I was not going to sit idly by and watch an incoming Opposition cut education, cut health and smash rights at work' (Gillard and Swan 2010). Nonetheless, the lack of a more explicit, broader ideological differentiation between Liberal and Labor might have contributed to the high rate of informal votes and was exacerbated by Labor's small-target strategy on social issues.

The scare campaign against Abbott was largely targeted at the alleged risk he posed on issues of economic management and industrial relations. He was not targeted for his views on social issues such as gender—including his claims during the campaign that Aussie blokes had trouble dealing with contemporary society because 'hard wired into just about every bloke is this kind of hunter warrior instinct' (cited in Kearney 2010). Worried about neutralising the effect of her unmarried, childless, atheist persona, Gillard acknowledged the importance of Australia's 'Christian heritage' for opposing same-sex marriage (cited in Shanahan and Kelly 2010), thereby continuing the previous Labor strategy of using same-sex marriage as a 'sign' of social conservatism.

On asylum-seeker issues, Gillard (ABC 2010a) aimed to steer a middle path between right and left, claiming that one should demonise neither as 'rednecks' people who were understandably anxious about boats arriving nor as 'bleeding hearts' those concerned about children behind razor wire, but feel empathy for both.

Consequently, Gillard (Oakes 2010) displayed little empathy for adult asylum-seekers, although showing motherly concern for their 'innocent' children. She did use figures on the low numbers of asylum-seekers to try to undermine Abbott's scare campaign (O'Brien 2010a). Nonetheless, her comments about a 'sustainable' rather than a 'big' Australia (Franklin 2010a) were commonly seen as a dog whistle on immigration issues as well as an attempt to address legitimate concerns about outer-urban infrastructure and transport issues. On both asylum and immigration issues, Gillard was trying to address the tensions that she had previously argued Howard and Abbott had exploited between Labor's 'blue collar' and 'tertiary educated' constituencies (Gillard 2003, 104). This framing of Labor's electoral problems risks reinforcing socially conservative constructions both of working-class attitudes and of working-class identity. It downplays the ethnic and social diversity within the Australian working class itself as well as potential links between the working class and other disadvantaged groups. It also reveals the ongoing influence on the Labor Party of Howard's neo-liberal constructions of so-called 'elite', politically correct issues and 'mainstream' issues (Johnson 2007, 39–50).

The result was an even less explicit differentiation on social issues than had occurred during the 2007 Rudd campaign. Admittedly, Gillard's gender was meant to be a sign of progressive social views, just as Rudd's multi-racial family and Mandarin-speaking abilities had been used to project this symbolically in 2007. Yet few of the differences between Gillard and Abbott on social issues were highlighted during the campaign, perhaps out of a belief that they would alienate the outer-suburban voters, such as those of western Sydney, to whom the campaign appeared to be held hostage (Jones 2010). Labor's paid parental-leave scheme was an important innovation for parents, although Abbott's scheme was arguably more financially generous, particularly to middle and higher income earners. Labor's announcement of support for an extra two weeks' support for fathers when the child was born also encouraged men to play more of a parenting role (ALP 2010). Gillard (2010a) claimed that the reason Labor reneged on its 2007 promises to massively extend day care and childcare centre provision was because of the collapse of the ABC Learning childcare centres.

Gillard's emphasis on work had more in common with a Blairite conception focusing on work as the key to social inclusion and less in common with the broader Keatingite conception of social inclusion that included social movement, Indigenous and multicultural issues (Johnson and Tonkiss 2002). Lowitja O'Donoghue complained during Gillard's *Q&A* appearance about the lack of content on Indigenous issues during the election campaign (ABC 2010a). Though Gillard's proposals for modernising welfare by increasing responsibility harked back to a Keatingite agenda of reciprocal obligation, measures such as partial income quarantining for those failing to act responsibly went much further than Keating's policies (Gillard and ALP 2010). The emphasis on hard work and responsibility to attract suburban voters also had echoes of Latham.

Overall, there was little new in Labor's strategy; it harked back to earlier arguments about information technology and the education revolution that had been used by Kim Beazley and Latham as well as by Rudd in 2007. It was, however, 'Rudd-lite' in its arguments about the need for a national broadband network and a carbon price but without the related emphasis on market failure driving the need for state action. It was arguably an even smaller-target campaign on progressive social issues than in Labor campaigns under Howard. Like previous small-target campaigns, it arguably reinforced, rather than undermined, the socially conservative views advocated by the Liberals. It also apparently drove many disillusioned former Labor voters to vote for the Greens—a result that saw a major reduction in Labor's primary vote with longer-term implications for ideological challenges from the left that Labor still has to come to grips with.

Significantly, Adam Bandt, the new Greens MP for Melbourne, ran not only on the basis of supporting a carbon tax and same-sex marriage and abolishing mandatory detention of asylum-seekers but also on a policy of abolishing Howard's draconian Australian Building and Construction Commission— retained by the Gillard Government. His reputation as an industrial lawyer was partly based on a successful appeal to the International Labour Organisation (ILO) against aspects of Labor's *Fair Work Act*. Meanwhile, former NSW Labor Premier Morris Iemma pointed out that the anti-immigration message of a sustainable Australia not a big Australia had led to a massive drop in the multicultural vote in Sydney electorates (ABC 2010b).

There were substantial swings against Labor in parts of the electorate of Minister for Sustainable Development Tony Burke which had a high migrant population (Saulwick 2010). Such developments problematise Labor's understandings of how 'progressive' social issues work out amongst working-class and suburban electorates—including overly simplistic conceptions of tensions between suburban 'blue collar' and inner-city 'tertiary educated' voters. Here, as elsewhere, Gillard's original arguments regarding how to defeat Howard fed into her views about how to defeat Abbott (whom she had identified as one of Howard's key henchmen).

Abbott

Despite Labor's small-target strategy, there were still underlying ideological differences between Labor and Liberal, even if they were not always highlighted in the election campaign. The differences on economic policy were apparent well before the election in a piece Abbott wrote in response to Rudd's (2009) article on the GFC in *The Monthly*. Abbott (2009) lauded the role of market forces, arguing that 'greater exposure to market forces over the last three decades has eventually led to more jobs, higher pay and much greater wealth'. He argued against Rudd's analysis of market failure as a cause of the GFC, claiming that Rudd 'has confused a cyclical (if severe) downturn with a fundamental crisis of capitalism' (Abbott 2009).

Consequently, Rudd's essay was 'a rallying cry for everyone who doesn't trust markets and who thinks that the government is far more likely to spend money wisely than misguided individuals' (Abbott 2009). Abbott (2009) argued that Rudd's second, $42 billion stimulus package was unnecessary—a sign of panic and a justification for shifting 'from being an "economic conservative" to a born-again socialist'. Furthermore, Abbott (2009) claimed that neo-liberalism had 'never really existed outside the theorising of the academic Right and the fantasising of the academic Left'. Abbott's emphasis on reducing government debt showed, however, clear neo-liberal influences, as did his arguments that markets, and the individuals involved, make better financial and investment decisions than governments.

Nonetheless, the Liberals had learned their electoral lesson about introducing extreme market policies in the workplace. Abbott (Mitchell 2010) claimed that WorkChoices was 'dead, buried and cremated'. He still managed, however, to mobilise anti-union arguments by suggesting that prominent unionists were amongst the 'faceless men' who had deposed Kevin Rudd (Curtis 2010). I have argued elsewhere that WorkChoices reinvigorated a class-based theory of exploitation in the 2007 campaign as opposed to the normal neo-liberal arguments that 'mainstream' taxpayers were being ripped off by government largesse given to politically correct elites and special interests (Johnson 2010). Abbott's proclaimed ditching of WorkChoices attempted to head off a Labor and union mobilisation of class issues. In addition, Abbott's arguments about 'all talk and no action' evoked a conception that opposed the Labor chattering classes with ordinary practical people who got the important things done.

The repeated images of Abbott in protective vests, driving forklifts or engaging in other 'action man' activities, reinforced that conception. Abbott's (2010a) critique of government waste suggested that taxpayers' dollars were now being ripped off, not so much because of 'special interests' as because of an incompetent, spendthrift government. He also suggested that the Government would be imposing big new taxes to further its environmental agenda, and that, at the least, climate change issues were exaggerated and could be dealt with by the Liberals' 'direct action' measures (Abbott 2010a). In the process, Abbott was mobilising a particular version of masculinity tied to a version of neo-liberalism.

At the same time, Abbott tried to tackle his problems in appealing to women voters by championing a generous parental-leave scheme funded from a levy on big business—a move that some commentators thought owed more to the past ideological influence of B. A. Santamaria on his thought than neo-liberalism (Kelly 2010). Abbott argued that it was 'not just a visionary social reform but it is an important economic reform too. It will…give women the real choice that they need and have been denied for too long' (Gillard and Abbott 2010). He also appeared regularly in public with his wife and/or daughters.

Abbott proposed a number of measures designed to increase employment participation—from an incentive to employers to take on seniors, relocation allowances and job commitment bonuses for long-term unemployed young people to training packages for job seekers. He acknowledged the influence of Noel Pearson on his thought on employment capability issues (Abbott 2010b). Abbott's (and Pearson's) arguments reflected a neo-liberal, individual capability approach (Jayasuriya 2006, 34–53, 161–2).

> My ambition is for us to make the journey from welfare state to opportunity society. An opportunity society which preserves the comprehensive safety net but which eliminates the cancer of passive welfare which has caused intergenerational welfare to become a tragic way of life for too many of our fellow Australians. (Abbott 2010b)

Abbott's key ideas were summed up clearly and succinctly in the Liberals' 'Action Contract: A strong plan for Australia'. Key elements of this plan included rejecting 'Labor's massive new mining tax and other taxes that hurt productivity', restoring budget surpluses and repaying Labor's debt, ending government waste, protecting the private health system while also improving the public one, border security and restoring work for the dole (Liberal Party of Australia 2010). Labor had been 'wasting billions on pink batts and overpriced school halls. They're borrowing $100 million every single day, and they're threatening our economic future with their great big new tax on mining' (Gillard and Abbott 2010).

Abbott's agenda was not a new one. He was in fact running on a very traditional Liberal agenda, revisiting strategies and familiar arguments used in past election campaigns. His border-security arguments drew heavily on arguments from the 2001 election campaign. His focus on economic management drew on arguments that John Howard had continually made that the Coalition was a better economic manager and that Labor was economically 'risky'. The difference was that Abbott was now focused on the Rudd and Gillard Governments' stimulus debt, new taxes and claims of waste, rather than focusing on Hawke and Keating Government issues of spending and interest rates.

The Election Aftermath

As discussed in depth elsewhere in this book, neither Labor nor the Coalition won the 2010 election directly. It is worth noting, however, that Abbott's problems gaining the support of the rural independents were partly a legacy of the neo-liberal ideology of the Howard years and the extent to which The Nationals had been pulled in to support their Coalition partner's free-market agenda, with its smaller role for government. Rob Oakeshott claimed to be 'more Liberal-leaning' on economic policy (cited in Silmalis 2010) than he was on social policy but still saw the importance of substantial government funding for broadband and hospitals as important (Oakeshott 2010). Tony Windsor (2010) also nominated government service provision—in the form of health care and broadband—as major issues for his constituents. Windsor (2010) justified his position to his conservative constituents by arguing that '[p]hilosophy, in terms of both these parties, died about a decade ago or probably longer'. He still said, however, that 'possibly the most critical' factor in his decision was broadband (Windsor 2010).

The Government's major role in providing broadband did display a different philosophical position from the Liberals (Johnson 2011). After all, Abbott (O'Brien 2010b) opposed Labor's broadband scheme by arguing that 'we just don't believe that re-creating a government-owned telecommunications monopoly is the way to go. We think that competition and diversity of technology is the way to go.' Despite his eventual support for the Coalition forming government, Bob Katter was even scathing of the impact on his constituents of the Coalition's deregulation (of milk), free-trade agreements (on sugar) and privatisation (of Telstra) (O'Brien 2010c).

Conclusion

The election outcome was influenced by multiple factors, including a Labor government that had failed to manage policy implementation or to communicate effectively, and a leadership coup. There was also the much criticised influence of NSW Labor powerbrokers on the campaign—although this chapter has identified some of the earlier antecedents in Labor strategy. Both parties now find themselves facing long-term ideological dilemmas. Under Rudd, Labor had been forging a relatively clear ideological narrative, involving critiques of neo-liberalism and market failure (even if it was increasingly poorly communicated by Rudd himself). According to that narrative, the inhumanity of extreme free-market policies, typified by WorkChoices, combined with the market failures typified by climate change, the GFC and the poor provision of infrastructure, such as broadband, demonstrated the failures of neo-liberal ideology. A social-democratic approach, based on a judicious use of market forces combined with government regulation, infrastructure spending and provision of services, was therefore necessary.

That narrative was not so clearly articulated by Julia Gillard. This is despite the fact that, while Gillard might be less critical of markets and neo-liberalism than Rudd was, she still has clear ideological differences with Abbott when it comes to the role of government in the economy and society, as her comments on issues ranging from health and education to broadband and industrial relations reveal. Labor is, however, now under challenge from more radical Greens perspectives, and Labor's small-target strategy and dog whistling on issues such as immigration saw very little said about broader conceptions of social inclusion. Gillard (2007) had celebrated the 'rebirth' of Labor's interest in ideas several years before, arguing that '[w]e must have the capacity to mould the wider political and intellectual agenda if we want to achieve government, hold on to it, and use it to change the country for the better'. The result of the 2010 election suggests that Labor still has a lot of intellectual work to do.

The Liberals are not, however, without their ideological dilemmas, too. The labour-market reform that Howard, Costello and Abbott himself had once seen as being crucial to their ideological agenda proved so electorally unpopular that Abbott had to declare its political cremation (although the Coalition might have tinkered with the existing regulations if elected). Meanwhile, free-market policies and problems of market failure (for example, in regard to broadband) increased support for independents in country and regional areas and contributed to the Coalition's failure to form government. In short, the 2010 election campaign demonstrated that both parties face ongoing ideological dilemmas.

References

Abbott, Tony. 2009. 'Misguided, would-be Messiah'. *The Weekend Australian*, 7 February, viewed 13 December 2010, <http://www.tonyabbott.com.au/LatestNews/ArticleswrittenbyTony/tabid/87/articleType/ArticleView/articleId/7045/MISGUIDED-WOULD-BE-MESSIAH.aspx>

Abbott, Tony. 2010a. Address to the Liberal Party, 151st Victorian Division, State Council, 17 April, Melbourne, viewed 15 July 2010, <http://www.tonyabbott.com.au/LatestNews/Speeches/tabid/88/articleType/ArticleView/articleId/7342/Address-to-the-Liberal-Party-151st-Victorian-Division-State-Council-Melbourne-17-04.aspx>

Abbott, Tony. 2010b. National Press Club address, 17 August, Canberra, viewed 3 September 2010, <http://www.tonyabbott.com.au/LatestNews/Speeches/tabid/88/articleType/ArticleView/articleId/7632/National-Press-Club-Address-Canberra.aspx>

Australian Broadcasting Corporation (ABC). 2010a. 'Julia Gillard joins *Q&A*'. *Q&A*, 9 August, ABC TV, viewed 28 August 2010, <http://www.abc.net.au/tv/qanda/txt/s2971154.htm?show=transcript>

Australian Broadcasting Corporation (ABC). 2010b. '"NSW disease" blamed for Labor loss'. *Stateline New South Wales*, 27 August 2010, ABC TV, viewed 6 September 2010, <http://www.abc.net.au/news/video/2010/08/27/2995969.htm?site=perth>

Australian Labor Party (ALP). 2010. Paid paternity leave, Australian Labor Party, Canberra, viewed 2 September 2010, <http://www.alp.org.au/agenda/more---policies/paid-paternity-leave/>

Curtis, Lyndal. 2010. 'Interview with Tony Abbott'. *AM*, 25 June, ABC Radio, viewed 3 September 2010, <http://tonyabbott.com.au/LatestNews/PressReleases/tabid/86/ArticleType/ArticleView/ArticleID/7486/Default.aspx>

Franklin, Matthew. 2010a. 'Not going forward PM'. *The Australian*, 21 July, 1–2.

Franklin, Matthew. 2010b. 'Mistakes, we made a few: Rudd shares the blame for Labor's errors'. *The Australian*, 24 November, 1, 4.

Gillard, Julia. 2003. 'Winning the culture war'. *The Sydney Papers* (Summer): 98–107.

Gillard, Julia. 2006. 'Courage, convictions & the community, the next ten years'. *The Sydney Papers* (Autumn): 102–10.

Gillard, Julia. 2007. Fabian Society Annual Dinner speech, 31 August, viewed 5 September 2007, <http://www.alp.org.au/media/0807/spedlop310.php>

Gillard, Julia. 2010a. Radio Interview, *ABC 774* [Melbourne], 27 April, ABC Radio, viewed 31 August 2010, <http://www.australia.to/2010/index.php?option=com_content&view=article&id=2413:julia-gillard-radio-interview-on-abc-774-melbourne-&catid=100:just-in&Itemid=176>

Gillard, Julia. 2010b. Australia's productivity challenge: a key role for education, Speech to John Curtin Institute of Public Policy, 10 June, Minister's Media

Centre, Department of Education, Employment and Workplace Relations, Canberra, viewed 31 August 2010, <http://www.deewr.gov.au/Ministers/ Gillard/Media/Speeches/Pages/Article_100610_130719.aspx>

Gillard, Julia. 2010c. Moving forward to a stronger and fairer economy, Speech to the National Press Club, 15 July, Canberra, viewed 6 July 2010, <http:// www.pm.gov.au/node/6892>

Gillard, Julia. 2010d. Interview transcript, Radio 2UE [Sydney], 21 July, viewed 21 July 2010, <http://www.alp.org.au/federal-government/news/transcript--2ue-interview/>

Gillard, Julia and Abbott, Tony. 2010. 'Leaders debate', National Press Club, 25 July, Canberra, viewed 3 September 2010, <http://www.tonyabbott.com. au/LatestNews/InterviewTranscripts/tabid/85/articleType/ArticleView/ articleId/7510/Leaders-Debate-National-Press-Club.aspx>

Gillard, Julia and Australian Labor Party (ALP). 2010. Modernising Australia's welfare system, Labor Party Policies, Australian Labor Party, Canberra, viewed 27 August 2010, <http://www.alp.org.au/agenda/more---policies/ modernising-welfare/>

Gillard, Julia and Swan, Wayne. 2010. Press conference with the Hon. Wayne Swan MP, Deputy Prime Minister, 24 June, Parliament House, Canberra, viewed 26 June 2010, <http://www.deewr.gov.au/Ministers/Gillard/Media/ Transcripts/Pages/Article_100624_152904.aspx>

Hetherington, David. 2010. 'A fairer design for markets'. *Per Capita*, viewed 31 August 2010, <http://www.percapita.org.au/01_cms/details.asp?ID=243>

Jayasuriya, Kanishka. 2006. *Statecraft, Welfare, and the Politics of Inclusion.* Basingstoke, UK: Palgrave Macmillan.

Johnson, Carol. 2004. 'Mark Latham and the ideology of the ALP'. *Australian Journal of Political Science* 39: 535–52.

Johnson, Carol. 2007. *Governing Change: From Keating to Howard* [Second edition]. Perth: API Network.

Johnson, Carol. 2010. 'The ideological contest'. *Australian Cultural History* 28(1): 7–14.

Johnson, Carol. 2011. 'The politics of broadband: Labor and new information technology from Hawke to Gillard'. *Australian Journal of Political Science.*

Johnson, Carol and Tonkiss, Fran. 2002. 'The third influence: the Blair Government and Australian Labor'. *Policy and Politics* 30(1): 5–18.

Jones, Tony. 2010. 'Labor campaign panned by pioneer pollster', [Interview with Rod Cameron], *Lateline*, 8 September, ABC TV, viewed 10 September 2010, <http://www.abc.net.au/lateline/content/2010/s3006629.htm>

Kearney, Simon. 2010. 'Blokes are doing it tough: Abbott'. *Sunday Mail*, 15 August, 11.

Kelly, Paul. 2010. 'Abbott plays a decisive card'. *The Australian*, 13 March, viewed 3 September 2010, <http://www.theaustralian.com.au/news/opinion/abbott-plays-a-decisive-card/story-e6frg6zo-1225840206167>

Latham, Mark. 2003a. Competitive capitalism versus crony capitalism: the difference between Labor and Liberal, Speech to the International Chief Executive Officers Forum, 19 August, Canberra, viewed 19 September 2005, <http://www.smh.com.au/articles/2003/08/19/1061261153599.html>

Latham, Mark. 2003b. *From the Suburbs: Building a nation from our neighbourhoods*. Annandale, NSW: Pluto Press.

Liberal Party of Australia. 2010. The Liberals Our Action Contract: A strong plan for Australia, Liberal Party Policies, Liberal Party of Australia, Barton, ACT, viewed 8 September 2010, <http://www.liberal.org.au/~/media/Files/Policies%20and%20Media/Our%20Action%20Contract.ashx>

Mitchell, Neil. 2010. 'Interview with Tony Abbott', *Radio 3AW* [Melbourne], 19 July, viewed 3 September 2010, <http://www.tonyabbott.com.au/LatestNews/InterviewTranscripts/tabid/85/ArticleType/ArticleView/ArticleID/7496/Default.aspx>

Oakes, Laurie. 2010. 'Interview with Julia Gillard'. *Today*, 27 June 2010, Channel Nine, viewed 29 June 2010, <http://today.ninemsn.com.au/article.aspx?id=1076748>

Oakeshott, Rob. 2010. 'Transcript of announcement'. *The Age*, 7 September, viewed 7 September 2010, <http://www.theage.com.au/federal-election/transcript-of-rob-oakeshotts-announcement-20100907-14zex.html>

O'Brien, Kerry. 2010a. 'Gillard's first day in office'. *7.30 Report*, 24 June, ABC TV, viewed 26 June 2010, <http://www.abc.net.au/7.30/content/2010/s2936464.htm>

O'Brien, Kerry. 2010b. 'Abbott quizzed on broadband and economy', [Interview with Tony Abbott]. *7.30 Report*, 10 August, ABC TV, viewed 31 August 2010, <http://www.abc.net.au/7.30/content/2010/s2979381.htm>

O'Brien, Kerry. 2010c. 'Independents: preparing for the pitches', [Interview with Tony Windsor, Rob Oakeshott and Bob Katter],.*7.30 Report*, 22 August, ABC TV, viewed 3 September 2010, <http://www.abc.net.au/7.30/content/2010/s2990184.htm>

Rudd, Kevin. 2006a. 'Child of Hayek'. *The Australian*, 20 December, 12.

Rudd, Kevin. 2006b. 'Howard's brutopia: the battle of ideas in Australian politics'. *The Monthly*, November, 46–50.

Rudd, Kevin. 2007. Radio interview, *ABC Melbourne*, 11 April, viewed 24 April 2007, <http://www.alp.org.au/media/0407/inloo111.php>

Rudd, Kevin. 2009. 'The global financial crisis'. *The Monthly*, February, 20–29.

Rudd, Kevin. 2010. Transcript of press conference with the Prime Minister, 23 June, Parliament House, Canberra, viewed 24 August 2010, <http://pmrudd.archive.dpmc.gov.au/node/6848>

Saulwick, Jacob. 2010. 'Upset migrants turn on ALP'. *Sydney Morning Herald*, 24 August, 6.

Schubert, Mischa. 2004. 'Labor must embrace market: Gillard'. *The Age*, 14 December, 4.

Shanahan, Dennis and Kelly, Paul. 2010. 'I'll do it my way, declares Julia Gillard'. *The Australian*, 20 August, viewed 4 September 2010, <http://www.theaustralian.com.au/national-affairs/ill-do-it-my-way-declares-julia-gillard/story-fn59niix-1225907498894>

Silmalis, Linda. 2010. 'Abbott warned: rein in your MPs'. *The Sunday Telegraph*, 29 August, viewed 3 September 2010, <http://www.news.com.au/features/federal-election/rein-in-your-mps-rob-oakeshott-warns-tony-abbott/story-fn5tas5k-1225911345298>

Taylor, Lenore. 2010. 'Decision that shattered faith in PM'. *Sydney Morning Herald*, 5 June, viewed 10 July 2010, <http://www.smh.com.au/opinion/politics/decision-that-shattered-faith-in-pm-20100604-xkiu.html>

Windsor, Tony. 2010. 'Transcript of announcement'. *The Age*, 7 September, viewed 7 September 2010, <http://www.theage.com.au/federal-election/transcript-of-tony-windsors-announcement-20100907-14zew.html?utm_source=twitterfeed&utm_medium=twitter>

Part 2. The Media and the Polls

5. The New Media and the Campaign

Peter John Chen

Over the past decade new media has moved from a marginal place in political campaigning in Australia to an integral element of the electoral strategies of political parties, candidates and some civil-society organisations. At the same time, the impact of these channels shifted from alternative avenues for political communication to intrinsic parts of coordinated and centralised multi-channel message distribution. In examining the role of new media in the 2010 election, this chapter examines the adoption and use of a variety of new and increasingly entrenched new media channels in the political communication mix in Australia. Using Norris and others' notions of 'modern' and 'postmodern' campaign strategies, this chapter identifies the current practices of the major parties in Australia as sitting between these two forms of meta-strategy. This is informed by a focus on a limited set of key media channels in Australia as the primary focus of political parties' attempts to define campaign narratives and the resultant dominance of the marketing model of political communication in Australian campaigns.

The narrow news agenda in Australia is the result of comparatively close relationships between campaign communications strategies and mainstream media production practices. In the 2010 electoral cycle, this was countered to some extent by a small number of civil-society actors who challenged media hegemony through deconstruction of contemporary media practice, as well as by new forms of political mobilisation led by the emerging third-party group GetUp!. To examine the place of new media in the 2010 election, this chapter looks at the media strategies of key actors: political parties and candidates, non-party organisations and alternative media (bloggers and micro-bloggers). Before we can discuss these actors, however, it is necessary to situate new media within its wider communication landscape. We see established and new media positioned within a complex media ecosystem of channels, actors and institutions that are bound together by competition, intersecting audiences, power relationships and inter-media agenda setting.

The Media Context for the Election

It is important to consider the role of new media in context. Elsewhere (see Chen 2010; Chen and Vromen 2010), we have established that an increasing amount of political content was consumed online compared with previous elections, and the consumption of political content increased during the electoral period (from circa 7 to 15 per cent of pages viewed). While this speaks to an increasing role for online media in electoral politics, we have also identified that the majority of this content is sourced from established commercial and public media channels (these factors are illustrated in Figure 5.1). Thus, while minor parties such as the Australian Greens might be encouraged by their comparatively high traffic rates given their voter share (Figure 5.2), this represents a tiny fraction of online content consumption overall.

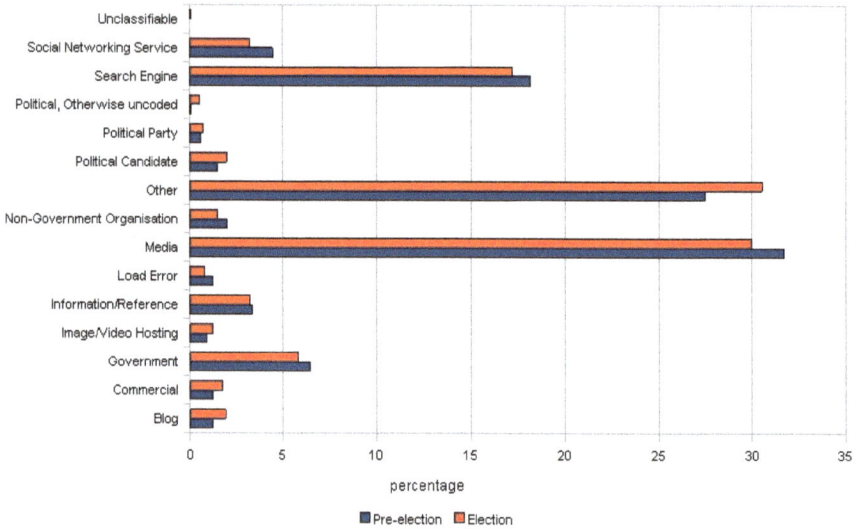

Figure 5.1 Average Users' Page Visits, Pre-Election and Election Period Compared

Source: Based on a panel study of Australian Internet users who were intending to vote in the 2010 election.

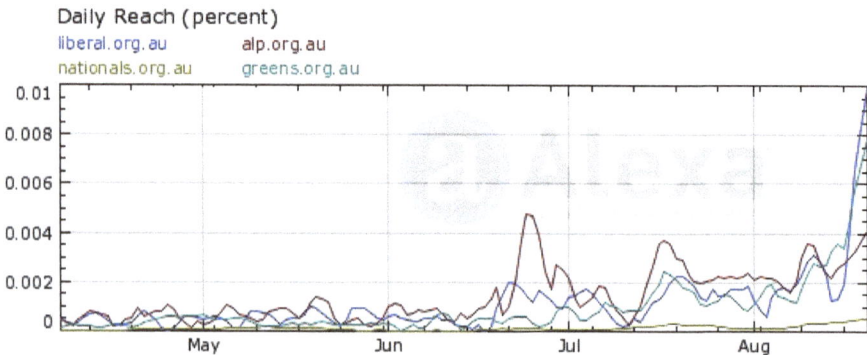

Figure 5.2 Web Traffic to Political Party Web Sites, April–August 2010

Source: Compiled from Alexa.

While this would speak to the 'normalisation' of new media's impact on politics (reversion to status quo and cooption by existing elites; Small 2008), the altering political economy of online news has seen a narrowing of political coverage online, with Goot (2008, 99) observing a greater bias towards coverage of the Government over Opposition or minor parties. Thus, while new media was expected to break free of hegemonic news agendas, the declining resource base for news construction online seems to have had the opposite effect overall. What we find interesting about the 2010 election, however, is not the prospect of mass conversion through online channels, but the relationship between new media and agenda-setting processes of control and resistance.

Insiders and the Battle for the Narrative

The Australian election in 2010 was interesting because of the comparatively small range of key themes and policies that consumed the campaign. While key policy topics are discussed in detail elsewhere in this volume, the political communication perspective leads to a focus on three meta-narratives that came to dominate coverage of the campaign and the immediate preceding period. These meta-narratives were: the 'horserace', illustrated in obsessive coverage of comparatively meaningless polling data (given the margin of error in close electoral contexts); the imposition of artificial relationship stories between key political actors (for example, Gillard–Abbott's 'flirting'; AAP 2009); and the engineering and disruption of pseudo-events, such as the insertion of Mark Latham into the election campaign as both an object of easy ridicule and a means of derailing planned campaign events (Esser and Spanier 2005).

The persistence of these meta-narratives is the result of situational and structural factors. While the comparatively late leadership change within the ALP was always likely to be a key story during the election given its novelty, gender clearly played a role in the fascination of political commentators with the relationship between Julia Gillard and Kevin Rudd. Unlike in the ascendency of Tony Abbott, here, a feminised role was projected on Julia Gillard through media frames that placed the emphasis on relationship repair (the quest for her apology; AAP 2010) and maintenance (Rudd's rehabilitation into the Cabinet) as obligations she had to meet—a narrative turn associated with an uncritical acceptance of Opposition and media claims of her unopposed election to leadership as somehow illegitimate due to the projection of presidentialism on the election of Kevin Rudd in 2007 (but more likely due to her gender). Structurally, the known length of the campaign and daily media packages provided by campaign teams have driven the focus on horserace reporting, with the resultant tendency to shift substantive coverage from policy topics into deconstruction of campaign strategies and the circular assessment by the media of campaign performance based on media performance and the capacity of candidates to 'win' each day's (or hour's) news cycle (Mutz 1995).[1]

None of the parties was able to break out of the constraints of these meta-narratives during the campaign, regardless of clear attempts by the Prime Minister to 'reboot' her campaign during the second week. This tends to demonstrate a number of factors about the Australian media ecosystem, but also about the way parties have responded to it. Overall, I argue that the political strategy of the major political parties can be seen to remain within the 'modern' paradigm identified by Norris (2000, 138): centralisation and emphasis on mass media, with largely undifferentiated messaging. This appears to be over-determined by the corresponding characteristics of media in Australia: its small number of major media channels, the tendency for increasing reliance on syndicated content, and the resulting narrowing of the media agendas reported across the country. The implications for this are both a loss of agenda-setting capacity to the media and a narrowing of the range of subject and depth likely to appear in political reporting.

Targeted Use of New Media

What is interesting is the extent to which parties were able and willing to move outside this model of communication. In this regard, there appears to be mixed results. On the one hand, it is clear that there are signs Lees-Marshment's (2001) marketing model has gained traction through the use of specialist consultancies and market research in shaping messages and campaign strategies. This picks up on the professionalisation approach developed in the United Kingdom during the 1990s (Gould 1999) to substitute for declining internal party resources. On the other hand, attempts to segment the marketplace and engage in diverse messaging strategies aimed at specific segments were considerably less successful.

Thus, while the Liberals largely 'went wide' with the three 'nos' (no to debt, boats and waste), the ALP employed the so-called 'small-bore' strategy pioneered by the Clinton campaign in the United States (Lowry 2003) and engaged in the cooption of policies associated with the Coalition, such as Internet filtering (Counihan 2010) and immigration policy. Without the extensive fragmentation seen in the United States through local media and particularly cable news channels, this failed to be effective. Targeted policy announcements ideal to this strategy were quickly coopted into national stories in the Australian media context; the use of the marketing approach itself was seen as a takeover of the

---

1   And increasingly the 'new-media' cycle, particularly given the ability of journalists to harvest numbers (followers, posts, and so on) from web sites. A good example of this is Guselli (2010).

federal ALP by the 'NSW disease', while issues focused on unrest in neglected areas of Sydney (such as rail announcements) were magnified into national stories. This was problematic given that their strategy relies on selective attention because of the inherent trade-off associated with the mass-party model it supports.

Here we see a weakness of Australia's increasingly cartelist party system.[2] Unable or unwilling to draw upon a wide range of policies initiated by the former leader during the election campaign, the ALP could not benefit from the advantages of incumbency. Under different circumstances, the Government would have entered the election with major advertising campaigns supporting both carbon trading and mining tax reform, bolstering their transition from government into the electoral process. In 2010, this was missing, providing a space for mining industry concerns and interventionist media to fill. In addition, neither party managed to fully capitalise on the online communities developed during previous elections. Thus, while previous leaders such as Rudd and Malcolm Turnbull had built up large numbers of followers on their various social networking services (SNS), their cultivation and use between elections were limited. This differs from the mobilisation of supporters undertaken by the administration of Barack Obama as a continuance of campaigning into government over key policy issues, which helps to sustain support networks developed during the campaign but also demonstrates that Australia's permanent campaign is more rhetorical than demonstrative. The tendency for campaign teams to mobilise late and demobilise quickly after elections undermines the community development value of these channels. That politics is increasingly mediatised is clear, but that is not the same as maintaining a constant campaign approach to all political communication.

This is not to say that segmentation and micro-channelling of messages were not employed in the campaign, but their capacity to realise significant benefits was limited. The most clear use of these types of new-media targeting was largely in the parody tactics employed by the ALP against Tony Abbott, including the establishment of the 'Phoney Tony' fake Twitter account (Kwek 2010a)—reusing the established online meme of parodying public figures on SNS—and the use of a customised billboard web site originally used in the 2010 UK general election. Figure 5.3 illustrates an example of the latter, which illustrate the connection between personal parody and policy criticism (in these examples, criticising Abbott's inability to articulate technical issues about the Coalition's alternative broadband policy). Other tactical approaches to market segmentation were less visible: the Australian Greens made a limited attempt to

---

2 Incumbency, however, still provides considerable advantages. In the case of new media, incumbency is positively associated with having a web site (0.39) and SNS (0.28).

69

mobilise voter enrolment through the use of a targeted YouTube video by Sarah Hanson-Young[3]—an approach dramatically overshadowed by GetUp!'s election trailer video.

Figure 5.3 Parody Billboards Posted at <www.tonyabbottisright.com>

Diversification in the Use of New Media

In examining the use of new media by candidates, we can identify that there are moves to shift campaigning from the mass model of modernism into a more postmodern style. This, Norris observes, employs overarching strategy with coordinated localism, allowing for message customisation at the local level. The Liberal Party, as an example, employed this in terms of television advertising at the lowest level of granularity for TV ad buying: using custom advertisements in Western Australia. They were also observed using Google AdWords to target key electorate searches (Howden 2010)—a tool that is much more surgical than mass media, but also requires a greater investment in human resources (time, decision making) for smaller audience yields.

---

3   'Don't waste your first time'—an entertaining spoof of the well-publicised advice of Tony Abbott to his daughters regarding their virginity (<http://sarah-hanson-young.greensmps.org.au/content/dont-waste-your-first-time>).

What is interesting is that the use of new media by candidates has considerably diversified over the years. This runs counter to our previous hypothesis (Chen and Walsh 2009) that greater provision of templated web sites and social networking profiles by parties would homogenise the representation of candidates online. This is illustrated in Figures 5.4 and 5.5.[4] The first illustrates the adoption of a range of new media channels by candidates in the 2010 election. What this shows is that there is considerable difference between the adoption of different channels between major parties (the ALP and Coalition) and minor parties, but that emerging minor parties (the Greens) appear to make up for areas of under-representation (web sites) with alternative channels (SNS)—a substitution effect previously observed. Importantly, Figure 5.5 (a compound figure that illustrates the visibility of candidates online based on the depth of content provided and the width of visible points of presence through multi-channelling) demonstrates the greater diversity of online performance in 2010 than in 2007. As a small number of key performers in all the three parties listed have dramatically increased their use of online media, this has shifted the average performance downwards on these relative scales.

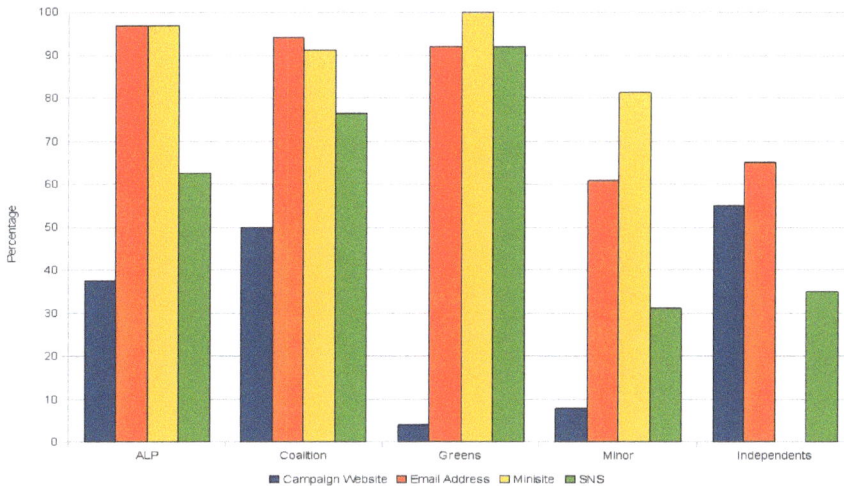

Figure 5.4 Candidates' Use of Online Communication Channels

---

4 These figures are based on the content analysis of 175 candidates.

Depth-Width, 2007 and 2010

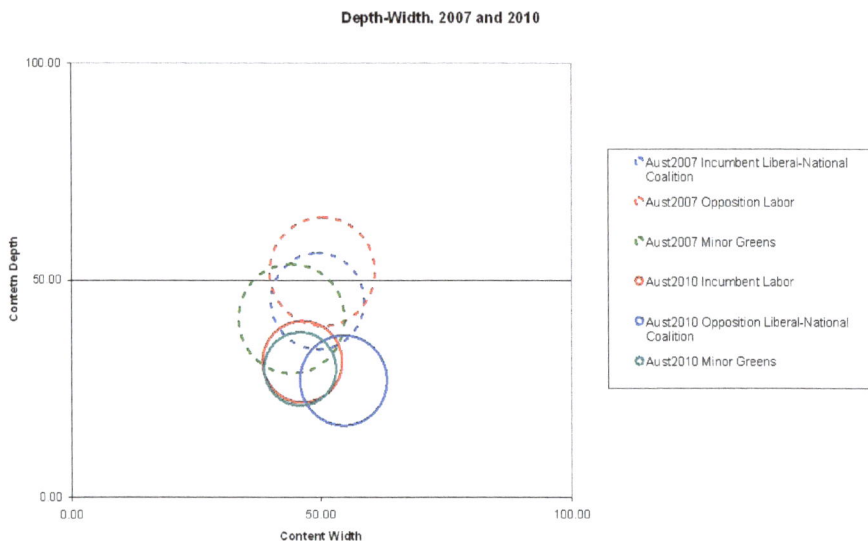

Figure 5.5 Candidates' Points of Presence Online: Clustered by party, 2007 and 2010

Equalisation and the Social Media Effect

Our assessment of previous elections has tended to follow Small's (2008) assessment of the Canadian experience: equalisation of access by minor parties without noticeable impact on their electoral performance. In one way, the discussion above demonstrates this to be the case in the 2010 election: regardless of the ability to present competitive online content, minor parties have entrenched disadvantages in the two-party system of Australia. This can be demonstrated better by looking at party systems, such as reports of major-party candidates developing the content of party databases using data mining and the freedom of information (FOI) requests of local government (Novak and Kenny 2010). While the Greens deployed new electoral-management technology in the lead-up to the 2010 election to increase their electoral intelligence, they were unable to make full use of this system due to issues of local training and capacity. This appears to reiterate previous findings from survey data that showed minor parties were far less likely to capture data into electoral-roll database systems during the campaign (Chen 2005); however, the building of capacity within the party, combined with the financial windfall associated with their strong result in 2010, could see this turn around in the next electoral cycle.

Additionally, it is not clear that internal capacity was as important as it has been in previous elections. A good example of this is the use of social networking systems within the party web sites—a practice undertaken in this election by the ALP (Campaign iQ) and Liberal (my Liberal) parties. This clearly follows the model used in the United States by the Obama presidential campaign: deliberate use of social networking (CeBIT 2010), but a focus on drawing communities into a domain controlled by the candidate, which provides greater control over what occurs,[5] but also better information about user behaviour for the purposes of mining information about participants. The success of this model in the Australian context, however, appears modest at best. As illustrated in Table 5.1, participation in these online forums was quite modest, and it is questionable whether the short time frame of the Australian electoral cycle is the best place to build these communities. Interestingly, in the case of the ALP, there appears to be no consistent plan to employ this platform post election, with the ALP's post-election review process using a separate submission system for members to submit feedback and input to the party, rather than the more interactive discussion forums established in Campaign iQ.

Table 5.1 Party Web Site Voter Engagement Performance

Party	Indicator	Week ending					
		21 July	28 July	4 August	11 August	18 August	25 August
ALP	Members	963	1325	1723	2073	2323	2608
	Groups	30	35	39	47	47	47
	Issues	2	2	2	2	2	2
	Ideas	60	101	162	238	267	287
	Comments	63	115	161	220	264	288
Liberal	Ideas	23	26	47	54	55	55
	Comments	209	400	550	737	804	854

Sources: Compiled from <www.alp.org.au>; <www.liberal.org.au>; <http://www.formspring.me/GreensMPs>

The capacity to draw supporters into your own social networking community requires considerable planning and incentives, which the Australian environment does not appear to provide. This meant that general SNS had greater appeal for members of the public who were more likely to use them as creative vehicles for political expression (see below) but also conventional political engagement. In this context, incumbency was less important than social capital, with the Greens able to exploit their comparatively younger audience to have greater traction through tools such as Twitter. Grant et al. (2010) identify presidentialism in services such as Twitter, which we discuss below; they also argue that the higher

---

5   It should be noted, however, that there appeared to be lower levels of message vetting on these systems than in previous years, with negative and critical messages allowed to stay up during the election campaign.

'conversational' nature of Greens politicians on this service leads to enhanced success and visibility for this group overall, which points to the increased potential for postmodern campaigning.

The shift away from static information repositories (Figure 5.6) has other implications for candidates' and parties' political communication. The narrative construction of the messages communicated through SNS (through successive chronological posts and RSS feeds) might serve to lock political actors more closely into the temporal flow of the campaign. While web sites have previously been criticised because of their static content and brochure-ware characteristics (for example, Gibson and Ward 2002), this is evidence of the way political actors will sometimes attempt to compress time—to capture key images and messages they wish to highlight and reiterate to audiences (Sanders 2009). While time compression can be misleading and distort the portrayal of events (indeed, it is the core aim of most political stunts and pseudo-events), it is a key means by which the relentless flow of news-cycle immediacy can be interrupted. Becoming embedded in a channel with a high rate of message decay both allows for adherence to the rapid response model of agenda management[6] and places weaker political actors into a subordinate position to major-media news issues of the day. This has considerable implications for power relations[7] within the Australian media ecosystem, which require further exploration.

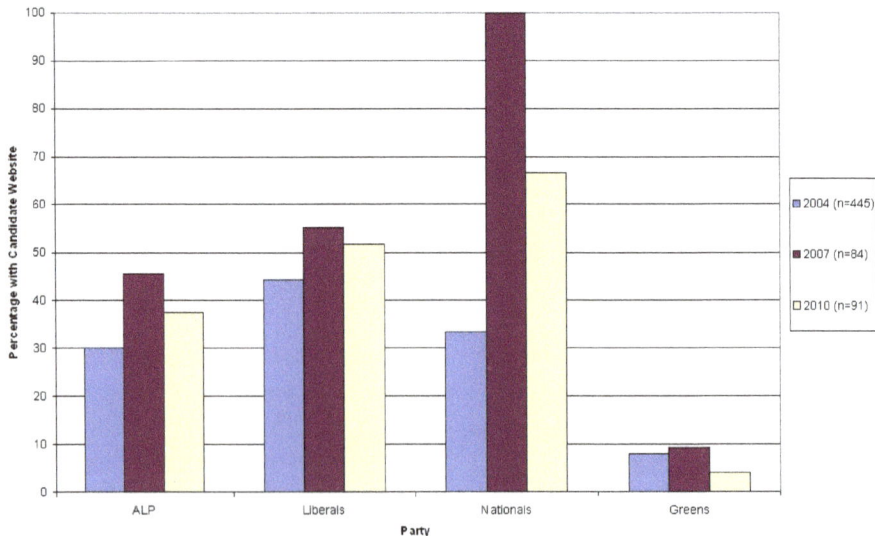

Figure 5.6 Candidates' Use of Personal Campaign Web Sites, 2004–10 by party

---

6   Additionally, digital video production and online distribution allowed services such as YouTube to be more important in the construction and distribution of quick-response ads and short videos (Gordon 2010).

7   For example, some politicians are using SMS and SNS messaging to enhance their source value (and influence) to journalists who are increasingly subject to the professional need for quick news production and instantaneous reporting (Meade 2010).

The Outsiders

Candidate-centric communication and journalist-source relations—while still critical in terms of the majority of online political content consumed—are increasingly challenged by outsiders. At the basic level, the rise of online media has undermined existing business models for news production and distribution, leading to the strengthening of a more limited range of meta-narratives, as previously discussed. On the other hand, new-media entrants have arisen that are increasingly interesting in terms of their ability to shape media agendas and mobilise political resources. These two political actors are seen in the rise of a new form of cultural production (gatewatching) and the virtualisation of interest groups and third-party political actors.

Gatewatchers

Bruns (2003) sees 'gatewatchers' as an emerging group of online content producers who observe, validate and criticise information produced by existing media organisations. He argues that due to the changing economics of information distribution, the privileged position the media channels to control access to information has been reduced through an increasing decline in scarcity. The implications of this are important: seeing the rise of new forms of content production (blogs, micro-blogs), new communities of interest (often gathered around specific interest areas that aggregate diverse content that might not have been economically feasible previously) and new forms of sociability.

The extent to which this dramatically alters the logic of political competition and performance is unclear. On one hand, it is possible to see the somewhat parasitic nature of some of these communities and channels as leading to an increased dependence on established content producers. This is visible in the tendency of SNS to be a virtuous circle for media and political celebrities. This was clear in the 2010 election when key political figures (leaders, but also individuals who remained strongly in the media spotlight as bitter ex-leaders) received considerable attention (both in terms of 'friendship' ties and as the subject of discussion). Figures 5.7, 5.8 and 5.9 illustrate this well: key figures receiving strong mainstream-media coverage benefit disproportionately in terms of online buzz. This reflects a tendency towards magnification of visibility online rather than diversity, which Hindman et al. (2003) refer to as the 'googlearchy'—a tendency also seen in Twitter coverage of election pseudo-events (Bourke 2010).

Twitter Followers (Sans Kevin Rudd)

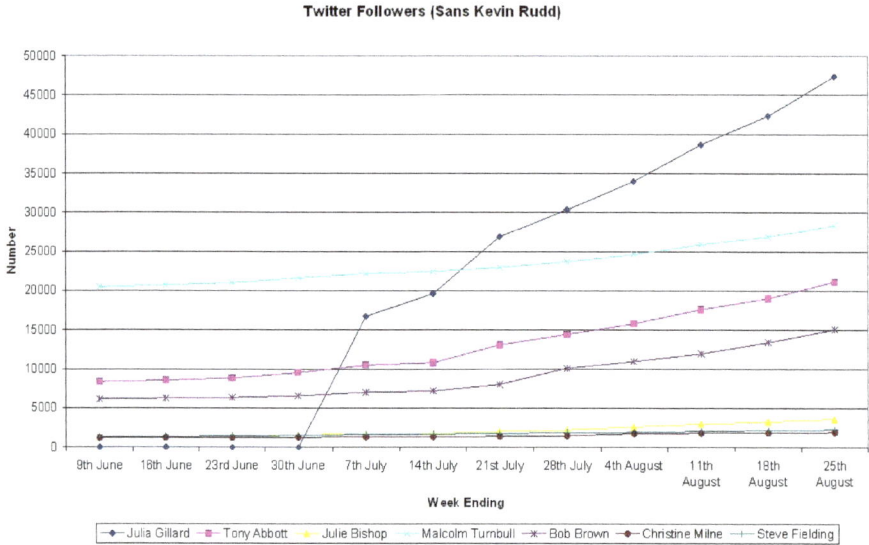

Figure 5.7 Party Leaders' Twitter Followers, June–August 2010

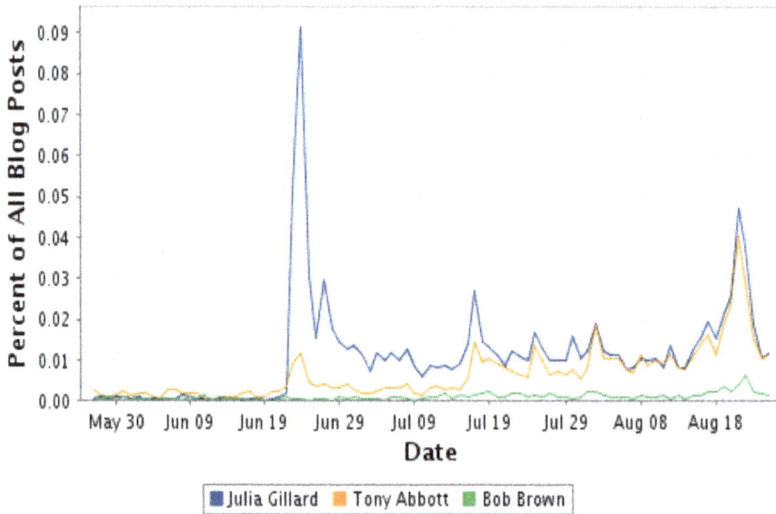

Figure 5.8 Comparative Attention Paid to Leaders in Blog Posts, May–August 2010

Tweet Contents

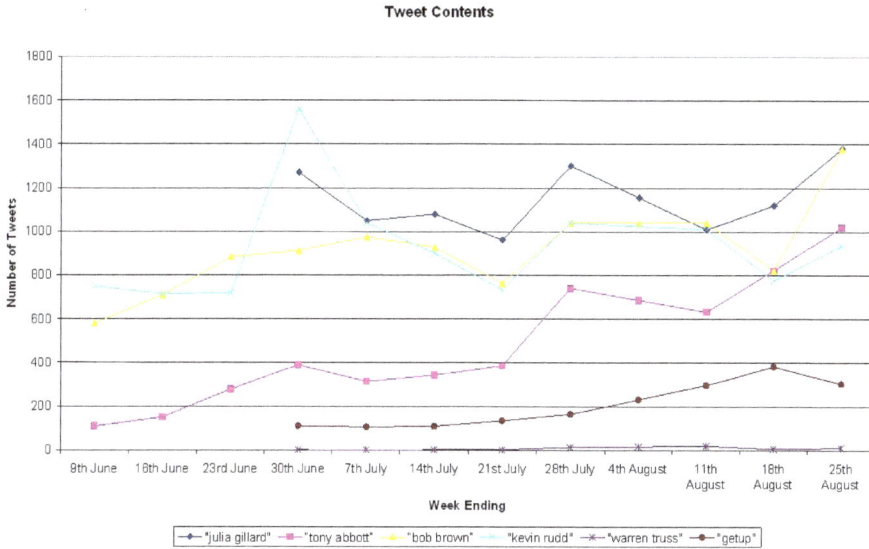

Figure 5.9 Content of Tweets Posted, June–August 2010

Source: Compiled from *Tweet Volume*.

Mass coverage is, however, only one aspect of this story and we have to recognise the growing importance of these forms of alternative media as scrutineers of journalistic practice (Cahill and Ward 2007). In the 2007 election this was seen in technical discussion of the use and interpretation of polling data in mainstream media (Flew 2008). Here the flipside of time-compression impacts is important. While we previously observed that this can make weaker actors subordinate to dominant narratives, services such as Twitter do allow time-compressed events to be unpacked. This was clearly the case in the relationship between Twitter-enabled audiences and key political pseudo-events.

While the integration (direct or indirect) of Twitter into campaign set-piece events generally fed into established meta-narratives (particularly an obsession with trivial issues, such as leaders' appearance; Buchanan and Elliott 2010), at times the online audiences were able to unpack mainstream-media claims about these events as legitimate places of public opinion formation, such as the identification of the son of a Liberal MP in the Rooty Hill leaders' debate (Kwek 2010b). This is significant in that the power of pseudo-events lies in the essential collaboration between politicians and journalists in the creation of reality and the suppression of its underlying artifice.

Audience deconstruction was a key area of gatewatching in the 2010 election, with a minor celebrity identified as a questioner in the ABC's *Q&A*, but also a degree of self-reflection about the very limited socioeconomic diversity among the gatewatchers themselves (Wilson 2010). In the post-election period, this has led to some tensions between established and online media, with journalists beginning to question and challenge the cultural norms of bloggers seen to be increasingly influential in shaping media coverage of electoral politics (Jericho 2010).

Emergent Models of Activism

The changing function of political parties and the resultant (or causal) impacts on political socialisation have undermined traditional means of defining political participation while generating new forms of activism. In the 2010 election, we can see that the expanding use of SNS within the community has opened new avenues for 'micro-activism', while the progressive advocacy group GetUp! had considerable success in mobilising resources in support of policies most clearly associated with the Australian Greens.

In previous elections, we have seen the use of parody web sites (Chen 2005) and videos as important vehicles for non-party political expression (Chen 2008). This online content has commonly taken the form of parodies of party leaders and signature policies. In doing so, they have tended to advocate, directly or indirectly, in favour of alternative voting decisions (a good example of the former would be <www.marklathamsucks.com> and of the latter would be the 'Johnny Overboard' web sites of the 2004 election). Over the past two election cycles in Australia these web sites have been in decline, as creative energy has shifted towards the more easily established and promoted use of groups on SNS. Examples such as 'Friends don't let friends vote for Tony Abbott' and 'That awkward moment when Julia Gillard takes your job' illustrate these types of group: each presents a specific party or party leaders (conservatism, disloyalty) while explicitly calling for votes against their respective parties.

Interestingly, while this form of campaigning has largely been discounted as low-engagement 'slactivism' (weak political engagement that demonstrates cynicism), Marichal (2010) argues that these channels of communication should be considered more carefully because of their increasing cultural pervasiveness, but also because of their capacity to provide a space for dialogue competing with and crosscutting political positions. This was previously observed in the use of online discussion forums behind 'Mark Latham Sucks', which presented a much more dynamic space for interaction than its (or its successors') name would suggest.

Even the comparatively non-directive version of these types of online expression (such as the women who changed their Facebook status to 'Julia' in celebration of the elevation of the first woman to the prime ministership; Tovey

2010) can be seen as interesting in the way this substitutes for other forms of political expression and alignment not generally seen in Australia (such as lawn signs, political discussions, or pins). These thus replace older forms of political expression, sustain social movement cultures, and import more public forms of political identity expression (or at least the public–private world of SNS).

More formally, the changing nature of advocacy politics saw the dramatic expansion of the influence of the left-wing group GetUp! in the 2010 campaign. Occupying a similar role to that of the 'Your Rights At Work' campaign from 2007, GetUp! aggregated membership donations and union funding towards a broad set of initiatives in the lead-up to and during the campaign. The media influence of the group is impressive—as illustrated in Table 5.2—pulling a far greater share of views to its video material than any of the political parties (largely due to the spoof movie trailer aimed at encouraging younger people to enrol to vote)[8] or the ABC's specific election parody YouTube channel. GetUp! is able to turn this online visibility into mainstream media visibility through targeted fundraising to take online advertisements onto commercial election coverage (Vromen 2008).

This demonstrates that virtualised interest groups of the model promoted by MoveOn.org in the United States have the potential to be effective in mobilising political resources outside that nation. Overall, this benefited the Greens most of all—highlighting issues most favourable to them, enrolling voters most likely to vote for them, and actively endorsing the Greens through their policy check list—an unsurprising outcome given the over-representation of Greens voters (Marks 2010) in the membership of the organisation.[9]

Table 5.2 YouTube Videos Posted Within 50 Days of the Election Date, 2010

		ALP	Liberal	Greens	GetUp!	ABC's 'Sledge'
	Views	256 279	290 444	84 290	549 244	16 319
2010	Videos	59	22	19	8	8
	Average views	4344	13 202	4436	68 656	2040
	Views	160 896	150 719	36 686	Not collected in 2007	
2007	Videos	14	25	14		
	Average views	11 493	6029	2620		

Source: Compiled from YouTube.

We have to recognise, however, that the ability of political parties to capture public resources remains a significant counterweight to the comparatively

---

8 'Election 2010 Spoof Trailer—GetUp': <http://www.youtube.com/watch?v=Qub4lWT6GNk>
9 In the lead-up to the election, GetUp! surveyed members to determine its policy position for the campaign, leading to this somewhat circular outcome.

modest budget of GetUp!. The ability of GetUp! to be effective outside its media niche is therefore questionable. Offline, the organisation has had its biggest victories (both directly and through the resultant exposure it gained) through litigation—a unique opportunity that is not easy to reproduce. The organisation's experience with mobilising members physically was mixed. As Table 5.3 demonstrates, election planning meet-ups were only modestly subscribed and the small organisation's ability to organise at the local level remained modest (Griffiths 2010). In future, the organisation is likely to shift back to a model that focuses on partnerships with other organisations that bring local resources (such as the capacity for offline mobilisation), rather than continue to expand into the type of organisational complexity more associated with parties.

Table 5.3 GetUp! Pre-Election Meet-Ups: Distribution and estimated attendance

Jurisdiction	Number	Percentage of total	Not fully RSVPd	Fully RSVPd
NT	4	2.040	75	25
NSW/ACT	56	28.57	76.78	23.21
Victoria	62	31.63	61.29	38.70
SA	12	6.12	25	75
WA	26	13.26	73.07	26.92
Tasmania	4	2.04	100	0
Queensland	32	16.32	78.12	21.87
Total	196	100		

Conclusion

Overall this chapter has presented a mixed picture of the role of new media in the 2010 election. For parties and candidates, new media has become an established, if not major, element of their marketing strategies. If Australia had structural characteristics more likely to encourage postmodern styles of campaigning, the current professionalism and platforms adopted within the major parties would provide for a more engaged and interesting set of campaigning strategies around market segmentation and local engagement. There is evidence that the major parties continue to experiment with these approaches, which indicates the strong influence of both UK and US campaigning approaches on the major parties. There remains, however, a tendency for media contraction towards a more limited set of policy topics, celebrity political actors and meta-narratives—a function of new media's impact on news production. This is countered to a limited degree by emerging civil-society organisations and citizen journalism, gatewatching and micro-activism, which have interesting potential to resist established ecosystem agenda-setting tendencies.

References

Australian Associated Press (AAP). 2009. 'No more flirting, Abbott tells Gillard'. *Sydney Morning Herald*, 1 December, viewed 30 September 2010, <http://www.smh.com.au/national/no-more-flirting-abbott-tells-gillard-20091201-k2ue.html>

Australian Associated Press (AAP). 2010. 'Gillard and Rudd won't campaign alongside each other after Brisbane meeting'. *news.com.au*, 7 August, viewed 30 September 2010, <http://www.news.com.au/features/federal-election/gillard-and-rudd-wont-campaign-alongside-each-other-after-brisbane-meeting/story-fn5taogy-1225902429876>

Bourke, Latika. 2010. 'Rooty Hill beats global pop culture'. *Sydney Morning Herald*, 13 August, viewed 13 August 2010, <http://www.smh.com.au/federal-election/rooty-hill-beats-global-pop-culture-20100813-121u0.html?utm_source=twitterfeed&utm_medium=twitter>

Buchanan, Matt and Elliott, Tim. 2010. 'Red alert for Gillard fans'. *Sydney Morning Herald*, 5 July, viewed 6 July 2010, <http://www.smh.com.au/national/the-diary/red-alert-for-gillard-fans-20100704-zvy2.html>

Bruns, Axel. 2003. 'Gatewatching, not gatekeeping: collaborative online news'. *Media International Australia Incorporating Culture and Policy* 107: 31–44.

Cahill, James and Ward, Ian. 2007. 'Old and new media: blogs in the third age of political communication'. *Australian Journal of Communication* 34(3): 1–21.

CeBIT. 2010. 'Labor gears up for Australia's first digital election'. *CeBIT Australia*, 15 July, viewed 17 July 2010, <http://www.cebit.com.au/news/government/Labor_gears_up_for_Australias_first_digital_election>

Chen, Peter John. 2005. 'e-lection 2004? New media and the campaign'. In Marian Simms and John Warhurst (eds), *Mortgage Nation: The Australian federal election 2004*. Perth: API Network, 129–135.

Chen, Peter John. 2008. 'Australian political parties' use of YouTube 2007'. *Communication, Politics & Culture* 41(1): 114–148.

Chen, Peter John. 2010. Online campaigning in Australia 2004–2010. Paper presented at the Elections, Campaigning and Citizens Online Workshop, 15–16 October, Oxford Internet Institute, Oxford.

Chen, Peter John and Vromen, Ariadne. 2010. Political web content consumption in the 2010 Australian election. Paper presented at Double Vision: Biennial Australian Studies Conference, 25–26 November, University of Sydney, Sydney.

Chen, Peter John and Walsh, Lucas. 2010. 'E-Election 2007? Political competition online'. *Australian Cultural History* 28(1): 47-54.

Counihan, Bella. 2010. 'Government tries to net votes in Howard's domain'. *Sydney Morning Herald*, 4 May, viewed 7 May 2010, <http://www.smh. com.au/opinion/politics/government-tries-to-net-votes-in-howards-domain-20100504-u4im.html>

Esser, Frank and Spanier, Bernd. 2005. 'News management as news'. *Journal of Political Marketing* 4(4): 27–57.

Flew, Terry. 2008. 'Not yet the Internet election: online media, political commentary and the 2007 Australian federal election'. *Media International Australia* 126: 5–13.

Gibson, Rachel and Ward, Stephen. 2002. 'Virtual campaigning: Australian parties and the impact of the Internet'. *Australian Journal of Political Science* 37(1): 99–129.

Goot, Murray. 2008. 'Is the news on the Internet different? Leaders, frontbenchers and other candidates in the 2007 Australian election'. *Australian Journal of Political Science* 43(1): 99–110.

Gordon, Josh. 2010. 'Pollies all atwitter as rapid-fire ads take cheap shots'. *Sydney Morning Herald*, 20 June, viewed 21 June 2010, <http://www.smh. com.au/technology/technology-news/pollies-all-atwitter-as-rapidfire-ads-take-cheap-shots-20100619-ynzq.html>

Gould, Philip. 1999. *The Unfinished Revolution: How the modernisers saved the Labour Party*. London: Abacus.

Grant, Will, Moon, Brenda and Busby Grant, Janie. 2010. 'Digital dialogue? Australian politicians' use of the social network tool Twitter'. *Australian Journal of Political Science* 45(4): 579–604.

Griffiths, Mary. 2010. 'Decidedly not in Sturt'. *Sydney Morning Herald*, 20 August, viewed 20 August 2010, <http://www.smh.com.au/opinion/politics/decidedly-not-in-sturt-20100820-138iy.html>

Guselli, Lachlan. 2010. 'Gillard v Abbott: who's winning on Facebook?'. *SBS*, 21 July, viewed 23 July 2010, <http://www.sbs.com.au/news/article/1306017/Gillard-v-Abbott---who-s-winning-in-social-media-->

Hindman, Matthew, Tsioutsiouliklis, Kostas and Johnson, Judy A. 2003. 'Googlearchy': how a few heavily linked sites dominate politics on the web. Paper presented at the Annual Meeting of the Midwest Political Science Association, 31 March, Chicago.

Howden, Saffron. 2010. 'Libs' Google-ad blitz sparks complaints'. *Sydney Morning Herald*, 9 August, viewed 10 August 2010, <http://www.smh.com. au/technology/technology-news/libs-googlead-blitz-sparks-complaints-20100809-11tpl.html>

Jericho, Greg. 2010. 'Spartacus no more'. *Grog's Gamut*, 27 September, viewed 27 September 2010, <http://grogsgamut.blogspot.com/2010/09/spartacus-no-more.html>

Kwek, Glenda. 2010a. 'Operation Phoney Tony: ALP uses Twitter to target Opposition Leader'. *Sydney Morning Herald*, 28 May, viewed 29 May 2010, <http://www.smh.com.au/technology/technology-news/operation-phoney-tony-alp-uses-twitter-to-target-opposition-leader-20100528-wkuf. html?autostart=1>

Kwek, Glenda. 2010b. 'Abbott v Gillard at Rooty Hill: Galaxy to investigate'. *Sydney Morning Herald*, 12 August, viewed 3 September 2010, <http:// www.smh.com.au/federal-election/abbott-v-gillard-at-rooty-hill-galaxy-to-investigate-20100812-1206t.html>

Lees-Marshment, Jennifer. 2001. *Political Marketing and British Political Parties*. Manchester: Manchester University Press.

Lowry, Rich. 2003. *Legacy: Paying the price for the Clinton years*. Washington, DC: Regnery.

Marichal, Jose. 2010. Political Facebook groups: micro-activism and the digital front stage. Paper presented at Internet, Politics, Policy 2010: An Impact Assessment, 16–17 September, Oxford Internet Institute, Oxford.

Meade, Amanda. 2010. 'New media has the press gallery all a Twitter'. *The Australian*, 26 June, viewed 28 June 2010, <http://www.theaustralian. com.au/politics/new-media-has-the-press-gallery-all-a-twitter/story-e6frgczf-1225884488511>

Marks, Kathy. 2010. 'Exclamation politics'. *The Monthly*, October.

Mutz, Dianna. 1995. 'Effects of horse-race coverage on campaign coffers: strategic contributing in presidential primaries'. *The Journal of Politics* 57: 1015–42.

Norris, Pippa. 2000. *A Virtuous Circle: Political communications in postindustrial societies*. Cambridge: Cambridge University Press.

Novak, Lauren and Kenny, Mark. 2010. 'Liberals' battle plan to win key marginal seats'. *Adelaide Now*, 28 May, viewed 28 May 2010, <http://www.adelaidenow.com.au/news/south-australia/liberals-battle-plan-to-win-key-marginal-seats/story-e6frea83-1225872263008>

Sanders, Karen. 2009. *Communicating Politics in the Twenty-First Century*. Basingstoke, UK: Palgrave Macmillan.

Small, Tamara. 2008. 'Equal access, unequal success—major and minor Canadian parties on the net'. *Party Politics* 14(1): 51–70.

Tovey, Josephine. 2010. 'Being a first will not get Gillard off the hook'. *Sydney Morning Herald*, 25 June, viewed 25 June 2010, <http://www.smh.com.au/opinion/politics/being-a-first-will-not-get-gillard-off-the-hook-20100624-z3br.html>

Vromen, Ariadne. 2008. 'Political change and the Internet in Australia: introducing GetUp'. In Tapio Häyhtiö and Jarmo Rinne (eds), *Net Working/Networking: Politics on the Internet*. Tampere, Finland: Tampere University Press.

Wilson, Jason. 2010. Twitter post, 11 August, viewed 3 September 2010, <http://twitter.com/jason_a_w/status/20871862706>

6. To the Second Decimal Point: How the polls vied to predict the national vote, monitor the marginals and second-guess the Senate

Murray Goot

From a poll-watcher's perspective, three things made the 2010 election distinctive. One was the unprecedented number of pollsters and the competition among them for media space. For the first time, seven companies were involved nationally—five from the outset of the campaign, one towards the end and one after respondents' had cast their votes—with others involved in particular States or in private polling for the parties. Polling was conducted both nationally and in marginal seats. Almost all the polling was focused on the election for the House of Representatives; only one set of results pretended to offer any sort of guide to the Senate. And no fewer than four companies conducted exit polls or day-of-the-election surveys.

A second feature was the record number of polls in the public domain not paid for by the press. Three polling organisations did have contractual relations with the press: Newspoll with *The Australian*, Galaxy with News Limited's metropolitan dailies and Nielsen with *The Age* and the *Sydney Morning Herald*. But Galaxy also polled for Channel Nine, and three firms produced 'exit' polls or election-day polls for television: Galaxy for Channel Nine, Auspoll for *Sky News* and Morgan for Channel Seven. And of the seven companies that conducted national polls during the campaign, three paid for the fieldwork themselves: Morgan, which posted the results on its web site and sent them to about 10 000 email addresses, gave some of its findings first to Channel Seven; Essential Research, whose results were distributed to some 400 email addresses and posted on the *Crikey* web site; and JWS, whose findings were taken up and published by the *Sydney Morning Herald*.

The third difference was the unprecedented range of data-gathering techniques these firms deployed. Morgan used face-to-face interviewing, a tradition that dates from 1941 when it ran the Australian Gallup Poll; but it also used phone polling and text messaging—an Australian first—for its exit poll. Galaxy used the phone, but switched to face-to-face interviews for its exit poll—a mode also used by Auspoll for its exit poll. Newspoll used phone interviewing. Essential Research ran its polling online. And JWS had respondents enter their voting intentions into a computer via their telephone keypads. The proliferation of polls was driven by new, cheaper technologies—the Internet and automated telephone polling lowering the barrier to entry.

This chapter outlines what the pollsters said about their own accuracy—an important part of their post-election marketing—before looking at the ways in which a more dispassionate observer might assess their performance. It traces the ways in which the polls tracked the parties' fortunes. It examines the uneven performance of the polls in the marginal seats—seats where, as the contest tightened, the pollsters put in a lot of effort. And it looks at their poor performance in relation to the Senate—an arena into which only one of the polls ventured.

Which of the polls performed best? That depends on the criteria against which their performance is measured; in any event, the differences were not statistically significant. Where the polls ran into most trouble was in marginal seats where they used small samples. Are the polls getting worse at measuring party support? Notwithstanding the decline of landlines and response rates, they are not. Are the polls getting better? Again, the answer is no. Indeed, anyone guessing that the two-party preferred vote at every election since 1993 would be evenly split would have as good a record for accuracy as any of the three polling organisations that have provided estimates at each of the elections since that date.

Bragging Rights

The day after the election a number of the pollsters released their own assessments of their performance and that of their competitors, though the parties' vote share was still unclear. The Morgan poll—keen to calibrate the errors of its rivals to two decimal places—was first in, though not necessarily best dressed. 'As of now', declared Gary Morgan on the day of the election—when the vote count had Labor on 38.5 per cent (it would finish with 38 per cent), the Coalition on 43.5 per cent (43.6 per cent), the Greens at 11.4 per cent (11.8 per cent) and Others at 6.6 per cent (6.6 per cent)—'the 7 NEWS Morgan Poll is easily the most accurate of the 4 major polls'. Morgan's 'Two Party preferred had an average error of only 0.3 per cent', meaning 0.3 percentage points; its 'Primary vote average error' (based on its estimate of votes for Labor, the Coalition, the Greens and Others) 'was only 0.5 per cent—probably our most accurate forecast', though whether it was the 'most accurate' ever or simply the 'most accurate' of the four 'final' polls he had conducted for the 2010 election was unclear. In addition,

Morgan had 'correctly predicted a Green controlled Senate', had predicted that 'the Greens would win their first House of Representatives seat' and had been 'the first to predict a hung parliament' (Morgan et al. 2010).

The poll on which Morgan based its claim to having produced 'easily the most accurate' poll was a strange hybrid—a mixture of initial interviews and selected 'follow-ups'. Morgan made no attempt to contact all the respondents; it simply assumed that the only respondents who might have changed their mind were the 'undecided' and those intending to vote Greens. While the original Morgan poll had the same two-party preferred count (51:49) as the adjusted poll, the average difference between the first-preference votes (Coalition, Labor, Greens, Other) and the election result was greater in the original poll (1 percentage point) than in the adjusted version (0.5 percentage points).

Another poll that might have formed the basis of its post-election comparison but did not was its day-of-the-election phone poll for Channel Seven. Described as an 'exit poll'—in fact, it was based on nationwide interviews on election day with respondents who had voted and those who had yet to vote—it reported a Labor two-party preferred vote of 51.5 per cent and a first-preference distribution of Liberal-Nationals 41.5 per cent, ALP 38.5 per cent, Greens 13 per cent and 7 per cent Other (Morgan 2010a). Less accurate than Morgan's pre-election poll in terms of the two-party preferred, it was no less accurate in terms of first preferences.

There was a third poll to which Morgan might have referred as well. Also described as an 'exit poll'—this time more accurately—it involved asking 2000 voters drawn from the Roy Morgan Elector Panel to text their vote to Morgan once they had voted. Since 'the original panel'—recruited over a number of years from Morgan's face-to-face surveys—was 'controlled' and 'their previous voting intention and their vote at the last election' in 2007 were 'known', it was 'possible to project from the sms [sic] "exit" poll', Morgan argued, 'to an Australia-wide vote'. While the response rate in this survey was high (1580 members of the panel responded), the last results, posted at 6.16 pm Eastern Standard Time, appear to have been entered into the system at 4 pm—two hours before polling booths in most of the country closed (Morgan 2010b). This means results from Western Australia—two hours behind the rest of the country—were under-represented.

Not to be outdone, Essential Research on the Monday after the election issued an 'election poll wrap' of its own, inscribed with the headline: 'Essential wins bragging rights.' In estimating the two-party preferred vote, it argued, '[a]ll pollsters performed well' because 'all were within 0.3% to 1.3% of the current result', which it reported as 50.7:49.3. 'The Essential Report and Morgan Research were closest with 51/49. Newspoll's 50.2/49.8 was next closest with Nielsen and

Galaxy 1.3% off at 52/48.' 'However,' it continued, 'a better way to compare the polls' was 'to look at their first preferences for the major parties'—by which it meant the Greens not just the Coalition and Labor—because the two-party preferred count was 'based on an assumed distribution of preferences' (not true of Morgan, Nielsen, Essential, Auspoll or JWS), 'not on the actual measurement of voting intentions'.

On this measure, 'all the polls'—it listed Newspoll, Nielsen, Galaxy, Morgan and Essential but not JWS—'were within the margin of error'. But 'Essential Research was clearly the closest', the 'average difference' between its estimates of the parties' performance and their support at the election 'being just 0.5%'; the equivalent score for Morgan (on the basis of its last complete poll not its subsequent adjustment) was 1.2 percentage points, for Nielsen 1.4, for Newspoll 1.7 and for Galaxy 1.9 percentage points. The Greens' support, it concluded, had been 'over-estimated' in 'most polls' (all polls, except the Essential, 'over-estimated' Greens' support), while support for Labor in Newspoll had been 'underestimated' (Essential 2010b).

Equally quick off the mark were the papers that had commissioned Newspoll and Nielsen. A headline inside Monday's *Australian* declared: 'Newspoll forecast right on the money again.' According to the report, 'Newspoll yet again' had 'taken out top polling honours'. With the official count showing Labor ahead 50.67 per cent to the Coalition's 49.33 per cent, Newspoll's 50.2:49.8 'came closest to precisely mirroring the outcome of the vote'. Nielsen and Galaxy—the 'other two major polls'—had 'overstated Labor's support'. (This was true, but they had overstated Labor's support by a smaller margin than Newspoll had overstated the Coalition's support.) 'Minor polls'—as the report called the Morgan and Essential polls, presumably on the grounds that they lacked media sponsors—had come 'closer than Nielsen and Galaxy to forecasting the outcome': the 'final Morgan telephone poll of the campaign' (its election-day phone poll), with a 51.5:48.5 split, and 'Essential Research's web-based poll', with a 51:49 split. As for '[t]he much ballyhooed "Robo-poll" automated telephone poll', produced by JWS and published by the rival Fairfax press, it 'also overstated Labor's two-party preferred vote' (Kerr 2010).

'It always seems risky to go with a number that's very different from other pollsters', Newspoll's chief executive officer, Martin O'Shannessy, was quoted as saying, 'but we have a very strict policy of always reporting the poll exactly and not adjusting it and that's why we reported this, not rounded in any way'. In fact, its 'very strict policy' of reporting the two-party preferred count to the first decimal point was relatively new; Newspoll had first adopted it in March 2009 on the eve of the Queensland election. This was the first national election at which Newspoll had reported its results to less than half a percentage point (Goot 2010, 78–80). O'Shannessy said nothing about how well Newspoll had done in predicting the first-preference vote for the various parties—again, as in Queensland and subsequently South Australia, reported to the first decimal point.

On the performance of the Galaxy poll—a poll with a very good record—not one of the News Limited dailies was prepared to comment. While the report in *The Australian* seemed happy enough to dismiss it—Newspoll and Galaxy were keen rivals—none of the other newspapers was prepared to defend it. Galaxy, however, was not to be counted out. On its web site, it insisted that its polling, which had shown Labor's two-party preferred vote at 50–52 per cent from the time Gillard became Prime Minister through to the election, was '[a] remarkable feat of consistency' (though what this proves is unclear); that it had predicted 'the closeness of the election' (though not the closeness that Newspoll had predicted); and that its 'Superpoll' in the last week of the campaign (discussed below) had 'provided the best guide to the swings in each of the states of all the published polls' (Galaxy 2010).

Writing on the Monday after the election in *The Age* and the *Sydney Morning Herald*—papers that had commissioned Nielsen, and, in the case of the *Sydney Morning Herald*, also published JWS—Mark Davis, the National Editor for the *Sydney Morning Herald*, awarded the palm not to Newspoll or Galaxy, not to the polls *The Age* or *Sydney Morning Herald* had published, but to Morgan's phone poll and the poll published by Essential; both had estimated Labor's two-party preferred vote at 51 per cent, which made them 'out by just 0.3 percentage points' but 'spot on if the election result is rounded to the nearest percentage point like most of the published poll predictions'. In contrast, Newspoll was out by 0.5 or by 0.7 percentage points if its estimates were rounded. JWS Research 'notched up an unrounded error [of] 0.9 percentage points'. Entering the contest, Nielsen's John Stirton noted that if it was a battle to the first decimal point, Nielsen's (unpublished) unrounded figure for Labor—51.8 per cent—'gave Nielsen a 1.1 per cent (unrounded) error', assuming Labor's two-party preferred vote remained at 50.7. Nonetheless, Davis stressed, the predictions made by all the polls were 'well inside their statistical margin of error'.

Each of these assessments—from *The Australian*, the *Sydney Morning Herald* and *The Age*—was confined to the way the polls had measured up to the two-party preferred vote. This was also true of *The Canberra Times* (2010), the only other daily to comment on the performance of the polls. Not until 1993 had all the polls published a two-party preferred figure (Goot 2009, 126). Now the two-party preferred score seemed to be the only measure that mattered.

Mirror, Mirror on the Wall...

Once the results were finally declared, the two-party preferred figures looked slightly different. So did the first preferences. If we focus on first preferences— the way polls everywhere else in the world are judged—there is more than one measure we can apply. With a variety of measures, a poll that scores well on one measure—whether it is the two-party preferred or some other measure—will not necessarily score well on others.

Labor's final two-party preferred margin was not 50.7 per cent, as it appeared on election night, but 50.1 per cent. On this measure, Newspoll, which had Labor on 50.2 per cent, performed best; it would have taken an even greater measure of luck to have performed any better. As Table 6.1 (pre-election polls) and Table 6.2 (election-day polls) show, the Essential poll, conducted online in the last week of the campaign, the Morgan pre-election phone poll, whether in its original or its adjusted form, the Morgan day-of-the-election (SMS) poll and the Auspoll were the next best with a Labor two-party preferred count of 51 per cent. These were followed by Morgan's day-of-the-election phone poll (51.5 per cent). Tied, at the back of the field, came half-a-dozen others: Morgan's final face-to-face poll, the final Nielsen phone poll, the two JWS automated phone polls (its campaign poll and its day-of-the-election poll) and the two Galaxy phone polls (its last campaign poll and its exit poll), all of which had Labor on 52 per cent. Morgan, with four runners in the race—almost certainly a world first—had two in the third (or second-last) bunch of finishers and two in the fourth (or last).

Table 6.1 Final Pre-Election Day Polls for the House of Representatives Election, 21 August 2010

Poll	Method	Date	Days before election	Lib*/NP**	LNP	ALP	AD	Greens	FF	Ind.	Other	Excl.	Total	N	2PP‡ (ALP)
Nielsen	Phone	17–19 Aug.	2	(39/2)#	41.5	39	1	13	1.5	2	2	n.a.	100	(2040)	52
Morgan	Face-to-face	14–15 Aug.	6	n.a.	43	40	n.a.	13.5	1.5	n.a.	2	[7]	100	(1049)	52
Morgan	Phone##	18–19 Aug.	2	(39/3)	42	38	n.a.	13	n.a.	n.a.	7	[9]	100	(1872)	51
Galaxy	Phone	17–18 Aug.	3	38/3	41	38	n.a.	14	2	n.a.	5	[5]	100	(1200)	52
Newspoll†	Phone	17–19 Aug.	2	n.a.	43.4	36.2	n.a.	13.9	n.a.	n.a.	6.5	n.a.	100	(2507)	50.2
Essential	Online	13–19 Aug.	2	(40/3)	43	38	n.a.	12	2	n.a.	5	[5]	100	(1077)	51
JWS	Phone–auto	14–15 Aug.	6	n.a.	42.2	36.5	n.a.	14.9	n.a.	n.a.	6.4	[3]	100	(28 000)	52
Election		21 Aug.		39.6/4	43.6	38	0.2	11.8	2.3	2.5	1.6		100		50.1

Note: Poll data to nearest integer or decimal point as reported by each of the polling organisations.

n.a. not available

* Liberal Party and Liberal National Party of Queensland

** The Nationals and Country Liberal (Northern Territory)

On 20 August, Morgan recontacted 187 'undecided' and Greens respondents and adjusted its figures to read: LNP 42.5 per cent; ALP 39 per cent; Greens 11.5 per cent

Separate figures for The Nationals not provided to the *Sydney Morning Herald* or *The Age*

† Based on the distribution of minor-party preferences at the 2007 election

Sources: For Nielsen, Coorey (2010, 1, 10) and Grattan (2010, 1); for the face-to-face poll, <http://www.roymorgan.com/news/polls/2010/4566/>; for the phone poll, <http://www.roymorgan.com/news/polls/2010/4567>; for the update, <http://www.roymorgan.com/news/polls/2010/4568> (viewed 21 August 2010); for Galaxy, Farr (2010, 4–5) and Shanahan (2010, 1, 6); Essential (2010a); JWS (2010); and for the election results, Australian Electoral Commission (<www.aec.gov.au>), viewed 5 October 2010.

Table 6.2 Election Day and Exit Polls, House of Representatives, 21 August 2010

Poll	Method	Lib*/NP**	LNP	ALP	AD	Greens	FF	Ind.	Other	Excl.	Total	N	2PP[†] (ALP)
Morgan	SMS	(39/2.5)	41.5	38.5	n.a.	12	n.a.	n.a.	7	n.a.	100	(1580)	51
Morgan	Phone	(39.5/3)	42.5	38	n.a.	13	n.a.	n.a.	7	n.a.	100	(1220)	51.5
Galaxy	Face-to-face	n.a.	44	41	n.a.	11	n.a.	n.a.	4	n.a.	100	(2959)	52[#]
JWS	Phone—auto	n.a.	42.5	37.2	n.a.	14.3	n.a.	n.a.	6	[2]	100	(17 851)	52
Auspoll	Face-to-face	n.a.	45	42	n.a.	9	n.a.	n.a.	4	n.a.	100	(3000)	51[##]
Election		39.6/4	43.6	38	0.2	11.8	2.3	2.5	1.6		100		50.1

Note: Poll data to nearest integer or decimal point as reported by each of the polling organisations.

n.a. not available

* Liberal Party and Liberal National Party of Queensland

** The Nationals and Country Liberal (Northern Territory)

[†] Except for Galaxy, based on preference flow at the 2007 election

[#] Exit poll conducted at 24 booths across Australia with respondents asked to fill out a form similar to the ballot paper

[##] Exit poll of 30 marginal seats

Sources: For the phone poll, <http://www.roymorgan.com/news/polls/2010/4571/> (viewed 30 September 2010); Morgan (2010b); for two-party preferred data, John Scales, 'JWS Research–Telereach election day poll results', Email to Steve Wilson [Channel Ten], 21 August 2010, 5.43 pm, Author's collection; for first preferences, John Scales, Email to Steve Wilson, 21 August 2010, 6.42 pm; for sample size and excluded (undecided/don't know), John Scales, Email to the author, 4 October 2010; for Galaxy, David Briggs, Personal communication; for Auspoll, Ross Neilson, and <http://blogs.crikey.com.au/pollbludger/2010/08/21/morgan-sms-exit-poll-51-49-to-labor/comment-page-13/>

Does the order of merit change if we change the measure of success from predicting the two-party preferred to one of predicting the primary or first-preference vote? In boasting of their success, both Morgan and Newspoll noted, after the final results were in, that the 'error' of their estimates for each of the parties was 1 percentage point or less—'well within the expected sampling error', Newspoll added, 'of +/− 2 percentage points' (Levine et al. 2010, 16; Morgan et al. 2010 for the poll cited in Levine et al. 2010; Newspoll 2010).

To compare like with like, we need to focus on those parties—Labor, the LNP (taken as a single entity), the Greens and 'Other' (the parties and Independents that make up the rest)—for which *all* the polls provided estimates (see Table 6.3a). On this measure, the Essential poll had an average error of just 0.3 percentage points. The next most accurate were three of the Morgan polls: the last of its pre-election phone polls (0.7), the phone poll taken on the day of the election (0.7) and the one taken on the day of the election via SMS (0.8). Less accurate were the final campaign polls conducted by Newspoll (1.1) and Nielsen (1.1), the last Galaxy poll of the campaign (1.3), and the day-of-the-election poll conducted by JWS (1.3). Least accurate were the JWS poll (1.6) and Morgan's face-to-face poll (1.9) completed six days before the election—three to four days before any of the other final pre-election polls; and two day-of-the-election polls, Galaxy (1.7) and Auspoll (1.8), conducted in less than one-quarter of the seats. (Given that Galaxy and Auspoll would have been delighted to have come up with figures that matched the national result, and in the absence of any statement about the electorates/polling booths they sampled, it seems reasonable—if less than ideal—to assess them on the same basis as their competitors.) If the polls taken early in the last week confirm one maxim—where voting intentions change, timing matters—the polls on election day confirm another: it is foolish to judge the whole electorate on the basis of sampling its (unspecified) parts.

Table 6.3a Magnitude of the Average Error in the Polls' Estimate of the Vote Share for the ALP, LNP, Greens and Others in the Final Polls of the Campaign and in Polls on Election Day, House of Representatives, 2010 (percentage points)

	Galaxy	JWS	Morgan	Auspoll	Essential	Nielsen	Newspoll
Campaign	1.3	1.6*	0.7, 1.9[†]		0.3[○]	1.1	1.1
Election day	1.7[†#]	1.3*	0.7, 0.8[∞]	1.8[†##]			

* Automated telephone call [†] Face-to-face [#] Exit poll conducted at 24 booths across Australia [##] Exit poll in 30 marginal seats [○] Online [∞] SMS

Note: Telephone interviews unless otherwise indicated.

Sources: As for Tables 6.1 and 6.2.

Since some polls estimated the distribution of the vote for a larger number of parties than just those with the most substantial support (Labor, the LNP, the

Greens plus Others), we can also measure the polls' performance by adopting a horses-for-courses principle—that is, by calculating the average error for each of the parties for which the polls provided an estimate (see Table 6.3b). On this measure, the order of merit is much the same, though there is nothing to choose between the Essential poll (0.6)—now looking slightly worse—and the two Morgan day-of-the-election polls (0.5, 0.6) at the top, followed by: the Morgan (0.8) and Nielsen (0.9) phone polls conducted in the last week of the campaign; the campaign polls of Galaxy (1) and Newspoll (1.1); the JWS day-of-the-election poll (1.3); with the Morgan face-to-face poll (1.5), the JWS campaign poll (1.6) and the exit Auspoll (1.8) retaining their places at the bottom.

Table 6.3b Averages of the Differences Between the Polls' Estimates of the Parties' First-Preference Votes for Each Party Polled and the Votes actually Recorded by Each Party, in the Final Polls of the Campaign and in Polls Conducted on Election Day, House of Representatives, 2010 (percentage points)

	Galaxy	JWS	Morgan	Auspoll	Essential	Nielsen	Newspoll
Campaign	1.0 [6]	1.6 [4]*	0.8 [4], 1.5 [5]#		0.6 [5]°	0.9 [8]	1.1 [4]
Election day	1.7 [4]†#	1.3 [4]*	0.5 [5], 0.6 [5]∞	1.8 [4]†##			

* Automated telephone call † Face-to-face # Exit poll conducted at 24 booths across Australia ## Exit poll in 30 marginal seats ° Online ∞ SMS

Notes: Telephone interviews unless otherwise indicated; the number in square brackets indicates the number of parties for which each poll provided an estimate; the Nielsen poll reported the widest range of estimates—for Liberal, Liberal National, Labor, Australian Democrats, Greens, Family First, Independents, and Other; for other polls, parties not reported are added to Other and the appropriate comparison is made.

Sources: As for Tables 6.1 and 6.2.

On any of these measures—two-party preferred, the parties for which all the polls offered estimates, and the estimates for the parties offered by each poll—there is no evidence of the polls doing either significantly better or significantly worse, in strictly statistical terms, than in the past. Nonetheless, some outperformed while others under-performed their medium or long-term average. In terms of the two-party preferred figures (Table 6.4), Galaxy recorded a relatively poor result. It overestimated Labor's lead by 1.9 percentage points in both its pre-election and its day-of-the-election polls; in 2004 and 2007, it had underestimated first the Coalition's, and then Labor's, winning lead, by just 0.7 percentage points. Nielsen, with the same size error, actually did markedly better than in 2007; its 2010 figure brought it back into line with its long-term average. Morgan's phone polls were slightly more accurate than their long-term average (though the variance in Morgan's performance has been high); Morgan's face-to-face poll—out by 1.9 percentage points—also beat its long-term average, which has been poor (see also Jackman 2005). Newspoll, too, outperformed its long-term average, while Auspoll did almost as well in 2010 as it did in 2007.

Table 6.4 Differences Between the Polls' Final Estimates of Winning Party's Share of the Two-Party Preferred and the Actual Two-Party Preferred Vote, House of Representatives, 1993–2010, for Polls that Estimated the Two-Party Preferred Vote at the 2010 election (percentage points)*

Election	Nielsen		Morgan		Newspoll	Galaxy		Auspoll	Essential	JWS
2010	+1.9		+0.9 +1.4	+0.9[∞] +1.9[‡]	+0.1[†]	+1.9[†]	+1.9[‡6]	+0.9[‡6]	+0.9[†z]	+1.9[o] +1.9[o]
2007	+4.3	+4.3[z]	+0.8[†]	+3.9[‡]	−0.7[†]	−0.7[†]		+0.3		
2004	+1.3		−3.7	−4.2[‡]	−2.7	−0.7[†]				
2001	+1.0			−5.5[‡]	+2.0					
1998	+1.0		+1.0	−1.0[‡]	−2.0					
1996	−2.6		−3.6		−0.1					
1993	+1.9	−0.4[6]	+0.9		+1.9					
Mean	2.0		1.8	3.3[‡]	1.4	1.1[†]		0.6	0.9[z]	1.9[o]

* Based on respondents' reports of their second preferences/preference between Labor and Liberal unless otherwise stated

+ Overestimate − Underestimate [†] Based on distribution of minor-party preferences at preceding election
[z] Online [o] Automated telephone calls [6] Exit polls [‡] Face-to-face [∞] SMS

Notes: Telephone interviews unless otherwise indicated; 1993 was the first election for which each poll estimated a two-party preferred count.

In terms of the first preferences that all the polls reported—for the ALP, LNP, the Greens and Others—Newspoll's performance was better than its long-term average, as were Nielsen's and Morgan's (both phone and face-to-face). Galaxy was the one poll to do noticeably worse than in 2004 or 2007 (Table 6.5a).

Table 6.5a Averages of the Differences Between the Polls' Estimates of the Parties' First-Preference Votes and the Votes Actually Recorded, House of Representatives, 1987–2010, for Firms that Conducted Polls During the 2010 Campaign (percentage points)*

Election	Parties	Nielsen†		Morgan		Newspoll	Galaxy		Auspoll	Essential	JWS
2010	4	1.1		0.8 0.7	1.1‡ 0.8∞	1.1	1.7	1.3‡è	1.8‡è	0.3ᶻ	1.6° 1.3°
2007	4	2.5	1.6ᶻ	0.6	2.1‡	1.2	0.6		2.5♭		
2004	6	1.7		1.0	1.8‡	1.1	0.5				
2001	7	1.5			1.9‡	1.3					
1998	7	1.0		1.2	1.1‡	1.5					
1996	5	1.4		1.8		1.0					
1993	4	1.9	1.9♭	0.7		1.7					
1990	4	2.2		1.7		2.7					
1987	4	2.6		1.1		1.6					
Mean		1.8		1.1	1.6‡	1.5	0.9		2.2♭		1.4°

* Phone poll unless otherwise indicated † Nielsen (2007–10), ACNielsen (1998–2004), AGB McNair (1990–96), McNair Anderson (1987) ° Automated telephone calls ‡ Face-to-face è Exit poll conducted at 80 booths in 40 electorates (AGB McNair); at 24 booths (Galaxy); in 30 marginal seats (Auspoll) ᶻ Online ∞ SMS

Notes: The period dates from the first national election to include Newspoll; restricted to the parties whose level of support was estimated by all the polls: LNP, ALP, Greens, Other (2007, 2010); Liberal, NP, ALP, AD, Greens, and Others (2004); LNP, ALP, AD, Greens, One Nation, and Others (2001); Liberal, NP, ALP, AD, Greens, One Nation, Others (1998); LNP, ALP, AD, Greens, and Others (1996); LNP, ALP, AD, and Others (1987–93).

In terms of the first preferences reported by individual polls—and for Newspoll and Galaxy these were the same as those reported by all the polls—the story is much the same. Nielsen—with its best figures since at least 1987—and Morgan did a bit better than average. Galaxy—whose record had made it think of itself as the best poll in the country—did worse than in 2004 or 2007. Most striking, perhaps, is how similar the long-term performance of Morgan, Nielsen, Newspoll and Galaxy has been—from one end (Galaxy, with an average error of 0.9 percentage points) to the other (Nielsen on 1.5), the range is just 0.6 percentage points (Table 6.5b).

Table 6.5b Averages of the Differences Between the Polls' Estimates of the Parties' First-Preference Votes for Each Party and the Votes Actually Recorded by Each Party, House of Representatives Elections, 1987–2010, for Firms that Conducted Polls During the 2010 Campaign (percentage points) *

Election	Nielsen†		Morgan		Newspoll	Galaxy	Auspoll	Essential	JWS
2010	0.9 [8]		0.6 [5] 0.5 [5]	1.5 [5]‡ 0.6 [5]∞	1.1 [4]	1.7 [4] 1.3 [4]‡ᵇ	1.8 [4]‡ᵇ	0.4 [6]ᶻ	1.6 [4]° 1.3 [4]°
2007	1.6 [8]	1.8 [8]ᶻ	0.6 [7]	1.5 [7]‡	1.2 [5]	0.8 [6]	2.5 [4]		
2004	1.4 [8]		1.1 [6]	2.1 [6]‡	0.7 [7]	0.5 [6]			
2001	1.4 [8]			2.6 [7]‡	1.3 [7]				
1998	1.3 [8]		1.1 [6]	1.2 [7]‡	1.5 [6]				
1996	1.4 [6]		1.8 [5]		1.0 [5]				
1993	1.9 [4]	2.1 [5]ᵉ	0.6 [5]		1.5 [5]				
1990	2.2 [4]		1.8 [5]		1.4 [5]				
1987	2.6 [4]		1.1 [4]		1.6 [4]				
Mean	1.5 [58]		1.0 [48]	1.8 [32]‡	1.2 [48]	0.9 [16]			1.4 [8]°

* Phone poll unless otherwise indicated † Nielsen (2007–10), ACNielsen (1998–2004), AGB McNair (1990–96), McNair Anderson (1987) ° Automated telephone calls ‡ Face-to-face ᵉ Exit poll conducted at 80 booths in 40 electorates (AGB McNair); at 24 booths (Galaxy); in 30 marginal seats (Auspoll) ᶻ Online ∞ SMS

Notes: The period dates from the first national election to include Newspoll; the number in square brackets indicates the number of parties for which each poll provided an estimate; mean is weighted; where separate estimates are provided, Liberal and Nationals are treated as two and the combined figure for the LNP is ignored; minor parties for which no estimates are provided are treated as 'Other'.

The Marginals

Overwhelmingly, the marginal-seat polling done for the press was commissioned in the last two weeks of the campaign by News Limited: *The Weekend Australian*, through Newspoll, and the metropolitan tabloids through Galaxy. Individual papers, including News Limited's Adelaide *Advertiser*, also commissioned or conducted marginal-seat polling of their own. In addition, Galaxy ran a marginal-seat poll for Channel Nine, and marginal-seat polling was conducted independently of the press (and of the parties) by JWS, which boosted it samples in marginal seats, and by Morgan.

The Newspoll survey, with 3351 respondents (close to 200 per electorate), covered Labor's six most marginal seats in New South Wales (Macarthur, Macquarie, Robertson, Gilmore, Bennelong and Eden-Monaro), Labor's eight most marginal seats in Queensland (Herbert, Dickson, Longman, Flynn, Dawson, Forde, Brisbane and Leichhardt) and the Coalition's three most marginal seats in Victoria (McEwen, La Trobe and Dunkley). The decision to poll in New South Wales, Queensland and Victoria was based on Newspoll's national polling, aggregated over time (two or more weeks) and disaggregated by State. Labor was travelling poorly in Queensland (46 per cent two-party preferred, across the two weeks 30 July – 8 August, down from 50.4 per cent in 2007), had slipped in New South Wales (from 53.7 per cent to 51 per cent), but was more than holding its own in Victoria (55 per cent compared with 54.3 per cent). True, Labor had also slipped in Western Australia (42 per cent compared with 46.7 per cent in 2007) and improved its standing in South Australia (56 per cent compared with 52.4 per cent) (*The Australian*, 11 August 2010; Mackerras 2009, 229–32, for 2007). But New South Wales, Queensland and Victoria accounted for three-quarters of the 150 seats in the House of Representatives: New South Wales, with 49, accounted for one-third (and Labor held 28); Queensland, with 37, accounted for about one-fifth (21 Labor); and Victoria, with 37, accounted for one-quarter (of which the Liberals held 14)—and the three States were *The Australian*'s biggest markets. Within each State, Newspoll's choice of seats fitted not only within the Australian Electoral Commission's definition of 'marginal'—seats requiring a swing of up to 6 percentage points (AEC 2010; see also Mackerras 1975, 5)—it also fitted the definition of 'ultra-marginal' (requiring a swing of up to 4.9 percentage points) rather than 'marginal' (requiring a swing of between 5 and 9.9 percentage points) developed by Hughes (1977, 281).

The results—released on the weekend before the election—pointed to a swing against Labor of 1.3 percentage points in New South Wales, which was a more modest swing than the aggregate data suggested but enough to cost it four of its eight most marginal seats; they suggested a swing against Labor of 3.4 percentage points in Queensland, which again was smaller than it might have expected but enough to cost it all six of its most marginal seats; and they indicated a swing to Labor of 6.2 percentage points in Victoria, which was completely out of line with its data for Victoria as a whole and enough to cost the Liberals at least five and possibly nine of its most marginal seats (*The Weekend Australian*, 14–15 August 2010). No reference was made, however, to the differences between the State-by-State data it had published from its national polls and the data from these marginal-seat polls. Earlier, Newspoll had reported that Labor was ahead in the NSW marginal seat of Lindsay (n = 609), where it had a buffer of 6.4 percentage points, but behind in Dawson (n = 601) (*The Weekend Australian*, 7–8 August 2010).

In their last pre-election editions—published the day after the Newspoll survey appeared—News Limited's Sunday papers carried front-page reports of what Sydney's *Sunday Telegraph* called a '4000-voter superpoll', the Brisbane *Sunday Mail*, a 'super poll', and the Adelaide *Sunday Mail*, an 'exclusive super poll'. The only Sunday papers in the News group not to refer to the poll on page one were Melbourne's *Sunday Herald Sun*, published in a city where Newspoll had said Labor would pick up seats, not lose them, and the *Sunday Territorian*, which had not mentioned the election on its front page since 18 July—the day after the election was called.

Conducted by Galaxy across four seats in each of the five mainland States, the poll was taken on 8–13 August and covered an arc on the Mackerras pendulum stretching from seats that required a swing of up to 4.5 percentage points to the Coalition to change sides, of which there were 26, to seats requiring a swing of up to 4.5 percentage points to Labor to change sides, of which there were 19 (Mackerras 2010)—all 'ultra-marginals'. Eight of the 20 seats were held by the Coalition; 12 by Labor at least notionally. Excluded were the three Labor seats in Tasmania that required a swing of less than 4.5 percentage points as well as the seat of Denison, held by a margin of 15.4 percentage points, which Labor was to lose to an Independent, Andrew Wilkie; the margin might have made it 'safe' (AEC 2010; Mackerras 1975, 5) or 'ultra-safe' (Hughes 1977) vis-a-vis the Liberal Party but not in relation to Wilkie. Excluded, too, was the Labor seat of Solomon in the Northern Territory, which required a swing of less than 4.5 percentage points and was also lost. Again, there were roughly 200 respondents per seat.

In Queensland, Galaxy reported a swing to the Coalition of 5.4 percentage points (not 5.4 *per cent*, as most journalists and others persist in calling such swings)—a greater swing than that reported by Newspoll; this was based on three of the four most marginal Labor seats (Dawson, Dickson and Flynn but not the equally vulnerable Longman) plus one Liberal National seat (Bowman, the party's most vulnerable seat, held by a margin of 0.1 percentage points). Galaxy also reported a swing of 2.4 percentage points to the Coalition in New South Wales. Based on four of the five most marginal Labor seats (Macarthur, Macquarie, Gilmore and Eden-Monaro but not the equally vulnerable Bennelong), this, too, was greater than that reported by Newspoll. And it found a swing of 2.1 percentage points to the Coalition in Western Australia based on Labor's two most marginal seats (Swan and Hasluck) and the Liberal's two most marginal (Cowan and Stirling). There was no net swing to the Coalition in the South Australia marginals— the three most marginal Liberal seats (Sturt, Boothby and Grey) and the only Labor seat (Kingston) vulnerable to a swing as high as 5 percentage points. In Victoria, there was a swing to Labor, though much smaller than that reported by Newspoll; the swing of 1.6 percentage points was based on the Coalition's two most marginal seats (McEwen and La Trobe) and Labor's two most marginal (Corangamite and Deakin).

Extrapolating from these results, Galaxy projected a loss in Queensland of 10 Labor seats, in New South Wales a loss of seven and in Western Australia a loss of two. In South Australia, there was likely to be no change but in Victoria the swing against the Coalition pointed to Labor picking up two. The extrapolations, prepared by Galaxy's CEO, David Briggs, were based on the Mackerras pendulum. One had to read well into the reports carried by all but one of the Sunday papers, however, to register Briggs' note of caution: each projection 'presupposes', he noted, 'that the swings in each state will be uniform and there are good reasons for thinking that this won't be the case' (Kearney 2010a, 2010b; Kearney and Campbell 2010; Passmore 2010).

As well as projecting State-wide swings based on polling in just four seats, three of the six News Limited papers projected the distribution of first preferences nationwide: Coalition 46 per cent, ALP 37.8 per cent, Greens 10.2 per cent, Family First 2.2 per cent and Others 3.8 per cent. In addition, all six projected a national two-party preferred vote of 51.4:48.6 to the Coalition. These projections assumed a 'uniform swing' in each of the five States—an assumption that each of the papers (other than the *Sunday Tasmanian* and the *Sunday Territorian*) qualified by quoting Briggs. They also assumed an equal number of voters in each State—clearly a mistake, as a couple of bloggers were quick to point out (see Bowe 2010; Green 2010). Weighted by State, the national figure should have been reported as 51:49 in favour of Labor. Briggs' estimate of a swing to the Coalition of 1.7 percentage points—published in News Limited's Sunday papers (except the *Sunday Tasmanian*)—appears to have been calculated simply by adding all the State swings and dividing by five (Briggs cited in Passmore 2010). And while the headline inside *The Sunday Telegraph* referring to '[a] neck and neck fight to the last' might have served to keep readers in the paper's thrall, the projected net loss of 17 Labor seats would have produced a comfortable Coalition win: 78:69 plus three Independents. While nothing was said about the exclusion of Tasmania (and the two Territories), the *Sunday Tasmanian* could not resist adding 'Tas 2' to its front-page table listing 'Labor seats at risk', and reporting that '[s]enior Tasmanian officials from both parties' were 'agreed' that 'the election could now be decided in the state's two most marginal seats—Bass and Braddon'. How anyone could have reached this conclusion the paper did not stop to explain. As with the 'officials', however, its reasons for promoting the idea seem fairly plain.

While this poll represented the largest number of marginal seats in the largest number of States Galaxy polled, it was neither the first nor the last of its marginal-seat polls. With its polling showing a swing to the Coalition, especially in Queensland and New South Wales, and with Queensland and New South Wales accounting for two-thirds (18) of Labor's 27 ultra-marginals, it was on Queensland and New South Wales that Galaxy focused—both for News Limited and in its four-seat poll (Eden-Monaro, Macarthur, Bonner and Bowman) for Channel Nine (4–5 August 2010). In New South Wales, a Galaxy poll conducted for *The Daily Telegraph* at the beginning of the second-last week of the campaign (11–12 August) in four seats—two Labor marginals (Greenway and Lindsay) and two ultra-marginals (Macquarie, Labor; and Hughes, Liberal)—found Labor trailing, 37:45 or 49:51 two-party preferred, which was a two-party preferred swing of nearly 4 percentage points against Labor. 'On that basis', Simon Benson (2010) wrote, 'Labor would lose the seat of Macquarie, fail to pick up Hughes… but hang on to Lindsay and narrowly win in Greenway'. This was correct. But the temptation to push the analysis where it was never meant to go proved too great. 'If the same swings [presumably the average swing] were repeated across other marginal seats in Sydney and the Central Coast', he argued, 'Labor would lose Bennelong [it did] and Robertson [it did not] and could struggle to hold on to Eden-Monaro [it did not] and Dobell [it did not]' (Benson 2010).

In Queensland, a Galaxy poll conducted during the last week of the campaign (15–16 August) for *The Courier-Mail* in four of Labor's ultra-marginals—Herbert, Longman, Forde and Bonner—revealed a similar swing with Labor trailing, 38:44 or 49:51 two-party preferred, which was an anti-Labor two-party preferred swing of about 3.5 percentage points. 'If such a swing was observed on a uniform basis across marginal electorates in Queensland', Briggs observed, 'this would result in the government losing six seats'. Keen to generalise the poll's findings, the paper led with a statement not about the four seats but about 'Labor in pain in six seats'. What the headline ignored was the last paragraph in the story, which referred to a 'separate Galaxy poll in the *Sunday Mail*' that 'showed a 5.4 per cent swing against the Government' in four other Labor ultra-marginals: 'Bowman, Dawson, Dickson and Flynn' (Balogh 2010). On that basis, the paper might have generalised not to six seats but to as many as ten.

The JWS Research poll, with 28 000 respondents, also conducted in the final week, included a 'boost sample' of more than 22 000 drawn from '54 key marginals', ranging from Lindsay in New South Wales, held by Labor on a margin of 6.3 percentage points, to McMillan in Victoria, held by the Liberals on a margin of 4.8 percentage points. Published as an 'exclusive' on the front page of the *Sydney Morning Herald* (19 August 2010), though not commissioned by it, the JWS poll was the biggest rollcall of individual marginal seats published in the course of an election by any Australian polling organisation; indeed, with its having made upwards of 250 000 calls to get a response of this size, it was the biggest polling effort undertaken by anyone in Australia in a single weekend.

It was also one of the most controversial, with the Association of Market and Social Research Organisations issuing—and then hastily withdrawing—a statement attacking its 'standards', the 'low participation rate' and the 'vast numbers of people' likely to end up 'annoyed' (see Burgess 2010). According to JWS, Labor would lose 15 seats: eight in Queensland (every seat, except Longman, on the Mackerras pendulum, from Herbert, its second most marginal, to Bonner); four in New South Wales (Macarthur, but not the equally marginal seat of Macquarie; Robertson, but not the almost equally marginal seat of

Gilmore; Bennelong and Lindsay); two in Western Australia (Hasluck and Swan); and one in Victoria (Corangamite). But JWS also had the Coalition losing seats: three in Victoria (McEwen, La Trobe and Dunkley), two in New South Wales (Cowper and Paterson) and one in South Australia (Boothby). The loss of six Coalition seats meant Labor would 'win with a four-seat majority'.

The last week also saw a marginal-seat result from Morgan for Bennelong. It suggested that Labor might hold on. A week earlier, Morgan had reported new results from three other seats it had polled before the election was called: Macquarie (NSW) and Leichhardt (Qld), both ultra-marginals, where the results pointed to big swings away from Labor in the previous six weeks; and Brand (WA), where little appeared to have changed. On the day of the election, Morgan conducted polls in the marginal seat of Lindsay (NSW) and the ultra-marginals of Leichhardt and La Trobe (Vic.).

The Canberra Times, a Fairfax daily that had no relationship with Nielsen; the Adelaide *Advertiser* and *Sunday Mail*, owned by News; and the *West Australian*, owned by neither Fairfax nor News; all either commissioned polls or conducted polls of their own. These polls focused on seats in which the papers' readers resided—marginals in particular. *The Canberra Times* commissioned Patterson Market Research, a firm it had used in the past, to conduct two polls across the border in the NSW seat of Eden-Monaro—a seat it promoted as a 'bellwether' (*The Canberra Times*, 26 July 2010 and 20 August 2010) on the grounds that since 1972 whichever party won Eden-Monaro had formed government (Richardson and Kerr 2007, 35).

The Advertiser and *Sunday Mail*, using their own staff, conducted polls in Kingston (*The Advertiser*, 23 July 2010), Boothby (*Sunday Mail*, 25 July 2010), Sturt (*The Advertiser*, 6 August 2010) and Hindmarsh (*The Advertiser*, 21 August 2010); *The Advertiser*'s practice of bypassing pollsters dates to the 1970s. And the *West Australian* commissioned Patterson—a local firm it had used since the 1980s—to conduct a poll across Western Australia (*West Australian*, 7 August 2010) and in four marginals (Hasluck and Swan, Labor; Cowan and Canning, Liberal), though the paper was confused about whether these were the most marginal seats in Western Australia (they were not) and which party held them (*West Australian*, 24 July 2010 and 21 August 2010). In those seats polled more than once, Labor's lead was narrowing.

How well did the marginal-seat polls perform? Some were accurate, others remarkably inaccurate. Of the pollsters that polled in batches of more than a dozen seats, Galaxy appears to have done best. In Queensland, where it marked down 10 Labor seats as potential losses, Labor lost nine. In New South Wales, where it saw seven potential Labor losses, Labor lost four. In Western Australia, it saw two Labor seats at risk and both were lost. And in Victoria, it saw Labor losing two seats and Labor lost them. This gave Galaxy a score of 17 out of 21; in none of its sets of four did the average error exceed 1.2 percentage points. Newspoll, in contrast, picked only 11 of the 15 marginals along the eastern seaboard that changed hands and identified another that did not—effectively, a score of 11 out of sixteen. Its biggest problem was in Queensland where it had marked as 'in doubt' only five of the nine Labor seats that fell. After the election, the result from its 17-seat poll did not appear on the Newspoll web site.

Morgan's predictions for individual seats, based on its State-by-State figures (Personal communication), were out by 12 (Morgan 2010a). It had the Coalition gaining seats it did not gain (Dobell, Lindsay, Page, NSW; Brand, WA), losing seats it did not lose (Herbert, Qld; Sturt, SA), and failing to win seats it actually won (Macarthur and Gilmore, NSW; Dickson, Brisbane and Bonner, Qld; and Swan, WA). Across the three seats Morgan polled on election day (Lindsay, NSW: La Trobe, Vic.; Herbert, Qld), the average error, two-party preferred, was more than 6 percentage points; in two of the three cases (Lindsay and Herbert), Morgan called it for the party that lost. In contrast, *The Advertiser/Sunday Mail* scored four out of four (Kelton 2010) and Patterson five out of five.

Of the predictions generated by the JWS day-of-the-election automated phone poll, no less than one-third turned out to be wrong. Among the 18 marginal seats it expected Labor to hold were five it lost (Bennelong and Macquarie, NSW; Hasluck and Swan, WA; Solomon, NT); among the 15 it expected Labor to lose were four it held (Lindsay and Robertson, NSW; Moreton, Qld; Corangamite, Vic.); and among the six it expected the Coalition to lose were four it held (McEwen and La Trobe, Vic.; Boothby, SA; Stirling, WA).

The Senate

Compared with the contest for the House of Representatives, the contest for the Senate attracted little attention. If the number of pollsters lining up to measure the parties' electoral support in the House of Representatives continues to grow, the number lining up for the Senate has fallen. In 2004—an unusual election that saw the government win a majority in the Senate—there were three polls: ACNielsen, Morgan and an ANU online poll (Goot 2005, 65–7). In 2007, there were two: Morgan and Galaxy (Goot 2009, 128–30). In 2010, however, there was just one. Even so, it was not the press that commissioned the poll; it was Morgan that chanced its arm.

Encouraged by the prospect of being the first poll to declare the Greens would hold the balance of power, Morgan went into the field early. Its series of face-to-face polls, from which it extracted its findings on the Senate, was conducted in different States at different times, with all the surveys under way before the election was announced and completed when the election campaign still had some way to run. In New South Wales (n = 1195) and Victoria (n = 731), the polling was conducted in July; in Queensland (n = 1497), South Australia (n = 591) and Western Australia (n = 622), it was conducted in June–July; in Tasmania (n = 451), in May–July; and in the Australian Capital Territory (n = 446), in February–July (Morgan 2010c.

Headed 'Greens set to hold Senate "Balance of Power" with 10 Senators' and released on 10 August, Morgan's findings put support for the Greens in New South Wales at 17 per cent (they finished with 10.7 per cent of the vote), Victoria at 14 per cent (14.6 per cent), Queensland 13 per cent (12.8 per cent), South Australia 16.5 per cent (13.3 per cent), Western Australia 18 per cent (14 per cent), Tasmania 21.5 per cent (20.3 per cent) and the Australian Capital Territory 27 per cent (22.9 per cent). On these figures, Morgan predicted, correctly, that the Greens would win one seat in each of the States; but its prediction that the Greens would win a seat in the Australian Capital Territory proved wrong. Morgan warned that to achieve the levels of support its polling reported, 'the manning of polling places' might be the 'biggest hurdle for the Greens to overcome'. Whether this helps explain the difference between Morgan's figures and the vote the Greens actually achieved is difficult to say. Certainly, Morgan overestimated the Greens' support in New South Wales, South Australia, Western Australia and the Australian Capital Territory, but it did not do so in Victoria or Tasmania. For Morgan to be right, the Greens would have to have been better at staffing the polling places in Victoria and Tasmania than they were anywhere else.

Morgan's overestimates for the Senate were not confined to the Greens. In New South Wales, it overestimated the Greens by 6 percentage points and Labor by 4; in Victoria, it overestimated Labor by 6; and in Western Australia it overestimated the Greens by 4 and Labor by three. The evidence that counts most strongly against Morgan's thesis about the Greens' 'biggest hurdle' is, however, its underestimate—not overestimate—of the vote for parties *other* than Labor, the Coalition or the Greens: in New South Wales, Victoria and Tasmania by a massive 8 percentage points, in Queensland by 6, and in Western Australia by five. If the Greens had trouble 'manning' polling places, one can only imagine the height of the hurdle confronting even smaller parties.

Overall, Morgan's figures were much less accurate in the Senate than in the House. Applying the formula used in Table 6.3a—the difference between the polled figures and the results for Labor, the Coalition, the Greens and Other, divided by four—the average error in New South Wales was 5.4 percentage points, Victoria 4.2, Queensland 3.7, Western Australia and Tasmania 3.4, the

Australian Capital Territory 3.2 and South Australia 2.6. In contrast, Morgan's average error for the House of Representatives election (Table 6.3a) was 1.9 percentage points.

It would be nice to say that things such as sample size, aggregating the data from several surveys, and the time of survey explain much of this—and perhaps they do. But two of the three largest errors, in New South Wales and Queensland, occurred in States with the biggest samples, and the four jurisdictions with the lowest errors—Western Australia, South Australia, Tasmania and the Australian Capital Territory—had the smallest samples. Moreover, polling in the Australian Capital Territory started in February while in Tasmania it started in May—earlier than in any of the other jurisdictions. Clearly, there are hurdles other than these to polling in the Senate. One of them—suggested by the underestimate of the vote for 'Others'—is that respondents do not know what choices they will face on election day. More to the point, by not presenting respondents with the full panoply of parties, polling of this kind cannot enlighten them about what their choices really are.

Conclusion

Based on their national estimates for the House of Representatives, the polls did well. Few tipped a hung parliament, but none tipped a Coalition victory. All the polls overestimated Labor's lead but all were within the margin of error. There was no sign that the increasing difficulty of reaching the required number and kind of respondents affected the polls adversely. While some polls were a little better than others, it was not a case of winner takes all. The poll that came closest to estimating each side's final share of the two-party preferred vote did not come out trumps on other criteria. Nor did phone polls always beat online polls or polls conducted via text messaging. While Newspoll stood out for its estimate of the two-party preferred count, it was the online Essential poll, followed by the Morgan phone polls (before the election and on election day) and the Morgan poll via SMS, that did best in estimating the parties' shares of first preferences. Nor was a two-party preferred count calculated on the basis of the 2007 results—Newspoll, for example—necessarily less accurate than one based on asking respondents directly.

Polling in the marginals was a good deal less impressive, with a number of seats being called by Galaxy and Newspoll—and more especially by Morgan and JWS—falling for the wrong side of the ledger. This could partly reflect the fact that things can change one way in one seat and in the opposite way in another seat—phenomena that wash out in the aggregate. But it is more likely to underline the most basic truth about survey research: sampling variance is not a function of the size of the population but a function of the size of the sample. As this election showed, yet again, conducting polls with very small samples in a number of seats and then focusing on how many interviews one has secured in the aggregate does not get around this problem; in close contests—and marginal seats fit this description almost by definition—sample sizes of 400 (JWS) let alone 200 (Galaxy and Newspoll) are too small.

With the Senate, the problem was less one of predicting the number of seats than of accurately estimating the parties' shares of the vote. While Morgan was able (almost) to predict the number of seats the Greens would win, and trumpeted that they would hold the 'balance of power' (something that was not really in doubt), it did poorly in estimating the parties' shares of the vote. Its samples were not big enough and it polled too early but it also did not fully inform respondents about which parties were running.

Measured against their final national figures, two-party preferred, for the House of Representatives, the differences among the polls are small; even the least accurate of the polls—and no fewer than six of the 12 final pre-election or day-of-the-election polls tied for this title—came within 2 percentage points of the correct result. In political terms, a difference of this magnitude can make a world of difference; but in statistical terms, it is not a matter of great consequence. To be sure, there is also the matter of bragging rights. But over the long term, differences between the polls are even smaller than the 2010 figures might suggest. Since 1993, when the pollsters began to report a two-party preferred count, the average two-party preferred error for the phone polls conducted by Newspoll has been 1.4, for Morgan 1.8 and for Nielsen 2.0 percentage points—a range across the three organisations not of 1.8 (the difference in 2010 between 1.9 for Nielsen and 0.1 for Newspoll) but of just 0.6 percentage points.

But while the average errors recorded by each of these organisations over the past seven or eight elections have been perfectly respectable, they have been far from remarkable. Writing nearly 40 years ago, David Butler suggested that if 'an enterprising rogue had set up a pseudo-poll that conducted no interviews' but simply worked on the assumption that at every election Labor and the Coalition would each get 46 per cent of the first-preference vote, they 'would not have had too bad a record'—an average error between 1958 and 1972 of 'under $2\frac{1}{2}$' percentage points (Butler 1973, 114). In a similar vein, we can now say that if in 1993 an enterprising rogue had set up a pseudo-poll that conducted no interviews but simply worked on the assumption that at every election Labor would get 50 per cent of the two-party preferred vote, he or she would have an even better record—an average error of just 1.8 percentage points. As it happens, 1.8 percentage points is the median error for the three polls—Newspoll, Morgan and Nielsen—with records that stretch back to 1993. Moreover, the range of deviations (0.2–3.6 percentage points) from a 50:50 two-party preferred result in elections held since then is not very different from the range of errors recorded by the polls (0.1–4.3 percentage points).

The point here is not to suggest that any of the pollsters are rogues; rather, as Butler put it, it is to show 'how limited has been the possibility of error' (Butler 1973, 114). Indeed, if one can work out which party is likely to get the majority of the two-party preferred vote—generally, not a difficult task—the possibility of error is even less. Operating in a competitive polling environment and able to take advantage of a late or last-mover advantage because one pollster can see what another has reported (Goot 2009, 128) reduces the possibility of error further. The increasing emphasis on the two-party preferred count as the measure of a poll's success might help to explain why the number of market research firms involved in polling has increased in recent years and why the methods deployed by the industry have expanded.

Acknowledgments

For information of various kinds, I am grateful to David Briggs (Galaxy), Angelos Frangopoulos (Sky News), Julian McCrann (Morgan), Ross Neilson (Auspoll), Martin O'Shannessy (Newspoll), John Scales (JWS), John Stirton (Nielsen), Ian Watson, and Kate Whelan (Essential). For their comments on an early version of the chapter presented to a post-election workshop at the ANU, I thank Marian Sawer and Marian Simms especially. Writing and research were supported by Australian Research Council Grant DPO 987839.

References

Australian Electoral Commission (AEC). 2010. *House Division Classifications*. Canberra: Australian Electoral Commission, viewed 2 October 2010, <http://vtr.aec.gov.au/HouseDivisionClassifications-15508-NAT.htm>

Balogh, Stefanie. 2010. 'Labor pain in six seats'. *The Courier-Mail*, 18 August.

Benson, Simon. 2010. 'Gillard set to be a Labor saviour'. *The Daily Telegraph*, 14 August.

Bowe, William. 2010. 'Galaxy marginal polls and the rest'. *The Poll Bludger*, 15 August, <http://blogs.crikey.com.au/pollbludger/2010/08/15galaxy-marginals>

Burgess, Rob. 2010. 'Poll position'. *Business Spectator*, 19 August, <http://www.businessspectator.com.au/bs.nsf/Article/POLL-POSITION-pd20100818-8ETYU?opendocument>

Butler, David. 1973. 'Polls and predictions'. In *The Canberra Model*. Melbourne: Cheshire.

Canberra Times. 2010. 'Pollsters were on the money'. *The Canberra Times*, 23 August.

Coorey, Phillip. 2010. 'Hanging on: Labor leads, Libs close in'. *Sydney Morning Herald*, 21–22 August, pp. 1, 10.

Essential. 2010a. *Essential Report*, 20 August 2010, Essential Media, viewed 20 August 2010, <http://www.essentialmedia.com.au/category/election-special-essential-report>

Essential. 2010b. 'Election poll wrap', 23 August 2010, Essential Media, <http://www.essentialmedia.com.au/category/essential-report-100823-23rd-august-2010>

Farr, Malcolm. 2010. 'Green deal to drag Gillard to victory'. *The Daily Telegraph*, 20 August, 4–5.

Galaxy. 2010. Galaxy Research. Chatswood, NSW, <http://www.galaxyresearch.com.au/>

Goot, Murray. 2005. 'The polls: Liberal, Labor or too close to call'. In Marian Simms and John Warhurst (eds), *Mortgage Nation: The 2004 Australia election*. Brisbane: University of Queensland Press.

Goot, Murray. 2009. 'Getting it wrong while getting it right: the polls, the press and the 2007 Australian election'. *Australian Cultural History* 27(2): 115–33.

Goot, Murray. 2010. 'Underdogs, bandwagons or incumbency? Party support at the beginning and end of Australian election campaigns, 1983–2007'. *Australian Cultural History* 28(1): 69–80.

Grattan, Michelle. 2010. 'It's down to the undecideds'. *The Age*, 21–22 August, 1.

Green, Antony. 2010. 'Galaxy marginal seat poll'. *Antony Green's Election Blog*, 15 August; <http://blogs.abc.net.au/antonygreen/2010/08/galaxy-marginal-seat-poll.html>

Hughes, Colin A. 1977. 'The electorate speaks—and after'. In Howard R. Penniman (ed.), *Australia at the Polls: The national elections of 1975*. Washington, DC: American Enterprise Institute for Public Policy Research.

Jackman, Simon. 2005. 'Pooling the polls over an election campaign'. *Australian Journal of Political Science* 40: 499–517.

JWS. 2010. Labor looks set to win with 4 seat majority, Media release, 17 August. Echuca, Vic.: JWS Research.

Kearney, Simon. 2010a. 'A neck and neck fight to the last'. *The Sunday Telegraph*, 15 August.

Kearney, Simon. 2010b. '17 key seats surge to Libs'. *Sunday Mail*, 15 August.

Kearney, Simon and Campbell, James. 2010. 'Abbott boost in close-run battle'. *Sunday Herald Sun*, 15 August.

Kelton, Greg. 2010. 'How we put you in the poll position'. *The Advertiser*, 23 August.

Kerr, Christian. 2010. 'Newspoll forecast right on the money again'. *The Australian*, 23 August.

Levine, Michele, Morgan, Gary and McCrann, Julian. 2010. *The state of the nation after the federal election*. Roy Morgan Research, <http://www.roymorgan.com/resources/pdf/papers/20101001>

Mackerras, Malcolm. 1975. *Elections 1975*. Sydney: Angus & Robertson.

Mackerras, Malcolm. 2009. 'Describing the results'. *Australian Cultural History* 37(2): 219–42.

Mackerras, Malcolm. 2010. 'Malcolm Mackerras pendulum two-party preferred 2007'. *The Australian*, 23 August.

Morgan. 2010a. Election day 7 NEWS Morgan poll too close to call—ALP (51.5%) cf. L-NP (48.5%) but hung parliament most likely outcome. Finding No. 4571, 22 August, Roy Morgan Research, <http://www.roymorgan.com/news/polls/2010/4571/> [Released initially under the heading 'Final...', Email, 21 August, 10.03 pm (Author's collection)].

Morgan. 2010b. 4 o'clock election day result—special SMS Morgan 'exit' poll: at 4pm Saturday August 21 a hung parliament still most likely outcome, (ALP 51% L-NP 49%) according to special Morgan SMS 'exit' poll. Email, 21 August, 6.16 pm, Author's collection.

Morgan. 2010c. Greens set to hold Senate 'Balance of Power' with 10 Senators. Finding No. 4554; <http://www.roymorgan.com/news/polls/2010/4554/>

Morgan, Gary, Levine, Michelle and McCrann, Julian. 2010. Morgan poll most accurate & first to suggest 'hung parliament'. Finding No. 4572, Roy Morgan Research, <http://www.roymorgan.com/news/polls/2010/4572/>

Newspoll. 2010. *Election 2010—Newspoll accuracy again superior*, Topic Paper for Newspoll Clients, <http://www.newspoll.com.au/system/files/f7/o137/2010%2009%20September%20-%20Newspoll%20topic%20paper%20election%202010.pdf>

Passmore, Daryl. 2010. 'Baseball bats ready for Labor yet again'. *Sunday Mail*, 15 August.

Richardson, Charles and Kerr, Christian. 2007. 'The best seats in the house'. In Christian Kerr (ed.), *The Crikey Guide to the 2007 Federal Election*. Ringwood, Vic.: Penguin.

Shanahan, Dennis. 2010. 'Gillard fights surge to fast-finishing Coalition'. *The Weekend Australian*, 21–22 August, 1, 6.

7. Debates, Town-Hall Meetings and Media Interviews

Geoffrey Craig

The issue of leaders' debates—their frequency, themes and formats—assumed key prominence in the political jockeying that occurred between Julia Gillard and Tony Abbott during the 2010 Australian election campaign. The uncertainty over the leaders' debates at times descended into farcical brinkmanship but it also underlined the political importance of debates in campaigns. The eventual hosting of two town-hall meetings late in the campaign, while not debates, represented a significant change in the recent history of the narratives of Australian election campaigns where a single televised debate has been held early in the campaign. The campaign was characterised by an unprecedented focus on the 'meta-campaign'—the influence of campaign managers, or the so-called 'faceless men', and the Prime Minister's declaration she was ditching the 'risk-averse orthodoxy of modern campaigning'—and the tortuous 'debate about the debates' contributed to an undue emphasis on campaign strategy.

While election campaigns are awash with media interviews, this chapter also focuses on interviews on high-profile national television and radio current affairs programs that play a major role in the establishment of the news agenda during election campaigns. Specifically, the monitored television programs were *Insiders*, *7.30 Report*, *Q&A*, *Lateline*, *Four Corners*, *Meet the Press*, *Insight*, *A Current Affair*, *Today Tonight, Sunrise* and *Today*. The monitored radio programs were *AM* and *PM* on the ABC and the *Alan Jones Breakfast Show* on 2GB (Sydney).

Leaders' Debates

The leaders' debate on 25 July at the National Press Club was generally judged to be uninspiring and in accord with many of the now established conventions in leaders' debate. The underdog, Tony Abbott, benefited from his participation in the debate and exceeded low expectations, establishing himself as a potentially viable prime ministerial candidate. Commentators lambasted the lacklustre content and the careful presentation of the leaders: 'The so-called positions adopted by the contestants during the televised debate added up to nothing more than regurgitated press releases with even less detail…They are as packaged as plastic wrapped cheese, and their careful marketing ensures they are as bland' (Wright 2010).

No new policies were announced during the leaders' debate, but a number of issues were canvassed including economic management, health, immigration, broadband, the paid parental-leave scheme and climate change.

Lyndal Curtis on *AM* noted that while both political leaders provided disciplined performances, the advantage of the leaders' debate was that 'for most voters it would have been their first chance to see the leaders' messages in full, not sliced and diced into the bite-size quotes seen in the media' (Curtis 2010). Although some commentators observed that the debate was a relatively even contest, the so-called 'worm'—measuring the responses of a panel of undecided voters on Channel Nine—gave the debate to Gillard, 63 to 37 per cent. Channel Seven deployed its 'polligraph', which is based upon a sample of voters across the political spectrum and different demographics. A novel feature of the use of the different viewer-response measurement systems was the breakdown into responses from women and men. On Channel Nine, women voted Gillard the winner of the debate, 66 to 34 per cent, while the men voted Gillard the winner, 61 to 39 per cent.

There was much media commentary about the timing of the leaders' debate and it was eventually rescheduled so it would not coincide with the screening of the final episode of the popular *MasterChef* program. The *MasterChef* finale attracted an average capital-city audience of 3.962 million viewers, but the debate also attracted interest, with more than 3.4 million viewers across the three free-to-air networks and the ABC (Bodey 2010).

The leaders' debate ended with Tony Abbott requesting further debates, following the Rudd Government's initial promise to hold three debates during the election campaign. Over subsequent weeks in the campaign there was a series of vacillations over participation in further debates and debate formats. Prior to the leaders' debate, the Prime Minister said there would be only one debate and brushed off calls for further debates, noting she had debated Abbott many times during their regular joint appearances on the *Today* breakfast program and elsewhere. After a poor second week of campaigning for the Labor Party, the Prime Minister took up an offer on the *Today Tonight* program on the Seven Network to debate the Opposition Leader on the subject of the economy, but Abbott then refused the offer. Paul Kelly (2010b) noted that the Opposition Leader's refusal to debate on the economy, after calling for further debates, was risky and arrogant, and Peter van Onselen (2010) also noted it was a missed opportunity. The challenges and accusations about a debate on the economy continued to dog the campaign but it was agreed that a town-hall-style forum, with separate appearances from the two leaders taking questions from the public, would take place on Wednesday, 11 August. Subsequently, Abbott agreed to a debate on the economy, but wanted to restrict it to a 30-minute debate on the ABC, while the Prime Minister called for an hour-long debate. The stand-off, culminating in the final week of the campaign, was not resolved, leaving a frustrated Kerry O'Brien (2010) to ask the Opposition Leader: 'Tony Abbott, do you accept that for many Australian voters, this spat about a debate that's chewed up so much energy on both sides must by now look like a couple of immature kids exchanging insults in the schoolyard?'

The farcical debate about the election campaign debates strongly emphasises the need for the establishment of a debate commission, similar to the bipartisan Commission on Presidential Debates that oversees the US presidential campaign debates. Such a commission would be a valuable instrument in a bid to de-politicise the issue of leaders' debates and ensure that valuable campaign energy would not be wasted on strategic positioning by the party leaders. The Opposition Leader pledged that if elected he would establish such a commission, and the Prime Minister has subsequently included the issue of a debates commission in her agreement with the Greens Party (Brown 2011).

There were also a number of other debates of various formats that featured during the election campaign. The customary series of National Press Club debates occurred between ministers and their shadows on areas such as the economy, foreign affairs, health and communications. The debate format extended to breakfast television, with the *Sunrise* program on Channel Seven featuring debates between Wayne Swan and Joe Hockey on the economy, and also debates between The Nationals and the Greens, and the Australian Sex Party and the Family First Party.

Another unusual feature was the hosting of a leaders' debate outside the formal election campaign on 23 March after the then Prime Minister, Kevin Rudd, accepted a challenge from Tony Abbott during a parliamentary exchange. The debate, on health policy and held at the National Press Club, was offered by the government as one of three leaders' debates. Although the apparently snap decision to have a debate seemed initially a risky strategy for the Prime Minister, the debate demonstrated the advantage of incumbency, with Rudd able to choose the debate topic on which he was able to expound on his recent work on hospitals policy. The debate unfolded as a quite lively exchange between the two participants. Barrie Cassidy (2010) noted: 'It was a very good debate…by historical standards. At times, the leaders actually engaged one another directly, contrary to the rules.' Rudd performed well and was generally judged to be the winner of the debate. Paul Kelly (2010a) wrote: 'This debate was a throwback to the confident Rudd of the 2007 campaign. It should delight Labor strategists.' In accord with previous experiences in leaders' debates, the deployment of a positive approach contributed to debate success; Rudd's invocation of his family background and his use of personal and homespun language were favourably received by the so-called 'worm' that recorded the responses of a panel of undecided voters.

Town-Hall Meetings

A highlight of the election campaign was the hosting of two town-hall meetings or 'community forums' (the events were promoted as the People's Forum) where both the Prime Minister and the Opposition Leader were separately subject to an hour of questions from an audience of uncommitted voters, selected by the Galaxy polling company. The first town-hall meeting, on Wednesday, 11 August, at the Rooty Hill RSL Club in western Sydney, featured aggressive questioning of Gillard on a number of subjects, including the dumping of Kevin Rudd, gay marriage, pensions and climate change. There was particular scepticism from the audience when Gillard talked about ALP advertisements that cited Peter Costello's criticisms of Tony Abbott's economic credentials, and also when the Prime Minister talked about a proposed rail link between Parramatta and Epping in Sydney that was announced earlier that day. The Prime Minister attempted to stress the government's competence in management of the economy throughout her appearance. This was underlined in her opening remarks when she asked for members of the audience to raise their hands if they had a mortgage or if they paid rent, and then asked those people to keep their hands raised if they could continue to make those payments if they did not have a job.

Abbott received a more favourable response from the audience, although he did receive some questions that were critical of his party's position on asylum-seekers and broadband policy. As one journalist noted: 'The audience took a more inquisitive line with Abbott, less interested in the finer details of policies and more keen for him to elucidate who he was' (Welch 2010). Abbott appeared more comfortable than Gillard with the audience, and was able to deploy effectively the populist form of discourse required of such a format, which was supported by his decision to speak from the forum floor, on the same level as his interrogators. The town-hall meeting bolstered the fortunes of the Opposition. *The Australian* reported:

> In a spirited and confident performance at a venue where he once boxed, the Opposition Leader marked himself as a man at ease in the suburbs and a leader who would not only listen, but would solve their problems: from health to congestion, drug abuse to the rising cost of living. (Dusevic and Maher 2010)

The mix of questions and the modes of delivery from voters at times provided a welcome contrast with the conventional, well-honed cut and thrust of news media interviews. The general predilection of the audience to favour Abbott did prompt some subsequent public discussion about the selection process for the forum, and this discussion received momentum when it was discovered that one of Abbott's questioners was the son of a former SA Liberal MP (Coorey 2010a).

The second town-hall meeting was held on Wednesday, 18 August at the Broncos Leagues Club in Brisbane, just days before the election. The forum, held amid the wrangling over a debate over the economy, was a more even affair, and the Prime Minister was judged to be the winner with 83 votes to 75 votes for Abbott (Coorey 2010b). The Brisbane town-hall meeting attracted more viewers than the earlier event in Sydney, which was restricted to pay television viewers, although neither town-hall meeting was screened by the commercial television networks. The Opposition Leader, speaking first, again took to the forum floor, stating 'this is an exchange, not a lecture', and the Prime Minister followed his lead and also spoke at the same level as her questioners. The more equal approaches to the leaders in the second forum was reflected in a contrast between the opening questions for the Opposition Leader in the two meetings: in Brisbane he was asked a challenging question about affordable housing and the cost of living and the Opposition Leader acknowledged his limited ability to effect change, while the initial questioner at the Rooty Hill town-hall meeting provided Abbott with an easy opportunity to exploit a political advantage when he was asked a question on climate change. The Opposition Leader was asked about a range of issues including apprenticeships, superannuation, abortion, medical research, pension increases, peak oil, computers in schools, drought assistance, Aboriginal disadvantage, and gay marriage. Indeed, Abbott received 27 questions in the Brisbane town-hall meeting—considerably more than a week earlier in Sydney. Going against the convention of such public events, the Opposition Leader flagged a new policy where students could help pay off their Higher Education Contribution Scheme (HECS) debt by doing volunteer work. The Prime Minister was again questioned several times about the ousting of Kevin Rudd. She was also asked questions about medical negligence, desalination plants, medical registration systems, death duties and capital gains tax, education policy, the budget surplus, refugees, broadband and the Resource Super Profits Tax.

The town-hall meetings were generally welcomed in the 2010 election as campaign events that would provide greater opportunity for members of the public to express their views. In this way, such meetings were responses to the increasing party control of election campaigns that had sidelined public engagement with their political leaders. As Paul Kelly (2010c) wrote after the second forum: 'These events in Brisbane and Rooty Hill should establish the town hall concept as basic to future election campaigns.' Although questions did often reflect the mainstream news agenda, the town-hall meetings did permit a broad variety of questions, and their expression by members of the public helped to personalise and embody particular public issues. The meetings also required both party leaders to use a more accessible discourse in their answers, and the events facilitated greater accountability than sometimes occurs in conventional media interviews. As Channel Seven political editor, Mark Riley (2010), said in his preview of the Brisbane meeting: 'They can expect some unscripted questions from real people that they'll have to answer unlike at press conferences when they avoid our questions entirely.'

In addition to these town-hall meetings, the election campaign also featured forum-style programs that provided members of the public with an opportunity to question the party leaders and other politicians. The *Q&A* program on the ABC featured singular separate performances by both Abbott and Gillard in the last two weeks of the election campaign, and earlier programs during the campaign featured a panel of participants. The SBS program *Insight* was also based on questions and comments from members of the public, although it featured a regular group of uncommitted voters from a range of marginal seats across the country. Both programs also built into their structure questions and comments from other members of the public through online program sites, Facebook posts and tweets (Twitter). *Q&A*, for example, ran tweets in a banner at the bottom of the screen as ongoing responses to the studio discussion. Similarly, *Insight* drew on reports from an online reporter who summarised Facebook debates. Inclusion of such online and social media responses further enhanced the dialogic nature of such programs, distinguishing them from conventional political television that largely excludes the public.

Media Interviews

Media interviews constitute the prime form of political communication in election campaigns, and the 2010 Australian election in particular was characterised by a blitz of such encounters. In the last couple of days of campaigning, the leaders of both the major parties conducted dozens of radio and television interviews although most were merely short recitations of well-worn campaign messages. There were, nonetheless, a significant number of interviews throughout the campaign that had an important effect on the shaping of the campaign narrative and these extended, formal interviews are the subject of discussion here. In addition, both party leaders and senior members of the Labor, Liberal, National and the Greens parties were frequently interviewed throughout the campaign across most of the monitored programs.

An early interview in the campaign was a performance by the Prime Minister on *60 Minutes*. The interview mixed policy discussion with a more human-interest inquiry into the character and life of Julia Gillard. In addition to questions on the change of leadership, trade union influence on the Labor Party and the war in Afghanistan, Gillard was also asked about her mother and her partner. The Prime Minister also tried to diminish the policy differences between Labor and the Coalition on asylum-seekers in an early bid to defuse the subject as an election issue.

Media interviews are forums where political leaders can promote their individual character, personality and 'life story', but they are also prime opportunities for political opponents to seize upon gaffes, any hesitation or prevarication, or any deviation from previously articulated views. In the first week of the campaign, Tony Abbott's attempt to remove the spectre of WorkChoices from the campaign was first illustrated in a media stunt in a 3AW (Melbourne) radio interview where he signed a 'contract' guaranteeing it would not return as Liberal Party policy, but then in subsequent remarks he stated: 'Obviously, I can't give an absolute guarantee about every single aspect of workplace relations legislation, but WorkChoices is gone, now and forever.' This statement provided the Labor Party with the opportunity to continue its claim that WorkChoices, or some form of it, might be resurrected by a Coalition government.

It was indicative of the muted impact of the leaders' debate that an interview of Tony Abbott by Kerry O'Brien on the *7.30 Report* on the following evening did not make mention of the debate. In a lively exchange, O'Brien questioned Abbott's economic management skills with reference to Peter Costello's previous comments about the Liberal Party leader, and he challenged the Coalition's stance on future immigration levels. In an unusual move, O'Brien also screened an extended excerpt from an interview with Abbott a year earlier in which the then Opposition frontbencher indicated a willingness to revisit the industrial relations policies of the previous Coalition government.

The Prime Minister was caught out the following day in an interview with Alan Jones on 2GB when she stumbled on naming the year that lower company tax rates would be introduced. The Prime Minister engaged in a lengthy process of stalling as she apparently sought an answer to Jones's question. It was also at this time, during the second week of the campaign, that it was observed that Gillard's 'favourability' rating with talkback calls around the country was falling (Elliott 2010). It was also during this week of the campaign, however, that the *Australian Women's Weekly* featured an extended interview and photo shoot with the Prime Minister. The article reflected more general news media interest in the personality and personal life of the new Prime Minister. While much of the news media reportage presented the persona of Gillard favourably, the matters of her de-facto relationship, her childlessness and her lack of religious faith were also subject to public discussion in both the tabloid and the quality media.

A significant amount of news media attention during the campaign focused on former Prime Minister Kevin Rudd, the circumstances of his ousting and the nature of his relationships with the woman who succeeded him as prime minister and his senior Labor Party colleagues. The third week of the campaign featured an interview of Rudd by Phillip Adams on the ABC radio program *Late Night Live* where the former Prime Minister, fresh from his gall-bladder surgery, declared that he would be campaigning for the Labor Party outside his electorate and that he did not want Tony Abbott 'sliding into office by default'. Rudd also recorded an interview with the Seven Network's *Sunday Night* program that screened later in the campaign, on 15 August.

Another interview that had an impact on the campaign narrative was an interview of Tony Abbott by Kerry O'Brien on the *7.30 Report* in the following week of the campaign, on 10 August. In the interview, O'Brien quizzed the Opposition Leader on the broadband policy that had been released by the Liberal Party earlier in the day and Abbott several times acknowledged his limited technical knowledge in the area: 'Again, if you're gonna get me into a technical argument, I'm going to lose it, Kerry, because I'm not a tech head' (ABC 2010). This less than convincing performance by Abbott contributed to subsequent journalistic scrutiny of both the Opposition's broadband policy and the Opposition Leader's command of technology and economic policy detail.

The final week of the campaign featured a number of major interviews of the major-party leaders in addition to the daily frenetic campaigning and major campaign events, including the Brisbane town-hall meeting and the late delivery of the Labor Party campaign 'launch'. On ABC Television, both major-party leaders were featured in an episode of *Four Corners* and both completed their third interviews on the *7.30 Report*. On commercial television, both Gillard and Abbott conducted interviews on *A Current Affair*.

Conclusion

The 2010 Australian election campaign offered a strong contrast between the blandness of a highly disciplined leaders' debate and the more informal, unpredictable and informative series of town-hall meetings. The debate throughout the campaign about the number and format of leaders' debates highlighted the need for pre-existing agreement about leaders' debates that could be facilitated through a debates commission. While we should always expect the performances of political leaders to be highly disciplined in debates, interviews and other media performances, the greater public involvement that occurred through the town-hall meetings and forum-style programs required party leaders to offer less-scripted responses across a broad range of issues, to appear more human and less combative. The campaign also emphasised the ongoing importance of media interviews to both scrutinise political performance and provide significant public platforms on which politicians can promote their own political and personal narratives. The character of the next Australian election campaign will be strongly influenced by the political uncertainty that arises from a minority government but hopefully it might also be shaped by recognition of the benefits of greater opportunities for public involvement and at least some questioning of the overwhelming influence of the 'risk-averse orthodoxy of modern campaigning'.

References

Australian Broadcasting Corporation (ABC). 2010. *7.30 Report*, 10 August, ABC TV, viewed 11 August 2010, <http://www.abc.net.au/7.30/content/2010/s2979381.htm>

Bodey, Michael. 2010. 'MasterChef tops 3.9m but debate not far behind'. *The Australian*, 26 July, viewed 26 July 2010, <http://www.theaustralian.com.au/business/media/masterchef-tops-39m-but-debate-not-far-behind/story-e6frg996-1225896908998>

Brown, Bob. 2011. 'PM confirms commitment on leader's debates'. *The Australian Greens*. 15 April, viewed 13 December 2011, <http://bob-brown.greensmps.org.au/content/media-release/pm-confirms-commitment-leaders-debates>

Cassidy, Barrie. 2010. 'Positivity the best policy as Rudd tweets ahead'. *The Drum*, 23 March, viewed 24 March 2010, <http://www.abc.net.au/news/stories/2010/03/23/2853911.htm>

Coorey, Phil. 2010a. '"Jobs" Julia grilled as Tony leads from front'. *Sydney Morning Herald*, 12 August, 6.

Coorey, Phil. 2010b. 'Abbott pledges to slash debt'. *Sydney Morning Herald*, 19 August, 1.

Curtis, Lyndal. 2010. 'Debate produces no clear winner'. *AM*, 26 July, ABC Radio, viewed 26 July 2010, <http://www.abc.net.au/am/content/2010/s2963851.htm>

Dusevic, Tom and Maher, Sid. 2010. 'People warm to a leader at their level'. *The Australian*, 12 August, 1.

Elliott, Geoff. 2010. 'PM's radio ratings in a downward spiral'. *The Australian*, 28 July, 5.

Kelly, Paul. 2010a. 'Rudd skates home with sweet reason'. *The Australian*, 24 March, viewed 24 March 2010, <http://www.theaustralian.com.au/news/opinion/rudd-skates-home-with-sweet-reason/story-e6frg6zo-1225844495756>

Kelly, Paul. 2010b. 'Abbott's rejection of debate betrays risky arrogance'. *The Australian*, 5 August, 1.

Kelly, Paul. 2010c. 'Julia improves, but Tony is a natural'. *The Australian*, 19 August, 5.

O'Brien, Kerry. 2010. 'Abbott gears up for election day'. *7.30 Report*, 17 August, ABC TV, viewed 18 July 2010, <http://www.abc.net.au/7.30/content/2010/s2985780.htm>

Riley, Mark. 2010. *Channel Seven News*, 18 August.

van Onselen, Peter. 2010. 'It's the economy, stupid, but let's not talk about it'. *The Australian*, 7–8 August, 14.

Welch, Dylan. 2010. 'Getting down to the nitty-gritty at Rooty Hill RSL'. *Sydney Morning Herald*, 12 August, 6.

Wright, Tony. 2010. 'Abbott and Gillard as packaged as plastic-wrapped cheese'. *Sydney Morning Herald*, 26 July, viewed 26 July 2010, <http://www.smh.com.au/federal-election/abbott-and-gillard-as-packaged-as-plasticwrapped-cheese-20100726-10r88.html>

8. May the Less Threatening Leader of the Opposition Win: The cartoonists' view of election 2010

Haydon Manning and Robert Phiddian

National affairs correspondent for *The Age*, Tony Wright, expressed widespread frustration at the media-managed frivolity of the 2010 federal election campaign when he asserted on radio that 'this campaign has been made for the satirists' (ABC 2010). From our observation of the editorial cartoons of the campaign, the level of engagement with significant issues was too slight even for the satirists to get much of a handle on events. Indeed, it was only the ABC TV show *Gruen Nation* that broke new satirical ground in this campaign, and that was because it focused on the advertising and spin rather than the political substance. It debuted in its election mode with an audience of 1.6 million, 'winning' the night against the commercial channels, and developed a strong following for the quality and wit of its attack on election advertising (*The Sunday Age*, 1 August 2010). The success of this meta-analysis of the political game reflects the trouble satirists in more traditional modes had in finding anything much to grasp. Wright was only half-right about the campaign for the cartoonists; it was a joke for them, certainly, but mostly a rather bad and empty one.

They had to rely a lot on physical caricature of the leaders, as there simply was not much more to work with than a woman with red hair and a big nose up against a man with big ears often photographed coming out of the surf in his 'budgie smugglers' (or bathers). The major parties did differ on some key policies, such as the virtue or otherwise of a mining tax, how to deliver Internet services to the nation, and how generous parental-leave provisions might be, but for many voters (the cartoonists included), these appeared rather insignificant when compared with the issues in recent elections. For the most part, Tony Abbott and Julia Gillard seemed keen to empty their own campaigns of policy content in the hope of slipping into office by dint of being less scary than the other party in the eyes of a majority of swinging voters. As Gillard put it in what might actually have been an unguarded moment: 'If you are looking for a prime minister with small ears, this is not your election' (*The Australian*, 18 August 2010). It would have been a good joke if one could be certain it was a travesty of clearly understood political differences. For many, however, it must have seemed a metaphor for the lack of significant choice on offer. The cartoons of this campaign brought to mind those of 1998—another election when a struggling first-term government was opposed by a small-target Opposition, and where the theme of the cartoons could be summarised as 'Australia deserves better' (Manning and Phiddian 2000). As the grandfather of current Australian cartoonists, Bruce Petty, shows, it was a long struggle to the polls for the voters and (by extension) for the cartoonists.

Figure 8.1 Bruce Petty, *The Age*, 16 August 2010

Democracy matters, this reminds us, even when it is arduous. Surely, it should be better than this? Two cartoons illustrate the basic negativity of this campaign, and point to the eerily symmetrical 'curse on both your houses' that almost suggested the result voters delivered on polling day.

Figure 8.2 David Rowe, *Australian Financial Review*, 26 July 2010

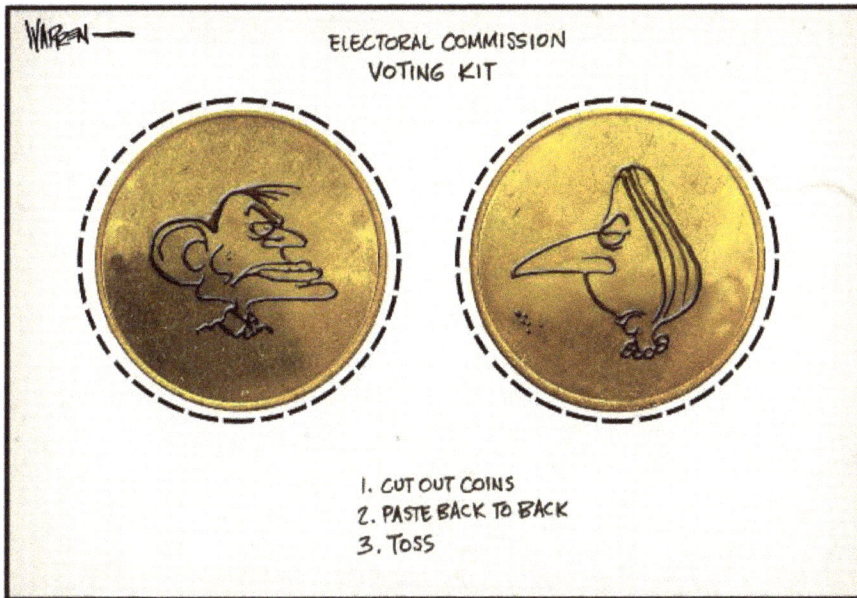

Figure 8.3 Warren Brown, *The Daily Telegraph*, 18 August 2010

The key theme in the cartoons that follow is voter disillusionment at two opposing leaders battling for attention when their platform and policies were demonstrably thin compared with campaigns in recent decades. Cartoonists tend to personalise and caricature issues, and they tend to focus particularly on the leaders of the major parties during the campaign. Our sample of all the cartoons appearing on the nation's capital-city daily newspaper editorial pages demonstrates this, although the presence of two former Labor leaders, Kevin Rudd and Mark Latham, provided some relief from the usual focus on the Prime Minister and the Opposition Leader.

For reasons that differed partially for each major party, negativity predominated in both campaigns. We will trace this through the cartoons, starting with the particular difficulties Labor faced in campaigning without being able to mention its achievements. After taking the prime ministership in extraordinary circumstances, Gillard said: 'I talked to many of my colleagues, and obviously my colleagues formed the same view I did that…a good government had lost its way. It was necessary to get the government back on track with me as prime minister' (*The Age*, 26 June 2010). Crafting a campaign based on an oxymoron of such profound dimensions was never going to be easy, and a messy campaign did indeed transpire for Labor.

Opposition Leader, Tony Abbott, was provided with plenty of ammunition but his cautious demeanour, constant negative carping and lack of economic knowledge meant his moment of mid-campaign dominance was only short lived. We will conclude by showing how some cartoonists predicted the evenness of the final result and commented pointedly on the insignificance during the campaign of important issues such as the rise of the Greens and environmental and Indigenous policies.

ALP Campaign

The *Sydney Morning Herald* cut to the quick in pointing to the difficulty that would so hamper Labor's campaign—namely, that they were a government with no choice but to stand on their record, while at the same time repudiating the recently deposed leader and implicitly supporting the general view of the Rudd Government as all talk but too little action.

Figure 8.4 Alan Moir, *Sydney Morning Herald*, 11 August 2010

The specific retreat from Rudd's rhetorical embrace of a big Australia to much hazy talk of what might constitute a 'sustainable population' and some associated dog whistling about there being too many migrants left cartoonists bemused, the general public confused and fourth-estate elites—particularly those writing for the Murdoch press—aghast. There can be no doubt Gillard's tilt at populism through variations on the term 'sustainability', which is often now little more than an appeal to anything and everything that might sound environmentally progressive, was one of the campaign surprises. Abbott announced that he shared Gillard's hostility to rising population rates, and was not keen to defend the tradition he inherited from Howard. As in the 2001 campaign, both leaders tried to outdo each other in their sympathy for those who felt pressured by immigration, as Nicholson points out.

Figure 8.5 Peter Nicholson, *The Australian*, 22 July 2010

After a fairly good opening week of campaigning, Gillard's second week fell apart when journalist Laurie Oakes reported he had received 'in confidence' information that, during Cabinet deliberations, she had opposed paid parental leave and questioned the size of a pension rise proposal. Cartoonists seized upon this news, as nothing quite beats conjecture about who might be the source of a leak. Suspicion fell upon the recently deposed prime minister, who now found himself well and truly back in the picture.

Figure 8.6 David Rowe, *Australian Financial Review*, 29 July 2010

The main upshot of these damaging leaks, combined with the prospect of more to come, was a truly remarkable twist to modern campaign strategy. The newly minted Prime Minister announced that she had had enough of the traditional finely honed campaigning and from now on would 'throw that rule book out and really get out there'; as she said, 'it's time for me to make sure that the real Julia is well and truly on display' (*The Canberra Times*, 3 August 2010; *The Advertiser*, 2 August 2010). With the announcement of the 'real Julia', cartoonists had a field day—cruelly and accurately suspecting they were observing yet another layer of spin. This proposition is elegantly summarised by Warren Brown.

Figure 8.7 Warren Brown, *The Daily Telegraph*, 5 August 2010

Whether the 'real Julia' line was really spin or substance, Gillard's moment of critical self-reflection served a good purpose in opening the way to one of the real innovations in the 2010 campaign. To prove how real she was, Gillard was suddenly determined to debate Abbott again, and he used his unexpected position of power to extort a new format out of his opponent: the 'town-hall debate'. While there is no doubting that this format played to his strengths, it is also arguable that it is a welcome democratic innovation in otherwise stage-managed campaigns. The cartoonists were not immediately convinced, with Mark Knight questioning the degree of engagement from the punters at the Rooty Hill RSL Club meeting where both leaders refused to appear simultaneously. It, and a follow-up event in Brisbane, did, nevertheless, break the mould of past campaigning by allowing for this more authentic interaction with citizen voters.

Figure 8.8 Mark Knight, *Herald Sun*, 12 August 2010

After the leaks forced Gillard's shift in strategy, any prospect of clear space to pump out the daily campaign message was further confounded when Rudd was hospitalised with a serious gall-bladder ailment. Cartoonists seized on the image of a deposed leader with a gall overload and questions of how 'sorry' Gillard might be for his discomfort. Then another former Labor leader, Mark Latham, captured national attention by sidling up to Gillard at Brisbane's annual agricultural show and, in an intimidating manner, questioning her about a complaint he thought she had made to the Nine Network about his working for them as a journalist. Latham also urged Gillard to expose Rudd's supposed duplicity as the source of Oakes' information. Labor's campaign looked decidedly derailed and in a state of despair, as Rowe and Knight so subtly point out.

Figure 8.9 David Rowe, *Australian Financial Review*, 13 August 2010

Figure 8.10 Mark Knight, *Herald Sun*, 31 July 2010

Finally, Labor's risibly late 'campaign launch'—well into the final week—brought this corrosive accusation of pointlessness from Alan Moir.

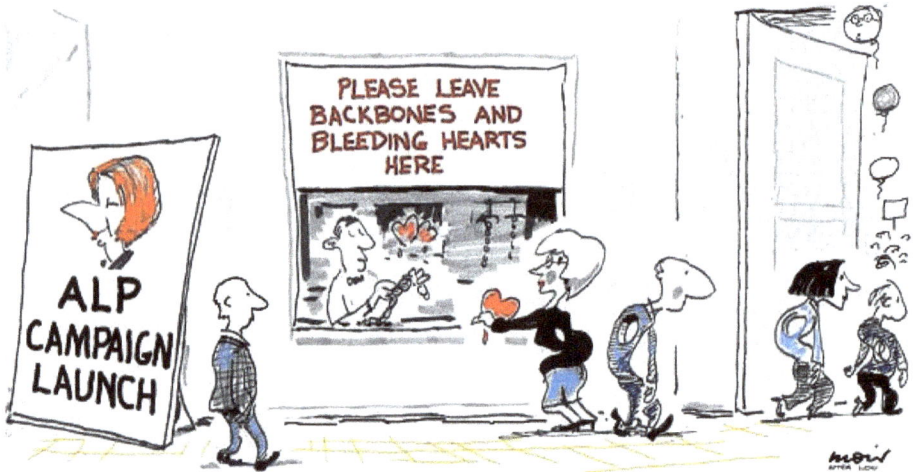

Figure 8.11 Alan Moir, *Sydney Morning Herald*, 17 August 2010

The 'true believers' had great difficulty getting excited by the Labor campaign at any point, even while most pundits continued to believe that they would survive as a government.

The Coalition Campaign

The Coalition campaign was clearly much more disciplined and 'on message' than Labor's. Apart from Abbott's difficulties explaining his policy on national broadband networking, there were relatively fewer cartoons poking fun at Abbott's campaign when compared with those aimed at Gillard. Interestingly, it was Rudd who made one of the more telling critiques of Abbott's campaign when he observed that '[t]here is a real danger at present because of the rolling political controversy about myself that Mr Abbott is simply able to slide quietly into the office of Prime Minister' (Gordon 2010). For the most part, cartoonists turned out similar caricatures of Abbott as an obsessed fitness fanatic perpetually dressed in only his swimming gear, and these became quite formulaic by campaign's end. Golding employs this caricature to make a further point that the opinion polls suggested a large gender divide had emerged, with women voters wary of Abbott. Worried by the prospect, Abbott employed his wife and daughters for as many photo opportunities as possible.

Figure 8.12 Matt Golding, *The Age*, 1 August 2010

The 'cartoonable' rough edges of the Coalition's campaign were most evident in their disarray over the costings of their promises. This raised questions about their economic credibility and was emphasised by the steady eclipse of the Shadow Treasurer, Joe Hockey, by the technically junior finance spokesman Andrew Robb.

Figure 8.13 Peter Nicholson, *The Australian*, 19 August 2010

Figure 8.14 Alan Moir, *Sydney Morning Herald*, 18 August 2010

Abbott himself deferred to these two on economic matters and, as noted above, he also had some trouble with his broadband proposal. The Coalition's policy on this matter might have been less wasteful, but it was certainly trumped by the grandeur of Labor's plan for a national network built upon optical fibre. It would transpire that this piece of product differentiation was crucial after the election in deciding the votes of three regional Independent MPs, and Sean Leahy's cartoon illustrates the fact that Abbott never looked in command of the issue or its implications for the future.

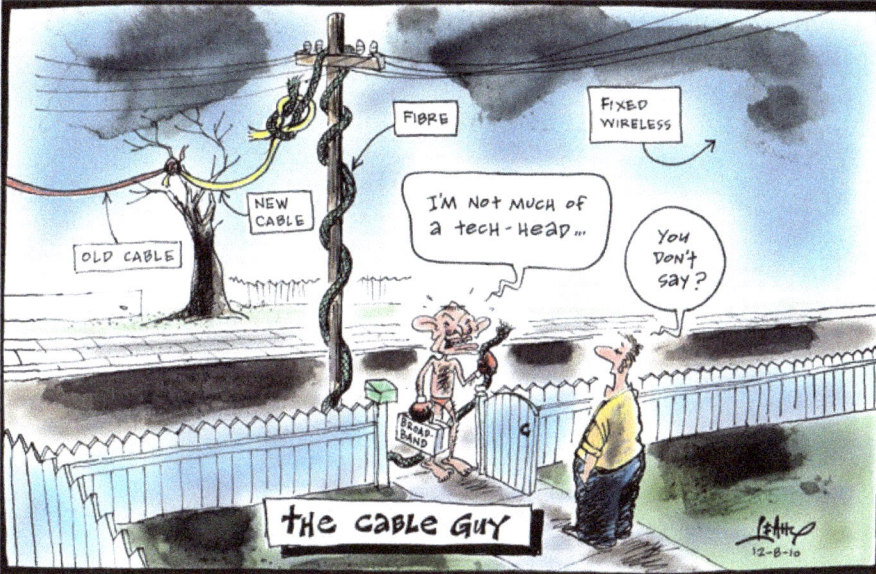

Figure 8.15 Sean Leahy, *The Courier-Mail*, 12 August 2010

Common Ground

The most obvious thing about the 2010 cartoons as a group is the extent to which they were dominated by the leaders, their images and machinations about tactics such as the endless dispute over the number and format of debates. Andrew Dyson neatly summarises the image primping—picked up particularly because of Gillard's appearance in a spread in the *Women's Weekly*, and capitalising on Abbott's long-term propensity to be photographed shirtless during hard physical exercise.

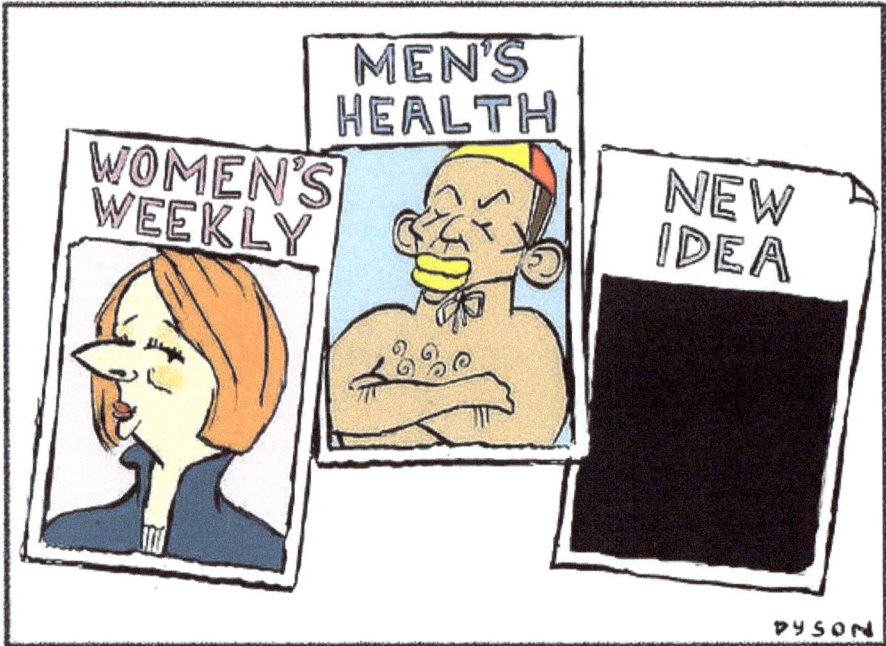

Figure 8.16 Andrew Dyson, *The Age*, 29 July 2010

Two points are worth making about the cartoon's focus on the two leaders. One is that, while leaders always dominate the image count, it was particularly so this time. This might well reflect the extent to which both Gillard and Abbott sought to draw attention to unpopular policies their opponents were associated with when ministers. For Gillard, it was the constant and obsessive attack on Abbott's supposed secret plans to reintroduce WorkChoices. For Abbott, it was the opportunity to chastise Gillard over rorting surrounding the Building the Education Revolution, plus her close association with Rudd's prime ministership as part of the so-called 'Gang of Four' whom many felt had displaced Cabinet decision making. These attacks—though focused on policy more than personality—too often caused the campaign to take on a snarling tone. The other point is that we found nothing systematically sexist in the representation of Gillard. She was caricatured—sometimes harshly—but her gender was, if anything, less often the focus of attention than Abbott's. If we are right, this supports Manning's earlier work (2008) on sexism in cartoons, and marks a small victory for equality.

A strong suite of cartoons focuses on one of the more nearly substantive debates of the campaign: the complicated situation concerning population size and both leaders' preparedness to doubt the decades-long bipartisan commitment to the so-called 'big Australia'. Much to the irritation of the business elite and many economists, Gillard and Abbott recognised that ordinary voters feel pressured in their daily lives by a growing population that in many suburbs is serviced inadequately by infrastructure. While these are innocuous enough as a set of observations, the leaders tended to conflate this matter with the problem of asylum-seekers arriving in boats. This never quite explicit connection of ideas became a proxy for conveying sympathy for voters living in middle to outer suburbs, especially the fabled land of western Sydney. Pope, Leak and Moir all found this politicisation of desperate people ethically dubious.

Figure 8.17 David Pope, *The Canberra Times*, 23 July 2010

Figure 8.18 Bill Leak, *The Australian*, 20 July 2010

Figure 8.19 Alan Moir, *Sydney Morning Herald*, 29 July 2010

In tune with the great cartooning cry of opposition in 2001 (the 'Tampa election'; see Manning and Phiddian 2002), this time, the cartoonists made a clear and valid accusation of scapegoating. The conclusion to draw from all this appears to be that an election campaign is not the best time to start a debate over something as complicated as population size. In practice, both leaders were rejecting one of Rudd's last prime ministerial thought bubbles—an expression of faith in a 'big Australia'. Clearly, without a prolonged pushing of the policy wagon in the years between elections, the sudden broaching of such issues runs the risk of drifting into appealing to nascent fears of many voters that immigration is 'getting out of control'. The alternative of growth by stealth—apparently preferred by an unusual coalition of business and cultural elites—seems little better than fearmongering from a democratic point of view.

Finally, some of the established elements of staged campaign conflict were becoming increasingly obvious as charades. Not only were the official campaign launches absurdly late in the piece (and consequently empty of content), the official leaders' debate was upstaged by a cooking show. After the usual charade with the Opposition Leader calling for more than one debate and the incumbent Prime Minister refusing to entertain such a proposition, the event failed to attract an audience of any consequence. Even after the debate was moved forward an hour to avoid clashing with the series final of *MasterChef*, it remained an object of bemusement to those voters who bothered to watch it.

Figure 8.20 David Pope, *The Canberra Times*, **29 July 2010**

Almost Missing Links

The main focus of the campaign in the cartoons was the uninspiring spectacle of a machine-politician prime minister trying desperately to simulate convictions confronting an Opposition leader assiduously trying to suppress the evidence of his lifetime of conviction politics. Nevertheless, satirists seized on a couple of issues of real significance that largely slipped underneath the campaigning radar. For example, apart from a couple of cartoons, there was precious little discussion of Aboriginal Affairs, as Moir acerbically points out.

Figure 8.21 Alan Moir, *Sydney Morning Herald*, 27 July 2010

Similarly, The Chaser's *Yes We Canberra* on ABC TV also hammered the self-indulgence (even the self-pity) of much of the campaign subject matter with a weekly segment in which Indigenous people were filmed in Arnhem Land commenting patronisingly on the campaign's machinations. It was a severe yet strangely cheerful comment on white, middle-class self-absorption, and neglect of real and urgent social issues.

Another missing link—all the more remarkable given that everyone (rightly) assumed that the Greens would come out of the election with at least the balance of power in the Senate—was the dearth of discussion of the Greens and most notably the question of putting a price on carbon during the next term. There was also little talk about the even more pressing issue of water for agriculture and environmental river flows. Both major-party leaders were happy to skate around the carbon question and were doubtless relieved to find that the Murray–Darling Basin Authority said it would delay release of its 'plan'—a document with potentially divisive recommendations. Given the urgency and prominence of water politics in South Australia, *The Advertiser* struck a chord with its aggrieved audience.

Figure 8.22 Jos Valdman, *The Advertiser*, 29 July 2010

The broader implications of growing Greens support were remarked on by John Spooner—often one of the most satirical observers. He reminds us that something major was happening and that joy on election night was less likely to visit Abbott or Gillard than it was the Greens leader, Bob Brown.

Figure 8.23 John Spooner, *The Age*, 21 August 2010

The Election Result and Aftermath

Sean Leahy in *The Courier-Mail* was—as far as we know—the first commentator of any kind to predict (as opposed to contemplate) a hung parliament. Perhaps his position in Queensland permitted him to sense that there was a bigger move on than other commentators envisaged.

Figure 8.24 Sean Leahy, *The Courier-Mail*, 18 August 2010

All pundits were instantly wise after the fact but, as usual, some of the best autopsy came in the cartoons. The week after the election provided some wonderfully incisive cartoons, of which we give only two examples that, we think, capture the mood of the moment precisely. Moir presents the sudden power of the rural Independents, and Nicholson deploys a strange pathos in his depiction of Labor's 'faceless men', who live only for electoral success and had clearly failed.

Figure 8.25 Alan Moir, *Sydney Morning Herald*, 27 August 2010

Figure 8.26 Peter Nicholson, *The Australian*, 25 August 2010

Summary: The opinion-poll election

Cartoonists working to interpret and satirise the 2010 election showed how difficult it was to locate some substance to grapple with, as both sides reduced the business of winning government to simply reflecting back to electors what the campaign strategists thought they wanted to hear. Perhaps the party operatives (especially on the Labor side, but also among the Coalition) had taken the developing psephological truism that electors make up their minds later and later in campaigns too much to heart. They appear to have forgotten that, if you want to have something convincing for the last week of the campaign, you need to start building the story months and years earlier. Moir's Labor launch cartoon (Figure 8.11), with 'true believers' leaving their hearts and backbones at the door, as if they were as dangerous as guns, makes this point particularly intensely. This election-day volley by Kudelka also nails it.

Figure 8.27 Jon Kudelka, *Mercury*, 21 August 2010

References

Australian Broadcasting Corporation (ABC). 2010. *Morning Program*, 5 August, 891 Adelaide, ABC Radio.

Gordon, Michael. 2010. 'Prime ministerial performance from ex-PM gets to the point'. *The Age*, 6 August.

Manning, Haydon. 2008. 'Australian cartoonists' caricatures of women politicians—from Kirner to Stott Despoja'. In *Comic Commentators: Contemporary political cartooning in Australia*. Perth: API Network, 125–47.

Manning, Haydon and Phiddian, R. 2000. 'Where are the clowns? Political satire in the 1998 federal election campaign'. In Marian Simms and John Warhurst (eds), *Howard's Agenda: The 1998 federal election*. Brisbane: University of Queensland Press, 48–63.

Manning, Haydon and Phiddian, Robert. 2002. 'Two men and some boats—the cartoonists and the 2001 election'. In John Warhurst and Marian Simms (eds), *The Centenary Election*. Brisbane: University of Queensland Press, 41–62.

Part 3. The Parties' Perspectives

9. The 2010 Federal Election: The Liberal Party

Brian Loughnane

The 2010 federal election campaign was one of the most remarkable in Australian history. Key elements of the election result include

- a net gain of 14 seats by the Coalition (including seats that became notionally Labor following redistributions)
- a net loss of 16 seats by Labor
- the first time a first-term government had lost its majority since 1931
- the largest loss of seats by a first-term government since 1931
- the fourth-highest number of seats lost by Labor in its history—only losing more seats in 1931, 1975 and 1996
- the Coalition received almost 700 000 more primary votes than Labor; on a two-party preferred basis, the ALP achieved 30 527 more votes than the Coalition
- Labor's primary vote (37.99 per cent) was the third-lowest recorded by Labor since 1949
- on a two-party preferred basis, the election result (50.12:49.88 per cent) was the second-closest since 1949, and represented a 2.6 per cent swing to the Coalition
- Labor won nine seats on preferences after trailing on primary vote.

Post-election analysis of the vote reveals interesting trends

- a primary-vote swing against Labor in every State except Tasmania
- two-party preferred swings varied across the country: the Coalition recorded positive two-party preferred swings in Queensland (+5.6 per cent), New South Wales (+4.8 per cent), the Northern Territory (+4.6 per cent), Western Australia (+3.2 per cent) and the Australian Capital Territory (+1.7 per cent), but recorded negative swings in Tasmania (−4.4 per cent), Victoria (−1 per cent) and South Australia (−0.8 per cent)
- at this election, the Greens' primary vote reached double digits in all States for the first time; NSW voters are the least supportive of the Greens while those in Tasmania and Western Australia are the most supportive; overall, 60 per cent of seats recorded a Greens primary vote of more than 10 per cent

- the Coalition won three more Senate seats than the ALP—the ALP's second-worst Senate result since 1984

- the Greens won a Senate seat in each State for the first time at a single election, with the ALP reduced to winning only two Senate positions in each State, except Tasmania

- of concern, the number of informal votes increased by 1.6 per cent nationally; 26 of the 30 highest informal votes were recorded in New South Wales and Queensland—the States with optional preferential voting for State elections

- the number of enrolled people turning out to vote is falling (from 95.8 per cent in 1996 to 93.2 per cent in 2010); in 1996, 92.7 per cent of all enrolled voters lodged a formal vote; in 2010, that number had fallen to 88 per cent

- some commentators have argued that the result was a protest against both major parties. In fact, while the major-party combined vote was marginally down on the previous two elections, it was above the 2001 and 1998 results. In the past six elections, the combined major-party vote peaked when there was a change of government in 1996 and 2007.

The reasons for the results recorded at this election are complex. Aided by Liberal Party research conducted following the election, I will set out below in some detail the factors we believe influenced the result. And though the campaign was an important influence on the result, it was far from the only influence. To properly understand what happened on 21 August, we must begin with the community expectations that Labor itself created in the lead-up to the 2007 election.

Despite significant hesitation, the community gave Labor a mandate in 2007 to implement what Australians considered significant promises to help make their lives better. Doubts about Labor's commitment to deliver on their promises, however, quickly began to appear.

We first saw those hesitations emerge in our research prior to Labor's first budget in 2008. Understandably, however, people found reasons to put off making a judgment, believing the budget would be the moment Labor would start to deliver on its promises. The Prime Minister and Treasurer at the time raised expectations with their talk of tough decisions.

The 2008 budget was a failure for Labor and marked the beginning of its electoral decline. Australians were underwhelmed by the budget and by the lack of any significant action on the issues for which Labor had sought and been given a mandate. The failure of the budget was quickly compounded by Labor's ambivalence towards rising petrol and grocery prices, and manifested itself in the swing against Labor at the Gippsland by-election.

Brendan Nelson's reply to the budget in May 2008 captured the mood of ordinary Australians and was the beginning of the Coalition's re-emergence as a viable alternative after the 2007 election. Brendan Nelson deserves great credit for instinctively understanding and clearly articulating both the expectations of Labor and the disappointment widely felt with the government across the community.

By mid-2008, our research was showing that while support for Rudd was apparently high, behind these top-line numbers were very deep frustrations. Labor appeared to ordinary Australians to be ignoring their legitimate concerns and obsessed with its own priorities and interests. This was particularly true of Kevin Rudd. Just seven months into office, Labor had begun to lose its way.

The government did receive some initial credit for its approach at the beginning of the global financial crisis. As the stimulus roll-out occurred throughout 2009, however, concern within the community quickly developed. Australians believed schools could use additional funding but were frustrated at the bureaucratic and poorly considered edict that the money had to be spent on school halls when, in many cases, there were obviously other clear priorities for their school.

The concern in the community at Labor's level of waste was deep. The school-halls and insulation fiascos cut through as practically every community in Australia had examples of mismanagement and waste and this was made worse by the government's exaggerated rhetoric and refusal to admit any level of problem.

The community reaction to the 2009 budget was that the government lacked a clear strategy to manage the economy and, in particular, to begin to repay debt. A sense began to grow that the government was losing control of the nation's finances with little to show in return. The time had come to begin delivering practical results on the ground, but instead the rhetoric continued, the debt grew and interest rates began increasing.

As he moved around the community, Malcolm Turnbull heard these concerns and articulated them. In contrast, Kevin Rudd and Labor continued to dismiss them, further fuelling community concern. Our feedback on Kevin Rudd in this period included representative comments such as: 'marvellous vision but can't put it into action', 'struggles to know how to implement things', 'badly targeted spending', 'always overseas' and 'just waiting for an opinion poll'.

It was clear to us the community had deep reservations about Labor and Kevin Rudd, after only two years in government, even if those reservations were not yet fully reflected in published opinion polls. The community was looking for a strong alternative and an opportunity was emerging for the Coalition. The latter part of 2009, however, was one of the most difficult periods in the history of the Liberal Party.

Labor was attempting to use its proposed emissions trading scheme (ETS) as an issue as much to divide the Coalition as to legislate what it considered to be important policy. As a consequence of the public spotlight being on us, growing community concerns with the Rudd Government were ignored. But they were there, they were real and they were growing. The community was actually more worried in this period about the inaction of the government than it was about the Opposition.

This is why Tony Abbott was able to so quickly and effectively unite the Coalition and take the fight to Labor. People wanted Labor held to account and wanted a strong alternative, and Tony Abbott provided that from the moment he became leader.

It also helps to explain the apparently sudden and dramatic collapse in support for Kevin Rudd. From our perspective, the collapse was neither sudden nor dramatic. As mentioned earlier, the signs of trouble for Rudd were there as early as six months into his term as Prime Minister. Rudd was cut an enormous amount of slack by the electorate. They wished him well. They wanted him to succeed. But Labor's performance never matches its rhetoric. Australians were waiting for something to change but after two years the government's priorities seemed to be overseas travel, photo opportunities and process rather than outcomes to improve people's lives.

In a professional political sense, Rudd was one of the most effective framers of a message we have ever seen in this country. But this was both his strength and the basis of his failure. He effectively positioned climate change as 'the great moral challenge of our time'. People believed he was serious and that he would do something about it. The failure of the Copenhagen climate change conference came as the wider frustrations of the community with Labor were coming to the surface. Why take 114 people to a conference unless you were certain it was going to achieve something? And what did the much-anticipated failure of the conference say about a leader's judgment?

After Copenhagen, people expected Rudd to find other ways to take action. Instead, he abandoned the ETS and moved to introduce a new tax on the mining sector—considered by most Australians a critical driver of our prosperity. This was the moment of no return for Rudd and the final straw that broke the very strained bond of trust he had with the Australian community.

Even a few months earlier, the Liberal Party would not have been able to use humour and ridicule against Kevin Rudd. But community sentiment had moved so quickly that our 'Kevin O'Lemon' advertisement accurately captured the mood.

We had obviously considered the possibility of Labor changing leaders before the election—indeed, we had prepared for it—so our campaign was able to quickly adapt to Julia Gillard. What was surprising, however, was the speed with which the Gillard skyrocket returned to earth.

As Deputy Prime Minister, Julia Gillard was directly linked to every major decision of the Rudd Government and as a minister was personally responsible for a significant number of the major failures. So while we thought the change would not fundamentally alter the community's problems with Labor, we did think she would have a longer honeymoon.

But after only three weeks it was clear the community's concern and frustration remained and that the way Kevin Rudd was removed by the faceless operatives of the Labor machine had, in fact, created a new and very deep hesitation about Labor.

Labor itself was obviously finding that Gillard's replacement of Rudd had not reversed its decline. The decision of the Labor machine to call the election early seemed to us not to have been a considered strategic decision, but rather an attempt to move the focus away from the day-to-day bungles that threatened to overwhelm the new Prime Minister.

Nonetheless, the task for the Coalition in the campaign was formidable. No first-term government had lost its majority since 1931. After the series of redistributions in New South Wales, Queensland, Western Australia, Tasmania and the Northern Territory, we needed to win 17 seats to obtain a majority. And Labor, of course, had the full advantage of incumbency to support it, together with the additional resources of the industrial arm of the labour movement and various complicit so-called third-party groups such as GetUp!.

Despite this, and given the challenges we faced throughout the term of parliament, our position at the start of the campaign was stronger than we would have expected even a few short months before. Tony Abbott's principled and decisive leadership had put us in a competitive position and had staked out clear policy positions. He had united the parliamentary team, seen off a first-term prime minister, restored the party's morale and established the Coalition as a credible alternative government. We were therefore able to begin campaigning strongly from the moment the election was called.

Our success in setting the strategic direction of the contest in the first week of the campaign was very important. Had we not laid the basis then, Labor's internal difficulties in the second and third weeks, while certainly not unhelpful, would have smothered any attempt by us to establish the terms of the contest.

Contrary to Labor's attempts to write their own history, the leaks from within Labor were not per se what had such a catastrophic impact on their campaign. Rather, it was the subject matter of the leaks and the fact that Julia Gillard failed to deny that she had opposed the introduction of paid parental leave; that she had opposed pension increases on the grounds that older Australians did not vote for Labor anyway; that she had sent a relatively junior staff member in her place to meetings of the National Security Committee of Cabinet; and that she failed to consult Cabinet about her citizens' assembly policy.

This focused voters' attention on the fact that Julia Gillard was not the politician Labor spin doctors wanted Australians to think she was. Those responsible for these internal Labor leaks in fact exposed the real Julia. In contrast, Tony Abbott was seen as a person with strong principles, highly disciplined, intelligent, energetic and with an easy rapport with people on the campaign trail.

In this campaign, every day mattered. In 2007, 68 per cent of voters told us they had made up their mind before the campaign. In 2010, only 49 per cent had decided before the campaign. In our polling, Labor had rebounded to a significant lead on primary votes immediately after Julia Gillard became Prime Minister. This was reversed to a six-point primary lead by the Coalition on election day. Analysis of voter groups over this period shows it was younger voters under thirty-five and those with families who were most responsible for this movement.

Shortly after becoming leader, Julia Gillard's margin over Tony Abbott as preferred prime minister was more than 25 per cent. By the last part of the campaign, however, Tony Abbott had drawn level as preferred prime minister—a remarkable achievement for an Opposition leader. Interestingly, our research showed that during the campaign Gillard's favourability fell below Rudd's and remained below it after the election.

There is no doubt that community revulsion at the way in which the faceless powerbrokers toppled an elected prime minister influenced votes, and this was also shown in our research. Economic considerations, however, were paramount: the economy, budget management, waste and taxes were all cited in our research as major spontaneous reasons for the way people decided to vote. The Coalition built and maintained a strong lead on key economic issues during the campaign.

The Coalition's policy agenda was encapsulated in our Action Contract. Tony Abbott made a cast-iron pact with Australians to 'end the waste', 'pay back the debt', 'stop new taxes', 'help families', 'stop the boats' and 'do the right thing'.

According to our research, our positive Action Contract advertisements featuring Tony Abbott were the most effective single advertisements of the campaign. The positive nature of our campaign was particularly important in building momentum, as our research showed 69 per cent of voters chose to positively endorse a party while only 28 per cent were motivated to vote against a party.

Our success in building this positive campaign was remarkable given the strength of our opponent's negative campaign against us. It is clear the Australian Council of Trade Unions (ACTU), other unions and other left-wing groups were fully integrated into Labor's campaign, as an analysis of television advertising spending during the campaign shows. The ACTU spent $3.8 million on anti-Coalition advertising during the election campaign. GetUp! spent $1.5 million on television advertising, assisted by union donations worth $1 million.

There was a period of 10 days—a lifetime in a political campaign—in the first half of the election in which Labor did not advertise at all except for a minor buy in one State. But during this period, the ACTU and unions were on the air nationally attacking Tony Abbott and the Coalition.

Our post-election research showed that our members and candidates added to the Liberal Party's vote across Australia while Labor's candidates were neutral or a negative influence on their vote. Considerable work and preparation went into our marginal-seat campaigning and it was important in securing 14 additional seats for the party.

Despite the massive opposition we faced, the Coalition held to its strategy and clearly won the campaign by focusing on the key voter concerns: the cost of living, debt, deficit, waste, new taxes, lax border security, lack of competence in government service delivery and integrity in government.

Labor had no positive agenda to move Australia forward, thereby undercutting their campaign theme from the beginning. They could only resort to the same tired scare campaign they have used in previous elections. Australians do not believe minority government is good for the nation.

In the period since the election, it has been apparent Labor is a mess and that Julia Gillard is struggling. As a result, Australia is drifting. At the core of Labor's problem is that it is unable to put Australia's interests first. Everything Labor does is driven by the need to survive. What do the Greens think? What do the Independents think? How will the factions react?

We are in an unprecedented political situation. We have a weak and unstable government that is in a mess and getting worse. We have a prime minister who is not up to the job. And we have a restless Labor Party that has already removed one prime minister and will remove another when desperation sets in.

Australia cannot afford another three years of weak government with limited ambition. The Coalition will hold Labor to account and we will push them to do better because Australian families deserve nothing less.

The contrast could not be clearer between an ineffective Labor government with no policies, no direction and weak leadership, and the Coalition with clear direction, good policies and strong leadership to make Australia a better country. Australia does need strong leadership and only one leader can provide it. Tony Abbott knows what he believes, will always make the right decision for the right reason and has what it takes to get Australia moving again to make life better for ordinary Australians.

The Coalition is the only path to a strong and prosperous Australia. We therefore have a great obligation to be ready to offer a strong alternative whenever the next election is held. Tony Abbott and the Coalition are determined to provide the leadership Australia needs and which Labor cannot provide.

10. The Australian Labor Party

Elias Hallaj

Before I begin the main arguments, I must respond to a few of the biased criticisms made of the Labor Party during the workshop and in some sections of the media.

The Australian Labor Party is not broken. It won the federal election (although the result was not clear until it also won the support of a majority of the Independents and the Greens MP). Of all Australia's numerous political parties (some of which do not exist anymore), the Australian Labor Party is the longest surviving, most democratic, most diverse and most successful. Of course it loses elections as well as winning them and like most major political organisations around the world its membership is slowly shrinking. We need to do more to retain and recruit members; there is no doubt about that. But unlike the grumpy armchair critics and their shrill chorus line, I firmly believe that amongst the membership and leadership of the party, we already have the answers to these universal challenges. We do not need to look too far because some States and Territories are retaining membership and providing a voice for their membership better than others. Rather than look to experiences in the United States or the United Kingdom for all our answers, I will argue we should develop our own answers by recognising existing best practice for recruitment, policy and leadership development, training and campaigning within the ALP.

To the pessimists who falsely claim that Labor is 'broken' or 'has no message', I will politely come back with a simple answer: you are wrong. The Australian Labor Party was founded on principles of social justice and equity and our current policies on education, health care, housing, workplace safety and security (as well as myriad other important policy areas) reflect our desire to make Australia a better place to live for all its citizens.

The Fundamental Challenges Facing Practitioners are Getting Tougher

For campaign practitioners, it is getting much harder to convey a message. Less people read newspapers, less people watch the news on free-to-air TV each evening, and less people listen to the news or current affairs on radio.

There has been an explosion of new media, and commercial marketing has overwhelmed our increasingly limited attention spans with a ridiculous amount of information clutter. This clutter is made even more impenetrable by increasing voter cynicism and aversion to political messages and election campaign material.

The increasing cynicism about politics amongst voters is fed on a regular basis by a tabloid media that focuses on conflict, scandal and attention-seeking headlines and images rather than mature and reasoned analysis. This should not be surprising given the fact that the mainstream media is fundamentally profit driven.

Whether it be Sky News or News Limited papers, there is more and more negative coverage with a conservative bias in Australia's mainstream media than there ever has been in the past. ABC News 24 and online sources have *very slightly* redressed this and turned what was an overwhelmingly large bias in the mainstream media against the ALP into something closer to a very large bias.

The media and the public's very high expectations of modern politicians are often impossible to meet. Although it was fundamentally a good government, Labor's achievements between 2007 and 2010 were selectively overshadowed in the media by short-term challenges and problems. This is not that unusual given the media's focus on conflict over analysis.

And this is by no means unique to Australian politics. There have also been high expectations—impossible to meet expectations—on Barack Obama, Tony Blair and Bill Clinton; all had tough first terms due to very high expectations, both in the media and amongst voters.

The two biggest constraints in any Australian election campaign, for any campaign practitioner, were very apparent in this election: time and money. Neither is likely to change in the short term.

Five Unique, 2010-Specific Factors Affected the Result

Every local, State-wide and national campaign is unique, and certainly the result of this one is very unusual from a federal perspective, although not so unusual for someone living in Canberra. We now have the first minority Federal Government since 1943. The federal campaign and election in 2010 were unlike any other campaign in recent history. Five unique factors explain the election result

1. Labor was already on a knife-edge-small margin

2. the leaks

3. a mistaken belief that Labor could not lose

4. Tony Abbott's unexpected success in his small-target strategy

5. third-party (Liberal-front) campaigns against Labor.

1.

Labor had a majority of only eight seats after the 2007 election and a margin of 1.4 per cent. Several of the Howard Government's 11-year marginal-seat members hung on in tight contests, delivering Labor a smaller majority than might have been expected from its 5.4 per cent two-party preferred swing in 2007.

That 2007 two-party preferred swing to Labor of 5.4 per cent is, amongst postwar swings, beaten only by the 7.4 per cent swing achieved by the Coalition under Malcolm Fraser in 1975, and the 7.1 per cent swing when Gough Whitlam took Labor close to victory in 1969.

There was bound to be a correction, as there was for John Howard in 1998. Seats such as Macarthur, Gilmour, Patterson, Bonner, Dickson, and so on, looked within reach but the tide was already turning against Labor in New South Wales and Queensland in 2008.

While Labor received a massive swing in 2007, the actual buffer or margin was still small because of the large swing required to win government after 2004.

Every first-term government in recent memory has suffered a swing against it in its second election: Whitlam in 1974, Fraser in 1977, Hawke in 1984, and Howard in 1998 all suffered swings against them.

Labor went into this election with a wafer-thin margin, and against the backdrop of the worst global recession in 75 years.

2.

The five-week campaign had a good start and Labor improved its position in the first week. When the election was called, Labor was ahead and, in the first five or six days of the campaign, we improved in our internal polling. The Nielsen poll after week one had Labor on 54 per cent two-party preferred.

Then the leaks hit and dominated all media for more than a week. During that period, Labor's vote collapsed and there was nothing Julia Gillard or the campaign could have done to stop that. After week two, Nielsen had Labor's vote down to 48 per cent—a drop of 6 percentage points in a week.

There were three major problems with the leaks

- Labor could not get any message across for more than a week. It did not matter what we did or said, it was just drowned out by the coverage of the leaks
- They caused people to think that Labor was divided
- The nature of the leak stories hurt Labor because they were false stories about Julia Gillard opposing pension increases and paid parental leave.

Labor suspended polling at the end of week two because of swings of about 10 per cent in every seat polled.

Now, we will never know for sure what would have happened if Kevin Rudd had remained leader, but Labor was behind in the polls before the leadership change. We were in danger of seeing a good government lose. The caucus decided that change was necessary to try to stop Tony Abbott from being elected and a return to bad policies such as WorkChoices.

Labor went into this election with a lead, and the leaks in week two caused a large swing against the government. The sudden reappearance of Mark Latham did not help.

3.

There was a mistaken belief that Labor could not lose and Abbott could not win. This freed up people who wanted to send Labor a protest message.

Only 23 per cent of people the day before the election thought Abbott was a chance of winning. Only half of the Coalition voters thought Abbott had a chance of winning. Not even Liberal Party true believers thought Abbott was a chance.

4.

Abbott had unexpected success in his small-target strategy. This was made all the worse by the clear run given to Tony Abbott. A leader who had a public reputation as a head-kicker and aggressive combatant suddenly transformed into a kinder, genteel and sensitive new-age guy. His long record in government seemed to be obliterated in the media and, despite Labor's best efforts, he was well and truly out of the spotlight. Tony Abbott went into this campaign with nothing but negativity. This follows his record of opposing everything that the Labor government did to strengthen the economy: the economic stimulus, national broadband, improvement in schools and better hospitals.

But we *never* saw the real Tony Abbott during this campaign; Abbott was scripted, controlled by minders and ran a *very* disciplined campaign, which aimed to limit or hide his attributes that concern voters. Attributes such as

- speaking without thinking
- his extreme attitudes on women, industrial relations and climate change
- his lack of interest in and understanding of the economy.

By making Abbott a small target, the Liberal campaign was able to make the election more of a referendum on the government's performance.

Also, low expectations of Abbott assisted him during the campaign. People had such low expectations of him, all he had to do was appear half-reasonable and people marked him up for it. At the same time, every criticism he made of Julia Gillard got a run in the media.

Well, you might say, he was not under scrutiny because he was not prime minister, but there are many examples of Opposition leaders under scrutiny (for example, Peter Debnam in 2007 and John Hewson in 1993) and it certainly did not happen to Tony Abbott.

Anyway, it is likely that Abbott's honeymoon might be coming to an end. Although we did not see journalists writing like this during the election campaign, this is what Laurie Oakes posted on the Internet late last year: '[t]he jetlag gaffe[1] was a corker, even by the standards of the old, loose-lipped Abbott we were used to before he took over the Opposition leadership.' And: '[b]ut it was even more startling in light of the iron self-discipline he maintained throughout the election campaign.' And: '[t]o imply that arriving well rested at a conference of British Tories was more important than visiting the Diggers who risk life and limb every day fighting the Taliban was breathtakingly stupid.'

5.

Several cashed-up groups ran damaging campaigns against Labor and assisted the Liberal Party during the 2010 federal election. *The Daily Telegraph* (11 August 2010), for example, reported that this election saw the largest number

---

1   When asked why he declined an invitation to accompany Julia Gillard on a visit to troops in Afghanistan, Tony Abbott initially stated that he had not wanted to arrive jetlagged at the British Conservative Party's annual conference.

of private firms lobbying during a federal election campaign since the 1970s. Following is a short list of some of the organisations that ran significant anti-Labor campaigns during this election.

Alliance of Australian Retailers

The alliance put out extensive TV, radio and print adverisements depicting small grocers complaining about Labor's excessive taxation, regulations and plain packaging. Here are some typical quotes from the ads: 'The Alliance of Australian Retailers Pty Ltd is fed up with excessive regulation that is making it harder for us to run our businesses.' And: 'In recent times we have been hit with an excessive tax hike that has made our businesses a target for theft and only further fuelled the flourishing black market in tobacco products.'

Association of Mineral Exploration Companies

The association opposed the government's proposed Minerals Resource Rent Tax (MRRT) with significant TV, print and radio advertisements. The ads argued that 'all Australians' cost of living would rise if the government's tax was implemented'.

Primary Healthcare Australia

This group campaigned against the government's priorities in health funding and against the government's health reforms using television and radio advertising, running the tag line 'Don't let Labor's health policies be the death of you'. The most vicious of their ads was a radio ad depicting a woman diagnosed with incurable cancer who allegedly could have been saved if Labor had not cut funding.

Australian Fishing Trade Association

This association asked people to vote against the Greens and the ALP because they would put an end to recreational fishing. They ran expensive newspaper advertisements in Western Australia, the Northern Territory, Queensland and New South Wales, claiming that if Labor and the Greens were elected people would be banned from fishing in many public waters. The ad had a picture of a child with a fishing rod.

Australians for Extradition Justice

Using well-funded radio advertising, a 'group of businessmen' launched a campaign against the Labor government's new treaty that they said could see Australians extradited to Arab countries and tried under harsh Islamic Sharia law.

Quote: 'Australians for Extradition Justice believe that as a modern, progressive democracy, Australia should not have extradition treaties with countries that practise torture, or with countries which treat women as property.'

Conclusion

The 2010 federal election reinforced the view amongst election practitioners that the tasks of governing and campaigning are becoming increasingly challenging due to the increasingly difficult electoral and media environment. The fundamental challenges facing election practitioners are getting tougher, with more cynicism, criticism and constraints, as well as higher expectations, than in previous elections.

In 2010, the federal election also saw the confluence of a unique set of circumstances that challenged the government throughout the election campaign. Before 2010, Labor was already on a knife-edge-small margin. A combination of damaging leaks in the middle of the campaign, a mistaken belief that Labor could not lose, Tony Abbott's unexpected success in his small-target strategy and a series of damaging third-party (Liberal-front) campaigns against Labor all contributed to a significant swing against the government in many electorates. Labor held some of the ground it was predicted to lose in 2010 (for example, holding five seats in Tasmania, and losing only one incumbent in New South Wales), but the unusual minority government that resulted has provided oxygen to an army of armchair critics. The frustrated Abbott-led Opposition still appears to be largely unified and refuses to acknowledge any faults in its record, policies or plans.

Although the formal ALP review of the 2010 campaign is still under way, the ongoing survival of the Gillard Labor Government has confounded a chorus line of conservative critics. The Prime Minister has not taken a step backwards from the constant barrage of unfair criticism thrown at her by Tony Abbott, the Liberal Party and much of the mainstream media.

Unless there is an unforseen by-election that could tip the balance of numbers within the House of Representatives, it appears the Gillard Government will continue to fulfil its legislative agenda. So far, they are winning the majority of votes on the floor of the House of Representatives, and the government's record on infrastructure investments and economic management is strengthening. The next election is still almost two years away—a very long time for Tony Abbott to survive as Opposition Leader.

11. The Greens

Andrew Bartlett

The 2010 federal election was undoubtedly a watershed for the Australian Greens as a political party at the national level. It produced a record high vote for third parties in a federal election in both the Senate and the House of Representatives, as well as a major breakthrough in winning a House of Representatives seat for the first time at a general election.

Historical Comparison

The Greens' 2010 vote was larger than any previous third party in modern Australian political history.

It was the first time a third party had a senator elected in every State.

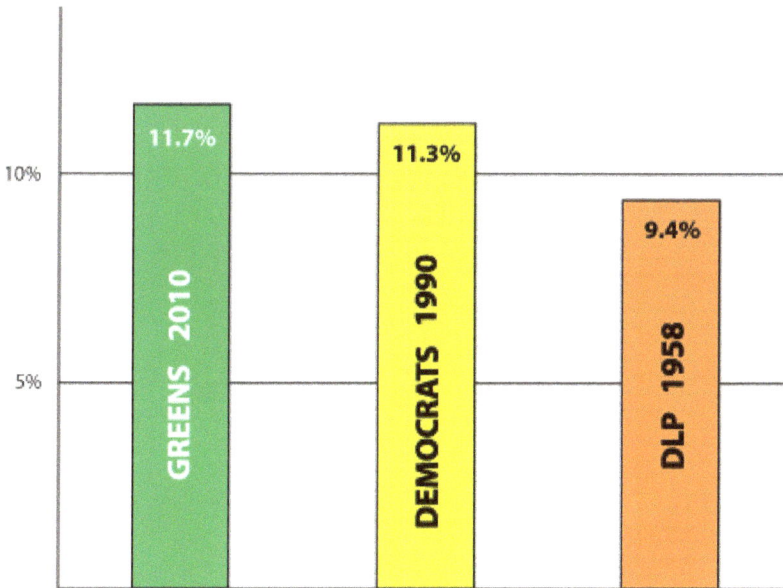

Figure 11.1 House of Representatives: Historical highs

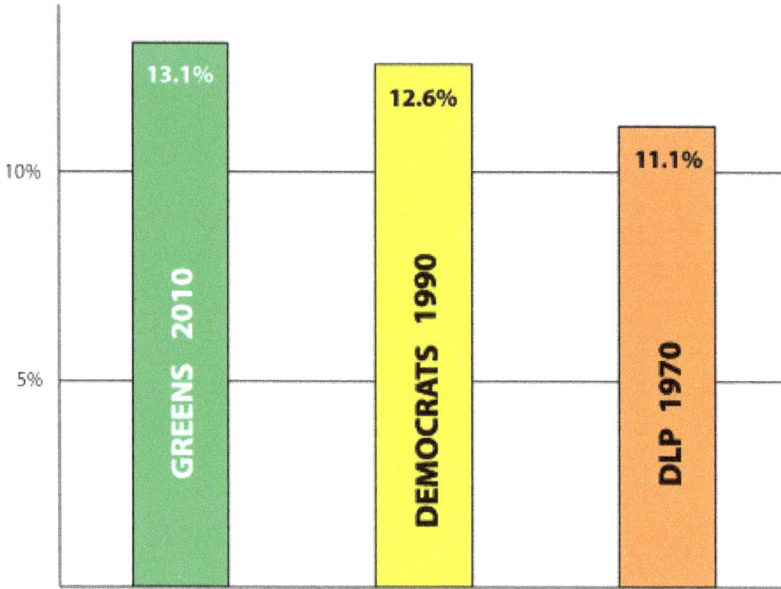

Figure 11.2 Senate: Historical highs

The election campaign and result can be assessed on both the Greens' policies and their positioning as a party competing against Labor and the Coalition in their own right, as well as in comparison with other third parties in Australian politics in the past.

Unlike other third parties of note since World War II, the Greens' vote in federal elections has built up gradually and consistently over a relatively long period. In contrast, both the Australian Democrats and the Democratic Labor Party (DLP) gained large votes early in their existence, and experienced notable peaks and troughs going forward. (The only other third parties to have gained a sizeable primary vote, the Nuclear Disarmament Party and One Nation, were even more rapid in their rise and fall.)

Growth of the Greens' Vote

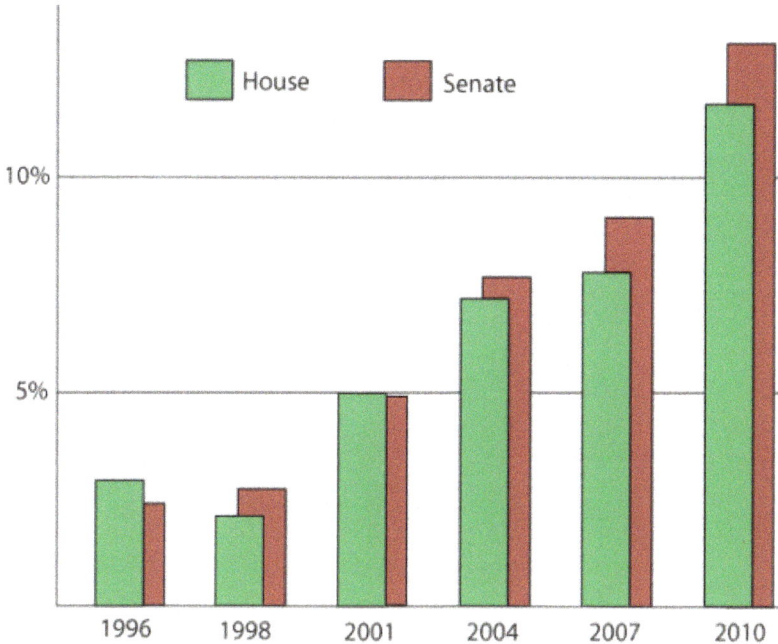

Figure 11.3 The Greens' Vote has Grown Substantially Over the Past 14 Years

Table 11.1 Growth of Greens' Vote

Election	1996	1998	2001	2004	2007	2010
House	2.9%	2.1%	5.0%	7.2%	7.8%	11.7%
Senate	2.4%	2.7%	4.9%	7.7%	9.0%	13.1%

Both the DLP and the Democrats had balance-of-power leverage from a relatively early stage, and both were relatively weakly represented in parliaments, assemblies and councils at State, Territory and local government levels. In contrast, much like the party's own organisational structure, the Greens have built up slowly but steadily over more than 20 years, gradually increasing their presence at these levels until the party now has well more than 100 representatives in local governments—including a number of mayors and deputy mayors—and has representation in all State and Territory Parliaments, except Queensland and the Northern Territory (although even in the Northern Territory Greens have been elected to local councils in both Darwin and Alice Springs).

Whilst the first senator was elected under a Greens banner back in 1987[1] and the party occasionally held a partial share of the balance of power on a few occasions, the 2010 election saw them gain sole balance of power in the Senate for the first time. The fact that the Greens had time to develop and become more of a known quantity to the public made it much easier to withstand the inevitable scare campaigns about 'extremist' Greens using the balance of power to destroy the country. Nonetheless, past experience at both State and federal levels made the Greens well aware that these types of scare tactics were inevitable, particularly in the final week or two of the campaign. A key part of the party's message and actions well before the election period was to demonstrate the Greens' capacity to be responsible and reasoned in the positions taken, including on Senate votes where their stance was crucial in a balance-of-power context.

The DLP, the Democrats and the Greens occupied different, though partly overlapping, positions on the political spectrum—especially the Democrats and Greens. But direct comparisons of this sort can only go so far, as the parties also operated at different times in history—again with some overlap between the Democrats' and the Greens' times in the Senate—and so have to be defined relative to the political environment and the positions of the major parties of the time.

Of course, a major difference is that neither the Democrats nor the DLP (nor One Nation) ever won a House of Representatives seat. Specifically targeting a House of Representatives seat as winnable in a planned, professional way far in advance of a general election was a new experience for the Greens. It also put the party in a political position where it is looking to fill the role not just of a third party with the balance of power in the Senate—vital though that is—but also of directly competing with the two major parties for House of Representatives seats and votes.

In an election campaign in which both major parties were widely seen to have difficulties in attracting new voters, rather than just consolidating their base, the Greens gained the bulk of the swing.

---

1   Jo Vallentine, first elected to the Senate for the Nuclear Disarmament Party in 1984; after that party suffered internal breakdown, she helped form the Greens WA and was re-elected at the 1987 election under the banner of that party.

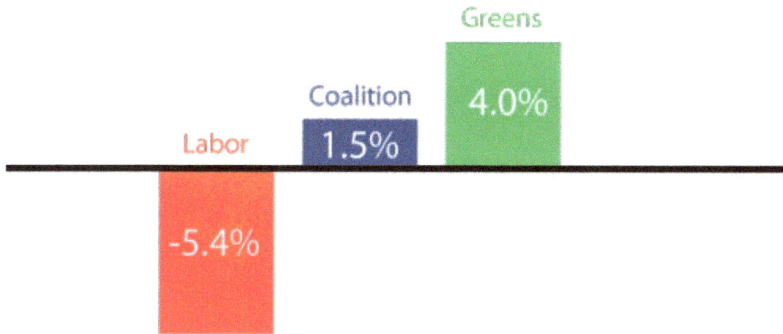

Figure 11.4 The Greens Received the Biggest Swing, 2010 Election

The Greens deliberately choose to campaign with positive messages and images, going so far as to modify the traditional design of the well-known traditional Greens' triangle to reinforce the suggestion of open horizons and a new dawn. The positive, enthusiastic theme was also a key part of the message for the target House of Representatives seat of Melbourne. All year in advance of the election being called, the voters of Melbourne were being informed that they had a real chance to 'make history' by electing a Greens member in their seat, with the focus on generating enthusiasm and positive potential rather than a more predominantly negative message.

The seat of Melbourne was the main target for the Greens, as it was clearly the most winnable, and when a convincing case can easily be made that a seat is winnable it in turn makes it easier to build better resourcing and planning. The campaign goal, however, was not just a Senate plus Melbourne one. There was determination to build a sizeable-base vote in a large number of seats, including the inner-urban seat of Brisbane, to provide more possibilities for the next election.

Whilst Melbourne was the standout with 36.17 per cent of the primary vote (just trumping the primary vote of 36 per cent gained by Pauline Hanson when she stood as One Nation candidate for Blair in 1998), the Greens gained more than 20 per cent of the primary vote in eight seats and more than 15 per cent in 36 seats—many of them a long way from the stereotype of a Greens' inner-city heartland. Despite strong results for Independents in some areas—and an understandable focus on them afterwards given the hung-parliament result—the Greens finished in a top-three position in 137 of 150 seats.

Over 20%

Over 15%

Over 10%

8 seats

36 seats

92 seats

Top 3 candidates

137 out of 150 seats

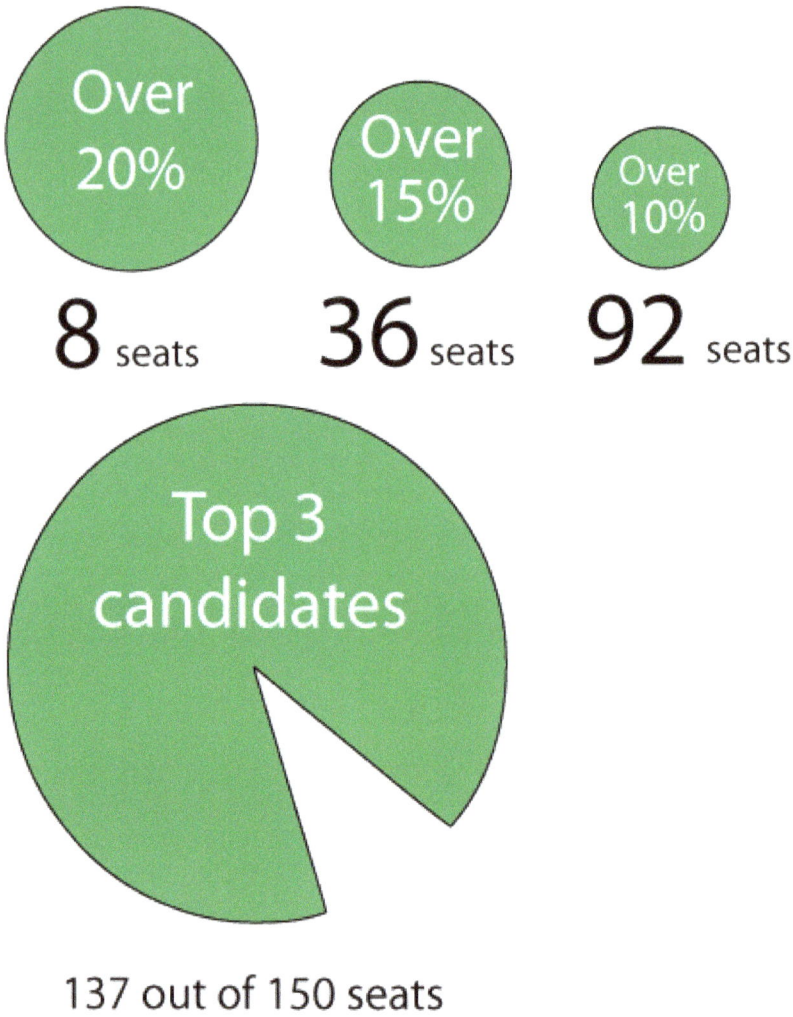

Figure 11.5 The Greens Finished in the Top-Three Candidates in 137 of 150 seats

The Greens focused on repeatedly promoting a consistent position on a number of identified key issues well in advance of the election. This included not only the traditional strengths of climate change and the environment, but also human rights, transport, a comprehensive dental-care policy, higher education, industrial relations and more.

As both Labor and the Coalition had undergone significant upheaval and leadership changes in the lead-up to the election, the emphasis on stability and reliability was particularly important for the Greens. There was a deliberate effort to communicate that the Greens were 'a safe pair of hands' not only with balance of power in the Senate, but also as a safe place for people to give their House of Representatives vote.

The Greens also put much greater effort into and had much greater success at fundraising and donations. The party's clear position to unwind WorkChoices and in particular to abolish the Australian Building and Construction Commission (ABCC) helped it receive some financial and other support from a number of key trade unions. As the party itself publicly revealed—in advance of the legally required reporting time line—it also received a very sizeable personal donation of more than $1 million. These resources certainly assisted the Greens in maintaining a significant public advertising presence in the crucial final weeks of the campaign when third parties are normally massively outspent by the two majors. Receiving sizeable donations does present some dilemmas for the Greens, given the party's history of campaigning for limits on political donations and expenditure, but the majority view is a pragmatic one that until such changes can be made law then it would put the party at too much of a competitive disadvantage to refuse donations, except from sources that are clearly antithetical to the party's values.

Note

All graphs taken from: <http://greens.org.au/content/greens-results-2010-pictures>

Part 4. The States and Regions

12. New South Wales

Elaine Thompson and Geoff Robinson

Labor's ability to minimise its losses in New South Wales despite a major adverse swing and the election of two rural Independents was central to Julia Gillard's ability to form a government. The result revealed remarkable patterns of swing and an exceptional informal vote. Labor did win a majority of the seats, and lost only two (or rather four with the redistribution); and their primary vote was higher than in either 2001 or 2004 (when they did not win a majority of seats); on the other hand, 2010 was the third-worst federal result for NSW Labor since 1975.

Political Context and Themes

The 2009 federal electoral redistribution abolished the Labor electorate of Lowe and incorporated much of its enrolment into Reid. The number of electorates was reduced to forty-eight. Any estimate of the political impact of changed electoral boundaries must be imprecise. The redistribution increased the urban component of Gilmore, Greenway and Macarthur and as a result they would probably have been Labor electorates on 2007 voting. The already marginal Liberal electorate of Hughes became more marginal as it now included more of the strong Labor areas of south-western Sydney. Macquarie's boundaries shifted into the conservative north-western outskirts of Sydney and it was weakened for Labor. Independent candidate Rob Oakeshott had an easy victory in the Lyne by-election that followed the retirement of former Nationals leader Mark Vaille in September 2008.

The incumbent State Labor Government was narrowly re-elected in 2007 but since then its fortunes had dramatically declined (Green 2010). Labor was racked by voter anger at perceived infrastructure deficiencies, ministerial scandals and an acrimonious internal conflict over privatisation of the power industry that contributed to the replacement of Premier, Morris Iemma, with Nathan Rees in September 2008 and then his overthrow by Kristina Kenneally in November 2009. The Coalition constantly linked State and federal Labor. The reappearance of debates about asylum-seeker policy on the national agenda also generated particular anxiety within NSW Labor. John Howard's vigorous advocacy of 'border security' was believed by many Labor activists to have been one reason for the Liberals' strong performance in outer suburban Sydney in 2001 and 2004.

Labor endorsed all sitting members except in Robertson where Belinda Neal lost a preselection vote to university lecturer Deborah O'Neill. Neal's tenure as an MP had been dogged by controversy—in particular, an episode where she was accused of abusing restaurant staff (Welch 2008). In Dobell, sitting Labor MP, Craig Thompson, easily won a preselection ballot despite controversies arising from his tenure as a Health Services Union office-bearer prior to his election (Bowe 2010a, 2010f; Davis 2009).

In ultra-safe Chifley, Roger Price retired and was replaced with Ed Husic who had been defeated as Labor candidate for Greenway in 2004 after a campaign in which his Muslim religion counted against him. Bob Debus retired in Macquarie and media consultant Sue Templeman was endorsed after an acrimonious contest (Bowe 2010e).

Julia Irwin's retirement in Fowler removed Parliament's most outspoken Palestinian sympathiser and initiated a complex reshuffle of Labor candidates. Laurie Ferguson vacated Reid in favour of John Murphy whose electorate of Lowe had been abolished. Ferguson was endorsed for the distant Werriwa whose member, Chris Hayes, then contested Fowler. Branch members were ignored (Bowe 2010b). This exercise in musical chairs assisted the Liberals' local narrative that Labor took voters in safe seats for granted (Dang 2010; Raue 2010a).

Labor's preselection battles received more coverage than disputes within the Liberals. Some Liberal (non-)decisions could have been important. Greenway MP, Louise Markus, chose to contest Macquarie. The Liberals were slow to endorse candidates for Lindsay and Greenway apparently because private polling suggested they had little prospects in these electorates (ABC 2010). Two sitting MPs did not contest their marginal seats. Danna Vale retired in Hughes and Pat Farmer lost preselection for Macarthur (Bowe 2010c, 2010d. The Liberals endorsed candidates from non–English-speaking-background ethnic communities in the safe Labor seats of Fowler, McMahon and Watson and the marginal Greenway. In Riverina, the retirement of sitting Nationals MP, Kay Hulls, enabled the Liberals to nominate a candidate.

The Senate tickets of Labor and the Coalition attracted little attention. The Greens endorsed as their leading Senate candidate fifty-nine-year-old Legislative Councillor Lee Rhiannon. Her past membership of the pro-Soviet Socialist Party of Australia attracted hostile comment (Rhiannon 2010).

The campaign in New South Wales largely reflected national themes—indeed, both Labor and the Coalition shaped their campaigns towards an imagined Sydney suburban audience. Labor candidates in Sydney suburban seats embraced Julia Gillard's rejection of a 'big Australia' (Keane 2010). The most notable election-specific promise was Labor's announcement of funding for a Parramatta-to-Epping railway link. Some argued that this would assist Labor to hold marginal Bennelong but others suggested that it merely increased voter cynicism given the State Government's perceived poor record on public transport (Alexander 2010; Saulwick and Besser 2011; Wanna 2010; West 2010).

Results

At the level of aggregate votes, New South Wales was a triumph for the Coalition. In 2010, New South Wales became the only State in which a majority of the anti-ALP swing in the House of Representatives went to the Coalition (a 4.6 per cent Coalition gain compared with a 2.1 per cent gain to the Greens). The 2010 primary vote for the Liberals was the highest since 1975, as was the 2010 vote for the Coalition, while The Nationals held their 2007 level.

Labor lost two seats to the Liberals: Bennelong and Macquarie. The Liberals were unable to retain Greenway after the unfavourable redistribution. NSW Labor strategists had complained in early 2010 that Kevin Rudd's policies failed the 'Lindsay test' (Crook 2011). Julia Gillard passed; Labor held Lindsay despite a two-party swing of 5.2 per cent. The Nationals outpolled the Liberals in Riverina almost three to one but were soundly defeated in Lyne. Oakeshott's fellow Independent from New South Wales, Tony Windsor, won easily in New England.

The success of Lee Rhiannon of the Greens to the Senate left Labor with two and the Coalition with three. The Greens' Senate vote of 10.7 per cent was, however, the lowest in Australia. The relatively poor Greens performance might have reflected a voter response to Rhiannon's perceived radicalism, or the particular hostility of leading NSW Greens to private education. It is also likely that Tony Abbott had a greater appeal to protest voters in New South Wales and that Labor's support base, with its large component of socially conservative ethnic communities, was less susceptible to the Greens' appeal. Many disaffected ethnic electors probably voted informally. The Greens also focused their national advertising more on the lower-cost markets of South Australia and Queensland.

Micro-parties polled poorly. The Christian Democratic Party, which was now more fixated on the Muslim threat than permissiveness, polled 1.9 per cent—more than double its more moderate Christian rival Family First, with 0.9 per cent. The Australian Sex Party challenged the Greens' appeal to social libertarians with 1.8 per cent. The informal vote of 4.2 per cent for the Senate was the highest in Australia.

There was a strong uniform swing from Labor to the Coalition and to a lesser extent the Greens within the Sydney metropolitan area. Greens' preferences reduced the two-party swing. Despite all the discussion and concern for Labor in the outer metropolitan mortgage belt and largely Anglo seats of Sydney, the swing against the ALP was greater in the inner metropolitan seats. Labor probably held most of its 2007 gains among outer-suburban working-class voters. The overall modest rural swing against Labor obscured good results for Labor members elected in 2007 but poor results elsewhere.

The Greens continued their advance in the inner city. In Grayndler, they won 25.9 per cent and outpolled the Liberals. They ended with 45.6 per cent after the distribution of preferences. In Sydney the Greens won 23.8 per cent but finished behind the Liberals. Compared with Victoria, in New South Wales, Labor's vote held up better in its inner-urban strongholds—a result that some Greens attributed to weaker candidates and a more narrowly focused appeal by their party than in Victoria.

While all States saw a rise in informal voting, New South Wales—with 6.8 per cent—registered by far the highest informal vote in the nation, even higher than the Northern Territory. Victoria recorded 4.5 per cent, Queensland 5.5 per cent and Western Australia 4.8 per cent, indicating something different occurring in New South Wales: were the NSW voters more alienated from both major parties than voters elsewhere?

The levels of informal voting were not related to the number of candidates, and appear to be part of the protest vote against Labor. While the ethnic make-up of electorates contributes to informal voting, it alone does not explain all the increases. There was also an element of disaffection in some electorates in terms of lower turnout, though this is more difficult to assess.

The nation's top-13 informal voting electorates were all in New South Wales, all metropolitan and all Labor. The fourteenth was also in metropolitan New South Wales: Macarthur, which the Liberals won. These seats recorded between 8.1 per cent and 14.1 per cent informal votes. No other seat anywhere in Australia saw the informal vote higher than 7.5 per cent.

Even Wentworth—the smallest electorate in Australia, one of the wealthiest and one with a highly educated electorate—recorded a 4.5 per cent informal vote, but it also was one of only two electorates in Australia to record a decrease in informal voting (−0.4 per cent).

Wentworth also recorded a turnout of 89.4 per cent—one of the lowest in Australia. There were only six electorates in Australia to record a turnout of less than 90 per cent, and none of the others has the affluent profile of Wentworth. Perhaps part of the reason might lie in the very limited campaigning by all parties, but especially the ALP, in the electorate.

The other electorate that recorded a decrease in informal votes was Lyne, with only 3.7 per cent informal votes, which was a decrease of 1.3 per cent. It also recorded the highest turnout in New South Wales, with 94.5 per cent. These results further emphasise the unique character of that electorate.

The level of the informal vote means that a focus on vote share understates the magnitude of Labor's setback. The number of Labor voters fell by one-sixth from 2007 to 2010.

Table 12.1 House of Representatives Party Votes in New South Wales, 2007–10

	2007	2010	Increase 2007–10 (%)
ALP	1 791 171	1 494 490	−16.6
Liberal-Nationals	1 555 493	1 788 013	14.9
Greens	230 031	410 405	28.2
Informal	211 519	293 763	38.9

Source: All electoral statistics are from the final Electoral Commission report (AEC 2010).

Only three seats swung to Labor in primary voting: Charlton on 53.2 per cent—a 0.1 per cent swing to Labor; Eden-Monaro, which swung to Labor both on primary votes, by 0.3 per cent to 43.6 per cent, and on the two-party preferred vote, by 2 per cent; and Page where Labor's primary vote increased by 4.1 per cent and its two-party vote by 1.8 per cent.

Even on the two-party preferred vote, there were only two more seats where Labor made gains: Dobell (1.1 per cent) and Robertson (0.9 per cent). Robertson was one of the most surprising results of the election; the likely explanation is that Belinda Neal's personality hampered Labor in 2007.

The Liberals defied the redistribution to hold Gilmore, Macarthur and Hughes despite the retirement of sitting MPs in the last two. In Macquarie Labor held the swing to 1.5 per cent but still lost. In Greenway Labor narrowly held on with 50.9 per cent after a swing of 4.8 per cent. The anti-Labor swing was lower in the parts of the electorate that had been in the pre-redistribution Greenway. Louis Markus's decision to contest Macquarie rather than Greenway probably did not cost the Liberals this electorate.

There was one exception to the pattern of good performances by the class of 2007. Bennelong, the seat in which the sitting Prime Minister, John Howard, was defeated in 2007, was widely predicted (by most) to be the first seat that Labor would lose. In 2010 the Liberals ran John Alexander, a well-known ex-tennis player and commentator. He won easily with a 48.5 per cent primary vote and 53.1 per cent of the two-party vote. In the words of former Labor State minister Rodney Cavalier, 'Maxine [McKew] could have won Bennelong only once since its creation and that was when she did—and only against John Howard. The Libs were very confident about getting it back a few months into 2008' (Cavalier 2010). The swing in Bennelong was, however, less than in all but one of the surrounding electorates and Labor's defeat might have been due to a Liberal rally among affluent voters and alienation of voters of Chinese background from Labor. Kevin Rudd's demise probably contributed to the latter.

Wealthy Sydney swung decisively to the Coalition. Malcolm Turnbull and Joe Hockey might have lost out to Tony Abbott for the Liberal leadership, but their electorates swung to the Liberals by 11 per cent and 8.6 per cent respectively. The Liberal base, at least in Sydney, returned after a flirtation with Labor in 2007 (Brent 2010).

The Coalition did well in rural marginal seats where Labor had come close in 2007 such as Paterson and Cowper. Notable was the 7.3 per cent swing in Calare, which gave The Nationals an easy win in an electorate Labor had held between 1983 and 1996 on similar boundaries. The Nationals carried Ben Chifley's hometown of Bathurst.

Lyne and New England registered extremely low votes for Labor, which polled 8.1 per cent of the primary vote in New England (−2.8 per cent) and 13.5 per cent in Lyne—dropping a massive 18.5 per cent in primary votes. There is irony here given the decisions by these two Independent MPs to support the new Labor government. In the 2008 by-election, Rob Oakeshott won with 73.9 per cent of the two-party vote. In 2010, Oakeshott retained the seat on 62.7 per cent of the two-party vote. Lyne had the highest turnout in New South Wales (95.4 per cent), and was amongst the top three in the country; New England also saw a healthy turnout with 94.8 per cent. New England and Lyne also had the lowest informal votes in New South Wales: 3.5 per cent and 3.7 per cent respectively. Lyne and Berowra—both NSW seats—were the only seats in Australia to record a drop in informal voting.

In 2007 there were 13 electorates with more than 25 per cent of their population born overseas in non–English-speaking countries, which we describe as 'ethnic' electorates. Labor's Bennelong victory gave it a clean sweep of these (Nelson 2007). In 2010 there were 27 electorates in this group. Labor's loss in Bennelong and the Liberals' retention of Menzies in Victoria meant that in 2010 Labor held 25 of 27 (Nelson 2010). There were, however, major swings against Labor in the Sydney ethnic electorates, driven by an increase in the Liberal portion of the vote and a major rise in the informal vote. The three electorates in 2010 with the highest portion born in a non–English-speaking country were Reid, Watson and Fowler. Swings against Labor on primaries in these electorates were 11.4 per cent, 9.9 per cent and 15.1 per cent respectively, and much of this swing went directly to the Liberals. The informal vote also increased notably in the ethnic electorates. The two seats with the highest informal vote across Australia were the NSW seats of Blaxland (14.1 per cent) and Fowler (12.8 per cent), and these also saw the greatest increase in informal votes (5.2 per cent and 2.4 per cent).

Former NSW Premier Morris Iemma complained that Labor's espousal of a 'sustainable Australia' had alienated voters in these electorates (Carleton 2010). This is plausible although Labor's good performance in Victorian ethnic electorates reminds us that the different political cultures of each State shaped the response of ethnic voters.

Rodney Cavalier (2010) has noted: 'Labor did not lose more in 2010 only because the margin of safety in what Morris Iemma calls the middle-ring of Sydney is so large to begin with.' Continued ethnic disillusion with Labor and gentrification could make electorates such as Reid and Banks in this middle ring more vulnerable in the future. At the March 2011 State election, NSW Labor lost many previously safe seats in this region.

A total of 13 women were elected out of 48 seats (27 per cent). Labor elected nine out of 26 (35 per cent) while the Coalition managed only four of 20—a mere 20 per cent. Equality moves at glacial speed in New South Wales. The election of Muslim Labor candidate Ed Husic in Chifley was noteworthy although his background as a union official recruited from Young Labor conformed to the modern Labor template. Women have usually been better represented in the Senate, but while there were three men and three women elected, there were no NSW Labor women elected to the Senate in 2010.

Conclusion

In 2010, as in 1998, the incumbent government fell over the line by the retention of traditional suburban marginal seats such as Lindsay and Robertson. The NSW Labor organisation remained effective in marginal-seat campaigning. The Liberals engaged in post-election speculation as to whether tactical errors cost them key marginal seats, as Labor had in 1998 (Coorey 2011). In 2010 Tony Abbott went a long way towards reforging a winning coalition of support but fell just short, as did Labor in 1998. Some things in politics remain the same.

References

Alexander, John. 2010. 'Trains, campaigns and broken promises'. *Sydney Morning Herald*, 10 November.

Australian Broadcasting Corporation (ABC). 2010. 'O'Farrell lying low after Twitter gaffe'. *ABC News*, 15 July, viewed 2 February 2011, <http://www.abc.net.au/news/stories/2010/07/15/2954909.htm>

Australian Electoral Commission (AEC). 2010. *The Official 2010 Federal Election Results*. Canberra: Australian Electoral Commission, viewed 21 January 2011, <http://results.aec.gov.au/15508/Website/default.htm>

Bowe, William. 2010a. 'Dobell'. *Electorate Form Guide*, viewed 2 February 2011, <http://www.crikey.com.au/fed2010-dobell>

Bowe, William. 2010b. 'Fowler'. *Electorate Form Guide*, viewed 2 February 2011, <http://www.crikey.com.au/fed2010-fowler/>

Bowe, William. 2010c. 'Hughes'. *Electorate Form Guide*, viewed 2 February 2011, <http://www.crikey.com.au/fed2010-hughes/>

Bowe, William. 2010d. 'Macarthur'. *Electorate Form Guide*, viewed 2 February 2011, <http://www.crikey.com.au/fed2010-macarthur>

Bowe, William. 2010e. 'Macquarie'. *Electorate Form Guide*, viewed 2 February 2011, <http://www.crikey.com.au/fed2010-macquarie/>

Bowe, William. 2010f. 'Robertson'. *Electorate Form Guide*, viewed 2 February 2011, <http://www.crikey.com.au/fed2010-robertson/>

Brent, Peter. 2010. 'Liberals still dominate the top end'. *The Australian*, 7 December.

Carleton, James. 2010. 'Morris Iemma rages against the Labor machine'. *Radio National Breakfast*, 25 August, ABC Radio.

Cavalier, Rodney. 2010. Email to Elaine Thompson, 26 September.

Coorey, Phillip. 2011. 'Abbott faces battle telling NSW Liberals what to do'. *Sydney Morning Herald*, 21 February.

Crook, Andrew. 2011. 'Bitar's email bombshell on the "Lindsay test"'. *Crikey*, 25 February.

Dang, Thomas. 2010. Thomas Dang Liberal candidate for Fowler, viewed 21 February 2011, <http://www.youtube.com/watch?v=14wsKnP-rDQ>

Davis, Mark. 2009. 'Labor MP accused of credit card rort'. *Sydney Morning Herald*, 8 April.

Green, Antony. 2010. 'Latest Newspoll has NSW Labor back to 1904 levels'. *Antony Green's Election Blog*, viewed 2 February 2011, <http://blogs.abc.net.au/antonygreen/2010/10/latest-newspoll-has-nsw-labor-back-to-1904-levels.html>

Keane, Bernard. 2010. 'Little Australia comes to Sydney'. *Crikey*, 14 July.

Nelson, Paul. 2007. *Electoral Division Ranking: Census 2006 first release (2006 electoral boundaries)*. Canberra: Parliamentary Library.

Nelson, Paul. 2010. *Electoral Division Rankings: 2006 Census (2009 electoral boundaries)*. Canberra: Parliamentary Library.

Raue, Ben. 2010a. 'Fowler—election 2010'. *The Tallyroom*, viewed 3 February 2011, <http://www.tallyroom.com.au/archive/election-2010/fowler>

Raue, Ben. 2010b. 'Macquarie—election 2010'. *The Tallyroom*, viewed 1 February 2011, <http://www.tallyroom.com.au/archive/election-2010/macquarie>

Rhiannon, Lee. 2010. Responding to attacks on my family and political background. Lee Rhiannon, viewed 2 February 2011, <http://leerhiannon.org.au/blog/responding-to-attacks-on-my-family-and-political-background>

Saulwick, Jacob and Besser, Linton. 2011. 'Transport stuff-ups cost state billions'. *Sydney Morning Herald*, 22 February.

Wanna, John. 2010. 'Both sides guilty in a cynical and shallow showdown'. *The Australian*, 21 August.

Welch, Dylan. 2008. 'Iguanas affair: Neal and Della off the hook'. *Sydney Morning Herald*, 3 September.

West, Andrew. 2010. 'Albanese coy on when rail link plan came up'. *Sydney Morning Herald*, 12 August.

13. Victoria

Nick Economou

If recent national elections were anything to go by, there was a prospect that the 2010 contest would bypass Victoria. This was despite the fact that the newly installed Labor leader and caretaker Prime Minister, Julia Gillard, represented the western Melbourne suburban seat of Lalor, and some of the party conspirators who helped Gillard displace Kevin Rudd, such as Bill Shorten (MHR for Maribyrnong) and Senator David Feeney, were also Victorians. Victoria's apparently secondary importance to the national contest had hitherto been due to the rather limited contribution the State had made to the transfer of marginal seats between the major parties. The 2010 election looked as if it would be a case in point. The Victorian 'pendulum' ahead of this contest (see Table 13.1) showed that the proportion of Victorian lower-house divisions considered to be ultra-marginal (that is, capable of shifting their representational alignment with a two-party swing of between 0 per cent and 4 per cent) (see Hughes 1983, 218) was a mere seven seats (or 19 per cent). This contrasted with New South Wales and Queensland, where the proportion of ultra-marginal divisions was 27 per cent and 57 per cent respectively.

At the completion of the election, however, the result in Victoria proved to be critical to the matter of who had actually won. Victoria, which has proven to be something of a Labor stronghold since 1993, made two major contributions to the national result. First, it returned the first representative of a political party other than Liberal, Labor or Nationals to the House of Representatives in a general election in the postwar period when Adam Bandt from the Australian Greens was elected as the Member for Melbourne. Second, despite the loss in Melbourne, Labor was able to defend its ultra-marginal seats while wresting the seats of McEwen and La Trobe from the Liberal Party. These were the only instances of Labor winning seats from the Liberal Party in the 2010 election and allowed Julia Gillard to have enough House of Representatives seats to be able to negotiate with the crossbenchers (including Bandt) to form a minority government.

The Campaign

There were two campaigns going on in Victoria in this election. The main campaign was clearly the contest between Labor and the Liberal Party for the most ultra-marginal seats. The Liberal Party was hopeful of winning back

Deakin and Corangamite, both of which were narrowly lost at the previous election (Economou 2010). Labor, meanwhile, had its eyes on La Trobe in the outer south-eastern suburbs of Melbourne and the semi-rural seat of McEwen to the city's north. Both seats had just eluded Labor in 2007, with McEwen needing a determination in the Federal Court sitting as the Court of Disputed Returns (*Mitchell vs Bailey [No. 2]* 2008 FCA 692). The major-party leaders made visits to the State, but had very little to offer by way of policies or regional pork-barrelling designed specifically for Victoria. The exception to this was a bidding war to subsidise redevelopment of the Kardinia Park football ground— home of the Geelong Cats AFL club and not far from the eastern boundaries of Corangamite. Tony Abbott appeared to win this tussle when the committee of the football club sent a flyer to its members urging a vote for the Liberals— much to the chagrin of AFL chief executive officer, Andrew Demitriou, who took steps to have this endorsement withdrawn (*The Age*, 11 July 2010).

The second significant campaign in Victoria was the contest between Labor and the Greens for the seat of Melbourne. Doubts about Labor's ability to withstand the growing momentum towards the Greens in this historically safe Labor seat increased with the announcement by sitting member and Finance Minister, Lindsay Tanner, that he would be retiring from politics immediately. Labor preselected former Australian Council of Trade Unions (ACTU) industrial advocate Cath Bowtell (*The Australian*, 5 July 2010). Bowtell was, however, done few favours by her Labor leaders. To the embarrassment of Julia Gillard, Victorian Labor Premier, John Brumby, used the election campaign period to announce that he would be committing his State Government to a 5 per cent emissions reduction and a 20 per cent increase in renewable-energy production (*The Age*, 21 July 2010). Gillard was also on the back foot on matters such as immigration, border protection and 'asylum-seekers'. Her decision to take a conservative position on these matters might well have been very damaging for Labor's chances in Melbourne with its concentrations of tertiary-educated, human-services-employed, young and affluent voters with social-progressive, post-materialist outlooks. Labor's approach to the national campaign appeared to be driving ever more former inner-city Labor voters to the Greens.

The Result

The notion of a two-dimensional campaign in Victoria was reflected in the results in both the House of Representatives and the Senate. In the case of the lower-house contest, the State-wide figures for Victoria are contained in Table 13.2, while the two-party swings for the ultra-marginal seats are contained in Table 13.1. Calculated by the Australian Electoral Commission as a contest between Labor and the Coalition, the Victorian two-party vote was counted to be 55.3 per cent—a swing to the Labor Party of 1 per cent. Based on results for each seat, however, Table 13.1 shows a bit more volatility than the overall State-wide figures, particularly on primary votes. The swings away from the ALP on primary voting varied across the pendulum, with some seats recoding quite big swings. In terms of two-party swings, however, movement was not particularly significant, save for the big 10.7 per cent swing to the Greens in Melbourne. The biggest two-party swing to the ALP was 6.6 per cent in Julia Gillard's seat of Lalor, after which the adjacent division of Corio (which includes the regional city of Geelong) returned a 5.3 per cent two-party preferred swing to Labor. A 5.3 per cent swing in McEwen rewarded Labor with a gain of the previously Liberal-held seat. Labor also enjoyed two-party swings of 3.5 per cent and 3.4 per cent in the regional city-based seats of Ballarat and Bendigo respectively.

Table 13.1 The 2010 Federal Election: The Victorian ultra-marginal seats (per cent)

Labor seat and two-party vote swing	Coalition seat and two-party vote swing
Corangamite −0.4 Deakin +1 Melbourne −10.7 **GRN gain**	McEwen −5.3 **ALP gain** La Trobe −2 **ALP gain** Dunkley 4–3 McMillan −0.4 Aston −3.3 Gippsland +5.4 Casey −1.7

Table 13.2 2010 Federal Election Result, House of Representatives: Victoria

Party	Primary vote (%)	Swing on 2007	Seats won
ALP	42.8	−1.8	22 (net gain 1)
Liberal	36.4	−1.6	12 (net loss 2)
Nationals	3.2	+0.2	2
Greens	12.6	+4.5	1 (net gain 1)
Family First	3.1	+0.2	
Others	1.6		
Informal	4.5	+1.2	

Source: <vtr.aec.gov.au/HouseStateFirstPrefsByParty-15508-VIC.htm 15/9/2010>

Of the 21 Labor-held seats in the pendulum going into the 2010 election, two-party swings to the Coalition occurred in only three seats, including Corangamite (0.4 per cent, and not enough to see it change hands), Bruce (0.2 per cent) and Batman (1 per cent). Of the 16 Coalition seats, however, two-party swings against the Liberal Party and towards Labor occurred in nine seats, including the two that changed hands (McEwen and La Trobe, 2 per cent), with the next two biggest swings occurring in Aston (3.3 per cent) and Dunkley (2.5 per cent).

In contrast, the strongest swings to the Coalition were mainly in rural seats, although Kevin Andrews won a two-party swing of 2.7 per cent in Menzies on Melbourne's eastern perimeter. In The Nationals-held seats, meanwhile, sitting members enjoyed an increase in their margins in Gippsland (5.4 per cent) and Mallee (3.1 per cent).

Labor's result in the second campaign in Melbourne was, however, not so positive. The momentum towards the Greens being indicated in the opinion polls duly occurred (*The Age*, 19 July 2010). Table 13.3 outlines the Melbourne result and shows that Labor's primary vote fell to the very low level of 38.1 per cent—an 11.4 per cent decline on the 2007 result. In the two-party vote, the Greens won 56 per cent and secured two-party majorities in 30 of the electorate's 41 booths. Labor was able to win only those booths within which could be found Housing Commission flats with concentrations of Labor's migrant-based core constituency. Melbourne was a Labor loss, but the distribution of Greens' preferences in Corangamite (where the Greens polled 11.4 per cent), Deakin (12.9 per cent) and La Trobe (12.3 per cent) were crucial to reversing the result on primary votes and allowing Labor to win these seats.

Table 13.3 2010 Federal Election Result: Division of Melbourne

Candidate	Party	Percentage of vote	Swing
Georgina Pearson	Family First	1.5	+0.5
Adam Bandt	Greens	36.1	+13.3
Joel Murray	Aust. Sex Party	1.8	+1.8
David Collyer	Aust. Democrats	0.6	−0.8
Penelope Green	Secular Party	0.6	+0.6
Cath Bowtell	ALP	38.0	−11.4
Simon Olsen	Liberal	21.0	−2.4
Informal		3.6	+0.8
Bandt	Greens	56.0	
Bowtell	ALP	44.0	−10.7

Source: <http://vtr.aec.gov.au/HouseDivisionFirstPrefsByVoteType-15508-228.htm> (viewed 12 October 2010).

Meanwhile, the strongest Greens seats apart from Melbourne were all Labor seats, including Batman (23.5 per cent), Wills (20.6 per cent) and Melbourne Ports (20.6 per cent). The 2010 election demonstrated once again that the Greens vote is at its most concentrated in the inner suburbs of Melbourne (see Economou and Reynolds 2003). The weakest Greens performances were in rural divisions, including Gippsland (6.5 per cent), Murray (6 per cent) and Wannon (6 per cent), with Wannon the only seat to record a fall in the Greens' vote compared with 2007 (down 0.9 per cent). After the Greens, the next biggest movement by way of primary swing was in the informal vote, which rose by 1.3 per cent to 4.5 per cent—the highest informal vote for the lower house in Victoria since 1987.

The Senate

In addition to its historic win in Melbourne, the Greens also secured a seat in the Senate—the first time the Greens had won a Senate position in Victoria despite coming very close in the 2004 and 2007 elections. The 2010 contest was a half-Senate election in which those senators elected in the 2004 contest were defending their seats. The 2004 contest was the election in which the Greens polled 8.8 per cent but were denied a seat by the ALP directing its preferences to the nascent Family First Party, which resulted in the election of Steve Fielding (Economou 2006). In the 2010 election, however, Labor issued a group ticket vote (GTV) that directed preferences to the Greens. As it turned out, the Greens won 14.6 per cent (see Table 13.4) and thus secured a full quota, which meant the party's lead candidate, Richard Di Natale, was elected without the need for Labor preferences. This meant that the left-of-centre parties secured three seats between them: two for the ALP, and one for the Greens.[1]

Table 13.4 2010 Federal Election Result, Victoria: The Senate

Party/ticket	Primary vote (%)	Quota	Seats
ALP	37.7	2.6	2
Liberal-Nationals	34.4	2.4	2
Australian Greens	14.6	1.0	1
Family First	2.6	0.1	
DLP	2.3	0.1	1
Australian Sex Party	2.2	0.1	
Other minor parties	5.2	0.4	
Others	0.3	0.0	
Informal	3.9		

Source: <http://vtr.aec.gov.au/SenateStateFirstPrefsByGroup-15508-VIC.htm> (viewed 15 September 2010).

There was another interesting twist to the result. At 34.4 per cent, the vote of the Liberal-Nationals Coalition was able to secure only 2.4 quotas. This meant that while Liberal Michael Ronaldson was returned, and Brigit McKenzie of The Nationals was elected (courtesy of the second position on the joint-party ticket), the third-placed Liberal on the ticket, Julian McGauran, was in real danger of not being returned. The Coalition ticket lost ground to the proliferation of right-of-centre minor parties that contested this election, whose accumulated vote was 9.3 per cent, or 0.65 of a quota. As the count unfolded, the significance of the cross-preferencing between the right-of-centre minor parties became apparent when the DLP ticket succeeded in getting ahead of Family First and finishing in second place to the ALP in the penultimate round of counting, with McGauran coming third. With Family First out of the count, the preferences

---

1   The idea of 'left-of-centre' and 'right-of-centre' parties is explained in Bowler and Denemark (1993), and Mackerras (1993).

from the Coalition ticket flowed to the DLP and pushed its candidate, John Madigan, ahead of Labor's Anthony Tow to secure the sixth Victorian seat. This was the first time since 1970 that a candidate running under the rubric of the DLP had been elected to the Senate from Victoria.

Conclusion

As it has been for so many federal elections in the past, this time, Victoria proved to be a very good State for the Labor Party, and the outcome in five electoral divisions proved to be crucial in allowing the Labor government to be returned, albeit as a minority administration. The notion of a strong regional variation within the national trend in this election can be highlighted by comparing the Victorian vote with the national result (see Table 13.5). Victoria was a very good State for the two parties of the left of centre: the ALP and the Greens. The State primary vote for both parties was higher than the national result, and Labor enjoyed a 1 per cent two-party swing compared with the 2.6 per cent swing against it in the national result. The swings were rewarded with seats: of the three seats that changed, two were to the ALP and one was to the Greens. Importantly, Labor defended its Victorian marginal seats. Labor did lose the seat of Melbourne to the Greens, and this was a major achievement for the minor party. In terms of securing executive power, however, the loss of Melbourne was not a disaster for Labor, as the newly elected Greens member stayed true to his campaign commitment and aligned himself with Labor in the event of a hung parliament. The left of centre also advanced in the Senate, rolling back the four–two right-of-centre outcome in the 2004 election by winning back the seat that had been surrendered by the ALP to Family First in that contest. Victoria, then, provided the basis upon which the ALP was able to retain government, and the Australian Greens was able to increase its parliamentary presence.

Table 13.5 Federal Election 2010, House of Representatives: Victoria and national compared

	ALP primary (%)	LNP primary (%)	GRN primary (%)	Others primary (%)	ALP tpv (%)*	Swing
Victoria	42.8	39.7	12.6	4.9	55.3	+1.0
National	37.9	43.5	11.7	5.0	50.1	–2.6

* tpv = two-party vote

Source: <http://results.aec.gov.au/13745/Website/HouseResultsMenu-13745.htm>

References

Bowler, Shaun and Denemark, David. 1993. 'Split ticket voting in Australia: dealignment and inconsistent voting reconsidered'. *Australian Journal of Political Science* 28(1): 19–37.

Economou, Nick. 2006. 'A right-of-centre triumph: the 2004 Australian half-Senate election'. *Australian Journal of Political Science* 41(4): 501–16.

Economou, Nick. 2010. 'Victoria'. *Australian Cultural History* 28(1): 81–6.

Economou, Nick and Reynolds, Margaret. 2003. 'Who voted Green? A review of the Green vote in the 2002 Victorian state election'. *People and Place* 11(3): 57–68.

Hughes, Colin A. 1983. 'A close run thing'. In Howard R. Penniman (ed.), *Australia at the Polls: The national elections of 1980 and 1983*. Sydney: Allen & Unwin, 216–247.

Mackerras, Malcolm. 1993. *The 1993 Mackerras Election Guide*. Canberra: Australian Government Publishing Service.

14. South Australia

Dean Jaensch

South Australia was not expected to loom large in the federal election, with only 11 of the 150 seats. Of the 11, only four were marginal—requiring a swing of less than 5 per cent to be lost. Three were Liberal: Sturt (held by Christopher Pyne since 1993, 1 per cent margin), Boothby (Andrew Southcott since 1996, 3 per cent) and Grey (4.5 per cent). Of the Labor seats, only Kingston (4.5 per cent) was marginal.

Table 14.1 Pre-Election Pendulum (per cent)

ALP			Liberal Party		
Electorate	FP	TPP	Electorate	FP	TPP
Kingston	46.7	54.4	Sturt	47.2	50.9
Hindmarsh	47.2	55.1	Boothby	46.3	52.9
Wakefield	48.7	56.6	Grey	47.3	54.4
Makin	51.4	57.7	Mayo	51.1	57.1
Adelaide	48.2	58.5	Barker	46.8	59.5
Port Adelaide	58.2	69.8			

FP = first preference

TPP = two-party preferred

Labor won Kingston, Wakefield and Makin from the Liberal Party in 2007. The Liberal Party could win all three back. But, in early 2010, it was expected that if there was any change in South Australia, it would involve Liberal losses.

The State election in March 2010, however, produced some shock results. The Rann Labor Government was returned to office, despite massive swings in its safe seats. In the last two weeks of the campaign, the polls showed Labor in trouble. The Rann Government—after four years of hubris, arrogance and spin—was in danger of defeat. The result saw an average two-party swing of 8.4 per cent against Labor—stronger in its safe seats, with an average of 11.6 per cent. But in the key marginal Labor seats, the average anti-Labor swing was only 4.2 per cent, and the Rann Government survived.

If these swings were repeated in the federal election, it would mean the loss of Adelaide, and possibly Hindmarsh and Kingston. Further, Labor would have no hope of picking up Boothby and Sturt. The key issue was whether South Australians would distinguish between federal and State politics, and whether they had exhausted their anger with the Labor badge in the State election.

A *Sunday Mail* poll (25 July 2010) found the Liberal Party leading in Boothby with a two-party vote of 52 per cent. An *Advertiser* poll (21 August 2010) found Labor had increased its buffer in Hindmarsh to 62 per cent. The key Liberal seat of Sturt had improved to a Liberal two-party vote of 55 per cent. At that stage local pollsters seemed to decide that there was nothing much exciting happening, and polling virtually ceased.

The federal party leaders had also decided that South Australia was unlikely to be fertile territory. Both Julia Gillard and Tony Abbott made fleeting visits to 'fly the flag', but that was it. According to *The Advertiser* (22 July 2010), this was a 'significant slap in the face to the electors of this state'. Without a raft of marginal seats that showed some signs of moving, the pork-barrels were distributed elsewhere. There were key projects in South Australia that would have benefited from federal funding. The redevelopment of Adelaide Oval kept blowing out in cost. The Rann Government would have welcomed a pork-barrel to assist in the funding of its new hospital. The desalination plant was also crying out for some federal funding, but no-one seemed to listen.

The most talked about issue in South Australia was water. The Murray River is crucial for the State—the parlous state of irrigation quotas, the collapse of the Lower Lakes and The Coorong, and Adelaide's dependence on the Murray for its water supply were themes of daily conversation everywhere. The decision of the Murray–Darling Basin Authority to refuse to release its report on proposals to save the basin until after the election did nothing to endear the voters to the Gillard Government.

The Advertiser (22 July 2010) expressed the view of most South Australians when it editorialised: 'Perhaps, when Ms Gillard and Mr Abbott visit this electoral backwater, they will come armed with transparent and accountable plans to save this state's lifeline—and possibly their own political careers.' During her fleeting visit to Adelaide, Julia Gillard did raise water as an issue. She travelled to the marginal Liberal electorate of Sturt to announce a stormwater-harvesting project for the eastern suburbs, which centre on Sturt. But as the Rann Government was refusing to fund the necessary pipelines, the announcement fell rather flat.

Sturt Labor candidate, Rick Starr, held a street-corner meeting. He stated that he was 'disappointed that the announcement Julia made a couple of weeks ago [for a people's assembly] didn't satisfy me that she was pushing climate change to the level of the agenda that it should be'. A recording of the comment was passed to the ABC. Starr, a law professor, emailed the ABC claiming that the 'recording device was concealed and in breach of the *Listening Devices Act*', and that he 'had not given the consent required' (*The Advertiser*, 3 August 2010). The affair was a storm in a teacup, but did show the extent to which parties are determined to keep their candidates either silent or on song.

The Greens decided that one of their key planks—opposition to anything related to uranium—held the possibility of winning votes in South Australia. Greens Senate candidate Penny Wright announced that the commitment to 'end the exploration for, and the mining and export of uranium' would be firmly applied (*The Advertiser*, 21 July 2010). The problem was that the Roxby Dam mine was involved in a massive $21 billion expansion project, involving thousands of jobs. This was a major economic plan of the Rann Government. Penny Wright was of the view that BHP could still operate, but with the uranium part shut down. BHP Billiton and the Rann Government had no public comment.

The Australian Democrats decided to re-enter the election contest in the State that had been their power base for more than 20 years. Their focus for the House of Representatives was Sturt. On the eve of the election, it was revealed that the Democrats' candidate had a conviction for a child sexual offence. He withdrew from the election, but his name remained on the ballot paper. Party leader, Sandra Kanck, admitted that this would 'damage the efforts of the other candidates for the party: for all of their bloody hard work, [he]…is going to undo it' (*The Advertiser*, 20 August 2010).

The count in the Boothby electorate had a problem. Following a complaint from the Labor Party, alleging improper practices in the counting process, the Australian Electoral Commission (AEC) agreed that a parcel of ballot papers 'had not been handled in accordance with the provisions of the *Commonwealth Electoral Act*'. A member of the commission's staff had transferred batches of votes (2977 ballot papers) from a number of boxes into one, for 'ease of handling'. The AEC, on legal advice, removed these votes from the count, but this did not affect the final result of a victory for the Liberal Party.

The Advertiser, South Australia's only local daily, published an editorial on 7 August that was essentially a call for a change in the parties' appeals, criticising them for 'wasting all of their energy sledging the other side'. On election eve, *The Advertiser* offered clear advice to the voters, based on the overriding issue of water: 'For South Australian voters, Labor's policy to return water to the River Murray is markedly superior [and]…Ms Gillard and Labor should be given a second chance' (20 August 2010).

Table 14.2 State-Wide Results, House of Representatives (per cent of votes)

Party	2007	2010	Swing	Two-party	Swing
ALP	41.8	40.2	−1.6	53.5	+ 1.1
Liberal	43.2	40.7	−2.5	46.8	−1.1
Greens	7.0	12.0	+5.0		
Family First	4.1	5.0	+0.9		
Other	3.9	2.1	−1.8		

Both Labor and Liberal suffered a small primary swing against them, with the Greens the major beneficiary. Six of the 11 seats were forced to preferences. But the overall result was that no seats changed hands, and all incumbents were re-elected. There was no sign of the State election landslide swings against Labor. In fact, in the former safe Labor electorates of Hindmarsh, Adelaide and Port Adelaide, which had produced the large anti-Labor swings, it was almost the status quo from 2007.

Table 14.3 2010 Election Pendulum (per cent)

ALP				Liberal			
Electorate	FP	TPP	Swing (TPP)	Electorate	FP	TPP	Swing (TPP)
Hindmarsh	44.5	55.7	0.7	Boothby	44.8	50.8	−2.2
Adelaide	43.9	57.7	−0.8	Sturt	48.1	53.4	2.5
Wakefield	49.2	62.0	5.4	Mayo	46.8	57.4	0.3
Makin	50.6	62.2	4.5	Grey	55.8	61.2	6.7
Kingston	51.1	63.9	9.5	Barker	55.0	62.9	3.4
Port Adelaide	53.8	70.0	0.3				

FP = first preference

TPP = two-party preferred

In the electorates of Kingston, Makin and Wakefield, there was a solid 'sophomore swing'. In all three, the Labor incumbent was first elected in 2007, and each had markedly increased support.

On the Liberal side, there was a swing against Labor in Grey—a massive electorate where the mining tax issue had an effect. The party narrowly held its two marginal seats of Sturt and Boothby.

The Senate election in South Australia offered more potential for change than the House of Representatives. The six senators elected in 2004 were split evenly: three Labor and three Liberal. Of these, only three—two Labor and one Liberal—renominated in 2010. Labor Senator Dana Wortley found herself relegated to the unwinnable third position after the party decided to select a union leader for the top spot.

There were 17 parties and three Independents—a total of 42 candidates. There was little doubt that Liberal and Labor would initially win two seats each. The two remaining seats were a contest between Labor, the Greens and Family First. The leading candidate for Family First was property developer Bob Day, who stood for the Liberal Party in 2007, then for Family First in the State election of 2010.

The electoral 'star' of SA politics, Nick Xenophon, did not have any nominations under his 'No pokies' banner in either the State or the federal elections. His record of pulling votes, however, made his endorsement potentially very valuable. Xenophon announced that his endorsement 'would not be given lightly' (*The Advertiser*, 14 August 2010), but Bob Day jumped the gun. After Day's full-page advertisement in *The Advertiser* (13 August 2010), Xenophon complained to the Electoral Commission that Day had implied he had Xenophon's endorsement.

Table 14.4 Senate Result, 2010

Party	Vote (%)	Quota	Seats
ALP	38.3 (+2.7)	2.67	2 (−1 on 2004)
Liberal	37.3 (+1.7)	2.02	3 (= 2004)
Greens	13.3 (+6.8)	0.93	1 (+1 from 2004)
Family First	4.1 (+1.3)	0.28	-
Other	7.0 (−12.4)	0.49	-

Labor's surplus was transmitted through preferences to elect Penny Wright for the Greens, giving South Australia two Greens senators. This left the Liberal Party and Family First to battle it out for the sixth seat, which eventually went to the Liberal Party.

A comparison of the SA and national results shows that Labor held up well.

Table 14.5 2010 Election: South Australia and national compared (percentage of votes)

	ALP	Liberal	Greens	Others	ALP	Swing
	Primary	Primary	Primary	Primary	TPP	Swing
South Australia	41.8	43.2	7.0	8.0	53.5	+1.1
National	37.9	43.5	11.7	5.0	50.1	−2.6

With all incumbents returned in the House of Representatives, the only change was the election of a second Greens senator at the expense of the Labor Party. The election in South Australia was all but a non-event.

15. The Northern Territory

Dean Jaensch

For 25 years after the first election for the Legislative Assembly in 1974, the Northern Territory's politics were dominated by a unique Country Liberal Party (CLP). The Labor Party could never lift its representation above one-third of the seats. In the 2001 election, however, patterns of party support, especially in the Darwin region, went into convulsions. Labor won its first election after a massive swing against the CLP in the Darwin region of almost 10 per cent. In the 2005 election, there was a further swing against the CLP, which was reduced to four seats out of twenty-five. In 2008, there was a landslide swing to the CLP that left Labor with the barest majority of 13 seats.

In House of Representative elections, the single elected member for the Territory received full voting rights in 1966, and the CLP dominated until Labor finally won the seat in 1983. For the next 15 years, the seat alternated between Labor and CLP, and Labor's Warren Snowdon held it from 1987 to 1996, and from 1998 to 2010. The redistribution of 2000 gave the Northern Territory two seats: Solomon was essentially the Darwin urban area, and Lingiari covered the rest of the Territory. Lingiari was a safe Labor seat from the beginning, with a majority of the Aboriginal population of the Territory. From its formation, it has been held by Warren Snowdon for Labor, and 2010 was likely to continue this, requiring a swing of more than 11 per cent to be lost.

The first election in Solomon in 2001 was won by the CLP, which retained the seat in 2004. In the 2007 election, CLP incumbent, David Tollner, led Labor on primary votes, but Greens preferences returned the seat to Labor with the narrowest margin in the nation of 0.2 per cent. The contest in 2010 was expected to be just as tight. A poll in Solomon revealed that 73 per cent of the voters believed 'at heart, I'm an environmentalist' (*Sunday Territorian*, 1 August 2010), and the demographics of the electorate showed 33 per cent under thirty-five years of age, and 32 per cent with an annual income of more than $100 000. Such data suggested that Solomon was prime space for the Greens.

The contests in both seats were essentially CLP versus Labor. But the usual crop of minor parties and Independents intervened. One Independent for the Senate had a single policy: 'I am a passionate Territorian, dedicated to the Territory. I am committed to growing the Territory and protecting our way of life.' The One Nation nominee ran on a policy of stopping all immigration for two years. The Indigenous Independent candidate for Lingiari proposed that the Territory be divided in two, with Alice Springs and Darwin as the two capitals.

Labor and CLP campaign policies were essentially national, but local issues intervened. The ALP incumbent was forced to defend his party's promise that GP 'super clinics' were the future when CLP candidate, Natasha Griggs, revealed that the only one in the Territory, at Palmerston, was closed on weekends. She also won points over the issue of 395 Royal Australian Air Force (RAAF) houses that Labor planned to demolish. Pointing out the serious shortage of housing in the Top End, she promised to retain the houses and offer them for private sale.

In content and style, CLP and Labor campaigns for Lingiari and Solomon are usually very different, but an internal dispute in the CLP threatened to wash over both electorates. The CLP candidate for Lingiari, Leo Abbott, an Aborigine, was revealed on 13 August to have breached a domestic violence order. On 14 August, Terry Mills, the CLP parliamentary leader, stating that he had not known about the order until it was published in the media, announced that he would move to de-select Abbott, although mobile polling had begun.

This prompted a serious internal dispute in the party. CLP Senator Nigel Scullion, former Member for Solomon, stated that the CLP had known about the matter, and that Abbott was an 'absolutely fantastic candidate' (*Northern Territory News*, 14 August 2010). Mills demanded that the de-selection proceed, arguing that 'domestic violence in any form is unacceptable, and retaining Mr Abbott would send the wrong message to the community' (*The Weekend Australian*, 14–15 August 2010). The CLP continued to rupture, with Solomon CLP candidate, Natasha Briggs, also arguing for de-selection. The CLP Management Committee refused to act. After a marathon meeting in which Mills argued for de-selection 'as a matter of principle', the CLP President stated that Abbott was 'one of the best Aboriginal people we have ever met' (*The Australian*, 16 August 2010).

Mills continued to argue that the Management Committee should support his position as leader of the party. The *Northern Territory News* (16 August 2010) agreed: 'the Management Committee…made up of faceless branch bosses… effectively told Mills to "go jump", humiliated Mr Mills, damaged the party's reputation and demonstrated who's boss—Senator Nigel Scullion.'

The dispute became more serious when one member of the Management Committee went public with the view that Mills was 'not the leader of the CLP: the Management Committee was', and Mills' proposal 'to dis-endorse was a low, mongrel act' (*Northern Territory News*, 17 August 2010). Two CLP Legislative Assembly members from Alice Springs electorates, including former parliamentary leader Jodeen Carney, stated that they would not campaign for Abbott, and would not vote for him. On election eve, Carney announced that she had 'quit the CLP' and the Assembly over the issue (*Northern Territory News*, 20 August 2010). Despite this internal brawl, the CLP won Solomon, with a two-party swing in its favour.

Table 15.1 Results and Swings, Solomon (percentage of votes)

Party	2007	2010	Swing	Two-party	2010 swing
ALP	41.9	36.1	−5.8	48.3	−1.9
CLP	46.8	46.4	−0.4	51.8	+1.9
Greens	9.1	13.3	+4.2		
One Nation	-	3.0	+3.0		
Other	2.3	1.3	−1.0		

In Lingiari, Labor's Warren Snowdon suffered a two-party swing of 7.4 per cent against him, and he was forced to preferences for the first time.

Table 15.2 Results and Swings, Lingiari (percentage of votes)

Party	2007	2010	Swing	Two-party	2010 swing
ALP	54.0	41.1	−13.9	53.8	−7.4
CLP	34.7	34.3	−0.4	46.2	+7.4
Greens	6.9	12.6	+5.7		
Other	-	3.9	+3.9		
Ind.	4.4	9.2	+4.8		

The patterns of voting in Lingiari were interesting. This is a very socially and politically fragmented electorate. The towns of Alice Springs and Katherine have a long anti-Labor history. Labor has never won a seat in either since the first Territory election in 1974, and they are usually solidly CLP. On the other hand, the outback, with a majority of Aboriginal people, has been the heartland of Labor support for a long time—a trend most obvious in the people covered by mobile polling, the overwhelming proportion of whom are Aboriginal. In 2010, however, there were significant differences from these essentially stable patterns. Table 15.3 shows the two-party preferred vote for Labor in these regions for the four national elections from 2001 to 2010.

Table 15.3 Results in Three Regions, Labor Two-Party (per cent)

Region	2001	2004	2007	2010	Change 2007–10
Alice Springs	45	33	35	52	+17
Katherine	40	45	42	44	+2
Remote mobiles	72	79	88	60	−28

The Katherine region showed little change in 2010, but there were significant changes in both Alice Springs and the remote polling regions. The swing against the CLP in the usually safe region of Alice Springs was major. It cannot be established how much the massive change in the aggregate patterns of support in the remote Aboriginal regions was due to the CLP candidate being Indigenous. But again, the change is significant.

The Senate campaign, and the result, caused little excitement in the Territory. With only two Senate seats, and a quota of 33.3 per cent, the CLP and Labor would win one seat each.

Table 15.4 Senate Result, 2010

Party	Vote (%)	Quota	Seats
ALP	34.4 (−12.6)	1.03	1 (= 2004)
CLP	40.6 (+0.6)	1.22	1 (= 2004)
Greens	13.6 (+4.7)	0.41	-
Other	10.8 (+7.3)	0.34	-

There was a strong swing of primary votes against Labor of more than 12 per cent, and the party was close to being forced to preferences. There was virtually no change to the CLP vote. The Greens, the Sex Party (5.1 per cent) and the Shooters and Fishers Party (4.8 per cent) shared the benefit.

16. Tasmania

Tony McCall

Prior to election day, Tasmania looked as if it was to be the State most likely to return to the status quo in terms of party support in the House of Representatives—five Labor members in five electorates—and a potential reverse of the major-party returns on the 2004 Senate result, with Labor this time edging ahead with three seats, Liberal two and the Greens one. It had been a dull and lifeless campaign with no reckless takeovers of regional hospitals (2007) or the theatre of forestry workers massing in Launceston in support of Prime Minister, John Howard (2004).

In contrast with those elections, in 2010, the volatile issue of forestry management lay dormant in the run-up to the vote. No political party, including the Greens, was prepared to risk the wedge effect of the forestry/pulp mill issue.

Tasmanians remained concerned about access to preventative and acute-care health delivery in remote rural and regional electorates—particularly Braddon in the north-west of the State, where a series of promises over cancer treatment facilities stretched the imaginations of the candidates and the bottom line of spending commitments.

Employment losses following industry closures in the vegetable-processing sector and paper mills in Burnie and Wesley Vale, east of Devonport, also heightened concerns in Braddon while uncertainty in the forestry industry was creating disquiet in Bass and Braddon. The impact of the proposed Mining Super Profits Tax on west-coast mining communities (which reverted to Braddon from Lyons in the 2009 redistribution) was a much discussed issue in early campaigning.

Labor made much of the National Broadband Network (NBN) roll-out in Tasmania, with the State the first cab off the rank for this ambitious project, and when the Coalition policy differed significantly in terms of cost and technology there was renewed focus on the impact these contrasting approaches might have in the electorates of Bass (Scottsdale), Lyons (Midway Point) and Braddon (Smithton), where fibre-optic connections had been operating during the election campaign.

Labor held Braddon and Bass but both were marginal. In Franklin and Lyons, Labor's margin was comfortable and Denison, a Labor seat for 23 years with a margin of 15 per cent, looked a relatively easy transition from retiring member, Duncan Kerr, to a member of a State Labor dynasty, Jonathan Jackson, son of former Tasmanian Attorney-General Judy Jackson.

In the Senate, the Liberals' team entered the election with an incumbent senator, Guy Barnett, shuffled to the vulnerable third place on the party ticket.

Labor endorsed Lisa Singh to run third on their ticket behind Senator Helen Polley and union delegate Anne Urquhart. Singh lost her State parliamentary seat—Denison—at the March 2010 election.

The Greens were confident of Senator Christine Milne's return with a comfortable result in contrast with the nail-biting wait in 2004.

Preselections, Parties and Candidates in Electorates

Incumbency would help Labor in Lyons where Dick Adams looked set to be returned on the back of an 8 per cent margin and in Franklin where Julie Collins was safe with a 4 per cent margin.

In Braddon, Sid Sidebottom was facing a bigger challenge with a 2 per cent margin, and in Bass, Labor faced the prospect of replacing the retiring Jodie Campbell, who had done little to advance Labor's prospects of holding the seat with a fragile 1 per cent margin. Labor was confident of securing a transition in Denison on the back of retiring Duncan Kerr's 15 per cent margin.

The Liberals preselected well-known candidates in Bass and Lyons. The party talked up the chances of media professional Steven Titmus ousting Labor in Bass on the back of Jodie Campbell's implosion. Rural services manager Eric Hutchinson was respected and well known in the sprawling rural electorate of Lyons and was a chance to eat into Dick Adams' margin. But the Liberals had to revert to relatively obscure candidates in Braddon and Denison. In Franklin, they endorsed a failed State candidate for Lyons, Jane Howlett, who switched electorates to run federally.

The Greens, buoyed by their 2007 results and successful State campaign, targetted Denison as a prospect and endorsed local medical doctor Geoff Couser. State campaign director, Sancia Colgrave, ran in Bass; long-time Tarkine activist and regular but unsuccessful State candidate Scott Jordan tackled Braddon;

unsuccessful State Legislative Council candidate Wendy Heatley was endorsed for Franklin; and party stalwart Karen Cassidy switched from State to federal electorates and ran in Lyons.

Two Independents nominated: John Forster in Franklin and Andrew Wilkie in Denison. Wilkie had narrowly missed out on a seat at the March 2010 State election on the back of an 8 per cent first-preference vote and the assistance of Hare Clark preference flows.

Campaign

Labor entered the campaign with confidence that they could hold all five House of Representative seats, and any opinion poll that was conducted locally reinforced that confidence.

Tasmanians focused on local and regional issues, especially health care, where discussion focused on governance arrangements for hospital administration within Labor's national health reform packages and the Liberal preference for regionally based boards. Support for road infrastructure projects was high on electoral agendas with local government mayors in the south of the State together bemoaning the lack of a share in infrastructure funds for their electorates; Franklin and Denison are not marginal and thus attract little interest from political parties and potential prime ministers who concentrated their pork-barrelling exercises in the winnable northern seats of Bass and Braddon.

Bass

Labor was nervous about Bass. The seat was very marginal and the rather unedifying exit of Jodie Campbell had the party concerned that too much damage had been done. The Liberals were running a well-known media identity as a candidate and Labor had endorsed a somewhat reluctant party stalwart, but well-respected community member, Geoff Lyons. The two major parties fought over silt removal in the Tamar River estuary, flood-levy infrastructure support and health packages.

Braddon

The Liberals felt that incumbent Labor member, Sid Sidebottom, might be vulnerable to an energetic, hardworking candidate. The Liberals had hoped failed State candidate Brett Whiteley might choose to run but after some months of speculation, he declined. The Liberals were left with little time to mount a convincing case around the endorsed candidate, Garry Carpenter. Carpenter had connections to the community through football and some exposure during a dairy farmer dispute with a milk processor in the electorate but was hardly well known outside that narrow gaze. Issues in Braddon focused on securing State and federal commitments for localised cancer services; employment losses in industry sectors struggling to compete globally such as paper and vegetable processing; and some early concerns that the proposed Labor mining tax might damage investment and job prospects in the State's west-coast mining area.

Denison

Pre-election expectations for Denison were aligned to a Labor transition. For a seat held by Labor with a 15 per cent margin, there was a seemingly quiet Labor preselection process, and Jonathan Jackson was regarded as a strong chance to replace the retiring Duncan Kerr. The Greens saw an opportunity to stake a claim at the federal level in a seat with very high Greens voting credentials, especially when Andrew Wilkie—an unlucky loser in the seat in the State election—decided to run as an Independent. The Liberals once again struggled to supply a high-profile candidate for this important capital-city seat, but eventually Cameron Simpkins nominated and was selected.

Most of the non-Labor candidates took the view that it was time Denison was again given the attention it deserved in the federal Parliament—particularly in relation to infrastructure—so their collective mantra was 'make Denison marginal'.

Franklin

Labor incumbent, Julie Collins, held a comfortable 4 per cent margin, and again the Liberals struggled to find a significant challenger and, in the end, in a rather desperate move, parachuted in a failed State election Lyons candidate, Jane Howlett. Wendy Heatley, the Greens' candidate, had received only 621 votes at the State poll. A contentious road-infrastructure development—the Brighton by-pass—threatened Aboriginal relics and this was a focus for considerable argument and debate about resolution and consultation with the Aboriginal community in Tasmania.

Lyons

The affable Dick Adams, Labor Member for Lyons, prepared for his sixth defence of his realm. The Liberals sought to challenge Adams by nominating a smart, well-known rural-based manager, Eric Hutchinson, who worked in the wool industry and had a high profile in the rural electorate. Adams had the advantage of the preference flow from the Greens in Lyons, and the Greens were able to coax party stalwart Karen Cassidy to nominate. Rural and regional challenges around liveability and sustainability dominated pre-election issues in Lyons.

Results

Labor retained four of its five House of Representatives seats. The Independent Andrew Wilkie won Denison. Tasmania defied the broad national swing against Labor by further endorsing the south-eastern (Victorian, South Australian) sentiment, with a two-party preferred swing of 4.4 per cent and 60.6 per cent vote. Labor increased its first-preference vote across the State by 1.2 per cent. The Liberals had an election meltdown and a post-election crisis. The party had a 4.6 per cent fall in its first-preference vote and could secure only 39.4 per cent of the two-party preferred State vote. In addition to the rout in the House of Representatives, Senator Guy Barnett lost his seat, with the Liberals securing two senators (Abetz and Parry), Labor three (Polley, Urquhart and Singh), and the Greens one (Milne).

Table 16.1 Two-Candidate Preferred Votes and Swings in Tasmanian Divisions, 2010

Division	Labor votes	Percentage	Liberal votes/ Wilkie Ind., Denison	Percentage	Percentage swing to Labor
Tasmania					
Bass	37 165	56.7	28 337	43.3	5.7
Braddon	37 650	57.5	27 855	42.5	5.2
Denison	31 642	48.8	33 217	51.2	
Franklin	39 856	60.8	25 675	39.2	6.8
Lyons	40 959	62.3	24 796	37.7	4.0
Total Tasmania	198 322	60.6	128 830	39.4	4.4

Source: Adapted from AEC Election Results 2010: <http://www.aec.gov.au/Elections/federal_elections/2010/index.htm>

Table 16.2 First Preferences in Tasmanian Divisions, 2010 (percentage preferences)

Division	ALP	LP	GRN	SPA	CEC	OTH/Wilkie/Denison
Bass	43.4	39.7	15.6	0.0	1.3	0.0
Braddon	48.7	39.4	12.0	0.0	0.0	0.0
Denison	35.8	22.7	19.0	0.0	0.0	1.3/21.3
Franklin	42.9	33.5	20.9	0.0	0.0	2.8
Lyons	48.9	32.7	16.8	1.7	0.0	0.0
State total	44.0	33.6	16.8	0.3	0.3	4.8

Source: Adapted from AEC Election Results 2010: <http://www.aec.gov.au/Elections/federal_elections/2010/index.htm>

Table 16.3 Senate First Preferences by Group: Tasmania, 2010

First preferences for Tasmania Quota: 47 242 Enrolment: 358 567				
Group	**Votes**	**%**	**Swing**	**Quota**
Liberal	109 023	33.0	−4.4	2.31
ALP	136 908	41.4	+1.3	2.90
Australian Greens	67 016	20.3	+2.1	1.42
Family First	4045	1.2	−0.8	0.09
DLP (Democratic Labor Party)	1560	0.5	−0.2	0.03
Shooters and Fishers	6649	2.0	+2.0	0.14
Australian Democrats	1608	0.5	+0.5	0.03
Secular Party of Australia	574	0.2	+0.2	0.01
Senator On-Line	1488	0.5	+0.5	0.03
The Climate Sceptics	766	0.2	+0.2	0.02
Unendorsed/ungrouped amalgamated	1054	0.3	−0.4	0.02
Senate Ghost Groups amalgamated	0	0.00	−0.9	0.00
FORMAL	330 691	96.8	−0.6	
INFORMAL	1047	3.2	+0.6	
TOTAL	341 738	95.31	−0.7	

Source: Adapted from AEC Election Results 2010: <http://www.aec.gov.au/Elections/federal_elections/2010/index.htm>

Labor's Geoff Lyons triumphed in Bass with a 6.1 per cent increase in Labor's first-preference vote supported by a high Greens vote that flowed through to a 56.7 per cent two-party preferred vote, representing a 5.7 per cent swing to the Liberals. The Liberal's Steve Titmus had to concede defeat on the back of a disappointing 3.7 per cent drop in first-preference votes. Bass was no longer highly marginal.

It was a similar story in Braddon. Labor's Sid Sidebottom had a decisive victory that moved Braddon out of highly marginal status. Sidebottom secured victory on the back of a 3.8 per cent swing in first preferences, an increase in the Greens vote of 3.8 per cent, and a lacklustre Liberal vote—a loss of 3.6 per cent on first preferences. Sidebottom secured a two-party preferred percentage of 57.5 per cent and a 5.2 per cent swing to Labor.

No-one predicted Andrew Wilkie's victory. When the counting was complete, he had secured 51.2 per cent on the two-candidate preferred basis over Labor's Jonathan Jackson (48.8 per cent). How did this happen? The short answer is that voters in Denison abandoned Labor (−12.4 per cent first-preference swing), once again could not support the Liberals (−7.3 per cent), and shifted to Wilkie rather than the Greens (+0.4 per cent).

Finishing ahead of the Greens candidate, Geoff Couser, and just behind Liberal, Cameron Simpkins, Wilkie was well placed to challenge Jackson when the distribution of preferences began and a two-candidate preferred battle ensued. Polling-booth analysis reveals that Wilkie had a significant 65 per cent two-candidate preferred vote in high-income, socioeconomically advantaged residential areas such as Sandy Bay, Battery Point, Taroona and Waimea Heights, and was able to maintain an approximately 60/40 per cent advantage in at least 17 other polling booths. These booths equate to just less than half the total in the electorate.

Julie Collins replicated Labor's victory march in Franklin. On the back of a 6.2 per cent increase in the Greens' first-preference vote, Collins managed a small 2.2 per cent increase and a two-party preferred vote of 60.8 per cent against a Liberal vote of 39.2 per cent and a swing of 6.8 per cent. The Liberals faced another compelling defeat, losing 7.8 per cent on first preferences in Franklin, and the electorate continued to display its Green tinge.

Labor's Dick Adams increased his two-party preferred vote on the back of a 5.4 per cent first-preference swing and a substantial Greens vote (16.8 per cent—a 5.8 per cent swing). Adams' two-party preferred vote improved from 58.3 per cent in 2007 to a massive 62.3 per cent in 2010—a 4 per cent swing. Liberal candidate, Eric Hutchinson, secured the smallest swing against the party on first preferences (−0.8 per cent), but that would have been little comfort. Lyons is Dick Adams' seat until he chooses to retire.

Post-Election Analysis

Two issues are worthy of some discussion post election: Andrew Wilkie's negotiation with Labor and the fallout for the Liberal Party in Tasmania.

The detail of Wilkie's agreement with Labor tells us much about his intentions in the Parliament. Wilkie knows well that his future as the Member for Denison will now be about outcomes rather than the rhetoric of 'new political paradigms'. Beyond his commitment to supporting stable government and principles around transparent and accountable government, some of Wilkie's proposals have been adopted within the *Agreement for a Better Parliament* document.

The Liberal Party in Tasmania is busily licking its wounds as a result of it poor results. An independent review is being undertaken of the campaign including preselection processes and campaign strategy, and a very public discussion is emerging, driven by defeated Senate candidate Guy Barnett, around the power and influence of senior Liberal Senator Eric Abetz within the Tasmanian Liberal Party organisation. Senator Barnett, who will depart the Senate in June 2011, described the Tasmanian result for the party as 'diabolical and disappointing', but State Liberal Party President, Sam McQuestin, a Liberal candidate for the Legislative Council seat of Launceston, said the party's comparatively poor performance in Tasmania was not a reflection of its candidates or volunteers (*Examiner*, 24 August 2010).

Conclusion

Tasmania bucked the national trend (−5.4 per cent against Labor on first preferences) to return four Labor members to the House of Representatives— all with significantly increased two-party preferred margins—and three Labor senators, all of whom were women and two of them newcomers to the Parliament.

The election of Independent Andrew Wilkie in Denison, and his extensive negotiated agreement with the Gillard Labor minority government, will continue to be the subject of much scrutiny over the course of the Parliament.

The Liberal Party in Tasmania is at a crossroads over its capacity to attract both the voting public and candidates who can connect with the constituency.

References

Australian Electoral Commission (AEC). n.d.(a). *Election Results—House of Representatives*. Canberra: Australian Electoral Commission, viewed 5 October 2010, <http://results.aec.gov.au/15508/Website/HouseDivisionMenu-15508-TAS.htm>

Australian Electoral Commission (AEC). n.d.(b). *Election Results—Senate*. Canberra: Australian Electoral Commission, viewed 5 October 2010, <http://results.aec.gov.au/15508/Website/SenateStateFirstPrefsByGroup-15508-TAS.htm>

17. The Australian Capital Territory

Malcolm Mackerras

Labor always seems to perform well in the Australian Capital Territory and the 2010 election was no exception. Easily winning both seats in the House of Representatives and getting the first senator elected proved to be the usual doddle for the party. Yet there were three interesting aspects of these elections and they will be considered in turn.

The first relates to the under-representation of the Australian Capital Territory in the House of Representatives to which I referred in my past two contributions in this series on this subject. Having discussed this subject, I noticed that there would, from time to time, be redistributions of seats in the Australian Capital Territory, purely to equalise the numbers, but *not* to give the Territory the third seat to which I have long thought it to be entitled. At the conclusion of one recent chapter, I wrote: 'All of this reassures us that the ACT seats will be the biggest two at the next election in 2007. The only thing we do not know is whether it will be Canberra or whether it will be Fraser in which the poorest vote value lies' (Mackerras 2005, 239).

A redistribution took place during 2005. All it did was shift 9176 electors from Fraser to Canberra. That meant the enrolment for Canberra (on the new boundaries) at 30 November 2005 was 119 422 while that for Fraser was 109 838. By the time the 2007 election actually took place, two years later, Canberra had 122 401 electors and Fraser 116 341. So Canberra had the biggest enrolment in the country and Fraser the second biggest. In 2010 the enrolments were 124 294 in Canberra and 123 647 in Fraser. It was very clearly 'one vote, one value' between Canberra and Fraser but not between each electorate and the rest of Australia.

If we compare the Australian Capital Territory with the Northern Territory, it can be noticed that, in terms of area, the larger division is Canberra and Lingiari, respectively. The smaller is Fraser and Solomon, respectively. So, how do their numbers compare? In Canberra in 2010 the enrolment was 124 294; in Lingiari, 61 168. In Fraser, it was 123 647; in Solomon, 59 891. Bearing in mind that the area of Solomon is approximately the same as that of Fraser, such a numerical discrepancy is very difficult to justify. In the comparison between Canberra and Lingiari, the justification is better. In area, Lingiari is huge while Canberra is quite small. It is worth noting that the boundaries of Lingiari and Solomon were the same for the 2001, 2004, 2007 and 2010 elections. The same map will apply again in 2013.

One would have to say that the 2005 ACT exercise, apart from meeting statutory requirements, was a quite unnecessary redistribution. Yet something else could be said in its defence. The 2007 and 2010 ACT map is more logical than that which applied in 2001 and 2004. The boundary between Fraser in the north and Canberra in the south runs from east to west along the Molonglo River, then Lake Burley Griffin and then the Molonglo again until it reaches the ACT boundary with New South Wales. Lake Burley Griffin itself lies wholly within the Division of Canberra, as do all the buildings one associates with the seat of government: Parliament House, The Lodge, Government House and the High Court. That is appropriate.

In my opinion, however, the case for restoring the third seat in the Australian Capital Territory is as compelling as ever but is not going to be recognised by the current legislation. I mentioned previously how, during the 40th Parliament (2002–04) there was enacted the *Commonwealth Electoral Amendment Act 2004* to implement the *Report of the Joint Standing Committee on Electoral Matters*. This was a contrivance to ensure that the Australian Capital Territory and Northern Territory would each have two seats, notwithstanding that the Australian Capital Territory's enrolment is more than twice that of the Northern Territory (see Table 17.1).

Table 17.1 Elector Numbers, Populations and Seat Numbers for the Australian Capital Territory and the Northern Territory

Territory	Electors enrolled 2010	Population 2003	Seats 2001, 2004, 2007, 2010	Seats by population 2003	Seats by electors 2010	Mackerras suggested entitlements
ACT	247 941	322 871	2	2	3	3
NT	121 059	199 760	2	1	1	2
Ratio	2.05:1	1.62:1				

Note: See also Tables 17.3, 17.4 and 17.5.

Source: Most of the above data come from Parliament of Australia (2003). Population and seat numbers can be found on page 18.

I wrote then:

> The contrivance enacted by the Parliament has produced a grotesque violation of the principle of 'one vote, one value'. If the formula now based on population were applied to elector numbers, there would be three seats for the ACT and one for the NT. The population formula actually produced two and one, respectively. The Parliament's contrivance restores the numbers as two each. However, it would be quite easy to

devise a formula, consistent with the Constitution, which would make the numbers three and two. I have devised such a formula but lack of space prevents me from giving its details here. (Mackerras 2005, 237)

It should be mentioned that Canberra and Fraser were not the only divisions with high enrolments at the 2010 election. In Victoria, the Prime Minister's seat of Lalor had 116 976 electors while McEwen had 115 811 and Gorton 113 675. There is, however, a difference between Lalor, McEwen and Gorton, on the one hand, and Canberra and Fraser on the other. During 2010 there was a redistribution of Victoria's federal divisions. It was not completed in time to apply for the August election. It is worth noting, however, that this Victorian redistribution gives 86 830 electors to Gorton, 85 898 to Lalor and 90 003 to McEwen. In other words, in the States, regular redistributions stop electorates from becoming too bloated. In the Australian Capital Territory, that is not so.

The second interesting aspect of the ACT elections relates to the fact that both the Labor members retired. Bob McMullan was Senator for the Australian Capital Territory from 1988 to 1996. Then he was Member for Canberra from 1996 to 1998. Consequent upon the 1997 redistribution (which reduced the Territory from three to two members), he was elected to Fraser at the 1998, 2001, 2004 and 2007 elections, retiring in 2010. Annette Ellis was a Member of the ACT Legislative Assembly from 1992 to 1995 and was elected in 1996 for Namadgi, a division that existed only at that election (see Table 17.2). At the 1998, 2001, 2004 and 2007 elections, she was elected for Canberra, retiring in 2010.

Table 17.2 ACT Shares of Two-Party Preferred Votes

Election	Number of members	Labor (%)	Liberal (%)	Swing (%)
1966	1	55.8	44.2	0.9 to Labor
1969	1	71.6	28.4	15.8 to Labor
1972	1	68.0	32.0	3.6 to Liberal
1974	2	59.7	40.3	8.3 to Liberal
1975	2	49.3	50.7	10.4 to Liberal
1977	2	54.3	45.7	5.0 to Labor
1980	2	58.6	41.4	4.3 to Labor
1983	2	65.5	34.5	6.9 to Labor
1984	2	62.0	38.0	3.5 to Liberal
1987	2	63.2	36.8	1.2 to Labor
1990	2	58.5	41.5	4.7 to Liberal
1993	2	61.2	38.8	2.7 to Labor
1996	3	55.4	44.6	5.8 to Liberal
1998	2	62.4	37.6	7.0 to Labor
2001	2	61.1	38.9	1.3 to Liberal
2004	2	61.5	38.5	0.4 to Labor
2007	2	63.4	36.6	1.9 to Labor
2010	2	61.7	38.3	1.7 to Liberal

Both the successor Labor candidates (former economics professor Andrew Leigh in the safer Fraser and former diplomat Gai Brodtmann in the weaker Canberra) had no trouble winning their respective seats. Both divisions, however, produced two-party preferred vote swings to the Liberals. I attribute those swings to retirement slump. My reason for saying that is my noticing the swing against Senator Gary Humphries (Liberal) at the same election. Why would there be a swing to Liberal for the House of Representatives but against that party in the Senate election? Retirement slump is the obvious answer.

The third interesting aspect of the ACT elections relates to the Senate election. Over the years there has always been speculation about the possibility that the Liberal Party might fail to get a senator elected. Thus, in 1998 it was thought that the candidate for the Democrats, Rick Farley, might take the seat from the then Liberal Senator, Margaret Reid, while in 2004 and 2007 it was thought that the candidate for the Greens, Kerrie Tucker, might defeat Humphries. This never happened, though it should be noted that Reid was able to secure a quota in her own right in 1984, 1987, 1990, 1993, 1996 and 2001, but not in 1983, nor at her second-last election in 1998.

Humphries has now been elected thrice: in 2004, 2007 and 2010. In 2004 the quota was 70 436 votes. Kate Lundy polled 85 616 votes and Humphries 79 264. That meant the surplus votes were 15 180 for Lundy and 8828 for Humphries. The 2007 vote saw Lundy's surplus expand to 16 107 while that of Humphries contracted to 1447. The quota in 2007 was 75 108 votes. The main point, however, is that both in 2004 and in 2007 there was no need to count votes beyond the first preferences.

The interesting feature of the 2010 count is that there was a need for further counting. The first-preference votes are set out in Table 17.5 and I now give a description of the further counts. Lundy's surplus of 15 846 was distributed as follows: 14 954 went to the second Labor candidate, David Mathews, 554 went to Greens candidate, Lin Hatfield Dodds, and 182 to Humphries. The remaining votes scattered to the other candidates or were exhausted. Consequently, Humphries led the count with 75 758 votes to 51 154 for Hatfield Dodds and 16 322 for Mathews. Following the exclusion of two further candidates, Humphries had 76 485, Hatfield Dodds 51 206, Mathews 16 381, Churchill 4050, Glynn 2675 and Parris 2032.

Table 17.3 Election of Member for Canberra, 2010

Electors enrolled	124 294	Formal votes	112 156 (95.1%)
Electors who voted	117 911 (94.9%)	Informal votes	5755 (4.9%)

Candidates	Votes	%	Swing (%)
Jones, Giulia (Liberal)	41 732	37.2	+2.1
Ellerman, Sue (Greens)	20 816	18.6	+5.6
Brodtmann, Gai (Labor)	49 608	44.2	−6.9
			−0.8
Two-candidate preferred			
Brodtmann (Labor)	66 335	59.1	−2.7
Jones (Liberal)	45 821	40.9	+2.7

Table 17.4 Election of Member for Fraser, 2010

Electors enrolled	123 647	Formal votes	111 541 (95.6%)
Electors who voted	116 712 (94.4%)	Informal votes	5171 (2.1%)

Candidates	Votes	%	Swing (%)
Milligan, James (Liberal)	36 148	32.4	+1.2
Hedges-Phillips, Quintin (Secular Party of Australia)	2175	2.0	+2.0
Leigh, Andrew (Labor)	51 092	45.8	−5.3
Esguerra, Indra (Greens)	22 126	19.8	+6.5
			−4.4
Two-candidate preferred			
Leigh (Labor)	71 613	64.2	−0.9
Milligan (Liberal)	39 928	35.8	+0.9

Table 17.5 Election of Senators for the Australian Capital Territory, 2010

Electors enrolled	247 941	Formal votes	229 272
Electors who voted	235 271	Informal votes	5999
Senators to be elected	2	Quota for election	76 425

	Candidates	First-preference votes	Surplus votes
Group A	Lundy, Kate (Labor)	92 271	15 846
	Mathews, David (Labor)	1368	
Group B	Churchill, Darren (Dems)	3758	
	David, Anthony (Dems)	299	
Group C	Hatfield Dodds, Lin (Greens)	50 600	
	Parris, Hannah, (Greens)	1946	
Group D	Humphries, Gary (Liberal)	75 576	
	Watts, Matthew (Liberal)	887	
Ungrouped	Glynn, John (Independent)	2567	

References

Australian Electoral Commission (AEC). 2005. *2005 Redistribution of the Australian Capital Territory into Electoral Divisions: Commonwealth Electoral Act 1918*, December, Section 75. Canberra: Australian Electoral Commission.

Parliament of Australia. 2003. *The Parliament of the Commonwealth of Australia, Joint Standing Committee on Electoral Matters, November 2003, Territory Representation: Report of the inquiry into increasing the minimum representation of the Australian Capital Territory and the Northern Territory in the House of Representatives*. Canberra: Parliament of Australia.

Mackerras, Malcolm. 2005. 'The Australian Capital Territory'. In Marian Simms and John Warhurst (eds), *Mortgage Nation: The 2004 Australian election*. Perth: API Network.

18. Queensland

Ian Ward

In mid-August and at the height of an election focused upon on the contest between the major parties and their leaders, the mayors of Richmond, Hinchinbrook, Mount Isa and several other north Queensland local councils announced they would lobby the Local Government Association of Queensland (LGAQ) to press for the creation of a separate State. In Kennedy, Bob Katter—en route to achieving a primary vote of 46.7 per cent and a comfortable victory—hoped this would be a spark to 'light the fuse' (Vogler 2010). This serves to remind readers that Queensland is a large, diverse, decentralised State with distinctive political geography and culture. There is a further lesson here. In the colourful language of Bob Katter, the north Queensland mayors had had 'a gutful of the blood-sucking establishment of the south' (Calligeros 2010).

In Queensland, the ALP suffered a (two-party preferred) swing of 5.58 per cent—larger than in New South Wales (4.84 per cent), and more than double the Australia-wide swing from Labor of 2.58 per cent. Prior to the 21 August poll, Queensland was widely tipped as a State in which the election would be decided because of the number of seats held by narrow margins. Each side 'launched' its campaign in Brisbane. In the last week of the campaign, Brisbane also played host to a televised forum in which the two leaders fielded questions from an audience of swinging voters.

As a further pointer to the State's perceived importance, beginning well before the campaign proper and when Kevin Rudd remained Prime Minister, the leaders of both major parties made repeated visits to Queensland regions. As it happened, the pundits and parties were right to identify Queensland as a key battleground. At its first federal outing, the new Liberal National Party (LNP) gathered 1.13 million votes and claimed 21 seats. Labor emerged with just eight seats. In all, seven ALP-held seats fell. Moreover, Labor failed to claim Dickson and Herbert—each transformed by the 2009 redistribution into 'notionally' Labor seats. Table 18.1 does show some variation in the swing against Labor in the seats it lost. It also shows that the newly created LNP took seats from Labor in areas where, prior to their 2008 merger, both the Liberal Party and The Nationals had held sway.

Table 18.1 Labor* Seats Falling to the LNP in Queensland

Electorate	Location	Pre-poll margin	2PP[a] swing	Party room
Bonner	Inner eastern Brisbane, urban	4.5%	7.35%	Liberal
Brisbane	Inner Brisbane, urban	4.6%	5.73%	Liberal
Dawson	Central Queensland, regional	2.6%	5.02%	Nationals
Dickson*	Northern outer Brisbane, urban	0.8%	5.89%	Liberal
Forde	Southern outer Brisbane, urban	3.4%	4.99%	Liberal
Flynn	Central Queensland, rural	2.2%	5.82%	Nationals
Herbert*[b]	Central Queensland, regional	0.0%	2.20%	Liberal
Leichhardt	Cairns and Cape York, regional	4.1%	8.61%	Nationals
Longman	Sunshine Coast, mostly urban	1.9%	3.79%	Liberal

* Includes two seats with sitting LNP members but which had been transformed into 'notionally Labor' by a redistribution completed in 2009

[b] 2PP = two-party preferred

Sources: AEC (2010); a ABC (2010).

'All Politics is Local'

James McGrath oversaw the LNP campaign in Queensland. McGrath had been recruited by Malcolm Turnbull and the federal Liberals to run their national marginal-seats campaign. A casualty of the Liberals' leadership change, McGrath was subsequently exiled to his home State as Queensland LNP campaign director after a falling out with Liberal Federal Director, Brian Loughnane. McGrath added a new level of professionalism to the LNP. Prior to McGrath's April arrival, the LNP had 'botched' several candidate preselections, failing to manage Peter Dutton's transition to the safe Gold Coast seat of McPherson in October 2009, and endorsing a teenage outsider in Longman in March. The party had also publicly pursued—and ultimately dis-endorsed—the Member for Ryan, Michael Johnson, for refusing to surrender a campaign war chest he had accumulated. McGrath's *vita* included a stint with the British Conservatives where the Party Chairman with whom he worked, Francis Maude, had observed his 'brilliant way of combining the ground war and the air war'—of shaping the campaigns fought by local candidates on the ground to feed off the overarching media campaign (Kerr 2010).

The variation in the swing away from Labor in the seats it lost to the LNP recorded in Table 18.1 suggests the 'air war' alone is an insufficient explanation and that local factors also contributed to the waning of Labor support in Queensland. Given Queensland's political geography, the 'ground war' in its 30 seats inevitably took different forms. In early August, Liberal polling reportedly showed an 'erratic pattern' across key marginal seats and volatility across Queensland, which pointed to the election being a series of 'individual battles' (Coorey 2010). It is often difficult to know just how much the ebb and flow of local issues, or the standing of local candidates, contributes to a final result.

At first glance, a solid 'ground war' would seem to require a strong candidate. In the north Queensland seat of Leichhardt, the LNP's endorsement of Warren Entsch appears to have been a key factor. Roy Morgan Research estimates it gave the LNP a 2 per cent advantage (see *Insiders*, 15 August 2010, ABC TV). The Labor incumbent, Jim Turnour, had been a 'diligent and committed MP'. But in the 11 years Entsch had spent representing Leichhardt before retiring in 2007, he had made his mark as—in the words of the *Cairns Post* (21 August 2010), which endorsed him as the 'experienced voice we need'—'a love-him or hate-him personality, a foot-stomper and table-thumper'. Entsch reclaimed Leichhardt for the LNP with a 9.1 per cent buffer. In the inner-urban seat of Brisbane, the LNP preselected another former Liberal MHR. Therese Gambaro had represented the outer-northern Brisbane seat of Petrie from 1996 until 2007. She defeated the ALP's long-serving Arch Bevis, although with a smaller 5.73 per cent swing. In Bonner, Ross Vasta recontested the same seat he lost after a single term in 2007 and gained a 7.35 per cent swing.

Yet despite injudiciously endorsing a teenaged and inexperienced Wyatt Roy, the LNP still claimed Longman. And for its part Labor appears not to have profited from endorsing several well-known candidates. In Dawson (where it suffered a 5.02 per cent swing), Labor's preselection of the well-known Mackay Mayor, Mike Brunker, to replace 'the rather odd James Bidgood' (Wilson 2010) did not secure it the advantage pundits had predicted. Nor did Labor benefit from running the former Townsville Mayor Tony Mooney in Herbert. But perhaps the ultimate folly of presuming local campaigns turn upon well-known and liked candidates is found in Griffith. The abrupt dumping of Kevin Rudd as Labor leader on 24 June triggered a flood of indignant calls to talkback radio stations in Brisbane. Anger at the manner in which a Queenslander prime minister had been summarily demoted was sufficiently palpable that the LNP considered how they might capitalise on this in their election advertising (Balogh 2010). Rudd's stoicism, his admission to hospital for surgery, and willingness to thereafter campaign for the re-election of the Gillard Government in marginal seats are all likely to have boosted his cause. Yet in Griffith (where he campaigned on his record in delivering to 'southside' voters), he suffered a sizeable 9.01 per cent contraction in his primary vote.

One test of on-the-ground organisation and staffing levels is the manner in which parties manage requests for postal votes. The LNP held an advantage in safe seats such as Groom. But in key marginal Queensland seats Labor was reported to be 'streets ahead' and eager to remedy an error made in its 2009

State campaign. For example, Australian Electoral Commission (AEC) data show that, up to 12 August, Labor had 'requested 4004 votes in the Gladstone-based seat of Flynn to the LNP's 1471' and 3864 to 1669 in Bonner (Chalmers 2010). As it transpired, the LNP received more postal first preferences in both Flynn (4805 to 2147) and Bonner (3643 to 2573), just as it did in other marginal seats such as Herbert (2069 to 1791) and Leichhardt (2289 to 1402). Indeed (as Table 18.2 records) Labor secured more postal votes in just six of the 31 Queensland seats decided on preferences. This lends credence to the argument that Labor suffered electorally because many of the postal vote applications it enthusiastically dispatched arrived in the second week of the campaign and at the very nadir of national Labor's fortunes.

In some seats the importance of individual events rather than individual candidates has been highlighted. Longman is a case in point. Labor had 'privately been counting on Longman as a win', believing that Roy's age 'was starting to count against him' (Chalmers and Dickinson 2010). During the last week of the campaign, however, the Labor incumbent, Jon Sullivan, tactlessly dismissed a constituent who complained at a public forum of the waiting list his son faced to see a paediatrician. Sullivan was jeered and this became the story of the moment. It is an episode Wyatt Roy believes contributed to his victory: 'The reality is it had some effect on people's votes' (Thomas 2010). He might be right; the polling of both parties suggests that Labor did suffer a decisive swing against it in Longman in the last two days of the campaign (Atkins 2010a). The Queensland election did yield a number of similar episodes. For example, suggesting that 'ground warfare' is a more than apt metaphor, Mike Brunker engaged in a widely reported 'punch-up' with the local turf club president over election signage (*World Today*, 16 August 2010, ABC Radio). In Dickson, where Dutton's much publicised efforts to find a safer seat appear to have had no lasting impact, Liberal campaign workers and a supposed Labor 'rent-a-crowd' exchanged push-and-shove politics outside his campaign office on a day Tony Abbot had scheduled a visit (*crikey.com*, 4 August 2010). Cameras captured a similar incident in Longman in mid-August. Such episodes might have added colour, but are unlikely to have turned the campaign.

Table 18.2 Queensland Seats Decided by Preferences, 2010

Division	Won by	Seat type	Changed hands	Most postal votes	First-preference swing against ALP	Two-party preferred swing against ALP
Ryan	LNP	Outer metro	No	LNP	13.54	5.95
Brisbane	LNP	Inner metro	Yes	LNP	13.22	5.73
Bonner	LNP	Outer metro	Yes	LNP	12.73	7.35
Moreton	ALP	Inner metro	No	LNP	12.12	4.88
Rankin	ALP	Outer metro	No	ALP	10.98	6.26
Dickson	LNP	Outer metro	Yes*	LNP	10.95	5.89
Oxley	ALP	Outer metro	No	ALP	10.91	5.57
Lilley	ALP	Inner metro	No	ALP	10.19	4.77
Capricornia	ALP	Provincial	No	LNP	9.57	8.40
Blair	ALP	Rural	No	ALP	9.23	2.74
Fairfax	LNP	Rural	No	LNP	9.07	3.98
Griffith	ALP	Outer metro	No	ALP	9.01	3.86
Forde	LNP	Outer metro	Yes	ALP	8.92	4.99
Kennedy	Ind.	Rural	No	Ind.	8.78	4.65
Leichhardt	LNP	Rural	Yes	LNP	8.37	8.61
Longman	LNP	Provincial	Yes	LNP	8.04	3.79
Dawson	LNP	Rural	Yes	LNP	7.35	5.02
Flynn	LNP	Rural	Yes	LNP	6.78	5.82
Petrie	ALP	Outer metro	No	LNP	6.27	1.70
Herbert	LNP	Provincial	Yes*	LNP	3.12	2.20
Fisher	LNP	Rural	No	LNP	2.71	0.60

* Dickson and Herbert were made 'notionally' ALP seats by the 2009 redistribution

Source: AEC (2010).

Pork-Barrel Politics

That 'all politics is local' is most visible when political leaders come to town to 'pork-barrel'. In their analysis of the advantage of incumbency made prior to Labor's leadership change and the formal campaign, Tom Dusevic and George Megalogenis (2010) observed how the Rudd Government had targeted, amongst other key marginal seats, Herbert, Longman, Flynn and Dawson with community Cabinet meetings and carefully focused economic stimulus and 'nation-building' spending on roads, education and health care. They described Herbert in north Queensland as 'the first stop on the pork express', noted that Rudd, as Prime Minister, 'has been a frequent visitor to Townsville', and that Labor had pledged to provide, amongst other initiatives, a $318 million Townsville hospital upgrade, a GP super clinic and $17.3 million of community infrastructure spending. The wider point here is that governments are alert to political advantage and that, in an era of continuous campaigning, the battle for key marginal seats commences well before the start of the declared campaign.

After the issue of writs, and when it became clear the party was tracking poorly in many Queensland seats, Labor candidates attempted to arrest the decline by 'localising' their campaigns (van Onselen 2010). Localising required digging into the pork-barrel. In early August, Gillard was dispatched—as *The Australian* disapprovingly reported—to 'improve Labor's stocks in far north Queensland with two days of cash handouts to the marginal seats of Leichhardt and Herbert' (Maher 2010). An analysis undertaken by an equally unimpressed *Courier-Mail* of Labor's efforts to 'sandbag' Leichhardt, Dawson, Flynn and Longman against a rising LNP tide showed that it had 'rolled out the most promises in Queensland in those seats as part of a defensive political strategy' (Wardill and Balogh 2010). For its part, the *Cairns Post* complained that Kennedy, 'Queensland's largest electorate has not been promised a single region-specific project by either of the major parties during the 2010 election campaign'. The reason for this, locals ventured, was that, unlike Leichhardt, 'we are not a marginal seat so we don't have the major parties bidding against each other for votes' (Eliot 2010).

Regional Issues

The adage that 'all politics is local' reminds us that issues that might drive voters need not be those which preoccupy party leaders. Of course all candidates pursue votes beneath the umbrella of their party's national campaign. Its influence cannot be discounted. For example, the Liberal leader pledged to 'stop the boats', and Michele Levin of Roy Morgan Research observed that this was a 'sleeper issue' in Leichhardt, where some 6 per cent of voters were 'mostly concerned about boat people and immigration' and intending to vote for Entsch (*Insiders*, 15 August 2010, ABC TV). But the campaign in Leichhardt was also coloured by the decidedly local Wild Rivers issue. It appears to have provided Entsch with Indigenous booth workers and cost Labor Aboriginal votes on which it might otherwise have counted. Entsch says that the unpopularity of the Queensland Government's 2005 legislation and the Wilderness Society campaign 'to lock away north Queensland rivers' contributed to his victory (*SBS News*, 21 August 2010).

In the central Queensland seats of Capricornia, which includes Rockhampton, and Flynn, based on Gladstone, Labor seemingly suffered a 'QR effect', with traditional supporters turning against it in protest at the Bligh Government's decision to privatise Queensland Rail (QR) (Atkins 2010b). Up and down the Queensland coast, recreational fishers and industry activists held 'rallies attracting hundreds of people' (Cleary 2010) in protest at, as Warren Truss put it, Labor's 'secret preference deal' with the Greens to 'close down more fishing areas off our coast' (Warren Truss, Media release, 27 July 2010). Labor's interest in pursuing a Coral Sea Conservation Zone stretching from south of Rockhampton to Cape York triggered fears that commercial and recreational fishing would be restricted that resonated in the central and north Queensland coastal seats of Flynn, Dawson, Herbert and Leichhardt, each of which Labor lost.

Mining appears to have also loomed large as an issue in central Queensland in ways it did not in the metropolitan south-eastern corner. Concerns generated by the hostile industry reaction to Labor's super-profits mining tax reverberated in seats such as Flynn, which encompasses Emerald, Blackwater and Biloela in addition to Gladstone—all centres largely reliant upon servicing the mining industry and fearful that companies might scale back or withdraw. Labor's deal to secure Greens preferences in 15 Queensland seats in return for Senate preferences ramped up this anxiety. As Senator Ron Boswell (whose web site curiously carried both The Nationals' and LNP logos) said in support of the LNP's Capricornia candidate, a Labor government with Greens in control of the Senate would stamp on coalmining, 'turn Rockhampton into a ghost town and decimate the Central Queensland economy' (Ron Boswell, Media release, 4 August 2010). The same issue will have resonated in Dawson—also covering the central and north Queensland coal belt.

'Queensland is Different'

Ahead of the election, pundits suggested it was likely that the high tide of ALP support Rudd achieved in Queensland would ebb in 2010. Figure 18.1 puts this prediction in context. It compares the two-party preferred vote achieved by the

ALP in Queensland with its wider electoral performance in postwar elections. Queensland and the town of Barcaldine might lay claim to being the birthplace of the ALP, but Queenslanders have long been more reluctant than the rest of the nation to embrace federal Labor. This reluctance was clearly evident in 2010.

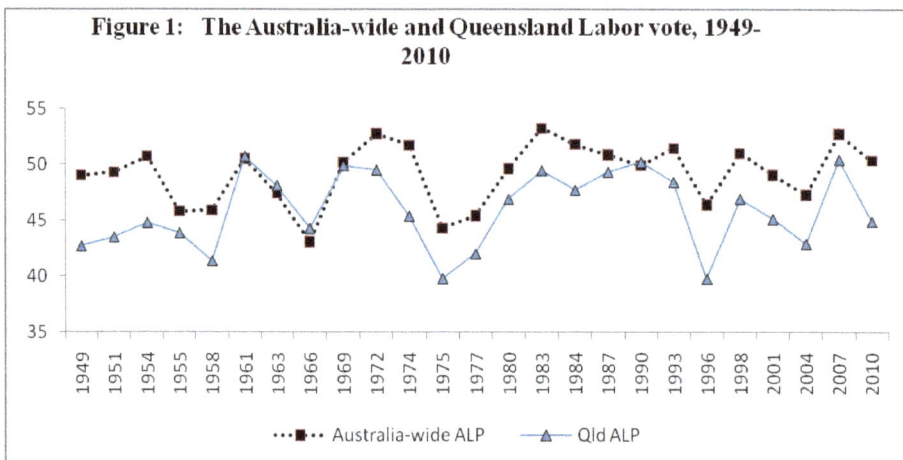

Figure 18.1 The Australia-Wide and Queensland Labor Vote, 1949–2010

Source: AEC (n.d.[b]).

It is true that, at the State level, Labor has governed Queensland (with a short interruption in 1996–98) since 1989. This has often been explained by the disinclination of 'Beattie Liberals' to install a State Government dominated by The Nationals. Figure 18.2 plots the percentage of Queenslanders intending to cast a primary vote for the ALP as measured by Newspoll. It suggests that for much of the past two decades Queenslanders have differentiated between State and federal Labor. The merger of the Liberal and National parties in 2008 to establish the LNP did not prove the hoped-for 'game changer' at the 2009 Queensland State elections. But it might after all have given Labor's opponents a fillip. Starting in 2008, but with a brief correction for the State election, the Queensland State Labor Government's popularity spiralled rapidly downward—collapsing by September 2010 to just 29 per cent. This evidently damaged federal Labor's prospects.

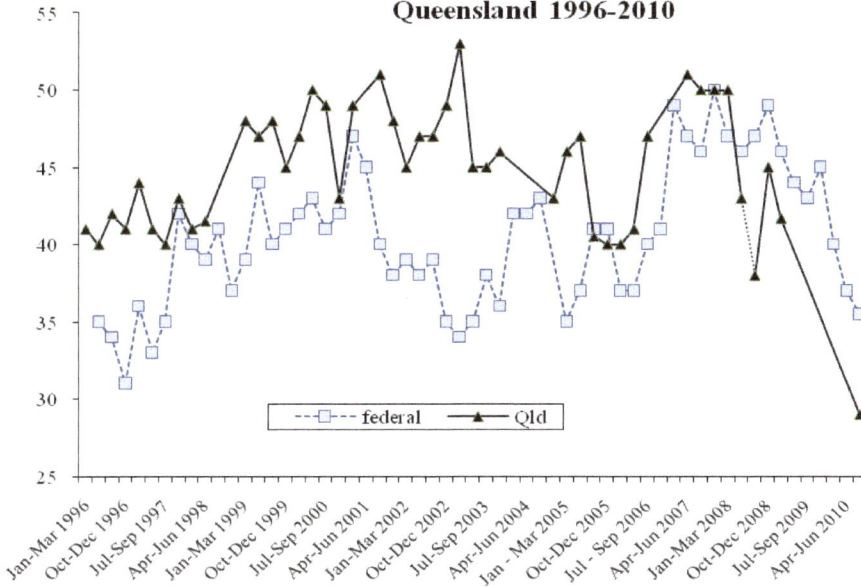

Figure 18.2 Newspolls: The State and federal ALP primary vote in
Queensland, 1996–2010

Source: Newspoll (n.d.).

Table 18.3 The Swing Against Labor in Different Regions (per cent)*

	NSW	Queensland	Australia
Inner metropolitan	6.5	5.1	3.3
Outer metropolitan	6.4	5.6	1.9
Provincial	1.7	5.6	1.7
Rural	3.4	5.4	3.1

* The AEC classifies inner metropolitan seats as those in capital cities comprising well-established, built-
up suburbs, and outer metropolitan seats as those containing large areas of recent suburban expansion.

Source: AEC (n.d.[a]).

Across Queensland, the two-party preferred swing away from Labor was much
more uniform than in any other State, including New South Wales, which
also had an unpopular State Labor Government. Table 18.3 is based on the
demographic classification of seats by the Australian Electoral Commission. It
suggests that voters in Queensland responded in a quite distinctive way and
that particular State-wide factors were in play. Chief amongst these will have
been the unpopularity of the Bligh Government. This was cleverly exploited
by the LNP whose internal research identified Bligh as Gillard's Achilles heel
(Wardill and Balogh 2010).

Air Wars

According to the media monitors Xtreme Info, the televised advertising campaigns of the two major parties 'intensively targeted' Queensland. During the five-week campaign, in Brisbane Labor aired 812 screenings of its advertisements, and the LNP, 706 (Crabb 2010). Labor's Queensland election advertising was heavily negative and involved a blitz in the 10 days before the media blackout. In keeping with Labor's national campaign, much of it sought to demonise Tony Abbott. The LNP, however, adopted a distinctive approach to its Queensland 'air war'. Taking a cue from Bligh's elevation to the federal ALP presidency at the beginning of August, the LNP warned that she had become 'Gillard's boss' and rolled out a message in leaflets, direct mail, via its candidates, in press and television advertising, and on YouTube. It was simple and direct: 'don't let Gillard do to Australia what Bligh has done to Queensland.'

The Bligh Government's standing had been dashed by its mishandling of health and water policies. It seems likely, however, that voter discontent with Labor owed much to the particular impact of the global financial crisis from which Queensland's economy had not rebounded. In the year to March 2010, the Queensland State final demand (SFD: in effect the GDP for the State) had risen by just 0.3 per cent and at a lower rate than any other State and significantly below the sister mining sate of Western Australia (6.1 per cent) and even New South Wales (4.7 per cent). Queensland experienced a 17.8 per cent dip in business investment—unparalleled among mainland States—and had the lowest level of consumption growth (1.8 per cent). Queensland's tourism industry had stalled (Battellino 2010). In the run-up to the 2010 poll, Queenslanders also faced an above-average, 12 cents-a-litre hike in petrol prices and escalating water and power utility bills. The State Labor Government, which had removed a longstanding petrol subsidy and privatised power companies, bore much of the blame. It was a ready and obvious target for LNP advertising.

As the election campaign closed, the LNP ran a full-page *Courier-Mail* ad that dwarfed its generic 'end the waste, pay back the debt, stop the boats' message with a blunt invitation to 'take the smile off [Bligh's] face' (see Figure 18.3). On polling day itself, the LNP State campaign director, demonstrating his 'brilliant way' of combining the ground and 'air war', reinforced this media campaign with a flood of SMS messages in key seats such as Herbert, and with, at polling places around Queensland, the same grainy pictures of Bligh and Gillard accompanied by advice to 'put Labor last'.

Figure 18.3 Last-Day LNP Print-Media Election Advertising

Source: Vexnews (2010).

With its pitch to punish the Bligh Government by voting against federal Labor, the LNP was a direct beneficiary of an extensive Queensland Council of Unions campaign launched in mid-2009 aiming to reverse a State Government decision to privatise rail and other public assets. This campaign fuelled popular disillusionment with the Bligh Government amongst a constituency on which Labor might otherwise have counted. It is also likely to have blunted—until the very last minute when an Abbott government and a resurrected WorkChoices loomed as very real prospects—the enthusiasm of unions such as the Australian Manufacturing Workers' Union and Australian Services Union to contribute organisers and other support to Labor's 2010 federal campaign.

A Final Note

The LNP's success in cultivating sullen resentment of Labor was not matched by an appealing positive message. Hence, the LNP was not the sole beneficiary of dissatisfaction with the Labor brand. Especially in metropolitan Brisbane, some erstwhile Labor voters split to the left and to the Greens. As Table 18.2 shows, in most metropolitan seats Labor's primary vote fell significantly but this translated into an appreciably smaller two-party preferred swing. While Labor bled primary votes to, it also secured preferences from, the Australian Greens (whose overall Queensland lower-house first-preference vote improved to 10.92 per cent). In the upper-house race, the Greens accumulated 12.76 per cent of first-preference votes and secured their very first Queensland Senate seat (at Labor's expense).

References

Atkins, Dennis. 2010a. 'Wave of anger sweeping Queensland'. *Sunday Mail*, 22 August.

Atkins, Dennis. 2010b. 'We'll be the swing kings next time we vote, too'. *The Courier-Mail*, 4–5 September.

Australian Broadcasting Corporation (ABC). 2010. 'Herbert'. *Australia Votes 2010*, ABC Elections, Last updated 7 September 2010, <http://www.abc.net.au/elections/federal/2010/guide/herb.htm>

Australian Electoral Commission (AEC). n.d.(a). *House of Representatives. Division classifications*. Canberra: Australian Electoral Commission, viewed 28 February 2011, <http://results.aec.gov.au/15508/Website/HouseDivisionClassifications-15508-NAT.htm>

Australian Electoral Commission (AEC). n.d.(b). *House of Representatives. Two party preferred results 1949–present.* Canberra: Australian Electoral Commission, viewed 28 February 2011, <www.aec.gov.au/Elections/ Australian_Electoral_History/House_of_Representative_1949_Present. htm>

Australian Electoral Commission (AEC). 2010. *Election 2010 Virtual Tallyroom.* Canberra: Australian Electoral Commission, viewed 28 February 2011, <http://results.aec.gov.au/15508/Website/HouseTppByDivision-15508-NAT.htm>

Balogh, Stefanie. 2010. 'Kevin Rudd the x-factor in Julia Gillard's election chances'. *The Courier-Mail*, 19 July.

Battellino, Ric. 2010. Address to the Moreton Bay Better Business Luncheon by the Deputy Governor of the Reserve Bank of Australia, 20 August, Brisbane, viewed 28 February 2011, <http://www.brr.com.au/event/67966/rba-mr-ric-battellino-deputy-governor-reserve-bank-of-australia-address-to-the-moreton-bay-better-business-luncheon>

Calligeros, Marissa. 2010. 'State split: north Queensland seeks independence'. *Brisbane Times*, 10 August, viewed 28 February 2011, <http://www. brisbanetimes.com.au/queensland/state-split-north-queensland-seeks-independence-20100810-11ui5.html>

Chalmers, Emma. 2010. 'Postals push in marginals'. *The Courier-Mail*, 14–15 August.

Chalmers, Emma. and Dickinson, Alex. 2010. 'Dad will vote for ALP after Longman MP Jon Sullivan says sorry over disabled remark at public forum'. *The Courier-Mail*, 20 August.

Cleary, Paul. 2010. 'Marine park push sees fishing lobby wade in for a fight'. *The Australian*, 31 July.

Coorey, Phillip. 2010. 'Research shows no big swing but local fights'. *Sydney Morning Herald*, 4 August.

Crabb, Annabel. 2010. 'Labor pips Coalition in election ad spending'. *ABC News*, 20 August, viewed 28 February 2011, <http://www.abc.net.au/ news/stories/2010/08/20/2988699.htm>

Dusevic, Tom. and Megalogenis, George. 2010. 'Power of incumbency'. *The Weekend Australian*, 5–6 June.

Eliot, Jennifer. 2010. 'Queensland's largest electorate snubbed'. *Cairns Post*, 18 August.

Kerr, Christian. 2010. 'Liberals praise McGrath magic'. *The Australian*, 24 August.

Maher, Sid. 2010. 'ALP pours millions into key seats'. *The Australian*, 6 August.

Newspoll. n.d. Queensland State and federal voting intention data collected by Newspoll. Commissioned by *The Australian*, viewed 28 February 2011, <http://www.newspoll.com.au>

Thomas, Hedley. 2010. 'Rival blames MP for lost seat'. *The Weekend Australian*, 4–5 September.

van Onselen, Peter. 2010. 'No warmth for ALP in north'. *The Australian*, 20 July.

Vexnews. 2010. 'Own goal: Queensland's disastrous Labor premier is Abbott's delight'. *Vexnews*, 19 August, viewed 28 February 2011, <http://www.vexnews.com/news/10673/own-goal-queenslands-disastrous-labor-premier-is-abbotts-delight/>

Vogler, Sarah. 2010. 'North Queensland mayors want to break free from the high-growth areas of the state'. *The Courier-Mail*, 10 August.

Wardill, Steven. and Balogh, Stefanie. 2010. 'Anna Bligh poisons Julia Gillard's election campaign'. *The Courier-Mail*, 12 August.

Wilson, Jason. 2010. 'Home town blues'. *NewMatilda.com*, 25 June, viewed 28 February 2011, <http://newmatilda.com/2010/06/24/home-town-blues>

19. Western Australia at the Polls: A case of resurgent regionalism

Narelle Miragliotta and Campbell Sharman

The 2010 election affirmed Western Australia's recent status as a conservative heartland State and one of the ALP's most unforgiving electorates. A significant swing was recorded against the ALP (−5.6 per cent), the severity of which can be largely attributed to the Federal Government's proposed mining tax. Labor's failure to assuage local concerns about this impost and the Liberals' deft exploitation of the issue served to reignite the anxieties of WA voters about Canberra's centralist ambitions and lack of responsiveness to State concerns.

The Election Context: It's the mining tax, stupid!

It was inevitable that Canberra's proposed resource rent tax on mining would prove a highly contentious election issue in Western Australia, which has a local economy heavily dependent on the wealth generated by mining activities in the State. A Newspoll conducted in June 2010 revealed that West Australians were more hostile to the tax than their counterparts elsewhere (Shanahan 2010). Voters in Western Australia's marginal electorates were not only less convinced that the tax would deliver any economic benefits but also more apprehensive about its negative effects on the economy.

While the announcement of the mining tax compromised Labor's electoral prospects in Western Australia, it presented its Liberal rivals with unexpected fundraising opportunities. In mid-May, the Liberals were reported to have sent hundreds of letters to various mining companies seeking a financial contribution for a marginal-seats campaign to fight the tax—a request to which the mining chiefs willingly acceded. The Liberals also received significant indirect campaign support from the mining industry. One of the more persistent opponents of the Gillard Government's policy was Andrew (Twiggy) Forrest, the CEO of the Perth-based Fortescue Metals Group, which led the push for a resumption of an advertising campaign against the proposed tax.

The anxiety the mining tax generated in Western Australia was symptomatic of deeper concerns held by its residents. The Rudd/Gillard Government's poor management of the issue reignited longstanding grievances about the failure of those situated east of the Nullarbor Plain to appreciate the State's unique circumstances and its fiscal contribution to the federation. In February, the Grants Commission announced that Western Australia's share of the Goods and Services Tax (GST) would be reduced from 8.1 per cent to 7.1 per cent of the estimated GST revenue for 2010–11 (The Australian 2010). In April, Premier, Colin Barnett, refused to relinquish one-third of the State's GST revenue ($350 million) that was part of a proposed federal–State arrangement for funding a national health and hospitals network. Barnett—who alone of the premiers refused to agree to the deal—justified his decision on the grounds that it would 'jeopardise the future autonomy of Western Australia to manage its own finances' (Maher 2010). Matters were little assisted by the Rudd/Gillard Government's decision to reopen the Curtin detention centre and to send asylum-seekers to the remote outback town of Leonora, prompting complaints from the Premier about the lack of consultation from his federal counterpart.

The Parties and their Campaigns

Coming into the election, the ALP held only four of the State's 15 lower-house electorates. Of these seats, two were especially vulnerable: Gary Gray's seat of Brand, which was home to a significant number of fly-in and fly-out mine workers, and Sharryn Jackson's seat of Hasluck, which contained one of the highest concentration of mining employees in the country. It seemed that federal Labor had all but conceded Western Australia even before the commencement of the campaign. In spite of regular visits by Gillard to Western Australia, the ALP appeared to focus most of its campaigning elsewhere. For its part, State Labor managed to contain much of the intra-party factional rivalries that had destabilised previous federal campaigns (Miragliotta and Sharman 2009).

While the ALP concentrated its attentions and resources on the more populous States of New South Wales and Queensland, the Liberals ran a disciplined local campaign that spoke directly to the concerns of WA voters. Its 'cash cow' advertisement reinforced fears that federal Labor was using the State's mineral wealth to underwrite its profligate spending initiatives. The Liberals' campaign was further enhanced by the party's incumbency at the State level, and the popularity of its premier.

The only irritant for the Liberals was The Nationals. The relationship between the parties has a long and fractious history in Western Australia. In 2006, The Nationals formally dissolved their coalition arrangement with the Liberals (Phillips and Kerr 2007, 310), although they agreed to support their former alliance partner in a minority government at the State level. The Nationals' decision to terminate the coalition, along with their successful negotiation of the 'royalties for the regions' scheme, served to reinvigorate the party's electoral stocks at the 2008 State election. Against this backdrop—and the absence of a coalition agreement that would ordinarily have prevented The Nationals from contesting Liberal-held seats—The Nationals fielded four House of Representative candidates, which was their largest contingent since 2001.

But it was The Nationals' decision to contest Wilson Tuckey's seat of O'Connor that proved most contentious, especially in light of a redistribution that had reduced the Liberals' margin in that electorate from 16.6 to 12.8 per cent. In a replay of previous campaigns, O'Connor became the flashpoint of disputation between the parties (Miragliotta and Sharman 2005). Tony Crook, The Nationals' candidate, exacerbated hostilities by announcing that, should he be elected, he would not align himself with the Coalition in the federal party room. A war of words erupted between the parties, with two prominent Liberal backbenchers charging that the WA Nationals were 'feral', while The Nationals' WA President countered by accusing the Liberals of putting politics ahead of the interests of regional voters (Jerga 2010).

For the Greens, the federal election began under less than propitious circumstances. In May, the Greens' first elected representative to the Legislative Assembly, Adele Carles, resigned from the party following disclosure of an affair with Troy Buswell, a high-profile and controversial minister in the Barnett Liberal minority government. Carles claimed that she had been forced to reveal the relationship under pressure from two of her colleagues—a circumstance that Carles declared had made it untenable for her to remain in the party (Thomson 2010). But the Greens' swift treatment of the matter appeared to suppress any negative publicity, with polling conducted in August showing that the party's support was at 14 per cent.

The Results

The ALP attracted 31.2 per cent of the State-wide primary vote in the House of Representatives—the lowest vote recorded against the party in any State or Territory. Its vote share fell to a historic State low: the lowest primary vote that has been recorded for the ALP in Western Australia at a House of Representatives election since Federation. Similar declines were recorded in its two-party preferred vote, which fell to 43.6 per cent (−3.2 per cent). Nor could the ALP take any comfort in its Senate result. A swing of 6.3 per cent was registered against the ALP, although it did manage to secure two of the six Senate vacancies. The ALP's share of the first-preference vote in the Senate fell to 29.7 per cent—the second-lowest Senate vote ever recorded for the ALP (the lowest was 19.5 per cent in 1901).

As a result of the collapse in its primary vote, the ALP failed to win a lower-house seat on first-preference votes. The preferences of Greens voters ensured the re-election of Gray in Brand, Parkes in Fremantle and Stephen Smith in Perth, but were insufficient to prevent the loss of Hasluck or to enable Labor to claim the potentially winnable seats of Canning and Swan. The only seat in which the ALP increased its primary vote (by 3.5 per cent) was in Canning. Labor's strong showing in Canning can be attributed to its star recruit, Alannah McTiernan, a former high-profile minister in both the Gallop and Carpenter State ALP administrations who had resigned her safe State seat of Armadale to contest Canning against controversial Liberal incumbent Don Randall.

The Liberal's performance in Western Australia was mixed. The Liberals won 47 per cent of the State-wide share of the primary vote in the House of Representatives and regained the seat of Hasluck—a historic event as their candidate, Ken Wyatt, was the first Indigenous person to occupy a seat in the House of Representatives. But the Liberals achieved only a slight bounce in their primary vote (0.7 per cent) and swings were recorded against their candidates in Canning (−2.2 per cent), Hasluck (−1.4 per cent) and Pearce (−0.3 per cent). The Nationals won O'Connor, despite the Liberals investing heavily in their campaign to retain the seat (−10.4 per cent). Further, a swing was registered against the Liberals in the Senate (−3.23 per cent), although they easily attained the necessary quotas to claim three seats.

The Nationals celebrated their best election outcome in more than 30 years, even if the overall increase in the State-wide share of their lower-house primary vote was comparatively small (2.4 per cent). The party achieved a strong result in Durack (formerly Kalgoorlie), gaining 17.7 per cent of the primary vote. They recorded their best result in the seat of O'Connor, where The Nationals won 28.9 per cent of the first-preference vote (a gain of 19.7 per cent) and won the seat with the assistance of ALP preferences; this was the first WA Nationals member elected to the House of Representatives since 1972. But in the Senate, the party's performance was lacklustre; while The Nationals benefited from the swing against the Liberals in the Senate, they still gained only 3.4 per cent of the primary vote.

The Greens continued to strengthen their support in Western Australia, attracting 13.1 per cent of the State-wide first-preference vote—the third-highest State-wide vote attained by the Greens at this election. The Greens recorded increases in all 15 lower-house seats and, in 10 of these seats, the party managed to gain more than 10 per cent of the primary vote—an outcome assisted by them drawing the number-one position on eight of the 15 lower-house ballot papers. The party's solid performance in the House of Representatives was mirrored in the Senate. The Greens attained 14 per cent of the vote and recorded a 4.7 per cent increase in their vote share, only narrowly failing to re-elect their number-one Senate candidate on a full quota. The result confirms that Western Australia is one of the Greens' most reliable strongholds.

There was the usual assortment of Independents and small parties contesting the election, although 33 fewer than in 2007. Family First fielded candidates in 14 of the 15 lower-house seats, managing to attract 1.7 per cent of the first-preference vote. Although Family First achieved a swing of 0.5 per cent, the party's poor result might suggest it has exhausted its electoral appeal. The Australian Democrats managed to organise candidates for the Senate contest but attracted only 0.4 per cent of the primary vote.

Conclusion

The WA branch of the ALP paid a high price for the failure of its federal counterparts to address local concerns about the proposed resource rents tax. Not only had federal Labor failed to consult the State branch prior to the announcement of the proposed tax, it had also issued a directive to its candidates to not speak about the levy. Instead, the ALP campaigned on the threat of a return to the unpopular WorkChoices policy under an elected Abbott government—a campaign that had failed to resonate with WA voters in 2007. In the aftermath of the campaign, one senior WA Labor member condemned the federal office's excessive reliance 'on a set of political clichés' and directives from 'Sussex Street [in Sydney]' (Parker 2010).

The ALP's poor result cannot, however, be attributed solely to its mismanagement of the mining tax. Over the previous two decades, the ALP's electoral record in Western Australia at both House of Representatives and Senate elections has been one of persistent and long-term decline in its primary vote. Since 1990, the ALP's State-wide share of the primary vote has not exceeded 40 per cent—down from 47.5 per cent in 1987—and it has not achieved a majority of the two-party preferred vote since 1987 (50.9 per cent).

Some of this loss of support can be traced to the rise in popularity of the Greens, but the WA trend also affirms that State's economic and political differences have effects on the outcome of federal electoral contests. When writing on the condition of Australian federalism in the 1970s, Epstein noted that Australia's social and cultural homogeneity might weaken the structural basis of its federal system but that the 'outlying states' possessed 'distinctive economic interests' that could provide the basis for 'centre–periphery conflict' (1977, 2–3). It seems that Epstein's observations remain valid and that Australia's State and Territory political communities continue to respond in ways that reflect their differing histories and socioeconomic concerns.

Table 19.1 Results for the House of Representatives, Western Australia

Party	First-preference vote (% swing)	Two-party preferred (% swing)	Seats
Liberal Party	47.02 +0.71	56.41 +3.15	11
ALP	31.18 −5.62	43.59 −3.15	3
Australian Greens	13.13 +4.21		0
The Nationals	3.58 +2.44		1
Family First	1.72 0.51		0
Others	3.36 −2.25		0

Table 19.2 Results for the Senate, Western Australia

Party	First-preference vote (% swing)	Quotas	Seats
Liberal Party	42.99 −3.23	3.0092	3
ALP	29.70 −6.3	2.0791	2
Australian Greens	13.96 +4.66	0.9774	1
The Nationals	3.43 +1.99	0.2401	0
Family First	1.15 +0.29	0.0808	0
Australian Democrats	0.38 −0.67	0.0268	0

References

Burrell, Andrew. 2010. 'Twiggy tour to preach evils of mining rent tax: Andrew Forrest'. *The Australian*, 11 August.

Butterfly, Nick and Boddy, Natasha. 2010. 'Boat people to be housed in NW'. *West Australian*, 19 April.

Epstein, Leon D. 1977. 'A comparative study of Australian parties'. *British Journal of Political Science* 7(1) (January): 1–21.

Jerga, Josh. 2010. 'Libs blast "feral" Nats as bitter coalition split emerges'. *WAtoday*, 3 August, viewed 6 December 2010 <http://www.watoday.com.au/federal-election/libs-blast-feral-nats-as-bitter-coalition-split-emerges-20100803-114ro.html>

Ker, Peter. 2010. 'How the west will stay won for the Coalition'. *Sydney Morning Herald*, 18 August.

Lawson, Rebecca. 2010. 'Mining tax is "economic terrorism"'. *Perth Now*, 2 August.

Maher, Sid and Parnell, Sean. 2010. 'Mining tax threatens Labor seats'. *The Australian*, 15 May.

Miragliotta, Narelle and Sharman, Campbell. 2005. 'Western Australia'. In M. Simms and J. Warhurst (eds), *Mortgage Nation: The 2004 Australian election*. Perth: API Network.

Miragliotta, Narelle and Sharman, Campbell. 2010. 'Western Australia at the polls'. *Australian Cultural History* 28(1): 87–93.

Newspoll. 2010. 'Geographic and demographic analysis—voting intention and leaders' ratings'. *The Australian*, 18 August.

Parker, Gareth. 2010. 'Alannah's exit interview'. *West Australian*, 23 August.

Phillips, Harry C. J. and Kerr, Liz. 2007. 'Western Australia'. *Australian Journal of Politics and History, Political Chronicle* 53(2) (June): 308–13.

Phillips, Harry C. J. and Kerr, Liz. 2009. 'Western Australia'. *Australian Journal of Politics and History, Political Chronicle* 55(2) (June): 286–91.

Probyn, Andrew. 2010. 'Labor in desperate dash to WA'. *West Australian*, 18 August.

Shanahan, Dennis. 2010. 'Mining tax hits ALP in marginals'. *The Australian*, 7 June.

The Australian. 2010. 'Western Australia suffers biggest cut in GST revenue'. *The Australian*, 26 February.

Thomson, Chris. 2010. 'Adele Carles quits Greens'. *WA Today News*, 7 May.

West Australian. 2010a. 'Time is right to put WA first'. *West Australian*, 22 May.

West Australian. 2010b. 'Forrest in blistering broadside on Greens'. *West Australian*, 4 August.

20. Rural and Regional Australia: The ultimate winners?

Jennifer Curtin and Dennis Woodward

On Tuesday, 7 September 2010, after 17 days of negotiations, two of the three rural Independents, Rob Oakeshott and Tony Windsor, announced their decision to support a Labor government. In justifying this outcome, Tony Windsor said that the vote of the country had been sidelined for too long and had been 'subsumed into two major parties which are dominated by city-based majorities and the elections have been fought on the western suburbs of our major cities so that country issues haven't really come to the fore'. He went on to say that 'the fact that there are country Independents in this building indicates that country people have had enough…so we are taking advantage of a particular political moment and sending a signal to country people that if you want to be taken for granted go back to the old parties' (Windsor 2010).

This sense of being forgotten, or ignored, has been a recurring theme in our analyses of the rural and regional vote in recent election campaigns (Curtin and Woodward 2002, 2005; Woodward and Curtin 2010; see also Costar and Curtin 2004; Curtin 2004). And little changed in the campaign of 2010; once again, The Nationals leader, Warren Truss, was virtually invisible in the media at the national level (Gannon 2010). The election-eve editorial of the *Weekly Times* lamented the fact that the 'needs of people outside metropolitan areas' had been overlooked and presciently argued: 'The best thing for regional Australia may be a hung parliament, with the three rural Independents—Bob Katter, Tony Windsor and Rob Oakeshott—as kingmakers' (*Weekly Times* 2010a). Even the Coalition's campaign launch made no specific reference to The Nationals. In contrast, Bob Brown, as leader of the Greens, made the headlines in the national print media almost daily during the campaign. And, in the main, major-party policy announcements focused on big-picture, nationwide issues and were most often launched in marginal electorates.

Yet while the campaign strategies might have reflected those of the past, the election result in 2010 was like no other: a hung parliament giving rural and regional Australia probably the biggest 'win' in decades. The three rural Independents, re-elected in safe country electorates, were placed in the unique position of ensuring rural and regional Australia were given the undivided attention of the major-party leaders, post election. The result: a rural package of $10 billion that was composed of existing and new commitments. The new (additional) funding for rural and regional Australia, which amounted to nearly

$4 billion, included $1.8 billion for health, $800 million for the Priority Regional Infrastructure Program, $573 million for the Regional Infrastructure Fund, $500 million for education, $125 million for reward payments to schools, $66 million for regional skills investment, $41 million for general practice and Aboriginal health, and $15 million for local school control. There was also a commitment to a national price for the National Broadband Network (NBN) and that the network would be built first in the regions (Oakes 2010).

The psephological analysis of the hung parliament outcome is outlined elsewhere in this book and is not solely a result of those in regional Australia who voted independent. The fact that the re-elected Independents prevailed and became critical players in their own right suggests, however, that the electoral story of rural and regional Australia has become increasingly complex. First, the issues of climate change and the mining tax complicated voting trends in rural and regional Australia. The final detailed Newspoll published in *The Australian* before election day revealed that the Coalition's support outside the capital cities had dropped by 4 per cent since 2007 (from 44.2 to 40 per cent) while the Greens' support in the same areas had increased by 6 per cent to 13 per cent (Newspoll 2010), indicating that regional voters were not universally opposed to some form of carbon pricing scheme. The election result reinforced this position. Similarly, there was no uniform rural and regional response to the revised 'mining tax'. While Bob Katter was inherently opposed to the tax, The Nationals had complicated the anti-tax message in the lead-up to the election, with Nationals leader, Warren Truss, and his maverick Senate colleague Barnaby Joyce demanding voters be given more of the spoils of the mining boom through a policy like the WA Royalties for Regions (Parnell and Barrett 2010).

Second, the election outcome was a mixed one for The Nationals. While its decision to merge with the Liberals in Queensland makes comparisons difficult, it arguably increased its representation in the House of Representatives from nine to 12, gaining two seats in Queensland from the ALP (Flynn and Dawson) and the wheat-belt electorate of O'Connor in Western Australia from the Liberals (although the elected National, Tony Crook, has chosen to sit on the crossbenches) (Taylor 2010). In addition, The Nationals successfully defended Riverina against a Liberal challenge. Their inability to win back the seats held by rural Independents bodes ill, however, for the once-dominant rural party. The Nationals seem unable to recognise and represent the diversity and heterogeneity that now constitute rural and regional Australia, both socially and economically, and they are increasingly invisible on the national stage on issues that matter outside the capital cities. The result is now electoral challenges on three sides: from the Liberals outside Queensland, from re-elected and now-powerful Independents who might well deliver, and from the Greens who are harvesting votes and directing preferences in ways that might yet prove difficult for conservative rural MPs.

Policy and Campaign Issues

In the lead-up to the 2010 election campaign, farmers seemed to have fewer economic concerns than in previous elections: drought fears had resided, wheat prices had climbed and the global economic crisis had not had the same negative impact on the agricultural sector as it had elsewhere. Agricultural production and growth, in seasonally adjusted terms, were up 10.9 per cent in the December 2008 quarter on top of the previous quarter's 13.4 per cent, and between November 2007 and November 2008, an extra 17 255 Australians found work in the farm sector (NFF 2010, 4).[1] In 2010 the National Farmers' Federation (NFF) shifted its focus to securing farmers' 'property rights' (in terms of access to water and environmental land-management requirements), trade liberalisation and population policy. Several of their demands, however, were such that neither of the major parties could attend to them without risking a political backlash elsewhere. For example, in an attempt to harness the implications of Treasury's population projections, the NFF's document (released in July 2010) demanded tax, immigration and welfare reform packages that provided incentives for relocation to regional Australia. Yet, by the time the campaign was under way, the idea of a 'big' Australia was becoming unpopular with voters and the rhetoric of both party leaders on cutting population growth and immigration was once again being seen as a negative. Also politically unpalatable to both the Liberals and The Nationals was the NFF's call for revisions to the *Fair Work Act*, reviving instead another version of WorkChoices. And, the NFF's simultaneous recommendations for further action on free trade and enhanced biosecurity once again revealed the tension that exists between trade liberalisation and border protection within the agricultural sector. This tension was highlighted clearly by Bob Katter in his post-election speech where, despite announcing his support for the Coalition, he berated Nationals leader, Warren Truss, for his role as Agriculture Minister in perpetrating the 'destruction of the sugar industry, the destruction of the fishing industry, the destruction of the tobacco industry and the potential destruction of the banana industry' (Katter 2010).

There were, however, some 'wins' for the NFF. Both the major parties committed funds to wide-ranging broadband initiatives, although Labor's NBN was more comprehensive and expensive (at $43 billion compared with the Liberals' $6

---

1   Federal Labor did not appear to use the May 2010 budget to shore up support in country Australia. There was $1 billion for rail freight and $700 million more for the infrastructure fund but little else—a departure from the strategy used by the Howard Government post Pauline Hanson.

billion plan). Yet despite the cost difference, Labor's initiative was critical in winning over the two NSW rural Independents. And although the NBN had already begun its roll-out in Tasmania, Labor (re)launched the program in the marginal Queensland seat of Herbert (Townsville) in the last week of the campaign (Berkovic and Cresswell 2010). Alongside this, Labor announced 23 new GP super clinics, a number of which were to be located in marginal regional seats as well as in Bob Katter's electorate of Kennedy (Dusevic 2010). Both were launched as national interest policies although both were cited as likely to have a strong resonance with bush voters. On top of this, Labor talked up its policy of telemedicine, which explicitly linked health services and the telecommunications initiative and found traction in the bush where access to specialist health services can often prove difficult (Cresswell 2010).

Around the edges, small announcements were made: both sides committed themselves to the uncosted 1700 km inland rail link between Melbourne and Brisbane; Warren Truss promised $1 billion for an education fund to upgrade regional universities and support remote students (Maher 2010); and there was much negative coverage of Labor's failed carbon emissions trading scheme and the rather weak alternative of providing funds for building community consensus for an alternative strategy through a range of 'talk fests' (Karvelas 2010). The ALP promised $200 million for its Building Better Regional Cities Program (Metherell 2010) and that half of its proposed $96 million for emergency-room doctors and nurses would go to regional and rural Australia (Arup 2010). The Nationals announced their intention to spend $300 million on bridge repairs in rural Australia (White and McKenzie 2010), and the Coalition offered a grab bag of election 'sweeteners': $150 million for rural research and development, $5 million in grants for agricultural science researchers, $20 million for feral animal control, $15 million for a biosecurity 'flying squad' (for serious quarantine risks), $10 million for early bushfire warnings and $2 million for an audit of 'green tape' (*Weekly Times* 2010b).

In addition, the ALP put forward a plan to develop a national food security strategy, which was welcomed by the President of the NFF (*Weekly Times* 2010b), while there were divisions between The Nationals and the Liberals over Nationals proposals for 'zonal taxation' and a registry of foreign-owned agricultural assets (White 2010). Two other issues that emerged in rural and regional Australia were concerns regarding (forestry) Managed Investment Schemes, where both Coalition partners resisted rural pressure to scrap their tax advantages (Dowler 2010), and opposition to ALP plans to extend marine parks, which Tony Abbott promised to halt (Needham 2010).

But the big issues for the bush that gained most attention were water policy and the findings of the inquiry into the Murray–Darling Basin, and the 'mining tax'. Although Gillard had renegotiated the parameters of the resource tax with three key mining giants, the smaller mine owners continued to rally voters against the Government. On 18 August, the coalminer New Hope was still urging shareholders to consider the impact of the resources tax when casting their vote (Tasker 2010). Labor promised to direct the funds raised into a regional infrastructure fund, but this seemed to be too little too late for those opposed to the idea. On the water issue, Labor promised voluntary water buybacks to return sufficient water to the Murray–Darling Basin (as would be recommended by the Basin Authority), $4.4 billion on water-saving infrastructure, and to pay off the water debts for the Snowy River (Arup and Harrison 2010; Arup and Welch 2010; Hunt 2010). The Coalition, in contrast, was less forthright on whether it would accept the Murray–Darling Basin Authority's recommendations, arguing that it would strike a balance between the environment and the needs of rural communities although it implied that it would match Labor's promise (although Barnaby Joyce suggested he would reject the recommendations; Wahlquist 2010). It specifically committed to a $730 million boost in water-saving infrastructure in rural areas and to purchase 150 billion litres of water for the Lower Lakes and Coorong in South Australia (Arup and Welch 2010).

Results

In the latter part of the last week of the campaign, it became increasingly clear from the polls that the result would be extremely close, with 16 of Antony Green's 'key seats to watch' located in regional Australia (ABC 2010). Despite the closeness, however, the Coalition maintained its dominance in non-metropolitan seats by securing 36 of the possible 62 seats on offer. In terms of first-preference votes, the swing against Labor in rural and regional Australia was 4.9 per cent—slightly lower that the national swing against them (see Table 20.1). The swing away from Labor, however, did not translate uniformly into a swing to the Coalition parties; the latter received 46 per cent of first-preference votes (up 2 per cent) while the Greens increased their share of first preferences by 2.9 per cent, bringing their total first-preference vote to 9.7 per cent. In Western Australia and Queensland, where the anti-mining tax lobbying was most evident, and where Senators Ron Boswell and Joyce were revealed as vociferously anti-Green (Franklin 2010), the Greens vote reached 13 per cent and 10.9 per cent respectively. Even in Katter's seat of Kennedy, the Greens won a respectable 4.5 per cent of the vote. Such an outcome seems to reinforce the points made by both Oakeshott and Windsor in their decision speeches to support Labor that climate change is a key issue for both regional and urban Australia, requiring meaningful attention and policy direction.

Table 20.1 House of Representatives, Rural and Regional First Preferences

Party	Non-metropolitan electorates			
	Seats won 2007	Vote 2007 (%)	Seats won 2010	Vote 2010 (%)
ALP	29	39.6	23	34.7
Liberal Party	22	31.4	15	24
Nationals	10	13	7	9
LNP (Qld)	-	-	14**	13**
Greens	0	6.8	0	9.7
Independents	2	4.4	3	5
Others	0	4.8	-	4.6
Total	63	100	62*	100

* The AEC has reclassified Forde (Qld) and Brand (WA) outer-metropolitan seats while adding the new rural seat of Durack (WA)

** Comparisons between 2007 and 2010 are inexact because of an inability to differentiate between Liberal and Nationals in Queensland

Source: AEC election results; Woodward and Curtin (2010).

While the swing against Labor was enough to almost lose them government, only 16 seats changed hands (discounting Lyne, which was held by Oakeshott going into the election), compared with 26 in 2007. Seven of these 16 seats were classified as non-metropolitan seats, but not all returned to the Coalition. The ALP lost six non-metropolitan seats, all of which were marginal, and most were surprising wins, courtesy of the massive swing against the Howard Government in 2007. Five of these were Queensland seats, where the protest vote against the Coalition had proved costly to The Nationals' rural Queensland heartland in particular. Labor's other rural loss in 2010 was the seat of Macquarie in New South Wales, but they picked up McEwen from the Liberals, while the Liberals lost O'Connor to the independently oriented Nationals member Tony Crook.

It is probably easier to analyse the ALP's losses than it is to measure the gains for The Nationals. Significant is the fact that the Greens' share of the first-preference vote was higher than that won by The Nationals (9 per cent compared with the Greens' 9.7 per cent) across all States except Queensland. While The Nationals hold only seven seats, all are relatively safe; the only marginal is Tony Crook's seat of O'Connor in Western Australia. And while The Nationals were unable to regain Lyne in New South Wales from Rob Oakeshott, they did win back both the seat they lost in Queensland in 2007 (Dawson) and the new seat of Flynn, which was nominally safe for them but which they failed to win—albeit under the banner of the Liberal National Party (LNP) of Queensland. Nominally then, The Nationals have 12 seats to their name, five of these in Queensland, compared with 10 won in 2007. Of course, the Liberals have also 'forfeited' their ownership of 10 seats as part of the new LNP but it is not yet clear what implications this merger will have on The Nationals' 'brand' in the longer term in Queensland or elsewhere. Certainly, in the seat of Kennedy, the newly merged party offered no challenge to the supremacy of Katter. And while the seats of Dawson, Flynn, Herbert, Leichhardt and Longman have been returned to the Coalition, the swing towards the new LNP was insufficient for these seats to regain their pre-2007 margin of more than 5 per cent. Instead, the Greens, Family First and at least one Independent picked up enough votes to ensure these four seats remained marginal.

In conclusion, just less than half (27) of the 58 marginal seats on offer in 2010 were classified as either rural (19) or provincial (eight), representing 43 per cent of rural and regional seats. This indicates that in one sense rural and regional Australia were not forgotten during the campaign, but were indeed targeted as part of the now-common major-party strategy of focusing on marginal seats. Ultimately, however, and largely thanks to the re-election of the three rural Independents, the result of the 2010 election will benefit rural and regional voters in both safe and marginal seats.

Table 20.2 House of Representatives, Rural and Regional Marginal-Seat Distribution

| Party | Number of non-metropolitan marginal electorates (and total non-metropolitan electorates) | |
	2007	2010
ALP	14 (29)	9 (23)
Liberal	11 (22)	4 (15)
Nationals	3 (10)	1 (7)
LNP (Qld)	-	6 (14)
Independent	0 (2)	0 (3)
Total	28	20

Source: AEC election results.

References

Arup, Tom. 2010. 'Gillard unveils $96m package for hospital emergency rooms'. *The Age*, 27 July.

Arup, Tom and Harrison, Dan. 2010. 'Labor promises more buybacks'. *The Age*, 11 August.

Arup, Tom and Welch, Dylan. 2010. 'Gillard, Abbott talk up water course'. *The Age*, 12 August.

Australian Broadcasting Corporation (ABC). 2010. Antony Green's election web page, viewed 15 August 2010. <blogs.abc.net.au/antonygreen/>

Berkovic, Nicola and Creswell, Adam. 2010. 'NBN sandbags marginal seats'. *The Australian*, 18 August, 1.

Costar, Brian and Curtin, Jennifer. 2004. *Rebels with a Cause: Independents in Australian Politics*. Sydney: UNSW Press.

Cresswell, Adam. 2010. 'Clever policy appeals on three fronts'. *The Australian*, 17 August, 5.

Curtin, Jennifer. 2004. *The Voice and the Vote of the Bush: The representation of rural and regional Australia in the Federal Parliament*. Canberra: Department of Parliamentary Services and the Parliamentary Library.

Curtin, Jennifer and Woodward, Dennis. 2002. 'Rural and regional interests: the demise of the rural revolt?'. In John Warhurst and Marian Simms (eds), *2001: The centenary election*. Brisbane: University of Queensland Press, 245-251.

Curtin, Jennifer and Woodward, Dennis. 2005, 'Rural and regional voters return home'. In Marian Simms and John Warhurst (eds), *Mortgage Nation: The 2004 Australian election*. Perth: API Network, 271-278.

Dowler, Kate. 2010. 'Bishop in MIS pledge'. *Weekly Times*, 28 July.

Dusevic, Tom. 2010. 'Clinics find favour where it counts'. *The Australian*, 19 August, 7.

Franklin, Matthew. 2010. 'Boswell blasts "Green lefties"'. *The Australian*, 6 August.

Gannon, Ed. 2010. 'Truss fails to hold up Nationals'. *Herald Sun*, 11 August.

Hunt, Peter. 2010. 'Gillard pledges to bridge basin gap'. *Weekly Times*, 11 August.

Karvelas, Patricia. 2010. 'Citizens' assembly a no-go zone for MPs'. *The Australian*, 13 August.

Katter, Bob. 2010. Press conference, 7 September, Parliament House, Canberra.

Maher, Sid. 2010. 'Nats flag incentives for students in the bush'. *The Australian*, 19 June.

Metherell, Mark. 2010. '$200m regional housing push'. *The Age*, 19 July.

Needham, Kirsty. 2010. 'Liberals to squeeze marine parks, ponder welfare quarantining'. *The Age*, 28 July.

Newspoll. 2010. 'Newspoll'. *The Australian*, 18 August, 6.

National Farmers' Federation (NFF). 2010. *2010 Federal Election Policy Platform*, National Farmers' Federation, Canberra, viewed 8 September 2010. <http://www.nff.org.au/read/1676.html>

Oakes, Dan. 2010. 'Windsor, Oakeshott secure extra $4bn'. *The Age*, 8 September.

Parnell, Sean and Barrett, Roseanne. 2010. 'Resource projects and boatpeople focus minds in mining towns'. *The Australian*, 21 July.

Tasker, Sara-Jane. 2010. 'Vote against ALP tax: New Hope'. *The Australian*, 18 August, 32.

Taylor, Robert. 2010, 'Crook to put WA ahead of politics'. *West Australian*, 8 September.

Wahlquist, Asa. 2010. 'Joyce opens basin divide'. *The Australian*, 13 August, 4.

Weekly Times. 2010a. 'Safe seats are duds for voters', *Weekly Times*, 18 August.

Weekly Times. 2010b. 'Where they stand', *Weekly Times*, 18 August.

White, Les. 2010. 'Disquiet in the united front'. *Weekly Times*, 4 August.

White, Les and McKenzie, David. 2010. 'Labor jumps the gun'. *Weekly Times*, 21 July.

Windsor, Tony. 2010. Press conference, 7 September, Parliament House, Canberra.

Woodward, Dennis and Curtin, Jennifer. 2010. 'Rural and regional Australia'. *Australian Cultural History* 28(1) (April): 113–119.

Part 5. Policies and Issues

21. Managing Gender: The 2010 federal election

Marian Sawer[1]

The 2010 federal election was the first in Australian history in which a woman prime minister was campaigning for the re-election of her government. Paradoxically, her party had no women's policy—or at least did not launch one publicly. Despite the avoidance of any policy focus on gender issues, gender was a significant undercurrent in the election, as reflected in consistent gender gaps in public opinion and voting intentions. Unusually, the management of gender turned out to be more of a problem for a male than for a female leader.

Gender Gaps and Gendered Coverage

Gender was expected to feature prominently in the 2010 campaign given the contest between Julia Gillard as Australia's first woman prime minister and Tony Abbott, a hyper-masculine Opposition leader and ironman triathlete. Abbott's persona was that of an 'action man' always ready to don lycra and a helmet for some strenuous sporting activity; the Coalition campaign slogan was 'Real action'. Abbott was also known for telling women how to live their lives, criticising them for taking 'the easy way out' by having abortions and blocking the importation of abortion drug RU486 while he was Health Minister. While the Abbott action-man persona might have been useful in a contest with Kevin Rudd, who was to be framed as 'all talk and no action', it was less useful in a contest with Julia Gillard. It required various forms of softening, particularly through referencing of the women in his life, but also through less-aggressive presentation and promises not to tinker with access to abortion. Despite these attempts to remake his image, Abbott was largely unsuccessful in presenting himself as a new man, at least in the eyes of women voters.

Fewer women than men approved of Tony Abbott and indeed Newspoll showed the gender gap increasing during the campaign (see Table 21.1). More women than men approved of Julia Gillard, but the gender gap was smaller (Newspoll and *The Australian* 2010). Nielsen also showed gender gaps in approval of

1   An earlier version of this chapter appeared in the *Australian Review of Public Affairs* (October 2010, <www.australianreview.net>). Marian Sawer also wishes to thank John Stirton of Nielsen and Gillian Evans and Kirsty McLaren for assistance with public opinion data, Janet Wilson for parliamentary data and Pam Debenham for permission to reproduce her 'It's about time' T-shirt.

Abbott and Gillard, with Abbott having the wider gap.[2] The gendered nature of the reactions to the leaders was also highlighted by Roy Morgan's 'polligraph', used on Channel Seven for the leaders' debate on 25 July. The polligraph (pink and blue worms charting audience responses) showed women reacting more favourably to Gillard than men and less favourably to Abbott, except when Abbott was talking about his paid parental-leave package.

Table 21.1 Gender Gap on 'Who Would Make the Better Prime Minister?'

	Date	Male (%)	Female (%)
Julia Gillard	23–25 July & 30 July – 1 August 2010	49	52
	30 July – 1 August & 6–8 August 2010	47	52
Tony Abbott	23–25 July & 30 July – 1 August 2010	38	31
	30 July – 1 August & 6–8 August 2010	39	30

Sources: Newspoll and *The Australian*.

In general, qualities associated with leadership such as strength, authority and decisiveness are regarded as male traits, while double standards are often applied to women displaying such traits (as illustrated by the 'Attila the Hen' description of British Prime Minister Margaret Thatcher). Women leaders generally have to work harder to manage their gender. If they are consultative and consensus seeking, they will be regarded as feminine and not tough enough for leadership. If they mimic what is regarded as a masculine leadership style, they may be put down as 'Attila the Hen' or, in any event, regarded as strident and overly ambitious (Kellerman and Rhode 2007, 7). The fact that there was a larger gender gap in approval of Abbott than of Gillard suggests that, unusually, it was the male leader who had the greater problem in managing gender. His portrayal of invincibility and invulnerability did not work in his favour, at least among women, while Gillard's leadership style was more likely to appeal to both men and women, even if particularly to women.

---

2   For example, Nielsen, 'Estimates of federal voting intention and leadership approval: three poll weighted average', 20–22 July 2010, 27–29 July 2010, 3–5 August 2010 (courtesy John Stirton, Nielsen). In contrast with the commercial polling organisations, the Australian Election Study found a larger gender gap in approval of Gillard than of Abbott.

The leaders' debate—at the end of a week in which Gillard was riding high in the polls—was promptly followed by what looked like an attempt to counter her advantage. Veteran political journalist Laurie Oakes was the recipient of yet another leak—this one to the effect that Gillard had opposed paid parental leave and the rise in old-age pensions when they came up in Cabinet. Both of these issues were of disproportionate importance to women, who might well be looking to women in government to champion them. Gillard's response to the leak—that she was simply being 'financially responsible' when querying the cost of paid parental leave and the old-age pension increase—was in tune with much of her campaign. Her focus on financial competence or 'managing the economy' accorded with the policy priorities usually identified with male rather than female voters, who generally place more emphasis on health and education (that is, on social expenditure rather than cuts to it).[3]

Given the continuing gender gap in voting intentions (Figures 21.1 and 21.2) Labor focused its attention on male voters. Hence the Prime Minister appeared wherever possible in a hard hat rather than playing to her advantage among women. The 'modern gender gap', with women to the left of men in voting behaviour, has appeared both in North America and in Europe (Inglehart and Norris 2000) and has been evident in New Zealand since 1996. The Australian Election Study (AES) has similarly shown fewer women than men voting for the Coalition since 2001 and a particularly big gap between university-educated men and women (Bean and McAllister 2009, 209; Wilson and Hermes 2009, 18). The 2010 AES data suggested that women were 9 percentage points less likely to have voted for the Coalition than men, and 8 points more likely than men to have voted for Labor (see Bean and McAllister in this volume). In other words, the modern gender gap had well and truly arrived in Australia; if women had voted the same way as men, the Coalition would have had an easy victory.

---

3   For example, Roy Morgan poll, 14 August 2010.

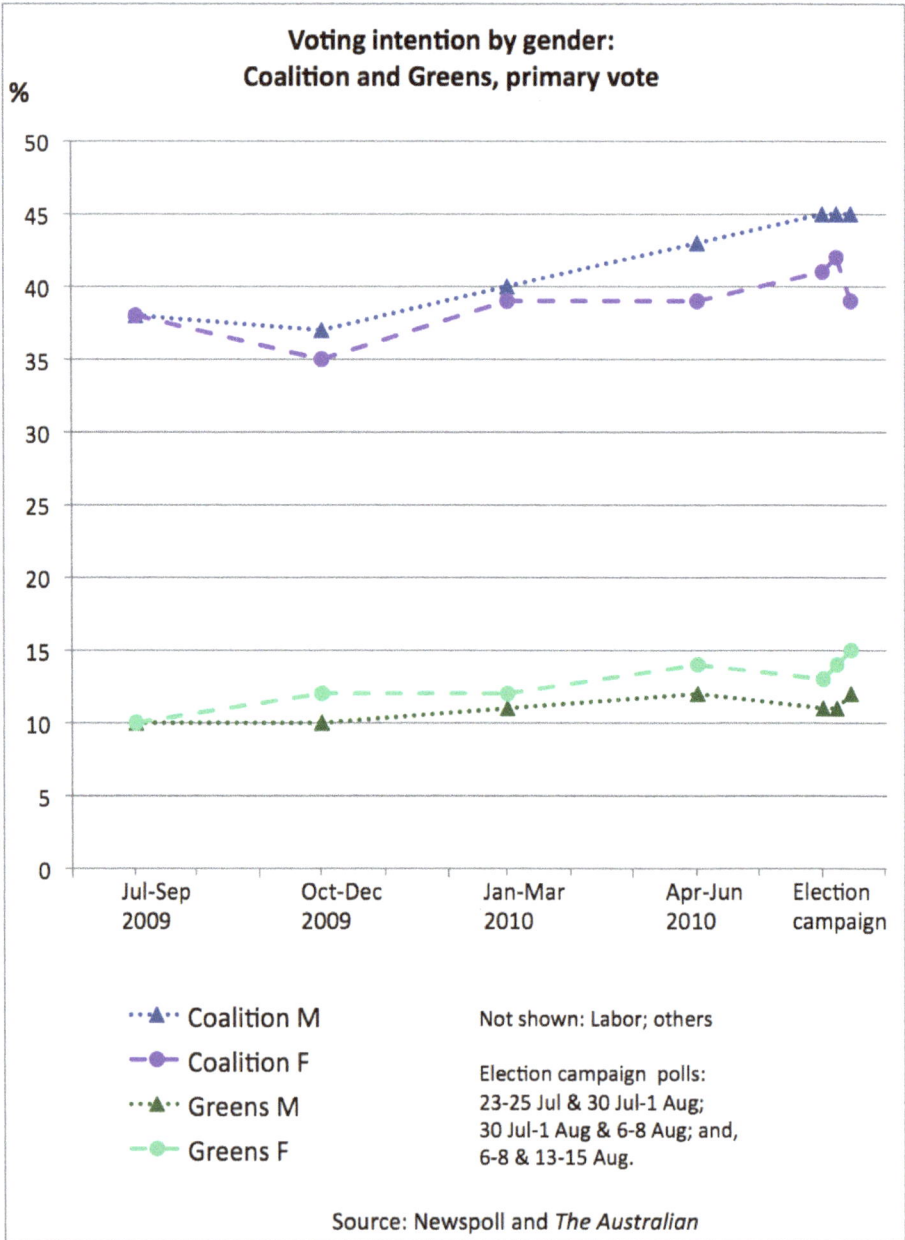

Figure 21.1 Voting Intention by Gender: Coalition and Greens, primary vote (per cent)

Source: Newspoll and *The Australian*.

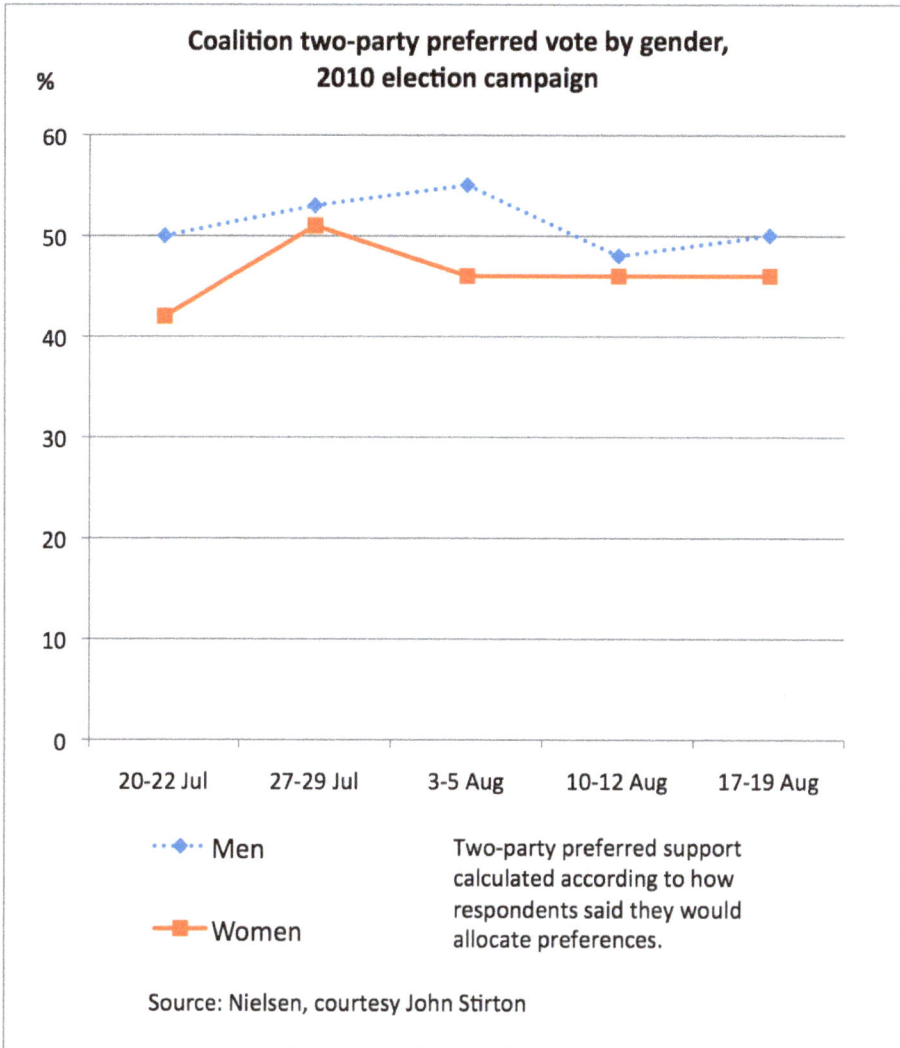

Figure 21.2 Coalition Two-Party Preferred Vote by Gender, 2010 Election Campaign

Source: Nielsen, courtesy John Stirton.

Despite the understandable preoccupation with male voters on the part of Labor strategists, others were more concerned at the possible effects of the Cabinet leak on women's votes and the boost it might provide to Abbott's campaign. In Victoria, 45 prominent women signed a letter to *The Age* (published on 10 August 2010) warning that Abbott's views and past policies would undermine the respect and equality women had fought to achieve and that there was good reason to fear that he would again try to impose his religious beliefs. Various incidents during the campaign seemed to confirm such fears, such as Abbott's inappropriate use of the anti-rape campaign slogan 'No means no' to attack Julia Gillard. When the media seized upon his repeated referencing of the slogan, Abbott accused Labor of a smear campaign to discredit him with women voters (Leslie 2010).

Gillard herself studiously avoided gender issues, including this one. She did benefit from the glamorous cover stories provided by *Women's Weekly*, *Women's Day* and *New Idea* and from the enthusiasm among many women, in particular, that a woman had at last reached the top job (see Figure 21.3). Such 'gender affinity' effects have been noted elsewhere, with parties experiencing a boost among women voters when they are led by women (Banducci and Karp 2000). EMILY's List, the fundraising and support mechanism for 'progressive' Labor women candidates, did attempt to persuade the Labor Party to capitalise on enthusiasm for a first woman prime minister by running a gender-based campaign. Its own gender-based polling in marginal seats suggested that women would respond to such a campaign and were wary of Abbott imposing his moral views. When it became clear that the party would not undertake such a campaign, EMILY's List undertook its own, designing and distributing women-centred election material including distribution of 20 000 'Why women can't trust Tony' leaflets in marginal electorates. It also engaged in online campaigning through Facebook and Twitter (Kovac 2010). Nonetheless, it pointed out in its submission to the party's post-election review that its campaigning work would have been much easier if the party had itself undertaken a high-profile launch of gender-based initiatives and ideas (see 'Campaign policies' below).

Despite her personal avoidance of gender themes, was Gillard singled out for gendered criticism? The following examples suggest that, as in the 2007 election, in 2010, sexist news coverage did little damage and was, if anything, counterproductive. It might also be—as found by a recent study of media coverage of Hillary Clinton's campaign for the White House (Lawrence and Rose 2010)—that the more aggressive forms of sexist bias have migrated to the Internet and are now to be found on blogs and other forms of social media.

Figure 21.3 Pam Debenham's 'It's about time' T-shirt

Source: Pam Debenham, Canberra artist.

Nonetheless, Gillard's private life was subjected to an extraordinary level of scrutiny, with even her 'de facto's' traffic offences becoming a front-page story in *The Daily Telegraph* (30 July 2010). Tony Abbott's references to knowing what it was like to bring up a family (for example, his first words in the leaders' debate) and his use of his eldest daughter, Louise, in the campaign were part of 'playing the family card'. Liberal Party research had suggested that family was a potent issue and campaign strategists were keen that Abbott's family be seen everywhere and often (Savva 2010, 307). The sight of Abbott's family was to serve as a reminder to voters that Gillard was unmarried and childless and hence supposedly out of touch on work/life issues. In 2007, Coalition Senator Bill Heffernan had suggested that Gillard was unsuitable to lead the nation because she was 'deliberately barren' (Sawer 2009,171).

Some went further, for the benefit of those who might forget that Gillard was not only out of touch with Australian families but also living in sin. While religious leaders largely abstained when asked to comment on Gillard's 'de facto' status, Jim Wallace of the Australian Christian Lobby was quick to say both that it would be 'a factor in the way that many Christians vote' and that Christians would be hoping 'her own arrangements' did not preclude Ms Gillard from empathising with traditional families wrestling with 'issues integral to raising children' (Morris 2010). The leader of the Family First Senate ticket in Queensland proclaimed that a prime minister in a de facto relationship was 'not a good role model' (*The Courier-Mail*, 10 August 2010).

The emphasis on Abbott's family credentials and Gillard's supposed lack of them is strongly reminiscent of the television advertisement used by the New Zealand National Party in 1999, which introduced its leader as 'mother of Ben and Anna, a wife and the New Zealand Prime Minister'. The intent was to remind the electorate that the Labour leader, Helen Clark, was not a mother and hence could not understand traditional family values or the issues involved in raising a family (Dore 1999). Clark differed from Gillard in that she did marry her partner before entering Parliament—under pressure from senior Labour Party officials. Gillard not only did not marry, she did not cook. Her lack of interest in the kitchen was not, however, interpreted as contempt for the values of 'homemakers', as happened to Hillary Clinton in 1992. Indeed attacks on Gillard's personal life if anything rebounded, as indicating a lack of respect for women's choices.

Campaign Policies

Despite the advent of Australia's first woman prime minister, neither the Coalition nor Labor appeared to have produced a women's policy for the 2010 election or any overall plan for achieving gender equality. This was in a context where the gender pay gap was widening, where there had been a major childcare crisis and where the participation of women in public decision making was going backwards relative to other democracies. In one of the best-kept secrets of the campaign, however, Labor did actually produce a policy—called Equality for Women—and released it the day before the election, without a launch or telling anybody. It was not included in the list of policies on the ALP web site, but could be located if you knew the name of the policy.

Relating to the portfolio, Labor launched two policies on specific matters. At a 'Women, Management and Work' conference in Sydney, on 29 July, Minister for the Status of Women, Tanya Plibersek, announced a policy to increase the number of women on boards through scholarships in the private sector and a 40 per cent target for Federal Government boards. Then on 9 August, she launched in Melbourne 'Federal Labor's National Plan to Reduce Violence against Women and their Children', a plan resulting from two years of consultation and evidence collection. There was a funding commitment of $44.5 million over four years, maintaining spending at a level similar to previous years (for example, $50.3 million for the Partnerships against Domestic Violence Strategy 1997–2005, followed by $75.7 million for the Women's Safety Agenda 2005–09).

The lack of focus on women's policy was highlighted when the Prime Minister 'forgot' to allocate the Status of Women portfolio when releasing the details of her new ministry on 11 September. By the time the ministry was sworn in by the Governor-General, Quentin Bryce, Status of Women had been added to the Employment Participation and Childcare portfolio of Kate Ellis. There was some comment on Ellis's lack of previous involvement with gender equity issues and her backing by the powerful right-wing trade union, the Shop, Distributive and Allied Employees Association (SDA)—noted for its anti-abortion stance (Vasek 2010). On the other side of politics, the previous Coalition Status of Women spokeswoman, Sharman Stone, lost her frontbench position and the portfolio was given to Shadow Parliamentary Secretary Senator Michaelia Cash, from the right of the party.

Over the years the status of Status of Women has slipped in Australia: originally the portfolio was located in the Prime Minister's Department and carried by the Prime Minister, with the help of a Minister Assisting the Prime Minister (also usually of Cabinet rank). In 2004, the portfolio was demoted to a line department but the Prime Minister continued to have nominal responsibility for it, assisted by a Cabinet minister. Under the Rudd and Gillard governments, the Prime Minister has no longer claimed the portfolio, which has been left with a junior minister (Tanya Plibersek and then Kate Ellis from September 2010).

The Equality Rights Alliance (ERA), based in the YWCA, represents more than 50 women's advocacy organisations and is one of the six women's alliances funded by the Rudd Government since 2010 to support policy engagement by women at the national level. Its mode of operation is similar to preceding women's peak bodies, with its policy work open to endorsement (or otherwise) by its member organisations but not requiring unanimity. For the election, it undertook the kind of rating of party policies previously the domain of the Women's Electoral Lobby (WEL), which still conducted its own rating exercise, assessing policies against responsiveness to feminist values.

The ERA ratings were arrived at by assessment of funding and other commitments made by the parties against policy priorities agreed by member organisations. There were some methodological difficulties caused by the late release by parties of funding commitments or the inability to provide them, and it seems likely that ERA will switch to the WEL methodology for the next election.[4] On the ERA ratings matrix, the Greens did best and the Coalition worst, with the Coalition failing to make any commitment to stronger sex discrimination laws or the improvement of government data collection, meaning data disaggregated by gender, age, location and disability to enable better responses to particular needs.[5]

The Coalition's paid parental-leave proposal was more generous than Labor's, at least for women earning more than the minimum wage, and included superannuation payments as well as being for a longer period (six months rather than 18 weeks). Nonetheless, there was distrust among women's advocacy organisations of the sudden policy turn-around by the Coalition on the issue. There was also criticism of the Coalition's proposal that the leave payments be made through the welfare system rather than by employers, on the grounds it would be seen as a form of welfare rather than an employment entitlement.

Labor fuelled this distrust through repeated reference to Abbott's earlier statement that paid parental leave would only happen 'over this Government's dead body' (*AM*, 22 July 2002, ABC Radio). It should be noted that in 2003 Abbot was also responsible for the abolition of the Work and Family unit in his Department of Employment and Workplace Relations, accepting the position of the Australian Chamber of Commerce and Industry that such matters should be the subject of negotiation between employers and employees rather than of government policy.

Interestingly, one of the most progressive elements of the Coalition policy—and one highlighted by the shadow minister in her second reading speech on the government's Paid Parental Leave Bill—was barely mentioned by Tony Abbott. Sharman Stone stressed that the Coalition would follow Sweden, Iceland and Norway in introducing a 'use it or lose it' paternity leave component, to encourage fathers to bond with their newborn babies and to share and diminish what would otherwise be the 'mother-only experience of an interrupted career' (Stone 2010). During the election campaign, Labor appropriated the Coalition's 'use it or lose it' component and committed to introducing it by July 2012.

The Coalition did not produce a women's policy for the election but did have a page on its web site entitled 'Advancing Women', which offered women a 'direct say' in Coalition policies: 'We know time is precious for all women… So we are making it as easy as possible to be involved. Send us your views directly by email.' The content or effect of this 'direct say' was not at all clear. Abbott's conversion to paid parental leave, for example, was repeatedly said to

---

4   Interview with Kathy Richards, Manager, Equality Rights Alliance, 21 September 2010.
5   It is interesting that for the NSW State election of 2011 the Coalition did make a commitment to the establishment of a Bureau of Women's Statistics within the (NSW) Office for Women's Policy.

have come about because he listened to his wife and children ('some of us have them', as Liberal frontbencher Bronwyn Bishop interjected in one of her male-identifying moments in Parliament; Bishop 2010).

The top item in the ERA's election priorities was 'closing the gender wage gap'. A poll commissioned by the Diversity Council of Australia during the campaign found that 76 per cent of Australians supported steps being taken to close the gap between men's and women's earnings (Auspoll 2010). Gender gap research commissioned by EMILY's List in June also suggested that pay equity was an important issue in its targeted marginal seats (EMILY's List Australia 2010). This priority was signally absent from the campaign debate despite at least three immediate issues being on the table. First, the Government response to recommendations of the House of Representatives inquiry into pay equity (Making it Fair, 2009) was still overdue. Second, government commitment to funding any increase in wages for community-sector workers resulting from the Australian Services Union equal pay test case was still unclear. Third, it was still not known whether the Government was going to address the widening gender pay gap in the Australian Public Service caused by agency-level rather than centralised wage fixing.[6]

The secretive Labor Party women's policy did in fact include the commitment 'to work through the funding implications of any increase in wages awarded as a result of the Australian Services Union's national pay equity case' (ALP 2010). After the election, there was a row over the Commonwealth submission to the case, which seemed to renege on prior commitments in the interests of returning the budget to surplus (Australian Government 2010, 10). After threatened strike action, the Commonwealth 'clarified' its position as not requiring that financial considerations take precedence over pay equity. Meanwhile, the Coalition made no commitment at all on the subject.

Contenders

The Greens continued to field the most women candidates while the gap between the ALP and the Coalition widened slightly due to the continued decrease in women Coalition candidates (Table 21.2). After the election, the number of Coalition men in the House of Representatives rose by eight, but the number of Coalition women remained constant at fourteen. Overall, the number of women in the House of Representatives fell to 24.7 per cent, with a significant gap

---

6 After the election the Special Minister of State announced that any reform of wage-fixing arrangements would be put off for another three years, despite the large gaps that had opened up between salaries paid to those at the same level, depending on whether they were employed in male-dominated or female-dominated departments and agencies.

between Labor and the Coalition (Figure 21.4). To use a term from international comparative studies, there has been 'stagnation' in women's representation in the House of Representatives over the past four elections; women's representation has been stuck at the 25 per cent level, with 2 per cent or less variation.

Table 21.2 Gender Breakdown of 2010 House of Representatives Nominations, Selected Parties

Party	Male	Female	Female (%)
Greens	88	62	41.3
ALP	103	47	31.3
Family First	76	32	29.6
Independents	65	17	20.7
LNP	24	6	20.0
Liberals/CLP	88	23	19.8
Nationals	15	1	6.2

Source: Australian Electoral Commission.

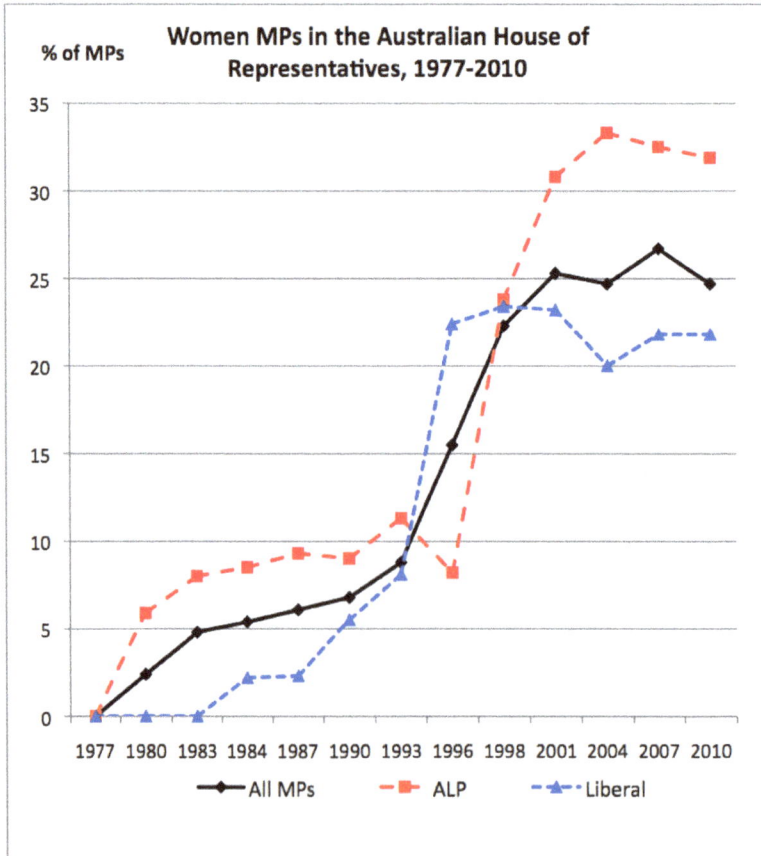

Figure 21.4 Women MPs in the Australian House of Representatives, 1977–2010

The number of women in the Senate, however, rose to the record level of 39.5 per cent (as of 2011), thanks largely to three new women senators for the Greens, although The Nationals also had a second woman senator (Tables 21.3 and 21.4).

Table 21.3 Gender Breakdown of the House of Representatives after the 2010 Election

Party	Male	Female	Female (%)
ALP	49	23	31.9
Liberals/LNP/CLP*	47	14	21.8
Nationals/LNP	11	0	0.0
Independents	5	0	0.0
Greens	1	0	0.0
Total	113	37	24.7

* MPs allocated in accordance with their party room (Crook allocated to Independents, Griggs to Liberals)

Source: Parliamentary Library.

Table 21.4 Gender Breakdown of the Senate, 1 July 2011

Party	Male	Female	Female (%)
Greens	3	6	66.7
ALP	17	14	45.2
Nationals/CLP*	4	2	33.3
Liberals	20	8	28.6
Other	2	0	0.0
Total	46	30	39.5

* Senator Scullion sits in The Nationals' party room

Source: Parliamentary Library.

One of the problems with allowing the number of women in Parliament to slip is the reduction in the pool of women available for entry into ministerial positions. Although the drop in the House of Representatives was partially compensated for in the Senate—from whence women ministers have been disproportionately drawn—the tradition of the Senate supplying only about one-third of ministers puts limits on this source. Australia already has a smaller proportion of women in its national Cabinet (20 per cent in the current Gillard Cabinet) than any comparable democracy apart from the new Cameron Government in the United Kingdom (17 per cent).

In some countries such as Finland and Spain, women are a majority of Cabinet members, while they are about half in Norway and Sweden, 37 per cent in Germany and one-third in France and New Zealand. Indeed the 2008 change of government in New Zealand illustrates how such proportions have become the norm under both social democratic and conservative governments. Interestingly, women tend to be 'over-represented' in Cabinets in other countries (relative to their presence in Parliament), as they were 20 years ago in Australia (Moon and Fountain 1997, 458). In Australia the opposite is now true. For example, women are 36 per cent of the Federal Parliamentary Labor Party but only 20 per cent of Cabinet (Table 21.5). One economical explanation is that while quotas apply to Labor parliamentary preselections they do not apply to ministerial selection.

While it was a difficult time for the most likely new candidate for Cabinet responsibility (Tanya Plibersek was expecting a baby in October), the general outcome was disappointing, with the number of women in Cabinet remaining the same and falling by one in the ministry as a whole (from seven to six). On the other hand, the allocation of the finance portfolio to Senator Penny Wong was the first time that a woman had held an economic portfolio in a federal Labor government.[7]

Table 21.5 Gender Breakdown of the Gillard Ministry and the Opposition Shadow Ministry, September 2010

Ministry category	Male	Female	Female (%)
Cabinet	16	4	20.0
Whole ministry	24	6	20.0
Parliamentary secretaries	6	6	50.0
Shadow Cabinet	18	2	10.0
Shadow ministry	26	6	18.8
Shadow parliamentary secretaries	11	3	21.4

Conclusion

It was paradoxical that while Australia had at last joined other democracies in having women in the positions of both head of government and head of state, Australia was slipping down the Inter-Parliamentary Union's (IPU) ranking of countries on representation of women in the National Parliament. Australia dropped from fifteenth place in 1999 to thirty-fourth place before the 2010 election and to fortieth place after the election (IPU, 30 September 2010). And this was at a time when there were a large number of gender issues requiring the attention of both the Government and the Parliament—most notably, the widening gender gap in wages and the urgency of funding equal pay for community-service workers. Australia was prioritising gender equity in its international development assistance to perhaps an unprecedented degree, but closer to home these issues were struggling to gain attention.

---

7   Senator Margaret Guilfoyle had become the first woman Finance Minister at the federal level 30 years before, in the Coalition Government of Malcolm Fraser.

References

Auspoll. 2010. 'Australian attitudes to pay equity'. *Auspoll*, 6 August.

Australian Labor Party (ALP). 2010. *Equality for Women*, 20 August. Canberra: Australian Labor Party. <http://www.alp.org.au/agenda/more---policies/equality-for-women>

Australian Government. 2010. Australian Government Submission to the Equal Remuneration Case, 18 November. Melbourne: Fair Work Australia.

Banducci, Susan A. and Karp, Jeffrey A. 2000. 'Gender, Leadership and Choice in Multiparty Systems'. *Political Research Quarterly* 53(4): 815–848.

Bean, Clive and McAllister, Ian. 2009. 'The Australian election survey: the tale of the rabbit-less hat. Voting behaviour in 2007'. *Australian Cultural History* 27(2): 205–218.

Bishop, Bronwyn. 2010. Interjection, Second Reading Speech by Maxine McKew on the Paid Parental Leave Bill 2010. *House of Representatives Debates*, 27 May, 4405.

Dore, Christopher. 1999. 'Mother of a challenge'. *The Australian*, 26 November.

EMILY's List Australia. 2010. *Gender Gap Research 2010—Recommendations for campaigning and policy*. Melbourne: EMILY's List.

Inglehart, Ronald and Norris, Pippa. 2000. 'The developmental theory of the gender gap: women's and men's voting behaviour in global perspective'. *International Political Science Review* 21(4): 441–463.

Kellerman, Barbara and Rhode, Deborah L. (eds). 2007. *Women and Leadership: The state of play and strategies for change*. San Francisco: Jossey-Bass.

Kovac, Tanja. 2010. *Winning elections for Labor women—a constant campaign*. Discussion Paper for EMILY's List submission to Federal Election Review 2010.

Lawrence, Regina G. and Rose, Melody. 2010. *Hillary Clinton's Race for the White House: Gender politics and the media on the campaign trail*. Boulder: Lynne Rienner.

Leslie, Tim. 2010. 'Abbott defends "no means no" remark'. *ABC News*, 3 August.

Moon, Jeremy and Fountain, Imogen. 1997. 'Keeping the gates? Women as ministers in Australia, 1970–96'. *Australian Journal of Political Science* 32(3): 455–466.

Morris, Linda. 2010. 'On PM's personal values, religious leaders keep respectful distance'. *Sydney Morning Herald*, 28 July.

Newspoll and The Australian. 2010. 'Who would make the better prime minister?'. Newspoll and *The Australian*, July–August.

Savva, Nikki. 2010. *So Greek: Confessions of a conservative leftie* [Second edn]. Melbourne: Scribe.

Sawer, Marian. 2009. 'Women and the 2007 federal election'. *Australian Cultural History* 27(2): 167–174.

Stone, Sharman. 2010. Second Reading Speech on the Paid Parental Leave Bill 2010, *House of Representatives Debates*, 27 May: 4383–4384.

Vasek, Lanai. 2010. '"Question mark" over Ellis'. *The Australian*, 15 September.

Wilson, Shaun and Hermes, Kerstin. 2009. Shifting Majorities: Examining class, birthplace and gender in the victories of Howard and Rudd. Paper presented to Australian Political Studies Association Conference, Macquarie University, Sydney, <http://www.pol.mq.edu.au/apsa/papers/Non-refereed%20papers/>

22. Immigration Issues in the 2010 Federal Election

James Jupp

One of only four stated objectives of the Liberals was to 'stop the boats'. Julia Gillard (a '10-pound migrant') and Tony Abbott (born in London) stressed their migrant origins where appropriate. Abbott's claim was almost ludicrous as he was only born in London because his Australian parents were there at the time. Gillard left Barry in south Wales when she was five, coming free with her Welsh parents. But immigration and population did not play the central roles that seemed likely at the start of campaigning. This followed in a consensual tradition in which such issues did not seriously divide the two major parties.

Public support for the 'White Australia' Policy in the past and for 'sending back the boats' recently has been such that the major parties have normally adopted a bipartisan approach to most immigration issues. Opposition to this now arises from outside the major parties: the Greens, churches and ad-hoc organisations; lawyers and non-governmental organisations (NGOs). The major claim made by Abbott was that continuing the Howard policy of 'offshore' detention and temporary protection visas would have diminished or ended the flow of boats.

In general elections for nearly 20 years there was agreement not to raise the issue of punitive detention for 'boat people' while also arguing that this and other practices remained within the UN Convention. Throughout the period 1990–2007, about 70 per cent in polls supported the bipartisan policies and kept the issues at a low level of partisan disagreement. Recent polls show that substantial majorities believe the Liberals are better able to cope than Labor, jumping to 44 per cent in April 2010 and staying there until the week of the election, with the ALP stuck at 29 per cent (that is, the majority favours stronger action). Morgan made sure of this majority by referring to 'illegal' migrants! It is therefore a key issue for Liberals, meaning Abbott was bound to use it. The Liberal-Nationals Coalition was also seen as better able to deal with population growth and to manage immigration (by 46 per cent to 28 per cent).

Bipartisanship on some issues was declining by 2001. One of many reasons for the defeat of the Howard Government was his breaking of bipartisanship over multiculturalism from 1998. But the attack on the World Trade Centre reinforced bipartisan agreement about the need to combat terrorism. This flowed over into an increasingly hostile attitude towards asylum-seekers, who were mainly Muslims at this time.

In 2002, ALP leader, Simon Crean, and Julia Gillard developed a more humane policy towards asylum-seekers arriving by boat, though keeping mandatory detention. This reflected growing opposition outside the party system and against the detention centres (*Protecting Australia and Protecting the Australian Way*). This policy was not publicised during the next election, which the ALP lost. It was close to that adopted by Senator Chris Evans after the Labor victory of 2007, but he was pushed aside as soon as it became an 'issue'. Party leaders and major media determine 'issues'. They might not seem 'major' to others (compare the small number of boat people with large increases in overall immigration—another but arguably less combustible issue). Abbott made it one of four major aims to 'stop the boats' because he was on to a winner.

Three Issues

There were three major migration-related 'issues' raised by the Liberals to which Labor reacted. Labor had no long-term policies on any of them and adlibbed. Indeed, policy making in either party was very short term and unduly linked to electoral outcomes as predicted by opinion polls or through focus groups. On refugee policy it was widely criticised as 'the race to the bottom'.

These issues were: the boat people; the size of the migration program; and the future size of the population. Put like that this might seem the order of increasing importance, but in practice the opposite was true, as measured by media responses. 'Stopping the boats' is easier than controlling population size.

Boat people have been a potential issue since the first Vietnamese arrivals in 1976. Australian governments then responded within the terms of the UN Convention and 1967 Protocol—that is, that they were refugees, if approved they would get permanent residence leading to citizenship, would be processed through an international agreement (orderly departure), would be assisted and accommodated like other non-English-speaking background (NESB) migrants but with limited additional services to take account of trauma and special needs. This continued under the Fraser and Hawke governments (1975–91) but started to change with the imposition of mandatory detention in 1991.

Policy changed with a large Cambodian intake, leading to mandatory and irrevocable detention with bipartisan agreement. This principle has remained and accounts for most of the administrative problems, including costs. It became even more important with the growth of numbers from Afghanistan, Iraq and Sri Lanka, leading to the so-called 'Pacific solution' of offshore processing, plus onshore internment in custom-built centres (Woomera, Baxter) administered by private prison companies and leading to temporary protection visas for those not rejected. The Crean/Gillard program wished to move away from this by reintroducing permanent visas, closing offshore camps (replaced with Christmas Island), limiting processing time, removing women and children from detention and responding to 'inhumane' practices as revealed by several inquiries. This created a clear-cut partisan division, with Abbott advocating a total return to the 'Pacific solution' despite its costs, damage to international reputation and unpopularity with Greens and some 'liberal' Liberals. The Howard Government had abolished several Labor measures such as permanent residence, special assistance for those from wartorn areas and easy access to citizenship.

The Labor program was, however, severely disrupted by a rapid increase of boat arrivals, made more burdensome by the collapse of the Tamil Tigers in the Sri Lankan civil war. Christmas Island became crowded and delays grew, partly due to final approval being left in the hands of the Australian Security Intelligence Organisation (ASIO). The Rudd Government took population policy away from the Department of Immigration and Citizenship (DIAC) and gave border protection to Home Security. As multiculturalism was dormant and settlement services mainly in State and NGO hands, this left DIAC significantly reduced from its rise under Howard and Phillip Ruddock. Senator Evans was pushed to one side and admitted that the policy had 'failed'. This raised the question of what policy should be—to implement the UN Convention or to stop the boats. This has never been properly debated at the national, partisan level. Liberal politicians frequently use the incorrect term 'illegal' and Labor speakers occasionally lapse into the same usage. That the Convention aims to assist (rather than resist) asylum-seekers was almost completely ignored in the partisan battle.

Immigration

The boat people are a very small part (1.5 per cent) of an immigration program that started to expand rapidly in the last two years of Howard's government and continued under Rudd. When the program began in 1947, and for at least the next 30 years, there was bipartisan agreement to 'populate or perish'. In the mid-1980s, some natural scientists, allied with some Australian Democrats and such inveterate opponents of expanding immigration as Bob Birrell, began to argue for limitation of numbers on grounds of sustainability (see Birrell et al. 1984). There was no major public debate about the ethnic content of the intake until the rise of Pauline Hanson's One Nation party in 1996. The election of that year saw John Howard—a critic of high migration and opponent of multiculturalism—become Prime Minister and start to move policy and public debate away from bipartisanship. The increasing concern with Islamic terrorism in Western democracies sparked off a long argument about the role of Muslims in societies such as Australia. While some Labor leaders joined in, the main thrust came from the Liberal Party and especially in Sydney, with the largest Muslim population in Australia. Labor was seen by many as the party of multiculturalism, and was rewarded by winning a solid block of metropolitan electorates with large ethnic minority populations. The price was anti-Labor voting in electorates such as Lindsay and Macarthur, which were adjoining the 'ethnic west' but which were less 'ethnic' than the metropolitan Australian average.

Eventually, Howard accepted increased immigration, but on the basis of temporary rather than permanent settlement. While no major party advocated a return to White Australia (and One Nation quickly disintegrated), by use of 'dog whistling', the Coalition in the cities began to appeal to working-class voters as defending the Australian way of life and (by implication) the limitation of Muslims and other unassimilable immigrants. This explains the heavy canvassing of western Sydney electorates by Abbott in the 2010 campaign. Howard's 'Aussie battlers' were unhappy for many reasons: congested traffic, poor services, distance from city centres and declining manufacturing. On the outer fringes of Sydney, there were 'borderline' electorates (Lindsay and Macarthur in particular) where there was considerable opposition to the spread of Muslim and non-European settlement. This explains the great emphasis on boat people in the last weeks of the campaign. Boat people did not come up the Parramatta River, but Muslims, Lebanese and Vietnamese were moving into 'white', working-class suburbs.

Opposition to population increase was based on very dubious figures, which the Coalition did little to illuminate. In particular, the projection of 35 million Australians within 30 years assumed the same level of temporary intake of students, 457 visa workers and working holiday makers—and not just the component of permanent residents used to predict numbers in the past. Kevin Rudd inadvertently fed fuel to the fire by saying he wanted a 'big Australia'— which most Australian political leaders had been saying for a century. But opinion polling showed that more than 60 per cent of Australians were content with remaining part of one of the least densely populated societies on Earth.

Sustainability

The reaction against increased population size was strong enough to sweep through both major parties. The Liberals clashed with employers crying out for labour. The ALP deserted its tradition of 'populate or perish' (and its strong immigrant base). Those in the Greens and the environmental and conservation movements could hardly contain their excitement. The Greens' vote had risen to its highest level in the polls since the party was founded and there was a prospect of holding the Senate balance of power and thus being able to do business with the major parties.

Essentially, this rather unexpected shift was a cry for stability and against rapid change. It also marked the rise of the educated young to a political influence they had previously lacked. Electorates thought susceptible to Greens campaigning included the inner-city seats of Melbourne, Sydney, Grayndler and Batman—all Labor strongholds gentrified by the expanding professional classes. On this dimension, the Greens are a threat to Labor. But their expansion also insulates many voters from turning directly to the Liberals. A Labor government was possible only if Greens' second preferences went to the party, as all indications suggest they did.

The ALP was slow to see what was happening. Many still adhere to Calwell's old adage 'I am Labor because I am Australian and Australian because I am Labor'. In other words, the ALP is the party of the common people and has no need of allies. But the manual working class is smaller than 50 years ago, the unions are less all-embracing, the Catholic Church is firmly based in the middle classes, the number of graduates is vastly greater and the proportion of Australians of British and/or Irish descent is much lower, especially in working-class suburbs. In the end Labor made a formal alliance with another party, the Greens, which has never happened before nationally, but is not unknown in State politics.

The Results

On the evidence available (which is slight), the 'boat people' issue was not decisive in the large swing nationally to the Liberals. In fact, the election could almost be seen as a 'declaration of independence' by Queensland, the State that gave us Joh Bjelke-Petersen and Pauline Hanson. In Western Australia there was only a limited swing and little change of seats, despite the potential impact of the asylum issue and the mining tax. In the south-east, the results in Victoria, South Australia and Tasmania were quite different from those elsewhere. In New South Wales only some of the 'western suburbs' turned strongly against Labor and only Bennelong, which is not essentially a western suburb, Greenway and those on the periphery, such as Hughes and Macarthur, conformed to the stereotype of a revolt against Labor by 'Howard's battlers'. In Melbourne similar suburbs did not move towards the Liberals at all.

Once again Labor representation was heavily dependent on two blocs of 'ethnic seats'—defined here as those with more than 25 per cent using a language other than English at home. Of the 72 electorates won by the party, 26 fall into this NESB category; one (Menzies) has never been Labor, Bennelong was not unexpectedly lost to the Liberals and Melbourne (more surprisingly) was lost to the Greens. One-third of all Labor-held electorates are 'ethnic'. Of Liberal counterparts, only Menzies and Bennelong have one-third or more speaking a language other than English at home. Of Labor seats there are non–English-speaking absolute majorities in Barton, Blaxland, Watson and Fowler—all in Sydney. The results between the two major States were quite different, with large swings against Labor in New South Wales and minor or negative swings against the Liberals in Victoria (see Table 22.2).

Table 22.1 'Ethnic Electorate' Results in the 2010 Election

Electorate	Result	ALP first preferences (%)	Swing to Libs (%)
Banks	ALP no change	43.3	+10.2
Barton	ALP no change	49.0	+10.2
Batman	ALP no change	53.1	−0.8
Bennelong	Liberal gain	37.0	+3.8
Blaxland	ALP no change	51.9	+7.2
Bruce	ALP no change	49.7	0.0
Calwell	ALP no change	57.4	−0.4
Chifley	ALP no change	52.4	+6.0
Chisholm	ALP no change	45.2	+1.0
Fowler	ALP no change	53.8	+15.1
Gellibrand	ALP no change	59.6	−0.1
Gorton	ALP no change	60.9	−0.8
Grayndler	ALP no change	46.6	+7.3
Greenway	ALP gain	42.6	+2.8
Holt	ALP no change	55.5	−3.0
Hotham	ALP no change	55.6	−0.3
Isaacs	ALP no change	50.0	−3.7
Kingsford-Smith	ALP no change	44.4	+7.7
Lingiari*	ALP no change	40.1	−0.5
McMahon	ALP no change	51.7	+5.5
Maribyrnong	ALP no change	56.2	−0.9
Melbourne	Greens gain	39.5	−3.5
Menzies	Libs no change	32.8	+3.0
Parramatta	ALP no change	44.8	+6.3
Reid	ALP no change	42.0	+7.8
Scullin	ALP no change	63.1	−0.2
Watson	ALP no change	51.3	+10.4
Werriwa	ALP no change	49.2	+8.2
Wills	ALP no change	53.2	−0.5

* In Lingiari many use Indigenous languages

Note: 'Ethnic electorates' are defined as having more than 25 per cent speaking a language other than English at home.

Source: ABC Elections.

Table 22.2a Selected Results from 'Ethnic Electorate' Polling Booths in Sydney, 2010 (per cent)

Electorate	Sydney	ALP % vote	Change since 2007	ALP 2PP vote since 2007
1	Cabramatta	54.26	−22.60	−23.08
1	Bonnyrigg	60.12	−19.27	−17.78
2*	Ashfield	50.75	−13.07	−9.1
2*	Leichhardt	44.32	−9.05	−4.6
3	Auburn West	52.17	−14.44	−5.63
3	Villawood	58.98	−5.87	−2.14
3	Bankstown Central	56.54	−11.92	−6.50
4	Auburn	56.91	−17.7	−12.73
4	Lidcombe	50.61	−13.77	−8.95
5	Lakemba	65.36	−5.44	−4.83
5	Canterbury	51.74	−16.99	−13.90
6	Blacktown	47.08	−14.63	−8.38
7	Eastwood	41.97	−10.33	−6.32
7	Ermington	43.29	−10.74	−9.11
7	West Ryde	40.22	−12.43	−6.31
8	Belmore North	57.29	−10.62	−10.49
8	Punchbowl	50.43	−9.77	−10.13
9	Rockdale Central	54.77	−11.09	−11.09
9	Arncliffe	52.98	−11.96	−12.72

Note: Electorates: 1 Fowler; 2 Grayndler (* PPV to Greens); 3 Blaxland; 4 Reid; 5 Watson; 6 Chifley; 7 Bennelong; 8 Watson; 9 Barton.

Table 22.2b Selected Results from 'Ethnic Electorate' Polling Booths in Melbourne, 2010 (per cent)

Electorate	Melbourne	ALP % vote	Change since 2007	ALP 2PP vote since 2007
1	Deer Park	63.19	−4.10	+1.37
1	St Albans	61.15	−1.76	n.a.
2	Springvale	68.29	−3.22	+4.52
3	Thomastown	66.38	−7.59	+4.96
4	Northcote	42.54	−7.37	n.a.
5	Broadmeadows	67.95	−4.32	−0.58
5	Craigieburn	63.36	−3.09	+2.07
6*	Carlton	46.39	−15.00	−15.31
6*	Richmond North	64.05	−10.82	+9.97
7	Brunswick North	51.02	−6.24	+0.45
8	Sunshine North	68.68	−1.85	+2.57
6*	Flemington	49.74	−9.69	−10.57
9	Clayton	60.10	−2.59	+0.58

* Two-party preferred vote with Greens

Note: Electorates: 1 Gorton; 2 Hotham; 3 Scullin; 4 Batman; 5 Calwell; 6 Melbourne; 7 Wills; 8 Maribyrnong; 9 Chisholm.

Federal electorates are now too large for analysis of specific group behaviour. Taking booth results is more fruitful, especially in those limited areas where NESB voters are numerically dominant. Table 22.2 shows clearly that there was a far greater 'revolt' in Sydney than in Melbourne. In general, the two-party preferred total suggests that voters went straight over from Labor to Liberal in Sydney, whereas many in Melbourne went to the Greens and returned their preferences to Labor. Another generalisation might hold that the Greens' vote was higher in former 'ethnic areas' (such as Carlton, Brunswick and Fitzroy) than in outer Melbourne suburbs with predominant NESB populations, such as Deer Park, St Albans, Springvale and Thomastown. A factor that needs also to be taken into account is that the Sydney 'ethnic areas' are much more likely to be populated from Asia and the Middle East, whereas many of the Melbourne districts have been 'ethnic' for much longer and are drawn from southern and Eastern Europe. Even so, it can be remarked that the East Asian districts of North Richmond and Springvale seem more loyal to Labor than their Sydney counterparts such as Cabramatta and Ashfield.

In both New South Wales and Victoria, Labor rarely rewarded its loyal supporters in national elections with 'ethnic' candidates, whereas the Liberals have now adopted a consistent strategy of 'horses for courses'. Nor were their nominees placed only in unwinnable electorates. Greenway, which Labor came very close to losing with a two-party preferred vote of only 50.9 per cent, has one of the largest Filipino communities in Australia. Both the Liberal Party and the Australian Democrats nominated Filipinos, while the ALP winner, Michelle Rowland, was born and raised locally. Apart from its large Filipino component, Greenway was one-third Catholic and the scene of a battle between a Pentecostal Christian Liberal and a Bosnian Muslim for Labor in 2007 (Jupp 2009). Both these candidates withdrew to neighbouring seats in 2010, where they were duly elected.

Other strong Liberal candidates chosen for their relevant ethnicity included Thomas Dang (of Vietnamese parentage) in Fowler where he gained a 13.2 per cent two-party swing in one of Labor's safest seats; Ken Nam in Watson with a 10.4 per cent swing against Tony Burke; Jamal Elishe, an Assyrian, with a swing of 5.5 per cent in McMahon; John La Mela, of Italian parentage, with a swing of 10.2 per cent in Barton; Fazal Cader, a Sri Lankan Muslim who won one-third of the vote against Simon Crean; John Nguyen, a Vietnamese Catholic, with a negligible swing in Chisholm; Venus Priest, a Filipina with a two-party swing of 7.3 per cent in Chifley; in Werriwa, Sam Eskaros from Egypt had a swing of 7.9 per cent against Laurie Ferguson; Ricardo Balancy, a Mauritian, gained a modest swing in Holt—home to the largest Mauritian community in Australia.

Not all candidates reveal their origins or birthplace but a generalisation is that the Liberals have advanced 'ethnic' candidates in 'ethnic' electorates, whereas Labor has not. This is starting to show results, especially in New South Wales where Labor was generally in retreat. One exception was in Menzies, held by former Minister for Immigration, Kevin Andrews. Joy Banerji from New Delhi was nominated by Labor, perhaps as a comment on Andrews' role in the botched case against Indian doctor Mohamed Haneef, in which he took a central role. The other important exception was also in Victoria, where Maria Vamvakinou from the Greek island of Lefkada was once again victorious for Labor against Wayne Teng, a Chinese-Vietnamese candidate for the Liberals.

There is obviously a brain at work now in the Liberal Party when it comes to seeking to attract 'ethnic' voters even in the strongest Labor areas. This is most marked in New South Wales, despite a substantial input of immigrants at the State and organisational levels of the ALP (Benson 2010). The Bennelong reversal in a middle-class area with large Chinese and Korean communities suggested that such environments could be very unpredictable for Labor. The contrast between New South Wales with its large swings and significant losses and Victoria, which behaved differently, suggests that 'ethnic' voters are strongly influenced by the local political atmosphere and media. There is no nationwide 'ethnic vote'. But there are very large and growing numbers of 'ethnic voters'. Labor needs to cultivate them more carefully now that the Liberals are coming out of their WASP ghettoes and provincial retreats. Sydney results showed very large swings to the Liberals in areas such as Cabramatta, Strathfield, Eastwood, Hurstville and Campsie—all with large East Asian populations (Stevenson 2010). This was not so marked for similar districts in Melbourne, where losses went to the Greens to a greater extent. A post-election warning note for NSW Labor was sounded by the Lebanese Muslim leadership at a mass rally at Lakemba mosque, celebrating the end of Ramadan. They threatened to run Muslim independents in appropriate seats because Labor had neglected them.

The Future

If the party system becomes more unpredictable and volatile over the next few years, it is reasonable to hypothesise (or even fantasise) about the shape of things to come. The 11 years of the Howard Government certainly had a conservative impact on many Australians and did much to prepare the ground for opposition to increased immigration and multiculturalism. Labor has responded by seeking a centrist role, which lays the basis for a continuing Greens presence in national affairs. This could well modify any tendency to move too far away from the ideal of a reforming, culturally varied society based on liberal values and a well-educated community. But Greens are not likely to be enthusiastic about increasing the present population even more than has already been added in the past 30 years. They could be a modifying influence on hostility to the small minority of asylum-seekers, even if the number of these increases.

A conservative victory would also have been a mixed blessing. Employers, backed by economists, favour growth. They might do so on the basis of temporary employment, but that is a dubious long-term approach. Those who arrive might well wish to remain. If not given this right, they are under no obligation to accept the 'Australian values' that are so important to conservatives. Universities are facing dramatic drops in income as overseas students turn away from a more restrictive visa system (Das 2010). Conservatives will also need to come to grips with the reality of global warming, as many have refused to do until now. But this is also a problem for many industries in which Labor voters and unions have a strong influence. This election—shaped by focus groups and opinion polls—showed little sign of a responsible and serious approach to the major issues of immigration, sustainable population and the impact of global warming. It is much easier to rail at the leaky boats and their desperate passengers.

References

Benson, Simon. 2010. 'Why did spurned ethnic voters turn to the Coalition?'. *The Daily Telegraph*, 14 September.

Birrell, Bob et al. (eds). 1984. *Populate and Perish?* Melbourne: Fontana/ACF.

Das, Sushi and Collins, Sarah-Jane. 2010. 'Turning off the tap'. *The Age*, 15 September.

Jupp, James. 2009. 'Immigration and ethnicity'. *Australian Cultural History* 27: 147–66.

Marks, Kathy. 2010. 'Mixing it up in Bennelong'. *Griffith Review* 29: 103–47.

Refugee Council of Australia. 2010. *Bulletin for Members and Supporters*, 8 September. Sydney: Refugee Council of Australia.

Saville, Margaret. 2007. *The Battle for Bennelong*. Melbourne: Melbourne University Press.

Stevenson, Andrew. 2010. 'A disaster of Labor's own making'. *Sydney Morning Herald*, 4–5 September, 11.

23. The Influence of Unions and Business in the 2010 Federal Election: Claims of 'slash and burn' and 'still no response and no answers'

John Wanna

In its own inimical way, the Australian Council of Trade Unions (ACTU) announced midway into the federal election campaign that Tony Abbott's 'slash and burn approach to the economy would jeopardise the recovery and jobs' (ACTU 2010a). Resorting to inflamed rhetoric, it accused Abbott of an 'obsession with cutting', of hatching 'dangerous plans…to bring back the worst aspects of *WorkChoices*', and being intent on slashing a 'further $1 billion from public spending [that] would send the economy in a dangerous direction and threaten thousands of jobs'. Not to be outdone, the Association of Mining and Exploration Companies (AMEC), which was locked in a dispute with the Labor Government over the mining-tax fiasco, declared that the new Prime Minister, Julia Gillard, had talked of 'throwing open the Government's door to the mining industry' but had then rebuffed the majority of industry players. AMEC declared that it had 'still [had] no response and no answers' to its questions and approaches to the Prime Minister to discuss the issues, and that accordingly it would 'relaunch its anti-mining tax media campaign' (AMEC 2010a, 2010b). AMEC was at the time fighting to be taken seriously in the taxation policy debate in the aftermath of the concessions given to the three multinational mining companies in the so-called 'secret deal'.

Despite a predictable level of hyperbole, the actual influence of unions and business on the 2010 federal election campaign was far more subdued and nuanced than it had been in the campaign of 2007, which had resulted in a change of government after 11 years. The voices of these powerful sectional interests were largely restrained and muted compared with the more aggressive campaigns they had run to coincide with earlier elections. The reasons for the subdued influence in 2010 were manifold. With Gillard opportunistically opting to call an early election (some three to four months early), both business and unions seemed taken by surprise at the sudden onset of the campaign. It was not clear which side of politics would win the election so many business groups remained neutral or did not commit to endorsing one side over the other. Business was still more than a little perplexed over the brutal execution of Kevin Rudd that happened just three weeks before Gillard raced to the polls. They were also unsure as to what exactly would be Gillard's new agenda as she put the government back on track. This did not necessarily translate into antagonism to her political priorities but uncertainty over what she would choose to change now that she was Prime Minister. She indicated her priorities were to take some action on climate change, to renegotiate the mining tax and to reduce the number of boats carrying asylum-seekers. In contrast, many in the union movement now considered they had achieved their ultimate ambition in deposing Rudd and were basking in the immediate afterglow, satisfied caucus had removed him (see Howes 2010).

There were some major differences between the federal elections of 2010 and 2007. First, in 2010 there was no highly orchestrated multimedia campaign run by the ACTU costing more than $20 million and extending over a two-year time frame (the 'Your Rights at Work' campaign, which ran from 2005 to 2007, supported by special levies on union members). This was an integrated campaign against WorkChoices involving mainstream TV and radio advertisements, new-media campaigns, union posters, stickers and buttons, and concerted advertorial coverage in Labor Party and union newsletters and web sites.

The 2010 federal election was not a referendum on WorkChoices as some believed was the case in the 2007 election (but see Wanna 2010), and overall there was far less attention given to industrial relations matters. Tony Abbott immediately attempted to defuse any potentially damaging industrial relations issues by claiming WorkChoices was 'dead, buried and cremated' and that the Coalition had no plans to reintroduce such radical measures. Labor meanwhile tried desperately to mount a scare campaign, claiming Abbot had an unfinished agenda and that he would undermine workers' rights after he was elected to govern (but this largely fell on deaf ears).

Arguably, the 2010 election was not really about policy differences or different ideological directions. There were few new policy announcements to swing undecided voters (except perhaps the different policies towards broadband, and Labor's 18-week minimum-wage parental-leave scheme worth $9800 to mothers versus the Coalition's policy based on the mother's average earnings over the past year up to $150 000, but far less generous to low-paid women or those not in the labour force). More importantly, there was no money available to fund new promises, without increasing government debt. So, both parties hitched their fortunes to uninspiring campaign messages, which uniformly failed to capture the electorate's attention. Labor's mundane slogan 'Moving forward' or 'Let's move Australia forward' excited no interest whatsoever, and was soon dispensed with after being widely lampooned. The Coalition's 'We will do the right thing…end wasteful spending, pay back Labor's debt, stop Labor's new taxes and stop the boats' was totally negative in tone if more stridently delivered.

Instead, with not much over which to argue, the election focused mostly on the competing leadership claims and credentials of Gillard and Abbott—despite the fact that both these leaders had been in the top job for a short period and each had relatively slight track records. The emphasis on leadership also kept attention on the sudden demise of Kevin Rudd, who was by now a damaged and enigmatic figure. But Rudd chose not to go quietly. His presence loomed over the entire election period and his antics sucked the oxygen from Labor's campaign. With some of Rudd's supporters deliberately playing a spoiler role in the first weeks of the campaign with embarrassing 'leaks', Gillard's judgments and motivations were repeatedly called into question. She was constantly accused of being disloyal and having given way to the 'faceless men' of Labor's murky factions. In interviews and in so-called 'town meetings', she was constantly called on to justify her actions in deposing Rudd as a first-term prime minister. The topic would not go away. But as the election campaign proceeded—principally focused on the prospective leadership qualities of Gillard and Abbott—business and unions did not appear to have much new to say or contribute on this question.

The Attitudes of Business

For most of its short life, the Rudd Government had been keen not to have an adversarial relation with business groups. It had courted the business sector and worked closely with some of its leading executives (not just within the peak groups but in the wider corporate sectors, especially banking and finance). Some business associations, such as the manufacturing-based Australian Industry Group (AIG), although steadfastly non-aligned, had developed close links with the Rudd Government and had been coopted on to a range of policy and advisory bodies. The CEO and chief spokeswoman of the AIG, Heather Ridout, had been used by the government as the constructive and sensible voice of business, and had developed close links to both Rudd and Gillard (with appointments to Skills Australia, Infrastructure Australia, the Business Advisory Group on Workplace Relations and the Henry Tax Review; see *The Weekend Australian* 2010). Ridout had notably refused to join with other business associations in a public campaign defending the WorkChoices legislation in the 2007 election, much to John Howard's disgust. By 2008, she was referred to publicly as the government's 'most influential public policy adviser' and a 'woman with the Prime Minister's ear' (*Sydney Morning Herald*, 24 May 2008).

Most other business associations, including the mining association, had maintained neutral and professional relationships with the Labor Government in its first term. The Australian Chamber of Commerce and Industry (ACCI) had initially been on the outer with Labor when its spokesman, Peter Hendy, was accused of being an extension of Howard's private office, but had since slowly tried to rebuild its links to government. The Business Council of Australia (BCA) had been chiselling away at longer-term challenges to business such as competition, innovation, productivity and the importance of taking adequate measures in the midst of the global financial crisis (GFC). The National Farmers' Federation (NFF) was concerned about the damaging aspects of the 'two-speed economy' rapidly enhancing the fortunes of some regions (Queensland and Western Australia) and industries (mining) while leaving other sectors falling behind in economic importance and living standards. The NFF had also developed extensive policy responses on climate change, environmental sustainability and water; population and regional development; economic policies and trade; and property rights (farmers' land rights). Finally, the Mining Council of Australia (MCA) was critical of infrastructural bottlenecks constraining exports, but then became seriously offside with the government over the mining super-profits tax (see below) announced jointly by the Prime Minister and Treasurer in May 2010.

Most of the corporate sector (finance and banking, insurance, retail, manufacturing, construction, real estate) was relatively comfortable with the first-term Labor Government, especially after its propitious and timely actions with the banking guarantees and stimulus packages to offset the worst aspects of the GFC. Those sectors of business dominated by consumer confidence and turnover had weathered the storm rather well due to concerted government action. So, for the most part, business remained relatively neutral and passive in the campaign. It did not mobilise its forces and did not aggressively campaign for one side or the other.

Many of the messages emanating from business during the campaign concerned the need to get crucial policy issues 'right' according to their assessments, while injecting some policy clarity and consistency. They used the opportunity to lobby for particular agendas of longer-term interest to business. They employed professional researchers to produce policy statements backed by evidence, and then put these preferences on their web sites without attracting much mainstream media attention. Business generally resisted the call for a 'small Australia' after Gillard distanced herself from Rudd's embrace of a 'big Australia' of 35 million by 2050. They were concerned about skills shortages, immigration levels, energy availability and the costs of utilities, and the need to have clarity about climate change policies (mitigation and adaptation). Some groups (for example, ACCI 2010, 1) stressed the need for government austerity and to return to budgetary surpluses as a basis for 'sound economic management'; others stressed the need for more extensive tax reform to promote growth. There were occasional complaints that the *Fair Work Act* had gone too far or included more generous concession to the unions than had initially been proposed, but other business leaders called for stability in industrial relations and for a chance to allow the new law to bed down. Overall, business tended to promote what they themselves referred to as 'sleeper issues' (QRC 2010, 1).

The Proposed Minerals Super-Profits Tax

The one exception to the relative complacency of business was the mining sector that waged a fierce public relations battle with the government throughout the last weeks of Rudd's leadership, and then with behind-the-scenes pressure on Gillard once she deposed Rudd. It was fought over a proposed 'super tax' on mining profits that would be shared by all Australians not merely those in the mining-rich States. While the proposed tax at first glance seemed a sound policy (reaping national benefit from the resource boom), it quickly became apparent that it was poorly designed and was being badly handled politically. The stoush ignited a political furore and led to the Labor factions toppling Rudd in late June.

Although a climate of opinion across business was largely accepting of increased taxes on the booming mining industry, the announcement of the Minerals Super-Profits Tax (MSPT) was both ill fated and ill thought out. It also followed closely on the heels of the government announcing it would abandon its attempts to introduce a carbon pollution reduction scheme. The idea behind the proposed rent tax had been floated in the report of the Henry Tax Review released on 2 May 2010, which advocated a 40 per cent resource rent tax on pre-tax profits of all mining firms in addition to company taxes and State royalties (although a 'tax credit' would be allowed for royalty payments). Some argued that in effect the super-profits tax was an 'equity' tax in that the government shared an extra dividend when the firms were highly profitable even though it had no direct ownership (Henry Ergas in *The Australian*, 6 May 2010, 12). Journalists had been briefed about the new tax in late April, with claims the new rent tax would raise about $5 billion, and initially the proposal received some good press. But when the tax was unilaterally announced by Prime Minister, Kevin Rudd, and the Treasurer, Wayne Swan, on 2 May 2010, they indicated that the estimated windfall to the government would amount to a total of $9 billion in its first two years, with the tax cutting in on all profits above the government bond rate of 5–6 per cent. Yet the estimate of the revenue likely to be raised itself kept rising, and soon it was claimed that the MSPT would raise $10.5 billion, then $12 billion over two years. The government did not appear to have had much consultation over the imposition of the new tax with the mining industry, which seemed genuinely taken by surprise.

In the face of the government's unilateral announcement, the immediate response from the mining industry was described as 'outrage' (*The Australian*, 3 May 2010, 5). Miners claimed that the new tax was unfair, too costly and would threaten future investment. Industry executives believed that not only were they not consulted over the decision but that also the government had deliberately double-crossed them by pretending to reassure them that there would be no taxation changes without extensive consultation. BHP-Billiton even claimed its effective tax rate would rise from 47 per cent to 53 per cent with the additional tax. Mining shares on the stock market were also severely hit over the days following the announcement, dropping some $16 billion in value in just two days (and more than $65 billion in three weeks). Crisis talks between the Prime Minister and mining executives were held during May, without either side giving much ground. Given the seriousness of the issue for the industry, the leaders of the mining industry (leading CEOs, mining firms and the various mining associations) began a massive, concerted advertising campaign to dissuade the government from its course of action (costing an estimated $22 million). Much of the pressure and criticism was personally directed at Kevin Rudd and to a lesser extent at Wayne Swan as the chief architects of the policy.

The advertising campaign ran pro-industry advertisements on TV with popular actors talking up the contributions mining made and the impact of the tax on jobs and economic growth more generally. These were supported by a blitz of other media advertisements, press releases and web-based promotions. For instance, full-page advertisements by the MCA talked of the fact that 'the minerals resources industry paid $80 billion in taxes and royalties in the past decade—the resources sector pays Australia's highest tax rate—that's a fair share'. The ad suggested that taxes on mining had risen from $2.6 billion in 1999 to $21.9 billion in 2009 (*The Australian*, 7 May 2010, 7). Miners claimed the super tax would raise more than $10.5 billion per year. Their campaign against the Commonwealth Government was supported by the State governments from the mining States (many that were led by Labor such as Queensland and South Australia), but not surprisingly, the main political opposition came from the Liberal WA Government (even though it cynically increased State royalties from 5 per cent to 7 per cent in case it was to receive compensation from the Commonwealth). The most vociferous political opponent was the federal Opposition whose leader, Tony Abbott, dubbed the tax as simply a resource grab and another 'great big tax', which he would abolish if he won government. The ferocity of the mining campaign saw the government respond in late May with a proposed advertising campaign of its own, estimated to cost $38 million.

The mining campaign was conducted with some vehemence until the day Rudd was deposed, after which Gillard called for a truce while she was given time to negotiate over the details. She did not conduct negotiations with the entire industry but instead chose to sign an agreement with the biggest three corporations (BHP-Billiton, Rio Tinto and Xstrada). Gillard retitled the tax the Minerals Resource Rent Tax (MRRT), and announced some major concessions: a lower rate of tax at 30 per cent (effectively 22.5 per cent), with super profits calculated after a rate of double the bond rate (about 12 per cent) and with the MRRT applying only to larger miners in the iron-ore, coal and oil and gas sectors. The immediate future of the MRRT was, however, still shrouded in uncertainty as many of the fine details had not been worked through, especially who would foot the bill for any additional increase in State royalties.

Mining associations such as AMEC representing the small and medium miners and exploration firms remained incensed that the government had not included them in the negotiations, and promised to maintain their anti-tax campaign even though the tax would hardly apply to their members. As Gillard moved to call the early election, she was still under attack from sections of the mining industry even though the concessions had been accepted by the big players.

The Unions' Softly-Softly Campaign

Sections of the union movement aligned with the Labor Party wielded considerable backroom influence in the change of leadership in June 2010 (Howes 2010), but played a relatively sedate role in the campaign itself. After the GFC, the union movement picked but a few small fights with the government. It largely chose to emphasise a limited set of policy issues on which to seek to exert influence. Some unions had become a little disillusioned by Gillard's industrial relations reforms in the *Fair Work Act*, believing worker and union rights had not been sufficiently restored (especially access rights to worksites). The government argued that if both sides of the industrial relations community were a little unhappy then it must have the policy 'about right'—a comment it used in other policy areas such as climate change and the resource tax. Building-industry unions were critical that the government had retained the controversial Australian Building and Construction Commission, an industry watchdog serving as a regulator of the unions in the industry and a body intended to eliminate intimidation on worksites. A few more militant or breakaway unions were more strident in their attacks on the government but were not supported by the majority of unions. Interestingly, a few unions (especially the Australian Workers' Union) ran advertisements in support of the mining tax, attacking mining executives personally for profiteering from the mining boom and having close political links with the conservative parties.

Once the election was under way, the unions largely left the running of their campaign to the ACTU leadership, which played a quiet, low-key role. The President, Ged Kearney, and Secretary, Jeff Lawrence, issued almost daily statements welcoming such announcements as school-based apprenticeships, work-experience trade cadetships and proposed increases in superannuation, but there was not much public visibility from these two. By far the majority of these media releases were commentary on and critiques of aspects of Tony Abbott's campaign. In contrast, the ACTU gave the Gillard Government an almost low-key endorsement, perhaps realising that union support for the Labor Government was soft and patchy. A short, small-scale advertising campaign was run in late July and early August (largely as a retaliatory strategy), costing less than $5 million and nothing compared with the scale of advertising the unions commissioned in 2007 (*The Weekend Australian*, 7–8 August 2010, 10). These ads asked voters to support the government's industrial relations laws, which were considered an improvement on the Howard years, and to prevent the return of WorkChoices. YouTube spoof ads depicting Tony Abbott in 'budgie smugglers' also attempted to suggest that he was planning to smuggle in harsh amendments to the fair work arrangements designed to undermine working conditions. Another amusing short video posted on YouTube by the Australian Workers' Union (AWU) depicted the Coalition as the Addams Family, featuring Tony Abbott as Gomez, Julie Bishop as Morticia, Joe Hockey as Pugsley and Barnaby Joyce as Uncle Fester (receiving about 25 000 hits). But these antics had amusement value rather than any real impact. More significant were ads attacking Abbott's leadership, suggesting he would slash the public sector, impose a $1 billion cut on government spending, and could not be trusted if he managed to form government (Abbott had earlier promised to make $47 billion in 'savings' from Labor's planned spending, much of which would come from scaling back the broadband initiative; see *The Australian*, 20 May 2010, 1). The ACTU claimed it had undertaken a survey and found 71 per cent of voters did not believe Abbott's denial that he would not amend fair work laws (ACTU 2010b).

Other unions used the election campaign as an extension of their industrial campaigns, taking the opportunity of getting their messages out to a wider audience. Unions ran public demonstrations against the WA Liberal Government over threats to local industrial relations provisions, and in Sydney over threats to jobs and employment. But the Queensland unions did not avail themselves of the opportunity of attacking the State Labor Government over its ambitious program of asset sales of public infrastructure. The AWU interestingly highlighted longer-term policy options for improved living standards, such as job security, retirement incomes and superannuation. The Construction, Forestry, Mining and Energy Union (CFMEU) called for greater certainty in the building industry and for action on climate change. The public-sector unions predictably argued for increased job numbers (with demands for an extra 12 000 from the Community and Public Sector Union), and against what they claimed was 'under-funding' of public services. Some, such as the National Tertiary Education Union, still campaigned against individual Australian Workplace Agreements (AWAs) in the workplace.

Political Donations from Business and Unions

Political donations to the major parties over 2009–10 totalled some $15 million: $8.2 million to the Liberals, $641 000 to The Nationals, and $6.1 million to the ALP. Funding to the Liberal and National parties from business was dominated by some of the large mining firms. Mineralogy Proprietary Limited (Clive Palmer) donated more than $1 million to State and federal branches of both conservative parties. Five of the six largest single donations were from mining companies— four to the Liberal Party and one to The Nationals. Many other businesses divided their donations roughly equally, giving similar contributions to both sides (for example, ANZ Bank, Westfield, Macquarie Group, Pratt Holdings, Wesfarmers, Coca-Cola, Clubs NSW, Australian Hotels Association, Tabcorp). Tobacco firms donated collectively some $240 000 only to the conservative side (ALP policy refuses funding from tobacco firms). The Liberals attracted a significant number of large donations from wealthy individuals.

Labor funds emanated predominantly from Labor funding arms (for example, Queensland Labor Holdings, $1.5 million), the Shop Distributors' Union ($310 000) and the AWU ($225 000), followed by other affiliated unions (Manufacturing Workers, CFMEU, Liquor and Hotel, Health Services Union, Australian Services Union, and Transport Workers' Union). Most other unions either did not make contributions or did not make significant contributions in the year before the election. Other sizeable donations came from legal and accounting firms with Labor connections, Labor clubs and hotel associations, construction companies and diverse investment entities. The CFMEU also donated $1.2 million to the left-of-centre lobby group GetUp! to feature ads attacking the Opposition Leader's attitudes to women and Indigenous issues (*The Australian*, 15 November 2010). This prompted the Liberal Senator Eric Abetz to claim GetUp! was a front for Labor and therefore ought to be investigated by the Electoral Commission as an associated entity of the ALP.

A Few Final Oddities and Quirky Moments

Not everything that occurred around the campaign was entirely predictable. The NFF talked of business suffering from 'reform fatigue' especially in the field of industrial relations. It volunteered to be 'part of the climate change solution' especially over carbon offsets, reafforestation and carbon sequestration in the ground (providing they were paid to participate). Meanwhile, an inept campaign funded by cigarette manufacturers using a hired lobby group lasted for about two days in trying to argue against proposed mandatory plain packaging legislation for cigarettes. After their first public salvo, the bogus group (the Alliance of Australian Retailers), which had some $5 million at its disposal, was exposed as a 'front' for the tobacco industry, and was publicly discredited.

The maverick Electricity Trades Union (ETU) in a statement of rebuke to the ALP publicly backed the Greens candidate, Adam Bandt, in the seat of Melbourne. The Victorian branch of the ETU not only provided public endorsement for the Greens as the only progressive alternative but also provided funding to the environmentalist party. The ETU apparently gave $325 000 to assist the Greens' campaign. Bandt in his maiden speech thanked the union for its support and announced that unions were becoming more independent and were not tied to the ALP automatically. The AWU's Paul Howes spoke out publicly against Bandt, saying there was no 'dawning of a new political era in which unions are no longer tied to the Labor Party' (*The Australian*, 8 October 2010).

Regulations on commercial and recreational fishing became an iconic cause for regional Australia. Bob Katter in particular embraced their cause, saying all manner of freedoms were being eroded by unnecessary regulation by big-brother governments. He claimed that pretty soon people would not be allowed to 'boil a billy' in Australia—a populist sentiment that resonated in regional Australia.

Conclusion

The 2010 election was highly unusual in many respects: the suddenness of its timing, occurring shortly after the removal of a first-term prime minister, the first to be led by a woman prime minister, the vacuity of the campaign and the lack of any real issues or policy contest. It was also unusual in that neither business nor the union movement played a pivotal role. The unions were at best lukewarm about Labor and predictably hostile towards Tony Abbott, but it was an understated and uninspiring campaign. Business was uncertain how to respond in the volatile political circumstances, finding it hard to 'read' the politics and unsure what the electoral outcome would deliver. Business largely sat on its hands and watched from the sidelines. The one exception was the mining industry that ran the high-profile anti–super-tax campaign lasting about two months; but even with the miners much of the heat of the issue had passed by the onset of the campaign and Gillard only had to deal with a few barbs from the smaller mining exploration firms who were nevertheless relatively restrained.

References

Association of Mining and Exploration Companies (AMEC). 2010a. Press release, 16 July. Perth: Association of Mining and Exploration Companies.

Association of Mining and Exploration Companies (AMEC). 2010b. Press release, 26 July. Perth: Association of Mining and Exploration Companies.

Australian Chamber of Commerce and Industry (ACCI). 2010. It's still the economy: economic management no. 1 business issue. Media release, 23 July. Sydney: Australian Chamber of Commerce and Industry.

Australian Council of Trade Unions (ACTU). 2010a. Press release, 10 July. Melbourne: Australian Council of Trade Unions.

Australian Council of Trade Unions (ACTU). 2010b. Media release, 25 July. Melbourne: Australian Council of Trade Unions.

Howes, Paul. 2010. *Confessions of a Faceless Man*. Melbourne: Melbourne University Press.

Queensland Resources Council (QRC). 2010. Election 'sleepers' demand attention. Media release, July. Brisbane: Queensland Resources Council.

The Weekend Australian. 2010. 'Change in leadership brings test for Ridout'. *The Weekend Australian*, 10–11 July, 29.

Wanna, John. 2010. 'Business and unions'. In *Australian Cultural History* 28(1) (April): 15–22.

24. Environmental Issues and the 2010 Campaign

Geordan Graetz and Haydon Manning

The 2010 campaign was notable for its dearth of significant environmental policy announcements and coverage of environmental issues. Despite this, there were pronouncements by the major parties on climate change, the Murray–Darling Basin, population, marine parks, the Queensland Government's Wild Rivers legislation and forestry and conservation measures. From this list of issues, however, it is difficult to divine a unifying theme; and Bean and McAllister's chapter in this volume also indicates that the environment trailed bread-and-butter issues such as health and Medicare, the economy and education as significant issues for voters. This all stands in contrast with the 2007 election, in which the government's response to climate change and management of the nation's water systems were front-of-mind issues for many voters and thus garnered sustained media attention.

Climate Change Responses

Climate change was one of the two major policy areas that saw Kevin Rudd swept to power in November 2007 (the other being industrial relations). Indeed, as Opposition Leader, Rudd had done much to paint John Howard as a ditherer on the issue. In government, Rudd was initially successful: he quickly ratified the Kyoto Protocol and travelled to the Bali Conference (2007 UN Climate Change Conference) in his first foreign foray as Prime Minister, and the Garnaut Climate Change Review, which he had commissioned while in Opposition, presented its final report in late September 2008. The government also commissioned a Green Paper (later a White Paper) on an emissions trading scheme and released its final report, *Carbon Pollution Reduction Scheme: Australia's low pollution future*, in December 2008. Rudd appeared to be taking action and he enjoyed high public approval ratings. The postponement of the emissions trading scheme, however— announced in April 2010 after several attempts to gain Senate support for the scheme—precipitated a fall in his popularity and his subsequent removal.

Clearly, there were 'hits and misses' in the Rudd Government's approach to climate change. Certainly, failure at Copenhagen and the postponement of the Carbon Pollution Reduction Scheme (CPRS) abraded Rudd's public standing and it was against this backdrop that the new Prime Minister went into the 2010 election campaign. Gillard argued that the domestic consensus on Australia's response to climate change had deteriorated in part due to the global financial crisis and the fear campaign spearheaded by Tony Abbott (he had labelled the CPRS a 'great big new tax on everything'). As a consequence, and during the campaign, Gillard proposed a 'citizens' assembly' on climate change: a panel of 150 citizens selected at random to be convened in 2012 to advise the government on the best way to achieve community-wide consensus on pricing carbon.

The 'citizens' assembly' was arguably the most derided policy initiative of the campaign, being condemned by the Opposition, Greens MPs, climate activists, scientists, economists and the media. Tony Abbott remarked: 'We already have a citizens' assembly; it's called a parliament. This is a decision for the Parliament. And [the Prime Minister] can't subcontract out leadership to some kind of giant focus group' (ABC 2010a). Even the Labor backbencher Steve Gibbons publicly criticised his leader's policy at a candidates' forum in his electorate, complaining that caucus had not been consulted and stating his opposition to the proposal (ABC 2010e). To be sure, Gillard had not even consulted her Cabinet over the plan (Tingle and Kitney 2010). Since the election, the 'citizens' assembly', which has been dumped as party policy, has again come under scrutiny, with Karl Bitar, Labor's serving National Secretary and Campaign Director, lambasting the scheme at his election wash-up speech to the National Press Club (Maher 2010).

Despite this misstep, during the campaign Gillard sought to affirm her climate credentials. She recommitted Labor to an emissions trading scheme and stated her opposition to a carbon tax; however, she upheld the Rudd Government's decision to delay putting a price on carbon until at least 2013. In a bid to appeal to the environmentally conscious voter, Gillard pledged $1 billion to connect renewable energy developments to the national electricity grid and proposed stricter environmental controls on new coal-fired power stations (Peatling 2010). In addition, Gillard promised $394 million for a 'cash for clunkers' scheme. Formally titled the 'Cleaner Car Rebate', the policy entailed supporting 'motorists to purchase new, low-emission, fuel-efficient vehicles'. Households, the policy envisaged, would 'be able to receive a $2,000 rebate towards a new vehicle by trading in their pre-1995 car for scrapping' (ALP n.d.). The rebate would be capped at 200 000 vehicles and run from 1 January 2011 to December 2014.

The Opposition took a substantively different approach as they aimed for a 'direct action' set of measures to lower emissions. Abbott promised $3.2 billion over four years for grants and subsidies to directly cut emissions and proposed to pay farmers to store emissions in their soil, creating 'carbon sinks'. The Opposition also proposed to pay brown-coal-fired power stations to convert to more environmentally friendly combined-cycle gas generation. In addition, Abbott undertook to plant 20 million trees in urban areas (to act as carbon sinks) and pledged to reward forestry companies that increased plantation numbers or that practised better forest management (Karvelas 2010a). In a further policy announcement, Abbott stated that the Coalition would axe funding to the Rudd Government's Global Carbon Capture and Storage Institute to the tune of $300 million, while also announcing plans to scrap Labor's $39.8 million program to assist small to medium-sized companies 'green up', as well as the government's $5 million fund for green buildings (Alexander 2010).

The Greens made a series of policy announcements on climate change; most notable was their call for an interim carbon tax. In addition, the Greens sought binding targets for emissions reductions in 2012, 2020 and 2050. The party also proposed national energy efficiency targets, a 30 per cent mandatory renewable energy target by 2020 (as opposed to the 20 per cent target that enjoyed support from both the Labor and the Liberal parties) and an end to taxpayer-funded subsidies for fossil-fuel industries (Peatling 2010). One of the Greens' largest policy announcements came at their campaign launch in early August in the form of a $5 billion loan guarantee scheme, which would provide eligible businesses willing to develop large-scale renewable energy projects with an opportunity to apply for loan guarantees at 100 per cent of the principal (ABC 2010c).

Water Politics

The management of Australia's water resources, particularly those in the Murray–Darling Basin, was also among the list of prominent environmental issues debated during the campaign. While the Murray–Darling Basin Authority (MDBA) delayed the release of its discussion paper, *Guide to the proposed Basin Plan*, until after the election, citing caretaker provisions—provoking anger among irrigators and regional communities—the major parties made several announcements pertaining to the future of the Basin (Beeby 2010).

Labor promised to continue voluntary water buybacks to return sufficient environmental water to the river system, having already purchased almost $1.4 billion of environmental water since 2008 (Morris 2010). The government also undertook to accept the recommendations of the MDBA regarding cuts to water allocations. In addition, Labor announced that it would commence water-saving works in the Menindee catchment area in October 2010. In contrast, the Coalition promised to strike a balance between the interests of the environment and those of regional communities, by undertaking an assessment of the social and economic consequences of the Basin Plan if it were to form government (Wahlquist 2010). Mick Keogh from the Australian Farm Institute pointed, however, to a potential problem for the Opposition with regard to this pledge:

the MDBA is 'required by legislation', introduced by the Howard Government in 2007, 'to consider only the environment' and not the interests of communities, industry or the economic consequences of its proposals (Wahlquist 2010).

Further to its pledge to balance the interests of the environment and regional communities, the Coalition announced $730 million for water-saving infrastructure to assist communities to change their irrigation practices. Part of the package included $300 million for improving on-farm water-efficiency measures. It also included funding for the Menindee Lakes region. Furthermore, the Coalition pledged to purchase 150 billion litres of water for South Australia's stricken Lower Lakes and Coorong region at a cost of $20 million (Arup and Welch 2010; Berkovic 2010). In a separate policy announcement, the Opposition Leader promised to hold a referendum on Commonwealth control of water if States refused to implement the reforms needed to restore the river system to health (Berkovic 2010).

In a different area of water policy, the Minister for Climate Change and Water, Penny Wong, undertook during the election to pay the water debts owed to the Snowy Hydro electricity scheme for the years 2002–05, which was part of an agreement with the NSW and Victorian governments to return water to the river. In announcing the policy, Wong stated that it would result in 56 billion litres of additional water for the river over the following two years and would remove environmental water flow caps earlier than had been envisaged. The cost of the proposal came to $13.7 million (Arup and Welch 2010).

The Population Debate

One of the more interesting policy issues to be discussed during the campaign was Australia's population trajectory. Population had grown to be a prominent issue in the months prior to the election because of Kevin Rudd's comments in October 2009 that he welcomed the prospect of a 'big Australia', after Treasury's *Intergenerational Report* projected a population of 36 million by 2050 (*7.30 Report*, 22 October 2010, ABC TV). Rudd's articulation of his vision for Australia—growing, prosperous, forward-looking, educated and globally engaged—failed to find favour with focus groups and he faced dissent within his own party. Recognising community anxiety over a growing population, and with the Opposition exploiting and further exacerbating the issue by tying population growth to the arrival of asylum-seekers by boat, Rudd created a new ministerial position within Cabinet in April 2010: the Ministry for Population.

In an interview with the Nine Network's Laurie Oakes just days after becoming Prime Minister, Julia Gillard, however, rejected her predecessor's vision, saying, 'I don't believe in a big Australia. Kevin Rudd indicated that he had a view about a big Australia. I'm indicating a different approach. I think we want an Australia that is sustainable' (Symons-Brown 2010). Under Gillard, 'sustainability' became the catchphrase of the campaign. In her ministerial reshuffle after assuming the prime ministership, she added 'Sustainable' to the title of the Minister for Population, Tony Burke, rendering him the Minister for Sustainable Population.

Gillard directed her words to voters in outer-metropolitan areas who were concerned about the impact of increased numbers of residents on service delivery and infrastructure capability, thus framing the debate in terms of maintaining Australians' unique lifestyle (Gordon 2010). But she also appealed to green voters with her emphasis on sustainability. Gillard's departure from the 'growth is good' mantra marked an end to the historical bipartisan consensus that held that Australians needed to populate or we would perish. But Gillard was not alone. Abbott and Opposition immigration spokesman, Scott Morrison, had abandoned the consensus position earlier in the year, and during the campaign called for the immigration intake to be reduced to 170 000 per year. Ironically, the Coalition's position is forecast to be achieved naturally as a result of normal immigration push/pull factors (van Onselen 2010).

The parties were responding to a shift in public opinion on the issue. Under the Howard Government, Australia had substantially increased its immigration intake, and the electorate had generally supported this program. But under the Rudd Government, the perception emerged, and was fostered by the Opposition, that the government had lost control of Australia's borders. Of course, this was a nonsense not supported by the facts, but the issue became more acute with cost-of-living pressures and shock jocks bemoaning infrastructure bottlenecks. A survey of Australians' attitudes to social issues, released during the campaign, found that three-quarters of Australians opposed the idea of a bigger Australia, with the figure reaching 86 per cent in regional Queensland. Blue-collar workers were most opposed to population growth (81 per cent), while social professionals were the least resistant (57 per cent) (Curtin 2010).

The media split over the issue, with the ABC airing during the campaign the controversial documentary *Dick Smith's Population Puzzle*. The broadcast was followed by a live *Q&A* population debate, which featured a number of prominent anti–population-growth campaigners. Smith argued that Australia needed to place a moratorium on population growth, stabilise the population at 26 million people, and reduce the immigration intake to 70 000 per annum, while doubling the humanitarian resettlement program to 25 000 (Meacham 2010).

The Australian took a different line and dedicated numerous pages throughout the campaign to pro-growth arguments. Political columnist George Megalogenis accused Gillard of 'dog whistling', while economics columnist Michael

Stutchbury denounced Dick Smith's position as rank protectionism and decried the retreat from Rudd's vision as 'zero-growth environmentalism' (Megalogenis 2010; Stutchbury 2010). Oliver Hartwich (2010) argued 'there is only one thing that's more unpleasant than dealing with the side-effects of growth. It's dealing with the side-effects of decline.' *The Australian*'s editorial column (26 July 2010) argued that Abbott and Gillard were engaged in an intellectually dishonest campaign and warned that imposing a cap on population growth 'will erode our economic prosperity'.

Business groups also voiced their concerns about the content and tenor of the public discourse on population. Heather Ridout, Chief Executive of the Australian Industry Group, said the 'hot-house atmosphere of the election campaign is not a proper one [in which] to have an analytical [debate] about population', while Chief Economist of the WA Chamber of Commerce and Industry, John Nicolau, submitted: 'It's a real concern…that we are looking at a more populist approach to the population debate' (Hewett 2010). Also throwing their support behind a big Australia were National Seniors Chairman, Everald Compton, a member of the government's demographic change and liveability advisory committee, and National Farmers' Federation President David Crombie (Karvelas 2010b). The wealth management (retirement savings) and property industries' lobbies also called for a bigger Australia (Charles 2010; Symons-Brown 2010).

In contrast, the Australian Conservation Foundation's Chuck Berger welcomed Gillard's nod to sustainability, and called on her to convert her commitment into a 'practical national population strategy'. Greens leader Bob Brown also called for a renewed focus on training local workers, as opposed to continued reliance on the skilled-migration program (Symons-Brown 2010).

It is worth pausing to reflect for a moment on the paradigmatic shift that has taken place in discussions about population. Continuous population growth driven by immigration has underpinned Australia's prosperity, and it is interesting to observe the shift in public sentiment in favour of the limits-to-growth thesis, which is so apparent in Dick Smith's public utterances. That significant sections of the Australian community now support lower growth is easily explained: politicians and anti-growth campaigners are not being truthful about the consequences of lower population growth on voters' standards of living. Indeed, it is difficult to imagine that the same voters who succumbed to Abbott's scare campaign on the CPRS because of concerns about cost-of-living increases will accept lower standards of living as a consequence of lower and continually declining economic growth. We need only look to Japan and Europe to see the ramifications of such an approach. Hartwich (2010) made a fundamental observation is his column for *The Australian*: 'Growth is not everything, but without growth everything is more difficult.'

Marine Parks

The issue of marine parks also received attention during the campaign, with the so-called 'tinny lobby' joining forces with Liberal and National party candidates and the Fishing and Lifestyle Party to target 13 Labor-held seats in New South Wales and Queensland that were likely to be affected by the plan of the then Environment Minister, Peter Garrett, to create a network of marine parks covering more than 5 million sq km (Cleary 2010a, 2010b). The issue, which was followed closely by *The Australian*'s Paul Cleary, 'sparked an underground political movement driven by blogs and social media pages' and led to a number of protests (Cleary 2010a).

Under the Howard Government, marine parks were successfully established off the coast of Victoria and Tasmania, and when the Rudd Government came to power, Garrett continued the program and identified new areas for protection. Garrett, however, came under sustained criticism from professional and recreational fishers for his failure to adequately consult affected communities and business operators, as well as his stance on compensation for those who were negatively affected by the conservation measures. Recognising that sentiment was turning against Labor, the Coalition argued for an additional period of consultation, and promised that operators who could provide proof of negative impact would be compensated (Cleary 2010c).

During the Coalition's campaign launch, Tony Abbott declared that one of his first acts as prime minister would be to stop Labor's proposed marine parks (Parnell 2010). Abbott did not promise, however, to abandon the marine parks plan altogether, merely to suspend the current process and to consult more widely. But the Coalition's position drew the ire of Minister Garrett, who dismissed the party's 'appeal to the fishing vote as a populist pitch that was inconsistent with past policy' (Cleary 2010b). For his part, Garrett postponed his final decision on the creation of a 1 million sq km conservation park in the Coral Sea until after the election, citing the need to engage with a wider section of the community before banning all fishing in the region, thus reneging on his promise of May 2009 to release a final schedule of proposed parks by the end of 2010 (Cleary 2010a).

Wild Rivers

In 2005, the Queensland Parliament passed the *Wild Rivers Act 2005*, designed to place limitations (environmental controls) on the kinds of developments that could occur in the declared high-preservation areas (wild river regions) of the Cape York Peninsula. The Act has been in force for several years now and has also been endorsed by Queensland electors at subsequent State elections. Protection of Queensland's 'wild rivers' came to prominence nationally, however, only recently after outspoken Indigenous leader and Director of the Cape York Institute for Policy and Leadership, Noel Pearson, launched a campaign against the Queensland Government and the Wilderness Society, which had supported the Act, arguing that it abrogated the rights of Indigenous peoples living on the Cape.

Tony Abbott has been a vocal critic of the Act since the legislation first came to his attention, and in early 2010 he signalled his intention to introduce legislation into the federal Parliament to overturn what he perceived as particularly odious aspects of the Act. His criticism of Wild Rivers grew stronger throughout the year and continued into the election campaign, when he again promised to introduce a Private Member's Bill into federal Parliament. In contrast, the federal Labor Party expressed support for its State Labor colleagues during the campaign.

Tasmanian Forests and Conservation Issues

During the 2004 election, John Howard had deftly outmanoeuvred Labor leader, Mark Latham, on forests policy and received the backing of the Forestry and Furnishing Products Division of the powerful Construction, Forestry, Mining and Energy Union (CFMEU). Forestry was thus pivotal to the campaign. In 2010, however, the management of Tasmania's forests and conservation issues more broadly barely rated a mention. Labor restricted its policy pronouncements to new bans on illegal timber imports, with Forestry Minister, Tony Burke, promising to introduce a 'mandatory code of conduct, requiring timber suppliers who place imports on the Australian market to check they are from a legal source'. The announcement came on the back of strong lobbying from Greenpeace and the corporate heavyweights Bunnings and Ikea, who warned of the impacts for the Australian timber industry of illegally logged imported timbers (Morris and Skulley 2010). The promise received widespread applause from green groups (ABC 2010d).

The focus of the Opposition differed from the government and concerned changes to managed forest investment schemes. Deputy leader, Julie Bishop, argued that there were problems with the current tax scheme that had resulted in the failure of some companies, and she flagged improvements to legislation governing tax arrangements (ABC 2010b). Taking the heat out of this issue were the groundbreaking talks on the future of the Tasmanian timber industry involving Timber Communities Australia, the National Association of Forest Industries, the CFMEU, Environment Tasmania, the Wilderness Society and the

Australian Conservation Foundation (ACF) that preceded the campaign. During the campaign, Coalition spokesman Eric Abetz said that the Opposition would oppose any deal that resulted in significant job losses even if the deal had the backing of industry representatives, while the Prime Minister expressed support for the negotiations and hinted that her government would consider funding an agreement if one were to transpire (Denholm 2010). While no agreement was struck during the campaign, a landmark deal was reached in October 2010 (Franklin 2010), and Regional Development Minister, Simon Crean, pledged to provide affected industry members with compensation (ABC 2010f).

Conclusion

The environmental issues that received attention during the 2010 election campaign were disparate and included climate change, the future of the Murray–Darling Basin, Australia's population, marine parks, Queensland's *Wild Rivers Act* and forestry and conservation. In its campaign evaluation of the major parties' environmental policies, the ACF, not surprisingly, awarded the Greens the highest mark, with a score of 90 per cent across four areas of focus: 1) the party's policies on reducing pollution; 2) making cleaner energy cheaper; 3) investing in cleaner, more sustainable cities and transport; and 4) protecting and restoring a healthy environment (ACF 2010). They awarded the Labor Party second position, with a score of 50 per cent, while the Liberal Party—the last of the major parties surveyed—scored only 22 per cent.

The issues that we have highlighted will be front of mind for the minority Gillard Government as it struggles to deal with community anxiety over climate change, increased living costs, the nation's water assets, infrastructure bottlenecks and a growing population, and in Queensland, threats to the commercial and recreational fishing industry. All of these issues are likely to reappear in the next campaign, but Tasmanian forest preservation—after so many campaigns on centre stage—looks like it will no longer feature so prominently.

References

Alexander, Cathy. 2010. 'Coalition to axe clean coal funding'. *Sydney Morning Herald*, 20 July.

Australian Broadcasting Corporation (ABC). 2010a. 'Gillard unveils climate change policy'. *Lateline*, 23 July, ABC TV, viewed 9 November 2010, <http://www.abc.net.au/lateline/content/2010/s2963020.htm>

Australian Broadcasting Corporation (ABC). 2010b. 'Libs flag forestry scheme changes'. *ABC News*, 30 July, viewed 31 October 2010, <http://www.abc.net.au/news/stories/2010/07/30/2969398.htm>

Australian Broadcasting Corporation (ABC). 2010c. 'Greens propose $5b renewable loans scheme'. *ABC News*, 8 August, viewed 31 October 2010, <http://www.abc.net.au/news/stories/2010/08/08/2976850.htm>

Australian Broadcasting Corporation (ABC). 2010d. 'Labor's logging ban wins applause'. *PM*, 10 August, ABC Radio, viewed 31 October 2010, <http://www.abc.net.au/pm/content/2010/s2979185.htm>

Australian Broadcasting Corporation (ABC). 2010e. 'Labor backbencher attacks climate change assembly'. *ABC News*, 12 August, viewed 31 October 2010, <http://www.abc.net.au/news/stories/2010/08/12/2981369.html>

Australian Broadcasting Corporation (ABC). 2010f. 'Crean prepared to help fund Tasmanian forest agreement'. *ABC Rural*, 22 October, viewed 31 October 2010, <http://www.abc.net.au/rural/news/content/201010/s3045778.htm>

Australian Broadcasting Corporation (ABC). 2010g. 'Abbott "playing politics" with wild rivers bill'. *ABC News*, 15 November, viewed 15 November 2010, <http://www.abc.net.au/news/stories/2010/11/15/3066469.htm>

Australian Conservation Foundation (ACF). 2010. *Election Scorecard: Party policy comparison table*. Melbourne: Australian Conservation Foundation.

Australian Labor Party (ALP). n.d. *Cleaner Car Rebate*. Canberra: Australian Labor Party, viewed 8 November 2010, <http://www.alp.org.au/agenda/connecting-renewables/cleaner-car-rebate/>

Arup, Tom and Welch, Dylan. 2010. 'Wong pledges water deal to save Snowy River'. *Sydney Morning Herald*, 12 August.

Beeby, Rosslyn. 2010. 'Irrigators irritated by "caretaker" gag on Murray–Darling plan'. *The Canberra Times*, 21 July.

Berkovic, Nicola. 2010. 'Abbott promises to save wetlands'. *The Australian*, 12 August.

Charles, Mathew. 2010. 'Call for big Australia'. *Herald Sun*, 9 August.

Cleary, Paul. 2010a. 'Garrett shelves fishing ban'. *The Australian*, 17 July.

Cleary, Paul. 2010b. 'Coalition fishes for coastal votes'. *The Australian*, 28 July.

Cleary, Paul. 2010c. 'Marine parks push sees fishing lobby wade in for a fight'. *The Australian*, 31 July.

Cleary, Paul. 2010d. 'Garrett loses his bottle in taking on the tinnies over marine parks'. *The Australian*, 14 August.

Curtin, Jennie. 2010. 'Big Australia vision goes down like a lead balloon'. *Sydney Morning Herald*, 4 August.

Denholm, Matthew. 2010. 'Gillard in danger of being wedged on forests with jobs on the line'. *The Australian*, 17 July.

Franklin, Matthew. 2010. 'Union declares forests war over'. *The Australian*, 23 October.

Gordon, Josh. 2010. 'Gillard rejects "big Australia"'. *The Age*, 27 June.

Hartwich, Oliver Marc. 2010. 'Europe shows alternative to growth is decline'. *The Australian*, 23 July.

Hewett, Jennifer. 2010. 'Business alarm at populist approach'. *The Australian*, 19 July.

Karvelas, Patricia. 2010a. 'Labor's plan to win back deserters'. *The Weekend Australian*, 14–15 August.

Karvelas, Patricia. 2010b. 'Keep growth out of the election: Ridout'. *The Australian*, 24 July.

Maher, Sid. 2010. 'Bitar lays out blame for poll'. *The Australian*, 10 November.

Meacham, Steve. 2010. 'Crusader Smith takes on his wealthy mates'. *Sydney Morning Herald*, 11 August.

Megalogenis, George. 2010. 'A sustainable idea of marginals'. *The Australian*, 19 July.

Morris, Sophie. 2010. 'Coalition could buy water: Joyce'. *Australian Financial Review*, 30 July.

Morris, Sophie and Skulley, Mark. 2010. 'Attack on imports of illegal timber'. *Australian Financial Review*, 11 August.

Parnell, Sean. 2010. 'Abbott spruiks Coalition, not LNP'. *The Australian*, 9 August.

Peatling, Stephanie. 2010. 'Critics blast emissions forum as more hot air'. *The Sun-Herald*, 25 July.

Stutchbury, Mike. 2010. 'Anti-growth stance a misty nostalgia for the little country that could'. *The Australian*, 14 August.

Symons-Brown, Bonny. 2010. 'Gillard rejects Rudd's "big Australia"'. *Sydney Morning Herald*, 27 June.

The Australian. 2010. 'The policy you have when you don't have a policy'. *The Australian*, 26 July.

Tingle, Laura and Kitney, Geoff. 2010. 'PM kept cabinet in dark on climate'. *Australian Financial Review*, 2 August.

van Onselen, Peter. 2010. 'Populist pitch on population'. *The Australian*, 26 July.

Wahlquist, Asa. 2010. 'Farmers cautious on Coalition pitch.' *The Australian*, 12 August.

25. Religion and the 2010 Election: Elephants in the room

John Warhurst

The 2010 Australian election continued a recent pattern in which religion has played a role in the campaign. This election continued some of the themes of recent elections such as Christian–Greens tensions, social morality and education politics, but with a new twist given the particular personal characteristics of the two major-party leaders: Julia Gillard, a declared atheist, and Tony Abbott, a conservative Catholic.

After the 2004 election campaign, prospective Labor leader, Kevin Rudd, concluded that the Coalition had captured the so-called 'religious vote'. This was a campaign conducted amid great publicity about the so-called 'Religious Right', the apparent rise of evangelical Christians, and the election of a Family First Senator, Steve Fielding. The established Christian churches, led by the Anglican and Catholic Archbishops of Melbourne and Sydney, had also campaigned against the education policies of Labor's agnostic leader, Mark Latham, apparently to great effect (Manning and Warhurst 2005). Rudd's subsequent project was to draw his party's attention to religious questions and to sell Labor's religious heritage and social gospel values to the electorate. It came to fruition in his article 'Faith in politics' for *The Monthly* magazine (Rudd 2006; reprinted in Macklin 2007).

The 2007 campaign saw this project in action (Warhurst 2010c). Rudd, an observant Anglican, attempted to sell his credentials to the evangelical constituency—in particular, through his participation alongside John Howard in the initial 'Making it Count' forum hosted by the Australian Christian Lobby (ACL). Here he combined personal social conservatism with social-justice principles based upon Christian socialism. Opinions vary as to how successful Rudd's ploy was. Rodney Smith, in his study of the ACL campaign (Smith 2009), doubts that it was. Others, such as former senator John Black and columnist Christopher Pearson, conclude that social conservatives in the church communities were drawn to Rudd, who promised, among other policies, not to advance the cause of gay marriage (Australian Development Strategies 2008). Certainly, religious belief was a notable aspect of Rudd's persona, and attention to his beliefs and church attendance continued throughout his term in office (Warhurst 2010a). Labor had a leader regarded as perhaps the most publicly religious of any prime minister in Australian history (Stuart 2009).

After Tony Abbott replaced Malcolm Turnbull as Opposition Leader in December 2009, he and Rudd were described as the most religious pair of leaders Australia had ever had (Young 2010). That was the state of play in the pre-campaign period when the ACL repeated its 'Make it Count' forum, held at Old Parliament House in Canberra, but also telecast to churches around Australia, on 21 June. This event—innovative in 2007—remains a notable part of the election campaign. Rudd and Abbott presented themselves as two pro-church leaders willing to endorse the ACL agenda on matters such as chaplains in schools, parliamentary prayers and opposition to gay marriage. Shortly afterwards, Rudd was deposed by Julia Gillard and this aspect of the election campaign was given a new twist.

The Beliefs of the Leaders

The two leaders offered a fascinating contrast in terms of religious beliefs. Arguably, they were both outside the Australian norm, despite a number of previous observant Christians and agnostics among previous prime ministers. Abbott's beliefs were always going to be an issue as his orthodox, conservative Catholicism had long attracted attention, especially the combination of his anti-abortion advocacy and his position as Howard's Minister for Health (Gleeson 2010; Warhurst 2007). This had come to a head when a conscience vote of the Parliament had removed his responsibility for the abortion drug RU486, in 2006.

Abbott's supporters claimed then that he was a victim of anti-Catholic sectarianism, while his critics claimed he was unelectable because of his relative unpopularity among women. During the campaign, some media certainly presented him as defined by his religious beliefs. The *Sydney Morning Herald* election special on the morning after the election was called, for instance, featured him in a large front-page cartoon wearing a clerical collar (*Sydney Morning Herald*, 19 July 2010). Afterwards *The Australian* claimed that the negative 'Mad Monk' image had been greatly overdone in various media (The Australian 2010).

Gillard's religious beliefs had not attracted attention when she was Deputy Prime Minister, being greatly overshadowed by her gender. But soon after she became the first woman prime minister, in stark contrast with both Abbott and Rudd, she declared herself to be an atheist (not an agnostic) in an ABC interview with Jon Faine, while stressing her Baptist religious upbringing and her respect for believers (Burchell 2010; Mullins 2010a). Thereafter her unbelief became part of her public identity as religious leaders cautioned against a growth in secular beliefs in the community. It was also frequently linked—directly and indirectly—with her de-facto relationship with her partner, Tim Mathieson.

The leaders themselves treaded cautiously and seemed not to wish to inflame the differences. Abbott was conciliatory (*Sydney Morning Herald*, 9 August 2010).[1] He promised not to attempt to change abortion laws if elected. Gillard engaged fruitfully with Cardinal George Pell in a Saint Mary McKillop fundraiser (Mullins 2010a), and maintained Rudd's policy opposition to gay marriage (Stockman 2010). She later apparently satisfied the ACL's Jim Wallace during a catch-up recorded interview (Stephens 2010).

Collective Church Lobbying

The major churches, church agencies and para-church groups traditionally undertake campaign advocacy across an enormous range of issues. This campaign was no different. The Australian Catholic Bishops' Conference, for instance, issued a statement identifying six essential criteria, beginning with '[t]he right of every person to human dignity' and mentioning 11 particular issues (Australian Catholic Bishops' Conference 2010).[2] The statement illustrates the frequent lack of focus in church statements, brought about by attempts to be inclusive of all religious points of view.

Particular church agencies and groups of agencies also entered the campaign. The social-justice agencies were unimpressed by both major parties on issues such as compassion for refugees and spending on foreign aid. Major church groups involved in social services called for greater investment in mental health. Various religious groups joined other groups in holding campaign meetings and hosting candidates' forums in local electorates (ACL, for instance, ran 20 such forums).

The ACL identified a range of concerns at the 'Making it Count' forum. These included seven topics covered in follow-up questions to each leader. These were: Indigenous affairs and the NT intervention, the continuation of parliamentary prayers, the treatment of asylum-seekers, the defence of traditional marriage and opposition to same-sex unions, the continuation of the school chaplaincy program, the alarming sexualisation of young girls, and climate change issues. Some of these questions would have graced any secular forum, while others clearly played to specialist church audiences.

---

1 A letter to the editor by M. Steffen noted Abbott's comments on ABC Radio the previous day: 'Just as my Catholicism should not be held against me, her views or lack of views on the subject should not be held against her [Gillard].'

2 The essential criteria were the right of every person to: human dignity; adequate food, shelter and protection; equality of access to education, health, employment and basic services; both present and future generations, to live in a safe, healthy and secure environment; and the duty to contribute to society to the extent that they are able; to live according to their own beliefs, to the extent that those beliefs do not impact upon the right of others. The issues were: health, social justice, migrants and refugees, overseas aid, women, Indigenous Australians, disability, the environment, education, religious liberty and human dignity.

Very little of this collective church lobbying had a high profile in the mainstream media, though it was mentioned, so that any influence was probably restricted to narrower audiences, including regular churchgoers. Much of it was deliberately bland, balanced and non-provocative. But this was not the case for some individual interventions.

Individual Church Lobbying

Gillard's beliefs were attacked by several unknown or marginal religious figures, such as Danny Nalliah of Catch the Fire Ministries. But the two most senior individuals who intervened in the campaign were Catholic archbishops: Barrie Hickey of Perth and George Pell of Sydney.

Hickey's comments decrying the growth of secularism were given a front-page headline ('Archbishop questions impact of Gillard's atheism') by the *West Australian* (29 July 2010). While he subsequently defended his comments as apolitical and misconstrued, they were certainly interpreted at the time as a veiled attack on Gillard and as being unhelpful to the Labor campaign. It drew an alternative view in *The Australian* by Anglican Archbishop of Perth, Roger Herft, that ethics were just as important as faith (*CathNews* 2010a).

Pell's initial comments were made in his regular column in *The Sunday Telegraph* and on the archdiocesan web site (8 August 2010). The main theme was a devastating attack on the Greens as 'anti-Christian'. He concluded that 'for those who value our present way of life, the Greens are sweet camouflaged poison'. Controversy followed. Bob Brown replied in equally provocative terms, questioning whether Pell represented mainstream Christianity (CathNews 2010b; Warhurst 2010a). Then an extensive online debate—some of it reported in the mainstream media—followed within the Catholic community. Some, such as Jesuit priest Frank Brennan and Catholic Social Services Australia's Frank Quinlan, attempted a conciliatory defence of the Greens (Brennan 2010; Quinlan 2010). Others, such as the Melbourne Director of Catholic Education, Steven Elder, claimed that support for the Greens was a vote against Catholic education (Elder 2010). The ACL supported Pell by uploading a second media release by the Sydney Catholic Archdiocese (9 August 2010). This bitter controversy had the potential to damage Greens support, especially in Sydney, where it contributed to a wider media attack on the Greens.

Secular Campaigning

Secular lobby groups are weaker in comparison. There is also the problem of which ones to include in such a category. The Atheist Foundation predicted that Gillard's beliefs would not be an electoral negative, while the national coordinator of EMILY's List rebutted the suggestion that to be pro-choice on abortion was anti-Christian (Sharp 2010).

Two minor political parties, the Secular Party and especially the Australian Sex Party, were probably of greater importance in this regard than any lobby group. The latter, launched in 2008, was convened by experienced lobbyist Fiona Patten. It campaigned against censorship and the Internet filter with the slogan 'Keeping politicians out of the bedroom', and had at least two prominent media supporters in David Barnett and Ross Fitzgerald (Fitzgerald 2010). It regularly portrayed itself as an opponent of religious hypocrisy.

Minor Religious Parties

Several smaller minor parties that can be described either as religious or as having religious overtones also campaigned nationally. The reborn Democratic Labor Party (DLP), buoyed by winning a seat in the Victorian Legislative Council in 2006, emphasised pro-life and pro-family issues and had Senate aspirations in its historical stronghold in Victoria. Family First, associated with evangelical churches, was led by Steve Fielding, hoping for election for a second term in the Senate contest in Victoria. The Christian Democratic Party (CDP) led by Reverend Fred Nile held seats in the NSW Legislative Council and always attracted votes in that State.

Impact on Voters

The evidence is slender so far but what there is suggests that on balance Abbott's religion was more of a negative than Gillard's atheism. Even when compared with Rudd in an earlier study by Graham Young of online opinion, Abbott's religion bothered more voters because they thought he was inflexible in his beliefs (Young 2010). Yet the chapter by Bean and McAllister in this volume indicates that although the pattern was 'unusual' in Australian political history, Catholics were inclined towards the Coalition.

The Canberra Times–Patterson poll in the electorate of Eden-Monaro, subsequently held by Labor, concluded that the religious views of the leaders when it mattered slightly favoured Gillard (McLennan 2010). It calculated that the net pro-Labor influence was 12 per cent while the net pro-Liberal influence was 9 per cent. Women, those under thirty-five and Greens voters were three categories noticeably drawn to Labor because of the religious factor, while men and over thirty-fives were more evenly split in this survey.

Conclusion

In this campaign religious belief or the lack of it threatened to become a major political issue. It pitted two political leaders whose attitude to religious belief was both out of the ordinary and markedly different. Gillard's public atheism contrasted clearly with Abbott's public Catholicism.

There was a range of interesting religion-related campaign phenomena, beginning even before Gillard became Prime Minister. Religious groups were active, as were prominent individuals such as Cardinal Pell. The religious groups predominantly advocated social-justice issues and, while apart from ACL perhaps marginally favouring Labor, were more often critical of both major parties for their inattention to their concerns.

But it turned out not to be a campaign in which support for the major parties turned on religion. To begin with Labor's Rudd and Gillard were both acceptable to the religious lobby. Gillard did receive some initial awkward negative publicity about her beliefs. But later both Abbott and Gillard softened their stances in order to build a more appealing centrist image.

The target of the religious lobbyists, as it had been in 2007, then became the Greens—regarded objectively as the most secular of the Australian political parties. Both Pell and the ACL targeted them on a range of issues, such as marriage, education and euthanasia, while they recognised the virtues of the Greens in other areas such as refugees and climate change.

The overall impact of the religion factor was probably slight, but in policy terms the religious groups did win concessions, including extensions of financial support for school chaplains and for private schools. The Greens polled exceptionally well despite the religious opposition to them. Their most contentious candidate, Lee Rhiannon, was elected to the Senate in New South Wales, though with the lowest Greens Senate vote nationwide.

The smaller religious parties had one surprising success. Fielding (2.64 per cent) failed in his bid for re-election in Victoria, but he was replaced with the DLP candidate, John Madigan, a blacksmith from Ballarat, who polled 2.34 per cent (Zwartz 2010). Family First went much closer to winning in South Australia where former Liberal candidate Bob Day (4.09 per cent) ran a well-funded personal campaign. The anti-religious parties, though unsuccessful, made their mark, too. The Sex Party, for instance, polled more than 2 per cent in a number of States.

The relationship between conservative religious groups and Gillard will be tested in the new Parliament on issues that the Greens will advance such as gay marriage and euthanasia, but so far Gillard has remained either opposed to or cautious about these parliamentary developments despite public debate and some Labor support (Maiden 2010).

References

Australian Catholic Bishops' Conference. 2010. 'Make your vote count say Catholic bishops'. Canberra: Australian Catholic Bishops' Conference.

Australian Christian Lobby (ACL). 2010. Web site: <australianchristianlobby. org.au/>. Canberra: Australian Christian Lobby.

Australian Development Strategies. 2008. *Profile of the 2007 Australian Election*. Brisbane: Australian Development Strategies.

Brennan, Frank. 2010. 'Why a conscientious Christian could vote for the Greens'. *Eureka Street*, 10 August.

Burchell, David. 2010. 'Power not a God-given right'. *The Australian*, 10–11 July.

CathNews. 2010a. 'Look at politicians' ethics not just faith: Anglican Archbishop'. *CathNews*, 2 August.

CathNews. 2010b. 'Greens closer to Christian ideals than Cardinal Pell, says Bob Brown'. *CathNews*, 9 August.

Elder, Stephen. 2010. 'A vote for the Greens is a vote against Catholic education'. *Eureka Street*, 12 August.

Fitzgerald, Ross. 2010. 'Welcome to the house of fun'. *The Australian*, 27 August.

Gleeson, Kate. 2010. Tony, Tony, Tony! Abbott and abortion. Paper to Australian Political Studies Association Annual Conference, Melbourne.

Macklin, Robert. 2007. *Kevin Rudd: The biography*. Melbourne: Viking.

McLennan, David. 2010. 'More flock to the fold under atheist Gillard'. *The Canberra Times*, 8 August.

Maiden, Samantha. 2010. 'Changing dying laws difficult, says PM'. *The Australian*, 22 September.

Manning, Hayden and Warhurst, John. 2005. 'The old and new politics of religion'. In Marian Simms and John Warhurst (eds), *Mortgage Nation: The 2004 Australian election*. Perth: API Network, 263–270.

Mullins, Michael. 2010a. 'Gillard's atheism belongs in the closet'. *Eureka Street*, 2 August.

Mullins, Michael. 2010b. 'Atheist "real Julia" courts Christian vote'. *Eureka Street*, 9 August.

Pearson, Christopher. 2007. 'Rudd's dog whistle days'. *The Australian*, 8–9 December.

Quinlan, Frank. 2010. 'Inside Canberra's Catholic lobby'. *Eureka Street*, 18 August.

Rudd, Kevin. 2006. 'Faith in politics'. *The Monthly*, October.

Sharp, Ari. 2010. 'Call for PM to outline her inspiration'. *Sydney Morning Herald*, 29 June.

Smith, Rodney. 2009. 'How would Jesus vote? The churches and the election of the Rudd Government'. *Australian Journal of Political Science* 44.

Stephens, Scott. 2010. 'The Prime Minister puts her faith in chaplaincy'. *ABC News*, 10 August.

Stockman, David 2010. 'No change to stance on gay marriage'. *The Canberra Times*, 1 July.

Stuart, Nick. 2009. 'Mixed in a miracle and a mess'. *The Canberra Times*, 22 December.

The Australian. 2010. 'The Opposition comeback at the August election forces a reassessment of the religion issue'. [*Cut and Paste*], *The Australian*, 13 September.

Warhurst, John. 2007. 'Religion and politics in the Howard decade'. *Australian Journal of Political Science* 42(1) (March): 19–32.

Warhurst, John. 2010a. 'Religion'. *Australian Cultural History* 28(1) (April): 31–37.

Warhurst, John. 2010b. 'Pell, Brown in unholy strife'. *The Canberra Times*, 12 August.

Warhurst, John. 2010c. The faith of Australian prime ministers. Presented to Australian Political Studies Association Annual Conference, Melbourne.

Young, Graham. 2010. 'It's real man versus metro man in the new culture wars'. *Online Opinion*, 2–3 January.

Zwartz, Barney. 2010. 'Ballarat blacksmith forges ahead with nod to DLP heroes'. *The Age*, 23 August.

Part 6. Election Results

26. The Results and the Pendulum

Malcolm Mackerras

The two most interesting features of the 2010 election were that it was close and it was an early election. Since early elections are two-a-penny in our system, I shall deal with the closeness of the election first. The early nature of the election does, however, deserve consideration because it was early on two counts. These are considered below. Of our 43 general elections so far, this was the only one both to be close and to be an early election.

Table 26.1 Months of General Elections for the Australian House of Representatives, 1901–2010

Month	Number	Years
March	5	1901,1983, 1990, 1993, 1996
April	2	1910, 1951
May	4	1913, 1917, 1954, 1974
July	1	1987
August	2	1943, 2010
September	4	1914, 1934, 1940, 1946
October	6	1929, 1937, 1969, 1980, 1998, 2004
November	7	1925, 1928, 1958, 1963, 1966, 2001, 2007
December	12	1903, 1906, 1919, 1922, 1931, 1949, 1955, 1961, 1972, 1975, 1977, 1984
Total	43	

The Close Election

In the immediate aftermath of polling day, several commentators described this as the closest election in Australian federal history. While I can see why people would say that, I describe it differently. As far as I am concerned, there have been 43 general elections for our House of Representatives of which four can reasonably be described as having been close. They are the House of Representatives plus half-Senate elections held on 31 May 1913, 21 September 1940, 9 December 1961 and 21 August 2010. There has, in my analysis, never been a close double-dissolution election or one for the House of Representatives only.

The 1913 and 1961 elections did not produce a hung parliament. They were so close, however, as to result in the early dissolution of the 5th Parliament and the 24th Parliament respectively. The 1940 election did produce a hung parliament, which ran its full term. (For a discussion of the expression 'full term', see below.) Eventually, we shall discover the history of the 43rd Parliament. My guess is that it will run to a full term, as did the 16th Parliament, elected in 1940.

Born in 1939, and professionally employed in politics since 1959, I have very good memories of December 1961 and August 2010. There are, in my opinion, two important differences. In 1961 two seats were very closely contested: Moreton, won by the Liberal Party, and Evans, won by Labor. In 2010 none was. For that reason, I consider 1961 to have been closer than 2010. More importantly, perhaps, the closeness of the 1961 election came as a complete shock. In contrast, in 2010 we had a predicted close election. I have been through the 2010 polling-day predictions of the experts. Every recognised analyst predicted a close result.

For 1913 and 1940, I must rely on the journalists of the day. For example, A. N. Smith wrote a magnificent book, *Thirty Years: The Commonwealth of Australia, 1901–1931*, which was published in Melbourne in 1933. Referring to the defeat of Andrew Fisher's Labor Government, he wrote, on pages 129 and 130:

> The elections took place on 31st May and were singularly inconclusive. The early counting showed that the party numbers in the House of Representatives were likely to be almost equal. For several days the result depended upon the counting of votes from the outer districts of two widely scattered electorates of New South Wales. In the Riverina Division the retiring Labor member was fiercely assailed by a strong opponent. In the adjoining Hume Division the veteran Sir William Lyne, who had supported the Labor Government, was also on the defence. The final returns were against both and the seats went to the Opposition. Against these was to be set Ballarat, vacated by Mr. Deakin, where, after a similar close contest, the seat went to Labor by a small majority.

> After ten or twelve days of doubt the Labor Party lost command of the House of Representatives by one member. Its losses included five seats in New South Wales and four in Victoria. But it won Bendigo from Sir John Quick, who had been a member of the Federal Convention, and to whom Federation owed so much, and also seats in Queensland, South Australia and Western Australia. The Liberals secured 38 seats against 37 gained by the Labor Party.

The records tell us that the second term of the Fisher Government ran from 29 April 1910 to 24 June 1913. More importantly, they tell us that in Hume the votes were 11 575 for Robert Patten (Liberal) and 11 236 for Sir William Lyne. In Riverina the votes were 11 674 for Franc Brereton Sadleir Falkiner (Liberal) and 11 208 for the sitting Labor Member, John Moore Chanter. These were close results but they were not nearly as close as Moreton in 1961. For that reason, I consider the 1961 election to have been closer than in 1913. The 5th Parliament first met on 9 July 1913 and was dissolved on 30 July 1914, so its length was one year and 21 days. Thus, here was a case of an early dissolution: a double dissolution.

The circumstances of the 1940 election are best described by Don Whitington in his book *The House will Divide*, which was first published in Melbourne in 1954. In his Chapter 9, 'The Menzies governments: 1939–1940', he writes:

> Just before the 1940 elections three senior ministers—the Army Minister, G. A., Street; the Vice President of the Executive Council, Sir Henry Gullett; and the Minister for Air, J. V. Fairbairn, were killed in an air crash near Canberra. It was alleged, but never proved, that Fairbairn was flying the machine, a service aircraft, as it approached Canberra airport to land. This was the worst misfortune the Government had experienced, for all three were capable ministers, and all were administering departments directly connected with the war effort.

> Worse was to follow, from Menzies' point of view, because at the general election in September 1940 the Government lost its majority. Government and Labor parties were returned with 36 each, two Independents holding the balance of power. Thus was ushered in what was probably the most fantastic era in Australian politics, an era in which the Commonwealth had a Government depending for survival on the votes of two Independents, but with elements within its own ranks which were not prepared to subjugate personal ambitions and prejudices to the prosecution of the war. (Whitington 1954, 73)

On page 74, in Chapter 10, 'Twelve months' turmoil', Whitington writes:

> As sometimes happens in politics, the minor issues of the 1940 election, which were virtually ignored, were more significant than the events which occupied the public eye.

> Not until the election was over, for instance, was the full importance appreciated of the two men who held the balance of power in the new Parliament. One was A. W. Coles, one of two brothers who had created what was by then one of the biggest chain store organizations in Australia; the other was Alex Wilson, a Victorian wheat farmer of the post World War I era, who, like most of his fellows, had financial dealings with the private banks about which he retained a sense of grievance.

> Coles entered the Parliament as the Independent member for the Victorian seat of Henty, but joined the U. A. P. [United Australia

Party] about eight months later. Wilson was elected as an Independent Country Party candidate, and announced that he would support the Government, though it was known his support would be conditional on the Government meeting his wishes on a number of matters, particularly financial policy.

Menzies lost the office of Prime Minister to Arthur Fadden on 29 August 1941. Then the Fadden Government was defeated in the House of Representatives on a vote described by Whitington in Chapter 10 (1954, 84–85) as follows:

> Curtin moved: 'That while agreeing that the expenditure requisite for the maximum prosecution of the war should be provided by Parliament, the Committee is opposed to unjust methods prescribed by the Budget, declares that they are contrary to equality of sacrifice, and directs that the plan of the Budget should be recast to ensure a more equitable distribution of the national burden.'

> Curtin knew—though few others did—that he would have the support of both Coles and Wilson. In a brief speech, Coles said: 'I regard the proposal of the Leader of the Opposition as a motion of want of confidence in the Government. [There is]…a loss of confidence in the Government's ability to carry on and to wage the maximum war effort. I told the Prime Minister I would vote against this Government today because he cannot give any assurance to the Parliament. He gave to the Governor-General an assurance he was not justified in giving because he had not consulted me. I told those Ministers who approached me when the ex-Prime Minister was being removed that I would not stand for it and that I would not support the Government.'

> Wilson said he would support Labor also because he disapproved of the Government's financial policy.

> Curtin's amendment was carried, and the Government resigned. Nairn, the U. A. P. Speaker, agreed to carry on under Labor, which gave it an extra vote in the House. The Curtin Cabinet was sworn in on October 7, 1941.

The truly interesting feature of the 16th Parliament is that it remained (until 2010) the sole hung parliament of the past 100 years. Yet it lasted for a full term of three years. Part of the reason for this stability was that there was a change of government during the term.

I remember the 1961 election very well indeed. From October 1959, I was a research officer with the Federal Secretariat of the Liberal Party and on polling night in 1961 I went into the tally room in Canberra with the same attitude as everybody else: Menzies was going to win, probably with minimal losses of seats. Menzies was a political genius who had always won bigger than expected so the same would happen again. There was only one opinion poll at the time. Released on Thursday, 7 December, it showed 47 per cent intending to vote Liberal-Country Party, 47 per cent for Labor and 6 per cent for the anti-Labor Democratic Labor Party (DLP)—a result that, in two-party preferred terms, represented an electorate dividing nearly 53–47 per cent in favour of Menzies. In other words, the swing to Labor was predicted to be only a little more than 1 per cent.

The polls closed at 8 pm in those days, and I gathered in the small tally room with the then Federal Director, Bob Willoughby. We were a bit shocked that Wide Bay was early looking like a loss to Labor, but it was a Country Party seat! We could not believe the figures being posted for Cowper where Sir Earle Page looked to be in trouble. In our disbelief, we asked Frank Ley, the Chief Electoral Officer, to check the Cowper figures, which, we thought, could not possibly be correct. Ley assured us they were correct. Anyway Cowper, like Wide Bay, was also a Country Party seat!

Willoughby was a bit disappointed at the emerging picture but he displayed no sign of recognising the danger to the government. *The Sun-Herald* on 10 December ran the headline 'LIBS BACK, but with a reduced majority'. Arthur Calwell was reported to have conceded defeat to reporters at 11 pm on election night. Late on that Sunday, Willoughby and I did some figure work and concluded that the probable result was a 61–61 seat draw. The press did not, however, seem fully to understand. The Monday-morning headline in the *Sydney Morning Herald* was 'Swing against Menzies grows', but the paper believed the government had been returned. In *The Canberra Times*, the swing was noted but '[t]he government will, however, retain a working majority in the House of Representatives'.

In our belief that the result would be a 61–61 draw, we were convinced there would have to be another election. If the Liberal Party agreed to provide the speakership then it would give Labor a one-seat majority. Anyway, on 18 December the result became known. The seat of Moreton in Queensland was retained by Jim Killen and the result was 62–60 in favour of Menzies.

I consider 1961 to have been our closest election so I explain by comparing Moreton in 1961 with Corangamite in 2010. In the Moreton case the final win by Killen was with a majority of 130 votes: 26 239 for Killen (Liberal) and 26 109 for O'Donnell (Labor). In percentage terms that was 50.12 per cent for Killen and 49.88 per cent for O'Donnell. In the Corangamite case, the final win by Darren

Cheeseman was with a majority of 771 votes: 47 235 for Cheeseman (Labor) and 46 464 for Sarah Henderson (Liberal). In percentage terms that was 50.41 per cent for Cheeseman and 49.59 per cent for Henderson.

The close 1961 and 2010 elections make for an interesting comparative exercise, with party roles reversed. In both cases a Queensland anti-government landslide nearly brought the government down. In both cases, however, Victoria saved the government. In both cases, the system of compulsory preferences saved the party in power. In 1961 the 80–20 distribution of DLP preferences in favour of the Coalition saved the Liberal Party the seats of Bennelong (NSW), Bruce (Vic.), Maribyrnong (Vic.) and Moreton (Qld) where Labor candidates led on the primary vote. In 2010 the 80–20 distribution of the preferences of the Greens in favour of Labor saved them the seats of Banks, Reid and Robertson in New South Wales, Corangamite, Deakin and La Trobe in Victoria and Lilley and Moreton in Queensland where Liberal candidates led on the primary vote.

The contrasts between the cases are, first, between a long-term Liberal prime minister (Bob Menzies) saved by the system and a short-term Labor prime minister (Julia Gillard) equivalently saved. Second, the Menzies 62–60 win gave him majority government, but the Gillard 76–74 win gave her only minority government. Against that it should be noted (see Table 26.5) that the Menzies Government failed to win a majority of the two-party preferred vote in 1961 whereas the Gillard Government succeeded in that respect in 2010.

The 24th Parliament first met on 20 February 1962 and was dissolved on 1 November 1963, so its length was one year, eight months and 13 days. The November 1963 general election was for the House of Representatives only, accompanied by one Senate casual vacancy election in Queensland. The 43rd Parliament first met on 28 September 2010 and we shall find out its history soon enough. I feel sure it will run full term.

The Early Election

To the best of my knowledge, I am the only person who has ever defined the term 'early election' and I shall do that below. In the meantime, I want to say something about the date 21 August, the date sensibly chosen by Julia Gillard. During the 1940s there were four general elections for the House of Representatives accompanied by the normal periodical election for half the Senate. They were held on 21 September 1940, 21 August 1943, 28 September 1946 and 10 December 1949. So the calendars for 1943 and 2010 were identical. Both in 1943 and again in 2010, the elections were the earliest in terms of the time distance from the expiry of the terms of existing senators—namely, 30

June 1944 and 30 June 2011. In 1943 the Australian people replaced a hung parliament with a Labor-majority parliament. In 2010 they did the reverse of that.

It is worth noticing that the Curtin election of 21 August 1943 was a one-option vote. There were no double-dissolution 'triggers' in 1943 so Curtin had to make it for the House of Representatives and half the Senate. In contrast, Gillard had a choice not available to Curtin: with 14 'trigger' bills on the list (11 of which related to the carbon pollution reduction scheme), there could have been a double dissolution. In the end, however, she made the same choice as Curtin. There have been three winter elections—all called by Labor prime ministers. The third was the double-dissolution election held on 11 July 1987, called by Bob Hawke. For a full list of the months of elections, see Table 26.1. That table leads me to predict that the next election will be in October 2013.

When I say I am the only person who has ever defined the term 'early election', I am referring to my article in *Politics* for May 1984 (Mackerras 1984, 73–84). In that article, I defined an early election as one that results from an early dissolution of the House of Representatives. I have kept that article up to date and the current version of it can be found on the web site of Old Parliament House where, now retired at the age of seventy-two, I am a volunteer guide.

The term 'early dissolution' is defined by me to be any dissolution occurring other than in the last six months of the life of the parliament. By definition, therefore, every double-dissolution election is an early election. Consequently, 2010 was self-evidently early. We know that because we know the double-dissolution option was available. So the three winter elections give us two early cases (1987 and 2010) and one case when the election was not early: 1943.

This was our forty-third general election for the House of Representatives and our nineteenth early election. The early elections were held in December 1903, September 1914, May 1917, December 1919, October 1929, December 1931, September 1934, April 1951, December 1955, November 1963, May 1974, December 1975, December 1977, March 1983, December 1984, July 1987, March 1990, October 1998 and August 2010.

In my article referred to above, I have a table entitled 'Early Dissolutions of the House of Representatives' in which I give all the information one needs to know. For the purpose of this chapter, the critical information is the length of the term and the reason to dissolve early. Without going into too much needless detail, I notice that the length of the first Lyons Parliament was two years, five months and 22 days, the first ('elected') Menzies Parliament, one year and 25 days, the third Menzies Parliament, one year, three months and one day, the sixth Menzies Parliament, one year, eight months and 13 days, the first Whitlam

Parliament, one year, one month and 15 days, the second Whitlam Parliament, one year, four months and two days, the first Fraser Parliament, one year, eight months and 25 days, the third Fraser Parliament, two years, two months and 10 days, the first Hawke Parliament, one year, six months and five days, the second Hawke Parliament, two years, three months and 16 days, the third Hawke Parliament, two years, five months and five days, the first Howard Parliament, two years and four months, and the Rudd–Gillard Parliament, two years, five months and seven days. Notice the striking similarity between the first Lyons Parliament and the Rudd–Gillard Parliament.

More interesting than the above, however, is the reason given by each prime minister for the early dissolution. The reason 'to preserve/restore simultaneous elections with the half-Senate' accounts for six cases: 1903, 1917, 1955, 1977, 1984 and 1990. Section 57 dissolutions (double dissolutions) also account for six cases: 1914, 1951, 1974, 1975, 1983 and 1987. There are three cases of the need for a new mandate for policies—1919, 1934 and 1998—and three cases coming under the heading 'instability in the House of Representatives': 1929, 1931 and 1963.

That left just one case for which I needed a description: the dissolution occurring on 19 July 2010. Gillard did not give one so I entered this as the reason: 'to enable Julia Gillard to become an elected prime minister.' I placed the term 'elected prime minister' in inverted commas.

Table 26.2 House of Representatives: Seats won, 24 November 2007 general election—actual

State/Territory	Labor	Liberal	Nationals	Independent	Total
New South Wales	28	15	5	1	49
Victoria	21	14	2	-	37
Queensland	15	10	3	1	29
Western Australia	4	11	-	-	15
South Australia	6	5	-	-	11
Tasmania	5	-	-	-	5
Australian Capital Territory	2	-	-	-	2
Northern Territory	2	-	-	-	2
Total	83	55	10	2	150

Table 26.3 House of Representatives: Seats won, 24 November 2007 general election—notional (including Lyne by-election)

State/Territory	Labor	Liberal	Nationals	Independent	Total
New South Wales	30	12	4	2	48
Victoria	21	14	2	-	37
Queensland	17	9	3	1	30
Western Australia	5	10	-	-	15
South Australia	6	5	-	-	11
Tasmania	5	-	-	-	5
Australian Capital Territory	2	-	-	-	2
Northern Territory	2	-	-	-	2
Total	88	50	9	3	150

Table 26.4 House of Representatives: Seats won, 21 August 2010 general election—actual

	Labor	Liberal	Nationals	Independent	Greens	Total
New South Wales	26	16	4	2	-	48
Victoria	22	12	2	-	1	37
Queensland	8	16	5	1	-	30
Western Australia	3	11	1	-	-	15
South Australia	6	5	-	-	-	11
Tasmania	4	-	-	1	-	5
Australian Capital Territory	2	-	-	-	-	2
Northern Territory	1	1	-	-	-	2
Total	72	61	12	4	1	150

Table 26.5 Aggregate Two-Party Preferred Percentages, 1940–2010

Election	Percentage Labor	Percentage UAP-Lib.-CP-Nats	Percentage swing
1940[a]	50.3	49.7	0.9 to Labor
1943[a]	58.2	41.8	7.9 to Labor
1946[a]	54.1	45.9	4.1 to Lib.-CP
1949[a]	49.0	51.0	5.1 to Lib.-CP
1951[a]	49.3	50.7	0.3 to Labor
1954[a]	50.7	49.3	1.4 to Labor
1955[a]	45.7	54.3	5.0 to Lib.-CP
1958[a]	45.9	54.1	0.2 to Labor
1961[a]	50.5	49.5	4.6 to Labor
1963[a]	47.4	52.6	3.1 to Lib.-CP
1966[a]	43.1	56.9	4.3 to Lib.-CP
1969[a]	50.2	49.8	7.1 to Labor
1972[a]	52.7	47.3	2.5 to Labor

Election	Percentage Labor	Percentage UAP-Lib.-CP-Nats	Percentage swing
1974[a]	51.7	48.3	1.0 to Lib.-CP
1975[a]	44.3	55.7	7.4 to Lib.-CP
1977[a]	45.4	54.6	1.1 to Labor
1980[a]	49.6	50.4	4.2 to Labor
1983[b]	53.2	46.8	3.6 to Labor
1984[b]	51.8	48.2	1.4 to Lib.-Nats
1987[b]	50.8	49.2	1.0 to Lib.-Nats
1990[b]	49.9	50.1	0.9 to Lib.-Nats
1993[b]	51.4	48.6	1.5 to Labor
1996[b]	46.4	53.6	5.0 to Lib.-Nats
1998[b]	51.0	49.0	4.6 to Labor
2001[b]	49.1	50.9	1.9 to Lib.-Nats
2004[b]	47.3	52.7	1.8 to Lib.-Nats
2007[b]	52.7	47.3	5.4 to Labor
2010[b]	50.1	49.9	2.6 to Lib.-Nats

Notes: [a] In respect of the 17 general elections from 1940 to 1980 (inclusive), the statistics are from *estimates* of the two-party preferred vote; [b] in respect of the 11 general elections from 1983 to 2010 (inclusive), the statistics are the percentages of the *actual* two-party preferred vote aggregates.

Table 26.6 Labor's Two-Party Preferred Percentages at Winning Elections

Election	Winner	Incumbent prime minister?	Percentage Labor
1943	Curtin	Yes	58.2
1946	Chifley	Yes	54.1
1983	Hawke	No	53.2
2007	Rudd	No	52.7
1972	Whitlam	No	52.7
1984	Hawke	Yes	51.8
1974	Whitlam	Yes	51.7
1993	Keating	Yes	51.4
1987	Hawke	Yes	50.8
2010	Gillard	Yes	50.1
1990	Hawke	Yes	49.9

House Seat Gains and Losses in 2010

In 1961, 1963, 1966 and 1969 seats in the House of Representatives changed hands only in one direction. In 1961 Labor gained 15 seats and lost none. In 1963 and 1966 Labor lost 10 and 11 seats, respectively, and made no gains. In 1969 Labor gained 20 seats and lost none.

Beginning in 1972, however, the normal pattern has been for seats to change hands in both directions. The exceptional cases were 1975 (Labor lost 28 seats and gained none), 1983 (Labor gained 22 seats and lost none), 1984 (Labor lost eight seats and gained none) and 1996 when Labor lost 33 seats and gained none. For all the 1998, 2001, 2004, 2007 and 2010 elections, seats have changed hands in both directions. The unusual nature of 2010 is the big difference with the result in 2007 when one compares the actual result (Table 26.2) with the notional result on the new boundaries in New South Wales, Queensland and Western Australia (Table 26.3). Consequently, I shall give the seat gains and losses in each of these States.

In New South Wales, Labor won 28 seats in 2007 and 26 in 2010. On an actual basis that is two losses, and one would identify the two as Bennelong and Macquarie. Only in Bennelong was a sitting Labor member defeated: Maxine McKew. If one takes the base as 30 seats, however, there were four losses: Gilmore and Macarthur, notional, and Bennelong and Macquarie, actual.

In Queensland, Labor won 15 seats in 2007 and eight in 2010. Actual losses were Bonner, Brisbane, Dawson, Flynn, Forde, Leichhardt and Longman. Additional notional losses were Dickson and Herbert. Of the new members, those in Dawson and Flynn joined the caucus of The Nationals, increasing the number of Queensland Nationals from three in 2007 to five in 2010: Dawson, Flynn, Hinkler, Maranoa and Wide Bay.

In Western Australia, the redistribution caused the Liberal seat of Swan to become notionally Labor; however, the sitting Liberal, Steve Irons, retained it. Labor lost Hasluck to the Liberal Party but Liberal Wilson Tuckey was defeated in O'Connor by Tony Crook of The Nationals.

There were no changes in party numbers in South Australia or the Australian Capital Territory. In Tasmania, Labor lost Denison to the Independent Andrew Wilkie. In the Northern Territory, Labor lost Solomon to the Country Liberals— the new member being Natasha Griggs who joined the party room of the Liberal Party. In Victoria (where there was no redistribution of seats), Labor gained La Trobe and McEwen from the Liberal Party.

American analysts of congressional elections have a term, 'retirement slump', which refers to the average fall-off in the party's vote when the incumbent retires. I think, in addition to that, the term 'retirement loss' is appropriate for Australia. The following members of our House of Representatives retired—and saw their seat lost to another party or to an Independent: Fran Bailey in McEwen, James Bidgood in Dawson, Bob Debus in Macquarie, Duncan Kerr in Denison and Lindsay Tanner in Melbourne.

Table 26.4 shows the current state of parties of the House of Representatives. As can be seen there are five 'others': the Greens Member for Melbourne and four Independents. When their intentions were finally revealed on the afternoon of Tuesday, 7 September, it was seen that only Bob Katter in Kennedy intended to support the Coalition, the others supporting Labor. This enables me to divide Table 26.4 into two: the mining States of Queensland, Western Australia and the Northern Territory, and the non-mining States of New South Wales, Victoria, South Australia, Tasmania and the Australian Capital Territory.

The 47 seats in the mining States divide 34 for the Coalition, one for the Independent (Katter) supporting the Coalition and a miserable 12 for Labor. The 103 seats in the non-mining States divide 60 for Labor, 39 for the Coalition and the four Labor-supporting 'others'. It is clear from where the Gillard Government and the Abbott opposition get their support.

My friend Martin Gordon points out that there is an alternative way to describe the above. If the outback SA seat of Grey is excluded from 'non-mining Australia' then that populous part of the country (New South Wales, Australian Capital Territory, Victoria, Tasmania and non-outback South Australia) accounts for 102 seats, of which Labor and its supporters have 64 and the Coalition thirty-eight.

Then 'mining Australia' would be Queensland, Western Australia, Northern Territory—and Grey. So the Coalition would have 36 seats in 'mining Australia' and Labor only twelve. In Grey itself, according to Gordon (in email correspondence in 2010):

> The striking thing is the swings to Liberal in Whyalla, 7.5 per cent, Port Pirie 10 per cent, Roxby Downs, 8.9 per cent, and also Andamooka and Coober Pedy. Whyalla has produced probably the best Liberal TPP vote (5,005 versus 6,461) for a long time. In fact the state seat of Giles would only have a Labor lead of 7,858 to 8,172…The Liberal TPP vote in Stuart and Frome is very impressive also.

Analysis of House Swings

Tables 26.7, 26.8, 26.9 and 26.10 set out the important information. Combining my look at these tables, I think the following observations can be made.

Table 26.7 The 10 Biggest Swings to Labor

Rank	Seat*	AEC demographic rating	% swing to Labor
1. (SS)	Kingston (Labor, SA)	Outer metropolitan	9.5
2. (SS)	Franklin (Labor, Tas.)	Outer metropolitan	6.8
3.	Lalor (Labor, Vic.)	Outer metropolitan	6.6
4.	Bass (Labor, Tas.)	Provincial	5.7
5. (SS)	Wakefield (Labor, SA)	Outer metropolitan	5.4
6. (RS)	McEwen (Liberal, Vic.)	Rural	5.3
7. (SS)	Corio (Labor, Vic.)	Provincial	5.3
8. (SS)	Braddon (Labor, Tas.)	Rural	5.2
9. (SS)	Makin (Labor, SA)	Outer metropolitan	4.5
10.	Lyons (Labor, Tas.)	Rural	4.0

SS = 'sophomore surge'

RS = 'retirement slump'

* The party shown is the one holding the seat before the 2010 election

Table 26.8 The 10 Biggest Swings to the Liberal-Nationals

Rank	Seat*	AEC demographic rating	% swing to Liberal-Nationals
1. (RS)	Fowler (Labor, NSW)	Outer metropolitan	13.8
2.	Wentworth (Liberal, NSW)	Inner metropolitan	11.0
3.	Bowman (Liberal, Qld)	Outer metropolitan	10.4
4.	Groom (Liberal, Qld)	Provincial	10.3
5.	O'Connor (Liberal, WA)	Rural	10.2
6.	Watson (Labor, NSW)	Inner metropolitan	9.1
7.	Banks (Labor, NSW)	Inner metropolitan	8.9
8.	Hinkler (Nationals, Qld)	Rural	8.9
9.	Maranoa (Nationals, Qld)	Rural	8.8
10.	Leichhardt (Labor, Qld)	Rural	8.6

RS = 'retirement slump'

* The party shown is the one holding the seat before the 2010 election

First, the Liberal National Party (LNP) performed very well in Queensland and the Liberal Party performed very well in those parts of the Sydney metropolitan area with a substantial Asian population. I argue that the sacking of Kevin Rudd was the main reason for these big swings.

Second, in the Northern Territory the Country Liberal Party (CLP) candidate for the substantially Aboriginal division of Lingiari secured a big swing. The candidate, Leo Abbott, was Aboriginal. I have not yet been able to examine the detail of swings within this division. My friend Martin Gordon has, however, done a thorough analysis and he assures me the swing was entirely due to the Aboriginal polling places. In the predominantly white polling places, there was no swing at all. In addition to this good performance in Lingiari, the CLP gained Darwin-based Solomon on a much lower swing.

Third, Julia Gillard in her western suburbs of Melbourne division of Lalor and Malcolm Turnbull in his eastern suburbs of Sydney division of Wentworth gained high levels of personal voting.

Fourth, Labor performed very well in Victoria and Tasmania.

Fifth, high levels of 'sophomore surge' were recorded. These deserve a special mention. According to Wikipedia, a sophomore surge is

> a term used in the political science of the US Congress that refers to an increase in votes that congressional candidates [candidates for the House of Representatives] usually receive when running for their first re-election. The phrase has been adopted in Australia by psephologist Malcolm Mackerras who is well-known for his electoral pendulums.

Under the heading 'etymology', it says the word 'sophomore' is commonly used to refer to someone in their second year of high school or college. Under the heading 'history', it says the phenomenon of sophomore surge was first noticed by political scientists in the 1960s.

The two biggest individual seat swings to Labor are both cases of sophomore surge. Otherwise, the two cases are rather different. Whereas Kingston is a case of South Australia as 'the State of sophomore surge', Franklin illustrates both retirement slump and sophomore surge. In 2007, Harry Quick retired from Franklin. The new Labor candidate, Julie Collins, was able to retain the seat. The swing to Liberal in Franklin in 2007 was, however, 3.1 per cent—the biggest swing to Liberal in Australia. So Franklin is the Australian equivalent of an American congressional district. First, there was retirement slump—but it was followed by sophomore surge. That is the typical American pattern.

South Australia is described above as 'the State of sophomore surge'. What is interesting about South Australia is that no division changed its member at this election. Grey, Kingston, Makin, Port Adelaide and Wakefield, however, changed their members in 2007, with Kingston, Makin and Wakefield Labor gains. In September 2008, Mayo changed its member at a by-election. In all of these six divisions, there was a swing in favour of the sitting member—the most notable cases being Kingston, Wakefield, Makin and Grey.

Table 26.9 Two-Party Preferred Votes and Swings in Each Division, 2010

Division	Votes preferring Labor		Votes preferring Lib-Nats		% swing to Lib-Nats
	Votes	%	Votes	%	
NEW SOUTH WALES					
Banks	43 150	51.4	40 719	48.6	8.9
Barton	44 742	56.9	33 941	43.1	8.1
Bennelong	40 166	46.9	45 518	53.1	4.5
Berowra	28 972	33.8	56 752	66.2	6.2
Blaxland	45 948	62.2	27 882	37.8	4.4
Bradfield	27 719	31.8	59 397	68.2	4.3
Calare (n)	35 033	39.3	54 209	60.7	7.3
Charlton	52 064	62.7	31 016	37.3	0.2
Chifley	50 103	62.3	30 268	37.7	7.3
Cook	33 450	37.3	56 138	62.7	6.3
Cowper (n)	34 691	40.7	50 477	59.3	8.0
Cunningham	56 234	63.2	32 780	36.8	3.7
Dobell	45 551	55.1	37 163	44.9	−1.1
Eden-Monaro	46 300	54.2	39 063	45.8	−1.9
Farrer	29 434	35.5	53 513	64.5	3.3
Fowler	45 178	58.8	31 704	41.2	13.8
Gilmore	38 649	44.7	47 850	55.3	5.7
Grayndler	58 789	70.6	24 450	29.4	4.2
Greenway	40 355	50.9	38 953	49.1	4.8
Hughes	38 688	44.8	47 619	55.2	4.6
Hume	36 337	41.3	51 679	58.7	3.4
Hunter (n)	50 803	62.5	30 511	37.5	3.2
Kingsford Smith	45 249	55.2	36 780	44.8	8.1
Lindsay	42 546	51.1	40 681	48.9	5.2
Lyne (n)	31 902	37.6	53 065	62.4	3.6
Macarthur	36 741	47.0	41 462	53.0	3.5
Mackellar	29 855	34.3	57 245	65.7	3.3
Macquarie	42 604	48.7	44 801	51.3	1.5
McMahon	46 170	57.8	33 690	42.2	6.0
Mitchell	27 500	32.8	56 229	67.2	7.5
Newcastle	51 220	62.5	30 744	37.5	3.4

Division	Votes preferring Labor		Votes preferring Lib-Nats		% swing to Lib-Nats
	Votes	%	Votes	%	
New England (n)	30 265	33.2	60 907	66.8	2.0
North Sydney	30 808	35.9	54 901	64.1	8.5
Page (n)	46 273	54.2	39 111	45.8	−1.8
Parkes (n)	27 946	31.1	61 789	68.9	5.2
Parramatta	42 583	54.4	35 734	45.6	5.5
Paterson	36 804	44.7	45 582	55.3	4.7
Reid	41 949	52.7	37 679	47.3	8.2
Richmond (n)	46 071	57.0	34 764	43.0	1.9
Riverina (n)	28 009	31.8	59 980	68.2	3.6
Robertson	43 520	51.0	41 821	49.0	−0.9
Shortland	52 612	62.8	31 101	37.2	1.9
Sydney	53 235	67.1	26 142	32.9	2.3
Throsby	51 909	62.1	31 662	37.9	4.7
Warringah	31 360	36.9	53 612	63.1	4.3
Watson	45 393	59.1	31 364	40.9	9.1
Wentworth	30 457	35.1	56 219	64.9	11.0
Werriwa	42 740	56.7	32 574	43.3	8.3
Total NSW	**1 958 077**	**48.8**	**2 051 241**	**51.2**	**4.8**
VICTORIA					
Aston	40 916	48.2	43 901	51.8	−3.3
Ballarat	55 188	61.7	34 251	38.3	−3.6
Batman	58 028	74.9	19 435	25.1	1.0
Bendigo	54 928	59.5	37 337	40.5	−3.4
Bruce	44 603	58.1	32 144	41.9	0.2
Calwell	61 045	69.7	26 509	30.3	−0.4
Casey	38 439	45.8	45 458	54.2	−1.7
Chisholm	43 459	56.1	33 991	43.9	1.3
Corangamite	47 235	50.4	46 464	49.6	0.4
Corio	53 083	64.2	29 578	35.8	−5.3
Deakin	41 927	52.4	38 073	47.6	−1.0
Dunkley	42 023	49.0	43 777	51.0	−3.0
Flinders	37 002	40.9	53 499	59.1	0.9
Gellibrand	61 531	73.9	21 732	26.1	−2.4
Gippsland (n)	34 199	38.5	54 513	61.5	5.5
Goldstein	36 811	43.5	47 747	56.5	0.4
Gorton	70 705	72.2	27 280	27.8	−0.9
Higgins	35 180	43.3	46 167	56.7	−0.3
Holt	60 412	63.2	35 133	36.8	−1.6
Hotham	50 394	63.5	28 966	36.5	−0.5

Division	Votes preferring Labor		Votes preferring Lib-Nats		% swing to Lib-Nats
	Votes	%	Votes	%	
Indi	33 916	40.1	50 755	59.9	0.7
Isaacs	55 721	61.0	35 594	39.0	−3.3
Jagajaga	52 868	61.5	33 075	38.5	−2.5
Kooyong	34 508	42.5	46 779	57.5	−2.0
La Trobe	45 308	50.9	43 689	49.1	−1.4
Lalor	74 452	72.1	28 736	27.9	−6.6
Mallee (n)	20 842	25.6	60 611	74.4	3.1
Maribyrnong	51 193	66.9	25 379	33.1	−1.5
McEwen	58 144	55.3	46 963	44.7	−5.3
McMillan	38 731	45.6	46 229	54.4	−0.4
Melbourne	65 473	73.3	23 854	26.7	−1.0
Melbourne Ports	48 819	57.6	36 002	42.4	−0.4
Menzies	33 811	41.3	48 102	58.7	2.7
Murray	23 882	29.7	56 666	70.3	2.1
Scullin	57 355	72.2	22 025	27.8	−1.4
Wannon	35 554	42.7	47 697	57.3	−0.2
Wills	61 297	72.6	23 091	27.4	−0.2
Total Victoria	**1 758 982**	**55.3**	**1 421 202**	**44.7**	**−1.0**
QUEENSLAND					
Blair	39 814	54.2	33 595	45.8	2.7
Bonner	38 765	47.2	43 400	52.8	7.4
Bowman	32 455	39.6	49 490	60.4	10.4
Brisbane	39 609	48.9	41 440	51.1	5.7
Capricornia (n)	43 150	53.7	37 230	46.3	8.4
Dawson (n)	39 455	47.6	43 494	52.4	5.0
Dickson	36 549	44.9	44 902	55.1	5.9
Fadden	26 356	35.8	47 236	64.2	3.8
Fairfax	34 034	43.1	45 032	56.9	4.0
Fisher	33 784	45.9	39 868	54.1	0.6
Flynn (n)	37 086	46.4	42 806	53.6	5.8
Forde	33 987	48.4	36 271	51.6	5.0
Griffith	47 007	58.5	33 405	41.5	3.9
Groom	26 589	31.5	57 912	68.5	10.3
Herbert	37 797	47.8	41 221	52.2	2.2
Hinkler (n)	31 993	39.6	48 770	60.4	8.9
Kennedy (n)	31 106	38.1	50 616	61.9	4.7
Leichhardt	36 273	45.5	43 539	54.5	8.6
Lilley	46 234	53.2	40 711	46.8	4.8
Longman	36 277	48.1	39 173	51.9	3.8

Division	Votes preferring Labor		Votes preferring Lib-Nats		% swing to Lib-Nats
	Votes	%	Votes	%	
McPherson	31 004	39.7	47 044	60.3	1.6
Maranoa (n)	23 625	27.1	63 520	72.9	8.8
Moncrieff	24 612	32.5	51 103	67.5	3.7
Moreton	41 447	51.1	39 612	48.9	4.9
Oxley	39 894	55.8	31 640	44.2	5.6
Petrie	40 097	52.5	36 267	47.5	1.7
Rankin	44 289	55.4	35 640	44.6	6.3
Ryan	38 138	42.8	50 896	57.2	6.0
Wide Bay (n)	28 029	34.4	53 484	65.6	7.2
Wright	30 049	39.9	45 358	60.1	6.4
Total Queensland	**1 069 504**	**44.9**	**1 314 675**	**55.1**	**5.6**
WESTERN AUSTRALIA					
Brand	41 610	53.3	36 418	46.7	2.7
Canning	38 303	47.8	41 818	52.2	−2.2
Cowan	34 992	43.7	45 062	56.3	5.0
Curtin	27 669	33.8	54 158	66.2	2.9
Durack	26 155	36.3	45 843	63.7	6.0
Forrest	33 257	41.3	47 343	58.7	3.3
Fremantle	45 858	55.7	36 478	44.3	3.4
Hasluck	40 774	49.4	41 722	50.6	1.4
Moore	31 901	38.8	50 302	61.2	2.3
O'Connor	22 029	27.0	59 555	73.0	10.2
Pearce	32 349	41.1	46 292	58.9	1.2
Perth	44 815	55.9	35 379	44.1	2.1
Stirling	35 832	44.4	44 775	55.6	4.3
Swan	37 710	47.5	41 729	52.5	2.8
Tangney	31 607	37.7	52 266	62.3	2.5
Total WA	**524 861**	**43.6**	**679 140**	**56.4**	**3.1**
SOUTH AUSTRALIA					
Adelaide	50 164	57.7	36 793	42.3	0.8
Barker	34 992	37.1	59 278	62.9	3.4
Boothby	42 042	49.3	43 317	50.7	−2.2
Grey	34 373	38.8	54 119	61.2	6.7
Hindmarsh	49 698	55.7	39 526	44.3	−0.7
Kingston	58 695	63.9	33 139	36.1	−9.5
Makin	53 014	62.2	32 219	37.8	−4.5
Mayo	39 201	42.7	52 702	57.3	0.3
Port Adelaide	63 295	70.0	27 084	30.0	−0.3
Sturt	41 113	46.6	47 172	53.4	2.5
Wakefield	54 528	61.9	33 485	38.1	−5.4
Total SA	**521 115**	**53.2**	**458 834**	**46.8**	**−0.8**

Division	Votes preferring Labor		Votes preferring Lib-Nats		% swing to Lib-Nats
	Votes	%	Votes	%	
TASMANIA					
Bass	37 165	56.7	28 337	43.3	−5.7
Braddon	37 650	57.5	27 855	42.5	−5.2
Denison	42 692	65.8	22 167	34.2	−0.5
Franklin	39 856	60.8	25 675	39.2	−6.8
Lyons	40 959	62.3	24 796	37.7	−4.0
Total Tasmania	**198 322**	**60.6**	**128 830**	**39.4**	**−4.4**
ACT					
Canberra	66 335	59.1	45 821	40.9	2.7
Fraser	71 613	64.2	39 928	35.8	0.9
Total ACT	**137 948**	**61.7**	**85 749**	**38.3**	**1.7**
NORTHERN TERRITORY					
Lingiari	23 051	53.7	19 876	46.3	7.5
Solomon	24 585	48.3	26 371	51.7	1.9
Total Northern Territory	**47 636**	**50.7**	**46 247**	**49.3**	**4.7**
Total Australia	**6 216 445**	**50.1**	**6 185 918**	**49.9**	**2.6**

Fairness of Our Electoral Boundaries

It is clear that Labor performed very well in Victoria and Tasmania and quite well in South Australia and the Australian Capital Territory. It is equally clear that the Coalition performed very well in the mining jurisdictions of Queensland, Western Australia and the Northern Territory. That leaves our most populous State of which the question must now be asked: who won in New South Wales?

Before I come to New South Wales, I want to give a brief consideration to the Australian Capital Territory. I argue that the swings to Liberal in both divisions were not real swings at all. They were cases of retirement slump, since both seats changed their Labor members through retirement. My basis for this assertion lies in the Senate vote. In 2007 Gary Humphries (Liberal) was elected to the second Senate seat with a quota in his own right. No distribution of preferences was necessary. In 2010, in contrast, he did not receive a quota on the first count. Before he could be elected, the surplus of Kate Lundy (Labor) needed to be distributed, then two other candidates (there were nine in all) needed to be excluded before Humphries was elected.

In New South Wales, Labor won in terms of seats but the Coalition won the two-party preferred vote (see Tables 26.4 and 26.9). That raises this question: can it be argued that the electoral boundaries in New South Wales were gerrymandered in favour of Labor? To so argue would go wholly against everything I have asserted about our federal redistributions since the electoral reforms of 1983 and 1984. I have asserted that the traditional pattern of boundaries being drawn in favour of the party in power would not happen again after those reforms.

In the case of this election, I point out that Labor won 50.1 per cent of the Australia-wide two-party preferred vote and the Coalition 49.9 per cent. The consequence in seats was that 76 recorded two-party preferred majorities in favour of the Coalition and 74 for Labor. Therefore, it is absurd to suggest that the boundaries were, in any way, loaded in favour of Labor. Quite the reverse! It is true that on my new pendulum the 76–74 distribution goes the other way; that is explained by Lyne and New England. As can be clearly seen from Table 26.9, Lyne and New England were easily won by The Nationals in terms of the two-party preferred vote. Their Independent members, however, decided to keep Labor in office.

Table 26.10 Median Seats on Mackerras Pendulum and Overall Labor Percentages Required for Government

Election year	Median seat	% swing needed	Seat held?	Coalition two-party preferred vote % at previous election	Labor % required on uniform swing
1961	Bowman (Liberal, Qld)	6.2	No	54.1	52.1
1963	Maribyrnong (Liberal, Vic.)	0.9	Yes	49.5	51.4
1966	Robertson (Liberal, NSW)	3.9	Yes	52.6	51.3
1969	Forrest (Liberal, WA)	7.8	No	56.9	50.9
1972	Griffith (Liberal, Qld)	1.6	Yes	49.8	51.8
1974	Mitchell (Labor, NSW)	1.3	No	47.3	51.4
1975	Isaacs (Labor, Vic.)	0.5	No	48.3	51.2
1977	Kingston (Liberal, SA)	6.6	Yes	55.7	50.9
1980	Fadden (Liberal, Qld)	6.1	Yes	54.6	51.5
1983	Bendigo (Liberal, Vic.)	1.4	No	50.4	51.0
1984	Dunkley (Labor, Vic.)	3.1	Yes	46.8	50.1
1987	Lowe (Labor, NSW)	2.3	No	48.2	49.5
1990	Aston (Labor, Vic.)	2.6	No	49.2	48.2
1993	Cowan (Labor, WA)	0.9	No	50.1	49.0
1996	Gilmore (Labor, NSW)	0.5	No	48.6	50.9
1998	Parramatta (Liberal, NSW)	3.9	Yes	53.6	50.3
2001	Moreton (Liberal, Qld)	0.6	Yes	49.0	51.6
2004	Eden-Monaro (Liberal, NSW)	1.7	Yes	50.9	50.8
2007	Bennelong (Liberal, NSW)	4.0	No	52.7	51.3
2010	Longman (Labor, Qld)	1.7	No	47.3	51.0
2013	Greenway (Labor, NSW)	0.9	?	49.9	49.2

Table 26.10 is entitled 'Median Seats on Mackerras Pendulum and Overall Labor Percentages Required for Government'; however, I faced a dilemma here. On the pendulum as actually published, the median seat is Greenway (Labor, NSW) where the Liberal Party needs a swing of 0.9 per cent to regain the seat. That means the overall share for Labor to govern is shown as 49.2 per cent. Those statistics only apply, however, because Lyne and New England have changed sides on the pendulum without having changed their voting patterns. If The Nationals had won both these seats then the Coalition number would have been 76 and the median seat would have been shown as Boothby (Liberal, SA), needing a swing of 0.8 per cent for Labor to win. That being so, the overall share needed for Labor to govern on the uniform-swing model would have been shown as 50.7 per cent—very close to the figure shown in the row above: the even 51 per cent.

Coming back to New South Wales, the argument to suppose a Labor gerrymander would lie in the very economical margins secured by Labor in Greenway, Robertson, Lindsay, Banks and Reid. Here I would say that good old-fashioned luck had a lot to do with those wins. I estimate the 'donkey vote' at this election in those seats to have been worth 1.2 per cent of the formal vote. It happens that Labor had the benefit of the ballot-paper draw in all five seats. If the draw had gone the other way, I think Labor would still have retained Reid but it would have lost Greenway, Robertson, Lindsay and Banks.

When I write of a 'donkey vote' in those seats to have been worth 1.2 per cent, I should mention the basis of that estimate. I went through all the preference distributions in seats in the Newcastle–Sydney–Wollongong conurbation and came up with that estimate. The single most interesting case is Reid where Christian Democratic Party (CDP) voters broke the 'how-to-vote' card that preferenced the Liberal Party. There were five candidates in Reid with the CDP first, Labor second, Greens third, Liberal fourth and Carolyn Kennett of the Socialist Equity Party bottom on the ballot paper. Kennett was first eliminated and CDP second. The CDP candidate, Bill Shailer, had 2445 primary votes and gained 167 from the Kennett distribution. His 2612 votes were distributed 1197 to Labor, 974 to Liberal and 441 to the Greens. My claim that Labor's Banks win was based on the 'donkey vote' is based on my analysis of the Greens distribution in that seat where they were on the top of the ballot paper and Labor was higher than Liberal. In Greenway and Lindsay the Labor candidate was actually on the top of the ballot paper.

Reference was made above to South Australia as 'the State of sophomore surge'. It is worth considering New South Wales in that context. Here I see a contrast between metropolitan Sydney and the country. In the north-western inner-metropolitan seat of Bennelong, Maxine McKew conspicuously failed to get any sophomore surge. I attribute that to her loss of Asian support—

a consequence of the dumping of Kevin Rudd. Also the unpopularity of the State Labor Government had the effect that she gained nothing from Julia Gillard's promise to build the Parramatta–Epping railway. McKew's fate contrasts greatly with that of Janelle Saffin in Page and Mike Kelly in Eden-Monaro. Both these country Labor members gained the benefit of sophomore surge.

The Senate Election

Given that the Australian Senate electoral system is semi-proportional rather than one of proportional representation, it is not surprising that one needs to go back to 1993 to find a truly proportional result. Indeed, depending on how one reads the Gallagher least-squares indexes of disproportionality, it can be argued that one needs to go back to 1987 to find a truly proportional result— and 1987 was a double-dissolution election in which one would expect the level of proportionality to be higher.

At this 2010 election, the Coalition won 18 seats, Labor 15, the Greens six and the Democratic Labor Party one seat—in Victoria. Table 26.12 sets out how these numbers affect the distribution of the seats in the whole Senate from July 2011. Converting percentages of votes into percentages of seats, I find that the Coalition's 38.6 per cent of votes becomes 45 per cent of seats, Labor's 35.1 per cent of votes becomes 37.5 per cent of seats and 13.1 per cent of votes for the Greens becomes 15 per cent of seats. So the big three parties are over-represented. In contrast, the category 'other' secured 13.2 per cent of the votes and only 2.5 per cent of the seats.

The senators elected in August 2010 have, from July 2011, replaced the senators elected in October 2004. For that reason it is sensible to compare the votes of 2004 and 2010. Whereas one speaks of a 'swing to the right' in the House of Representatives election (comparing 2010 with 2007), one speaks of a 'swing to the left' in the Senate election by comparing 2010 with 2004. That there was a swing to the left is made clear from Tables 26.13 and 26.14.

The seats followed the votes. In all of Queensland, Victoria and Tasmania, the left gained a seat from the right in 2010. In Queensland and Victoria that meant converting a four–two right–left distribution in 2004 into a three–three distribution in 2010, with the Greens gaining a seat in each State. In Tasmania it meant the Labor Party gaining a seat from the Liberal Party.

Can we, however, compare 2007 and 2010 and assert that the swing was to the left? Can we assert the swing was to the right? The answer is in the negative for both questions. All we can say is that the result in Tasmania was the same on each occasion: three Labor, two Liberal and one for the Greens. In the five mainland States, the distribution between left and right was three–three, both in 2007 and in 2010. The difference is simply that Labor performed better in 2007 and the Greens in 2010.

At the 2013 election can the Greens increase their Senate numbers yet again? Probably—but there is no certainty. If that election follows a double dissolution, the Greens would surely lose a seat in South Australia—and possibly in Western Australia also. If there is a premature House-only election then the half-Senate election might be deferred to May 2014. My prediction, however, is that we shall have a House of Representatives plus half-Senate election in October 2013. The Greens would have only three senators coming up for re-election—one each in Tasmania, Western Australia and South Australia. In that case it would be likely they could increase their numbers yet again.

Table 26.11 State of Parties in the Senate from 1 July 2008

Party	NSW	Vic.	Qld	WA	SA	Tas.	ACT	NT	Total
Labor	6	5	5	4	5	5	1	1	32
Liberal	4	6	5	6	5	5	1	-	32
Nationals	2	-	2	-	-	-	-	1	5
Greens	-	-	-	2	1	2	-	-	5
Independent	-	-	-	-	1	-	-	-	1
Family First	-	1	-	-	-	-	-	-	1
Total	12	12	12	12	12	12	2	2	76

Table 26.12 State of Parties in the Senate from 1 July 2011

Party	NSW	Vic.	Qld	WA	SA	Tas.	ACT	NT	Total
Labor	5	5	5	4	4	6	1	1	31
Liberal	4	4	4	6	5	4	1	-	28
Nationals	2	1	2	-	-	-	-	1	6
Greens	1	1	1	2	2	2	-	-	9
Independent	-	-	-	-	1	-	-	-	1
Democratic Labor Party	-	1	-	-	-	-	-	-	1
Total	12	12	12	12	12	12	2	2	76

Table 26.13 Labor and Liberal–Country Party–Nationals Senate Percentages

Election	Labor	Lib.–CP–Nats	Excess Lib.–CP–Nats over Labor
1949	44.9	50.4	5.5
1951	45.9	49.7	3.8
1953	50.6	44.4	−6.2
1955	40.6	48.7	8.1
1958	42.8	45.2	2.4
1961	44.7	42.1	−2.6
1964	44.7	45.7	1.0
1967	45.0	42.8	−2.2
1970	42.2	38.2	−4.0
1974	47.3	43.9	−3.4
1975	**40.9**	**51.7**	**10.8**
1977	36.8	45.6	8.8
1980	42.3	43.5	1.2
1983	45.5	39.9	−5.6
1984	42.2	39.5	−2.7
1987	42.8	42.0	−0.8
1990	38.4	41.9	3.5
1993	43.5	43.0	−0.5
1996	36.2	44.0	7.8
1998	37.3	37.7	0.4
2001	34.3	41.8	7.5
2004	**35.0**	**45.1**	**10.1**
2007	40.3	39.9	−0.4
2010	35.1	38.6	3.5
Average	41.6	43.6	2.0

Note: Cases where excess is 10 per cent or more are shown in bold.

Table 26.14 Greens Performances, 2007 and 2010

Jurisdiction	Senators	Half-Senate election 2007			Half-Senate election 2010		
		Votes	%	Total formal	Votes	%	Total formal
Australian Capital Territory	2	48 384	21.5	225 321	52 546	22.9	229 272
Tasmania	6	59 254*	18.1	326 846	67 016*	20.3	330 691
Victoria	6	320 759	10.1	3 182 369	471 317*	14.6	3 218 751
Western Australia	6	111 813*	9.3	1 202 750	172 327*	14.0	1 234 219
Northern Territory	2	8870	8.8	100 569	13 105	13.6	96 687
South Australia	6	65 322*	6.5	1 006 809	134 287*	13.3	1 009 578
Queensland	6	177 063	7.3	2 418 907	312 804*	12.8	2 450 511
New South Wales	6	353 286	8.4	4 193 234	443 913*	10.7	4 152 524
Total	40	1 144 751	9.0	12 656 805	1 667 315	13.1	12 722 233

* A senator was elected on this vote. In all there were three in 2007 and six in 2010, for a total of nine from 1 July 2011

Table 26.15 Winners and Losers for Last Senate Places, 2010

State	Quota	Last winners		Best losers	
		Fifth	Sixth	Best	Second best
NSW	593 123	Fiona Nash (Nationals)	Lee Rhiannon (Greens)	Steve Hutchins (Labor)	Glenn Druery (Liberal Democrats)
Vic.	459 822	Bridget McKenzie (Nationals)	John Madigan (DLP)	Antony Thow (Labor)	Julian McGauran (Liberal)
Qld	350 074	Larissa Waters (Greens)	Brett Mason (Liberal)	Keith Douglas (Aust. Fishing & Lifestyle Party)	Desiree Gibson (Aust. Sex Party)
WA	176 318	Judith Adams (Liberal)	Rachel Siewert (Greens)	John McCourt (Nationals)	Wendy Perdon (Labor)
SA	144 226	Penny Wright (Greens)	David Fawcett (Liberal)	Dana Wortley (Labor)	Bob Day (Family First)
Tas.	47 242	Stephen Parry (Liberal)	Lisa Singh (Labor)	Guy Barnett (Liberal)	Peter Whish-Wilson (Greens)

References

Mackerras, Malcolm. 1984. 'The Early Dissolution of the House of Representatives'. *Politics* 19(1): 73–84.

Smith, Arthur Norman. 1933. *Thirty Years: The Commonwealth of Australia, 1901–1931*. Melbourne: Brown, Prior.

Whitington, Don. 1954. *The House will Divide*. Melbourne: Lansdowne Press.

27. Electoral Behaviour in the 2010 Australian Federal Election

Clive Bean and Ian McAllister

All elections are unique, but the Australian federal election of 2010 was unusual for many reasons. It came in the wake of the unprecedented ousting of the Prime Minister who had led the Australian Labor Party (ALP) to a landslide victory, after 11 years in Opposition, at the previous election in 2007. In a move that to many would have been unthinkable, Kevin Rudd's increasing unpopularity within his own parliamentary party finally took its toll and in late June he was replaced with his deputy, Julia Gillard. Thus, the second unusual feature of the election was that it was contested by Australia's first female prime minister. The third unusual feature was that the election almost saw a first-term government, with a comfortable majority, defeated. Instead it resulted in a hung parliament—for the first time since 1940—and Labor scraped back into power as a minority government, supported by three Independents and the first member of the Australian Greens ever to be elected to the House of Representatives at a general election (previously, the Australian Greens' candidate Michael Organ was elected at a by-election in 2002). The Coalition Liberal and National Opposition parties themselves had a leader of only eight months' standing, Tony Abbott, whose ascension to the position had surprised more than a few. This was the context for an investigation of voting behaviour in the 2010 election.

The analysis in this chapter is based on the 2010 Australian Election Study (AES), conducted by Ian McAllister, Clive Bean, Rachel Gibson and Juliet Pietsch immediately following the federal election in August (McAllister et al. 2011). The data come from a national survey of political attitudes and behaviour using a self-completion questionnaire mailed to respondents just after the federal election. The survey was based on a systematic random sample of enrolled voters throughout Australia, stratified by State, drawn by the Australian Electoral Commission (AEC). After the initial mailing, the response rate was boosted by several follow-ups to non-respondents. The final response rate was 42 per cent. The data were weighted to reflect population parameters for gender, age, State and vote, giving a final sample size of 2061.

Campaign Orientations

The election was held less than two months after the replacement of Rudd with Gillard, with that event still clearly on people's minds. Nonetheless, public attention to the campaign was no greater than in the last election in 2007 and less in some respects, although it was greater for the most part than at the elections of 2001 and 2004 (Table 27.1). Fewer voters than in 2007 took a general interest in the election campaign (34 per cent compared with 40 per cent in 2007) or cared which party won (68 per cent compared with 76 per cent). Levels of attention to the campaign through the media, on the other hand, were almost identical to 2007, with 62 per cent, 77 per cent and 48 per cent saying they paid a good deal or some attention to the campaign in newspapers, television and radio respectively in 2010. Attention to the campaign via the Internet, however, almost doubled, with 29 per cent of the AES sample saying they paid attention to the campaign on the Internet in 2010, compared with 16 per cent three years earlier.

Another question asking respondents whether they used the Internet to get news or information about the election showed a similar increase—the proportion rising from 20 per cent in 2007 to 36 per cent in 2010. The 2010 percentage is four times what it was back in 2001 and it would be surprising if we were not seeing such strong growth in the use of the Internet for political purposes. Table 27.1 also shows that some 47 per cent said they watched the televised leaders' debate, held early in the campaign—almost identical to 2007. Nearly four in 10 (37 per cent) judged Gillard to have won the debate against Tony Abbott, with only 22 per cent awarding the contest to the Leader of the Opposition.

Table 27.1 Engagement with the Election Campaign, 2001–10 (per cent)

	2001	2004	2007	2010
Took 'a good deal' of interest in the election campaign overall	31	30	40	34
Cared 'a good deal' which party won	65	72	76	68
Paid 'a good deal' or 'some' attention to the campaign:				
in newspapers	53	57	61	62
on television	69	69	77	77
on radio	43	44	50	48
on the Internet	-	-	16	29
Used the Internet for election news or information	9	12	20	36
Watched the televised leaders' debate	40	35	46	47
Thought Howard (2001–07)/ Gillard performed better in the debate	18	25	13	37

Sources: Australian Election Study, 2001 (n = 2010), 2004 (n = 1769), 2007 (n = 1873) and 2010 (n = 2061).

For some time there has been evidence that the numbers of voters leaving their final voting decision until into the election campaign is increasing in various democracies (McAllister 2002). In Australia, however, this trend, which developed pace in the 1990s (Bean and McAllister 2000), reversed in the early part of this century to the point where in 2007 it was back to the low levels of the 1980s (Bean and McAllister 2009). But the uncertain context of the 2010 election sent the proportion of late-deciding voters back up to near the levels of the late 1990s, with 47 per cent saying they definitely decided how they would vote during the election campaign (Table 27.2). At the same time, 29 per cent said they seriously thought of giving their first-preference vote in the House of Representatives to a different party from the one for which they eventually voted.

Table 27.2 Volatility, Stability and Partisanship, 2001–10 (per cent)

	2001	2004	2007	2010
Decided definitely how to vote during campaign period	41	39	29	47
Seriously thought of giving first preference to another party in the House of Representatives during election campaign	29	25	23	29
Always voted for same party	48	50	45	52
Identifier with one of the major parties	77	77	77	78
Not a party identifier	15	16	16	14
Very strong party identifier	19	21	25	19

Sources: Australian Election Study, 2001 (n = 2010), 2004 (n = 1769), 2007 (n = 1873) and 2010 (n = 2061).

Party identification, which declined somewhat in the late 1990s (Bean and McAllister 2000, 183), has been very steady since the beginning of the twenty-first century. A little less than 80 per cent of the electorate now identifies with one of the major parties (78 per cent in 2010) and about one in six or seven claims not to be a party identifier at all (14 per cent in 2010). Given the volatile nature of the 2010 election, as reflected in the success of Independent candidates and minor parties and in the suboptimal outcome for the two major parties, it is perhaps a little surprising that party identification did not slip further in 2010. In continuing to exhibit relatively high levels of party identification, even in such circumstances, Australia stands apart from many other countries, where party loyalties have been in decline over the past few decades (Dalton and Wattenberg 2000; Webb et al. 2003; White and Davies 1998). On the other hand, the proportion of very strong identifiers has settled back to where it had been (19 per cent) after an increase in 2007 that now appears to have been an aberration rather than the beginning of a trend.

Socio-Demographics and the Vote

While relationships between social structure and voting are now consistently weaker than they used to be (McAllister 2011), the extent to which demographics and social location align with support for different political parties nevertheless continues to warrant attention. With the first female prime minister contesting an Australian national election, gender is a variable of particular interest. The traditional association between gender and party, in which women voted more conservatively than men, has not been in evidence in Australia for some time (Bean and McAllister 2009). The evidence for 2010 suggests that having a woman leading the government might make a difference to how women vote, with 8 per cent more women giving their first-preference vote in the House of Representatives to the Labor Party than men, and 9 per cent more men voting Liberal-Nationals than women (Table 27.3). This, of course, represents a reversal of the traditional gender gap.

Table 27.3 Gender, Age, Region, Religion and Vote, 2010 (per cent)

	Labor	Lib-Nats	Greens	Other	(n)
Gender					
Male	36	50	12	2	(976)
Female	44	41	13	2	(977)
Age group					
Under 25	37	41	19	3	(189)
25–44	43	39	17	2	(666)
45–64	43	44	11	2	(707)
65 and over	33	61	4	2	(391)
Region					
Rural	35	51	11	3	(434)
Urban	42	44	13	1	(1502)
Religious denomination					
Catholic	41	48	9	2	(510)
Anglican	35	56	8	1	(385)
Uniting	38	53	6	3	(220)
Other	38	47	13	2	(297)
No religion	45	32	21	2	(534)
Church attendance					
At least once a month	34	54	8	4	(300)
At least once a year	41	50	8	1	(440)
Less than once a year	31	51	17	1	(313)
Never	45	39	15	2	(885)

Source: Australian Election Study, 2010 (n = 2061).

Reminiscent of the 2004 election, in 2010, Labor fared badly with both young and old voters, despite the fact that the more usual pattern is for Labor to show a significant degree of appeal to younger voters (Bean 2007). The Greens, who usually attract good support from the young, appear to have been the main beneficiary again on this occasion, while the advantage enjoyed by the Coalition among voters aged sixty-five and over has grown quite large, with the Greens as well as Labor faring particularly poorly among this cohort.

The traditional urban–rural divide remained clearly in evidence in 2010, with the Coalition favoured in rural areas. With respect to religion, Protestant denominations preferred the Coalition, as usual, and those with no religion preferred Labor or the Greens. Catholics, however, although more favourable to Labor than Protestants, were more inclined to opt for the Coalition than Labor—a situation that, though unusual in Australian electoral history, has occurred before—in the elections of 1996 and 2004 (Bean 2000; Bean and McAllister 2005). For the other dimension of religion—church attendance—as we have come to expect, frequent attenders favoured the Coalition and non-attenders Labor (and the Greens), but in between the patterns lacked consistency.

Table 27.4 turns the focus to socioeconomic status variables. In terms of education, the Coalition appears to have done best among electors who have some post-school education but not at the university level, while the Greens did particularly well among the university qualified (with 20 per cent of such voters giving the Greens their first preference). In attracting the votes of the university educated in such large numbers, the Greens completely eliminated the advantage Labor has had over the Coalition among this group in recent elections (Bean and McAllister 2009).

Table 27.4 Education, Occupational Indicators and Vote, 2010 (per cent)

	Labor	Lib-Nats	Greens	Other	(N)
Education					
No post-school qualification	43	46	10	1	(594)
Non-degree qualifications	39	49	9	2	(785)
University degree	39	39	20	2	(541)
Occupation					
Manual	46	42	10	2	(549)
Non-manual	37	47	14	2	(1199)
Employment					
Self-employed	27	60	12	1	(292)
Government employee	48	36	14	2	(447)
Trade union membership					
Union member	53	31	14	2	(426)
Not a union member	36	50	13	2	(1412)

Source: Australian Election Study, 2010 (n = 2061).

Table 27.4 also shows that the tendency in recent elections for the strength of occupational voting to be variable (Bean and McAllister 2009; McAllister 2011) continued in 2010. Once the rock of Australian electoral choice, class voting (as measured by the difference between the non-manual vote for Labor and the manual vote for Labor) has dipped below 10 per cent at some recent elections, but has reached as high as (a still modest) 17 per cent at others (Bean and McAllister 2009). In 2007 it was 15 per cent. In 2010, class voting was down again, at 9 per cent, continuing the trend for it to be up at one election and down at the next.

The last two sections of Table 27.4 show that employment sector and trade union membership continue to shape the vote. For instance, 48 per cent of government employees reported voting Labor, compared with 27 per cent of the self-employed, while 53 per cent of union members voted Labor compared with 36 per cent of voters who were not members of a trade union.

Leader Evaluations

Party leader evaluations play a consistently significant role in Australian elections, although, despite some speculation to the contrary, there is little indication that their impact is on the rise (Senior and van Onselen 2008). The impact of leadership varies in different circumstances. In 2010, the presence of a female prime minister, as well as the fact that both major-party leaders were relatively new in their roles, generated additional attention for the leadership factor. Compared with past elections, in 2010, no leader rated highly. Table 27.5 has the relevant data. Gillard herself received a mean rating of 4.9 (on a scale where zero represents a strong dislike, five represents a neutral position and 10 represents a strong liking for the leader). While not a strong rating, it was considerably higher than that for Abbott, whose mean score was only 4.3. Ironically—but probably of no surprise to many—the politician with the highest rating was deposed leader Rudd, who slightly outdid his successor by recording a mean rating of five. A question in the AES, specifically included to gauge voter reactions to the overthrow of Rudd, found that virtually three-quarters of the electorate (74 per cent) disapproved of the way the leadership change was handled by the Labor Party.

Table 27.5 Ratings of Leaders and Parties, 2010 (means on 0–10 scale)

Leader	Mean	Std dev.	Party	Mean	Std dev.
Julia Gillard	4.9	3.1	Labor	5.1	3.0
Tony Abbott	4.3	3.1	Liberal	5.1	3.3
Warren Truss	4.1	2.2	Nationals	4.3	2.7
Bob Brown	4.1	2.9	Greens	4.2	3.0
Wayne Swan	4.0	2.5			
Kevin Rudd	5.0	3.1			

Source: Australian Election Study, 2010 (n = 2061).

The Labor and Liberal parties as such were more popular with the public than the party leaders—both recording mean ratings of 5.1. The leaders of the smaller parties—Warren Truss of The Nationals and Bob Brown of the Greens—were also marginally less popular than the parties they led.

The data in Table 27.6 also show that gender again played a role in leadership evaluations (see also Denemark et al. 2011). Women rated Gillard considerably higher and Abbott somewhat lower than men. Viewing the same information from a different perspective, we see that men rated Gillard and Abbott equally (both at 4.5), while there was a very large difference among women in favour of Gillard, who received a mean rating of 5.3 among women compared with Abbott's four. Two other patterns stand out in Table 27.6. Abbott was the only politician of the six included in the survey who was rated more favourably by men than by women. As well as Gillard, Truss, Brown, Wayne Swan and Rudd all had higher scores among women than among men. As a result, at least in the election of 2010, women voters emerged as having a considerably more positive view of politicians overall than men. The mean rating of the six leaders by women was 4.6. The mean rating by men was 4.3. And the final point of interest in Table 27.6 is that Rudd was almost as popular among women as Gillard.

Table 27.6 Ratings of Party Leaders by Gender, 2010 (means on 0–10 scale)

Leader	Men mean	Std dev.	Women mean	Std dev.
Julia Gillard	4.5	3.1	5.3	3.0
Tony Abbott	4.5	3.0	4.0	3.1
Warren Truss	4.0	2.1	4.2	1.9
Bob Brown	3.8	3.0	4.5	2.8
Wayne Swan	3.9	2.6	4.1	2.4
Kevin Rudd	4.8	3.1	5.2	3.0

Source: Australian Election Study, 2010 (n = 2061).

Gillard's advantage over Abbott remained when individual leadership qualities were examined. Respondents were asked how well a list of leadership qualities described each of the two major-party leaders. Gillard outscored Abbott on all nine items. Gillard's best quality was deemed to be her intelligence (87 per cent of AES respondents judging this quality to describe her extremely or quite well), followed by her being seen as knowledgeable. She also was rated highly for being competent and sensible, while at the other end of the scale she was not seen as trustworthy or inspiring. Interestingly, Abbott's image largely shadowed Gillard's—at both ends of the scale—but always with lower proportions of voters rating him well on the particular trait and in some cases much lower. The only instances in which the difference between Abbott and Gillard was minimal occurred with respect to traits on which both were judged poorly: trustworthiness, honesty and, to a lesser extent, strength of leadership.

Table 27.7 Leadership Qualities Ascribed to Julia Gillard and Tony Abbott, 2010 (percentage saying quality describes leader extremely well or quite well)

Quality	Julia Gillard	Tony Abbott
Intelligent	87	69
Compassionate	58	44
Competent	70	54
Sensible	70	48
Provides strong leadership	58	52
Honest	48	43
Knowledgeable	78	57
Inspiring	42	28
Trustworthy	40	36

Source: Australian Election Study, 2010 (n = 2061).

Issues

The policy issues debated in election campaigns involve a mix of the perennial and the topical. Recent research on Australian elections has pointed to the importance of issues for voting choice and election outcomes (Goot and Watson 2007) in contrast with the conventional wisdom that election campaigns and therefore election issues make very little difference (see, for example, Aitkin 1982). The 2010 AES asked respondents to rate 12 issues in terms of their importance (Table 27.8). Health is always on the agenda in modern elections. But irrespective of how prominent they are in the parties' campaigns, the issues of health and Medicare are invariably the issues of most concern to voters. And so it was yet again in 2010, with 73 per cent of voters saying the issue was extremely important—clearly ahead of any other issue. Next came management of the economy (70 per cent rated it extremely important) and then education (with 61 per cent seeing it as extremely important).

Table 27.8 Importance of Election Issues (percentage describing issue as extremely important) and Party Differential (percentage saying Labor closer on issue minus percentage saying Liberal-Nationals closer), 2010

Issue	Importance					Party differential
	All voters	Labor voters	Lib-Nats voters	Greens voters	Other voters	
Global warming	30	40	16	55	33	+11
Taxation	40	37	46	34	40	−6
Education	61	67	55	67	63	+17
Unemployment	40	45	38	34	43	+7
The environment	41	48	28	72	43	+13
Interest rates	43	43	48	31	42	−9
Industrial relations	28	35	22	29	31	+9
Health and Medicare	73	78	70	71	74	+11
Refugees and asylum-seekers	37	32	42	37	46	−17
The resources tax	30	25	37	22	38	−5
Population policy	32	30	36	26	37	−5
Management of the economy	70	68	80	51	74	−9

Source: Australian Election Study, 2010 (n = 2061).

No other issue had as many as 50 per cent calling it extremely important. In fact the drop-off to the next issue was huge—nearly 20 per cent. Interest rates (43 per cent), the environment (41 per cent), taxation and unemployment (both 40 per cent) were next, but a very long way behind. Two topical issues in the campaign, the mining resources tax and population policy, rated only 30 per cent and 32 per cent respectively. Likewise, global warming was seen as extremely important by only 30 per cent of the sample and industrial relations rated least important of all with 28 per cent.

Of the three top issues, the far right-hand column of Table 27.8 shows that Labor had an advantage on health and education, in that voters reported that Labor's policies on these issues came closer than the Coalition's policies to their own views, while the Coalition had an advantage on management of the economy. Labor's advantage on education in particular was quite large, with 17 per cent more voters saying the Labor Party was closer to them on this issue than the Coalition.

The middle columns of Table 27.8 demonstrate that the concerns of Labor voters largely mirrored those of the electorate as a whole. Labor voters showed particular concern about health and education. The concerns of Liberal-Nationals voters represented greater extremes, with 80 per cent citing management of the economy as extremely important, on the one hand, and only 16 per cent showing such concern about global warming, on the other. Coalition voters also displayed a relative lack of concern about the environment in general and considerably more concern than Labor voters about the resources tax. As would be expected, the environment was the greatest concern for Greens voters, albeit closely followed by health and with education also not far behind. Greens voters showed a comparative lack of concern about management of the economy, but were much more concerned than others about global warming.

Explaining the Vote

But how much if at all did these issues and other factors matter for the decision by individual voters to give their first-preference votes to one party over another? To round out the analysis, we look collectively at the key variables we have been considering above to estimate their independent impact on the vote in the 2010 election. This is achieved through the application of multivariate analysis that estimates the net effect of each factor on the vote while controlling for all the others. The analysis includes each of the socio-demographic variables examined earlier in the chapter, the party leader ratings and the campaign issues, plus party identification. For ease of presentation, only the variables whose effects are statistically significant are shown in Table 27.9. Methodological details are provided in Appendix 25.1.

Table 27.9 Multivariate Analysis of Significant Influences on Voting Behaviour, 2010

	Non-standardised regression coefficient	Standardised regression coefficient
Gender (male)	0.03	0.03
Education (university degree)	0.03	0.03
Religious denomination (Catholic)	0.04	0.04
Region (rural)	0.03	0.03
Party identification	0.55	0.52
Julia Gillard	−0.24	−0.16
Tony Abbott	0.15	0.10
Education	0.08	0.06
Management of the economy	0.13	0.10

Note: R-squared = 0.74. Entries in the table are statistically significant at $p < 0.05$ or better. Further methodological details can be found in Appendix 25.1.

Source: Australian Election Study, 2010 (n = 2061).

Table 27.9 shows that four socio-demographic variables—gender, education, religious denomination and region of residence—had statistically significant effects on the vote in 2010, albeit of very modest size. With all other factors in the model taken into account, males, the university educated, Catholics and rural residents all showed a greater inclination to vote Liberal-Nationals rather than Labor compared with females, those without a university degree, Protestants (the reference category for religious denomination in the multivariate analysis) and urban residents. For gender and religion, these results represent the reverse of the traditional associations between these variables and the vote (McAllister 2011), and in the latter case it means that Labor can no longer claim to always be the party that attracts the Catholic vote.

It remains important to emphasise, however, the small size of all these social-structural effects, particularly in contrast with party identification, which as usual had far and away the largest effect. The non-standardised regression coefficient shows that Liberal-Nationals identifiers were 55 per cent more likely to vote for the Coalition parties than Labor identifiers after all the other variables were taken into account.

Though small by comparison, leadership, too, had a significant impact on voting behaviour in 2010 and larger than at some recent elections (Bean and McAllister 2009; Senior and van Onselen 2008). Voters who strongly liked Gillard were 24 per cent more likely to vote Labor rather than Liberal-Nationals compared with voters who strongly disliked her (the negative sign in front of the coefficient in Table 27.9 simply indicates that positive sentiment towards Gillard was associated with a preference for Labor). By the same token, voters who strongly liked Abbott were 15 per cent more likely to vote Liberal-Nationals than those who strongly disliked him. Interestingly, there was no effect for the man who had been prime minister until less than two months before the election: Kevin Rudd.

Of the 12 issues included in the analysis, only two had statistically significant effects on the 2010 vote. Not surprisingly, given the focus on economic management during the global financial crisis over the two years leading up to the election, management of the economy was the strongest issue, with those who rated it as extremely important and were closer to the Coalition on the issue some 13 per cent more likely to vote Liberal-Nationals than Labor compared with those who rated economic management as extremely important and were closer to Labor on the issue. Education, which has become more prominent as an issue in recent times (Bean and McAllister 2009; McAllister 2011), was the other significant issue, although its effect was more modest. Issues such as health and taxation, which have consistently affected voting behaviour over the past two decades (Bean and McAllister 2009), did not reach statistical significance on this occasion. And no other issues featured, including the topical issues of population policy and taxing of the mining industry.

But what did the influence of the two leaders and the two significant issues on individual voting choice mean for the outcome of the election? We can make such calculations by combining estimates of their effects on individual voting behaviour with the extent of bias inherent in each variable towards one major party or the other. The technicalities of the calculations are detailed in Appendix 25.1. We have already seen in the earlier parts of the chapter, for instance, that the Coalition had an advantage among the electorate on management of the economy, while Labor had an advantage on education, and that Gillard was more popular (or, to be strictly correct, less unpopular) than Abbott.

By combining the effect (the regression coefficient) and the bias towards Labor or the Coalition (derived from the mean of the variable), we are able to estimate the net impact of each variable on the balance of the party vote. These calculations show that, ironically, each of the party leaders conferred a benefit, not on their own party, but on the rival party. In Gillard's case, it was very small (about 0.2 per cent), while for Abbott it was more than 1 per cent, reflecting his substantially greater unpopularity. Combining the two, we arrive at a net leadership effect of 0.9 per cent in favour of the Labor Party.

The two significant issues, on the other hand, virtually cancelled one another out. Management of the economy produced a net effect of 0.7 per cent to the Coalition, while education produced a net effect of 0.6 per cent to Labor, giving the barest advantage of 0.1 per cent to the Liberal-National parties for the two issues together. Subtracting this from the 0.9 per cent leadership effect, we get an overall effect for leaders and issues of 0.8 per cent in favour of Labor. While this advantage might seem slim, its significance is seen when we consider that in the final vote count in the 2010 election the Labor Party edged out the Coalition by an extremely narrow margin of 50.1 per cent to 49.9 per cent in the two-party preferred vote.

Thus, in the end, amidst such a closely fought election, the leadership factor was crucial. Both major parties approached the election with leaders who were relatively inexperienced, untried and who lacked popularity within the electorate. But Abbott's greater unpopularity meant that the toll was higher for the Coalition than for Labor. All other things being equal, the analysis in this chapter suggests that had the Coalition gone to the 2010 Australian federal election with a leader who was viewed more favourably across the electorate, the outcome probably would have been a narrow victory for the Liberals and Nationals.

References

Aitkin, Don. 1982. *Stability and Change in Australian Politics*. [Second edn]. Canberra: Australian National University Press.

Bean, Clive. 2000. 'Who now votes Labor?'. In John Warhurst and Andrew Parkin (eds), *The Machine: Labor confronts the future*. Sydney: Allen & Unwin, 73–88.

Bean, Clive. 2007. 'Young people's voting patterns'. In Lawrence J. Saha, Murray Print and Kathy Edwards (eds), *Youth and Political Participation*. Rotterdam: Sense Publishers, 33–50.

Bean, Clive and McAllister, Ian. 2000. 'Voting behaviour'. In Marian Simms and John Warhurst (eds), *Howard's Agenda: The 1998 Australian election*. Brisbane: University of Queensland Press, 174–192.

Bean, Clive and McAllister, Ian. 2005. 'Voting behaviour: not an election of interest (rates)'. In Marian Simms and John Warhurst (eds), *Mortgage Nation: The 2004 Australian election*. Perth: API Network, 319–334.

Bean, Clive and McAllister, Ian. 2009. 'The Australian election survey: the tale of the rabbit-less hat. Voting behaviour in 2007'. *Australian Cultural History* 27: 205–18.

Dalton, Russell J. and Wattenberg, Martin P. (eds). 2000. *Parties without Partisans: Political change in advanced industrial democracies*. Oxford: Oxford University Press.

Denemark, David, Ward, Ian and Bean, Clive. 2011. Gender and leader effects in the 2010 Australian election. Paper prepared for presentation at the International Political Science Association Conference: What Ever Happened to North–South?, 16–19 February, São Paulo, Brazil.

Goot, Murray and Watson, Ian. 2007. 'Explaining Howard's success: social structure, issue agendas and party support, 1993–2004'. *Australian Journal of Political Science* 42: 253–76.

McAllister, Ian. 2002. 'Calculating or capricious? The new politics of late deciding voters'. In D. M. Farrell and R. Schmitt-Beck (eds), *Do Political Campaigns Matter? Campaign effects in elections and referendums*. London and New York: Routledge, 22–40.

McAllister, Ian. 2011. *The Australian Voter: Fifty years of change*. Sydney: UNSW Press.

McAllister, Ian, Bean, Clive, Pietsch, Juliet and Gibson, Rachel. 2011. *Australian Election Study, 2010: Codebook*. Canberra: Australian Social Science Data Archive, The Australian National University.

Senior, Philip and van Onselen, Peter. 2008. 'Re-examining leader effects: have leader effects grown in Australian federal elections, 1990–2004?'. *Australian Journal of Political Science* 43: 225–242.

Webb, Paul, Farrell, David and Holliday, Ian (eds). 2003. *Political Parties at the Millennium: Adaptation and decline in democratic societies*. Oxford: Oxford University Press.

White, John Kenneth and Davies, Philip John (eds). 1998. *Political Parties and the Collapse of the Old Orders*. New York: State University of New York Press.

Appendix

The results shown in Table 27.9 are based on ordinary least squares multiple regression with pair-wise deletion of missing data. The dependent variable—first-preference vote for the House of Representatives in the 2010 federal election—is scored 0 for Labor, 0.5 for minor parties and Independent candidates and 1 for Liberal-Nationals. Similarly, party identification is scored 0 for Labor, 0.5 for minor parties or no party identification and 1 for Liberal-Nationals. Apart from age, scored in years, all other independent variables are either 0–1 dummy variables or scaled to run from a low score of 0 to a high score of one.

The issue variables are derived from a combination of the importance ratings and the party closer to the respondent, so that at one end of the scale those who rated the issue as extremely important and felt closer to the Labor Party on the issue are scored 0 and at the other end those who rated the issue as extremely important and felt closer to the Coalition parties on the issue are scored one.

The calculations for the effects of the leaders on the balance of the party vote involve taking the difference between the neutral point of 0.5 on the 0–1 leadership rating scale and the mean score for each leader and multiplying that by the non-standardised regression coefficient for the leader. This is perhaps the best of several defensible ways of calculating leadership effects on the balance of the party vote (Senior and van Onselen 2008:233–6). So for Gillard, the calculation was $0.49 - 0.5 = -0.01$ x $-0.24 = 0.2$ per cent to the Coalition. For Abbott, the calculation was $0.43 - 0.5 = -0.07$ x $0.15 = 1.1$ per cent to Labor. These two results are then added together to arrive at the net leadership impact on the vote of 0.9 per cent to Labor.

Similarly, the calculation for the impact of each significant issue on the party balance involves subtracting the neutral point on the 0–1 scale of 0.5 from the mean of each variable and multiplying that difference by the non-standardised regression coefficient for the variable. For education, the difference score was −0.08 (and the regression coefficient 0.08) and for management of the economy the difference was 0.05 (and the regression coefficient 0.13).

28. Seventeen Days to Power: Making a minority government

Brian Costar[1]

The 2010 federal election produced two major surprises. A first-term government whose electoral position had seemed unassailable as recently as six months earlier was almost defeated; had it been, it would have been the first to suffer that fate since the Great Depression election of 1931. And Australia witnessed the first 'hung' parliament—an 'unavoidable idiom' (Justice Committee 2010, 2; 7)—and subsequent minority government since the one that emerged from the 1940 election when the nation was at war. The first of these surprises is the subject of detailed analyses in the earlier chapters of this volume. This chapter's purpose is to examine the dynamics of the 17 days from 21 August to 7 September, which produced a minority Labor administration supported by three Independents and one Greens MP. Tempting as it is to provide a day-by-day account, this chapter emphasises the major issues and developments during those days against the background of political and personal ambition and established constitutional principles—with many of the latter appearing novel to some of the contestants and commentators.

Responses

As soon as it became clear that neither the Australian Labor Party nor the Liberal-National party Coalition was likely to obtain a clear majority (76 of 150 members) in the House of Representatives, observers were quick to prognosticate as to the implications for the future and especially the economic future. There were pessimists, generally in the business sector and the media, and optimists, generally among political scientists. Some predicted 'an unprecedented period of political uncertainty' (Marks 2010) blighted 'by minority rule without any clear policy mandate' (Stuchbury 2010) because the 'stability of the de facto two-party system has…been shaken' (Ashdown 2010). Many business leaders and financial journalists were concerned about the lack of economic certainty that could 'stifle' Australia's economic reforms (Asiamoney.com 2010) because 'business owners and investors in business love certainty' and regard 'policy negotiation' as 'romantic' and 'decidedly unstable and short-term' (Bouris 2010). Not all of business was so despondent: Shane Oliver, chief economist at

---

1   I would like to thank Peter Browne of the Institute for Social Research at Swinburne University for his assistance in the preparation of this chapter.

AMP Capital, drew attention to the fact that the Senate was frequently 'hung', which meant that 'having to negotiate policy through parliament has always been a fact of life in Australia' (Asiamoney.com 2010).

In fact, some of the more senior business-oriented economists were in the optimist (or, at least, realist) camp. Ed Shann, a former Treasury official and now an independent economist, expected that the hung Parliament would actually improve public policy debate 'because the minority government would be forced to provide better information to the Parliament and the public'. He was not fazed by the possibility of 'ineffective' government because Australia's economic growth was driven by external factors and the independent Reserve Bank would control monetary policy and inflation (Shann 2010). Saul Eslake, the former chief economist at ANZ Bank now working for the Grattan Institute, agreed and predicted accurately that the financial markets would not be panicked by the inconclusive election result because they had experience of minority governments in Europe and elsewhere—including the Australian States. He argued that those experiences 'don't justify the conclusion that hung parliaments necessarily result in bad or ineffectual governments, at least from a business or financial markets perspective' (Eslake 2010).

Others had more specific hopes, with Frank Zumbo, a consumer-law academic, welcoming a minority government of either persuasion because it would 'dampen the power of the faceless power-brokers' and open up the policy debate 'about the poor state of our competition laws' (Zumbo 2010). A more sectional angle was represented by a journalist at the rural *Weekly Times*, who looked forward to a 'bonanza' for the 'bush' because of the likelihood of three regional Independents being 'kingmakers' in the new Parliament (White 2010).

The political-science optimists generally were more concerned with accountability and the capacity of a hung parliament to restrain the executive arm of government. John Uhr of The Australian National University represented the consensus by making the early prediction of a transformation in politics for at least the next three years because the big parties would have to negotiate with Independents in the lower house and, after 1 July 2011, with the Australian Greens in the Senate. While he thought it unlikely that a hung parliament would occur twice in a row, open government, and parliamentary and electoral law reforms enacted during the next three years 'might prove difficult to reverse even under a majority government' (Mannheim 2010).

It is not surprising that the first federal hung parliament in 70 years was regarded as a novelty given that, other than in the Senate, Australia's two-party-dominant configuration has proved remarkably resistant to the political fragmentation common in comparable Western democracies. At the last federal election to produce a hung parliament, in 1940, the Coalition and Labor each won 36 seats and two Independents held the balance of power.[2] The two initially supported Prime Minister Robert Menzies, but in 1941—by which time Menzies (like Kevin Rudd in 2010) had been removed by his party—they switched their support to Labor and John Curtin became Prime Minister. Political historian Rodney Cavalier has fairly judged that the hung Parliament of 1940–43 'served Australia well' (Cavalier 2010), but the passage of time and the vastly different circumstances of a world war reduce its comparative relevance to the twenty-first century.

Of course, Australia has had much more recent experience of hung parliaments and minority governments. At various times since 1989, all the States and Territories have been governed by minority administrations, some of them more than once and some for a considerable period (Griffith 2010, 11–37). The last was formed as recently as March 2010 in Tasmania when, following the State election, a minority Labor government was sustained in office by the Greens, one of whom joined the cabinet and another of whom was appointed a parliamentary secretary. Nevertheless, as numerous as these recent examples are, they have occurred only in the sub-national jurisdictions in a federation in which the central government is far more powerful and important.

The Crossbenchers

Australians expect to know the result of federal elections within hours of the close of voting. But this was the first genuinely close election since 1961, and its impact on the final composition of the House of Representatives was not settled until more than a week later. Yet it was clear from election night that neither Labor nor the Coalition would harvest the 76 seats necessary to form a majority administration. This immediately brought into play the crossbench MPs, some of whose votes would be required to create and sustain a government. Who were they? The three sitting Independents, each of whom was comfortably returned, were Bob Katter, in the Queensland division of Kennedy, and NSW Independents Tony Windsor, in New England, and Rob Oakeshott in Lyne. On election night they were joined by two new members not formally aligned with Labor or the Coalition: Adam Bandt, who won the division of Melbourne for the Australian Greens, and Tony Crook of the WA Nationals, who defeated long-term Liberal MP Wilson Tuckey in the division of O'Connor.[3] Four days

---

2   In fact, it was slightly more complex than that, with the Coalition actually winning 37 seats but including the highly 'independent' Country Party Member for Wimmera, Alex Wilson; the Victorian Country Party was then deeply divided over its support for the federal Coalition. The one Independent was Arthur Coles who, despite being a member of the United Australia Party, won the Victorian division of Henty as a 'non-party' candidate (Martin 1993:302 ff.).

3   Tony Crook described himself as a member of 'The Nationals Western Australia' rather than as a member of the federal Coalition. He was reluctant to attend Coalition party meetings and decided to sit on the

after polling day, these five were joined by Independent Andrew Wilkie, who wrested the Tasmanian division of Denison from Labor despite securing only 21 per cent of the primary vote.

Given that the crossbench MPs, the Prime Minister, the Leader of the Opposition and their senior colleagues and advisers would all be involved in negotiations to produce a government, the personalities and political backgrounds of the players were of significance. Katter, Windsor and Oakeshott all represented regional constituencies (commonly referred to as 'rural') and were experienced politicians at either federal or State level. All three had previously been associated with The Nationals but had departed it in acrimony; in Windsor's case the breach ran so deep that he responded to election-night criticism from The Nationals Senator Barnaby Joyce by describing him as 'a fool' (Murphy and Arup 2010). Windsor had been in a similar position once before, as one of three Independents who had supported the Greiner Coalition Government in New South Wales when it almost lost office at the 1991 election; later that year, he was a signatory to an agreement with the government that ushered in a series of parliamentary reforms.[4] Andrew Wilkie had an entirely different background: once a member of the Liberal Party, he joined the Greens and ran unsuccessfully against John Howard in Bennelong in 2004. A former army officer, he had resigned as an intelligence analyst with the Office of National Assessments in 2003 'in protest at the Howard government's deceitful justification for joining in the invasion [of Iraq]' (Wilkie 2010, ix). Bandt, an industrial lawyer, had been a branch member of the Labor Party but contested the seat of Melbourne for the Greens in 2007 before winning it in 2010. Crook was a product of the often rancorous relations between the Liberal and Nationals parties in Western Australia and his attitude to supporting the federal Coalition was unpredictable. In short, despite commentary linking four of the six to the conservative side of politics, none of them had a strong emotional attachment to the non-Labor parties.

Negotiating Government

On Wednesday, 25 August, the Independents gathered in Canberra to begin discussions with the major parties and each other. After meeting Julia Gillard and Tony Abbott, they were joined by Adam Bandt before a large audience at the

---

crossbenches, but his uncertain affiliation meant he played little part in the negotiations over government formation.

4   Among the reforms were a referendum on four-year parliamentary terms (which was held and passed), a referendum on the independence of the judiciary (also passed) and the introduction of parliamentary estimates committees and whistleblower protection for public servants. According to Rodney Smith (2006:157), 'most of the reforms were achieved in some part, easily making the "fabulous fiftieth parliament" the period in which independents played the greatest legislative role since 1910'.

National Press Club. Their presentation was a relatively light-hearted affair with little policy or other detail revealed, though the bonhomie on display suggested that the four could operate as a bloc—or, as they described themselves, 'the gang of four' (Murphy and Arup 2010). As to be expected, the crossbenchers were on the receiving end of an avalanche of 'advice'—some public and some private. The News Limited Press, supported by conservative radio commentators, strongly pushed them in the direction of a Coalition minority government (ABC 2010c) because they represented 'conservative' electorates. On 4 September, *The Australian* continued its campaign with the publication of Newspoll findings that suggested voters in the three Independents' seats wanted them to support the Coalition.

A range of commentators and political figures argued that the Independents had a 'moral' duty to support whichever party won a 'majority' (ABC 2010a). This contention—of dubious constitutional provenance—became a moving narrative, with seats, first-preference and two-party preferred votes used interchangeably as the decisive factor (Brent 2010). Privately, they were bombarded with phone, email, text and tweet messages. Senator Bill Heffernan created controversy when he phoned Rob Oakeshott's home and introduced himself as 'the devil'—apparently a habitual greeting for this high-profile parliamentarian. Unfortunately, Oakeshott's wife, who took the call, 'thought it was a kook and hung up'. Heffernan later tried to apologise (Coorey 2010a).

The pressure on the three regional Independents—much of it partisan, ahistorical or misinformed—continued until day seventeen. Commentator Tony Smith was scathing in his assessment of the role of the media: 'the independents have been treated contemptuously…as opportunists, impractical idealists and vengeful egotists', which he explained was the result of too many journalists' inability to transcend the 'in–out' nature of the Westminster system (Smith 2010, 5).

Enter the Governor-General

Because of majority results in the 27 successive federal elections held since 1940, the role of the Governor-General in choosing a prime minister has been constitutionally anodyne. As constitutional expert Anne Twomey has correctly observed: 'While the role and powers of the Governor-General in relation to the formation of government in a hung Parliament are uncertain to the extent that they are not codified, they are strictly confined by convention' (Twomey 2010, 25). Yet memories of Remembrance Day 1975—when the Governor-General dismissed a government because of its failure to secure the passage of supply through the Senate—remain strong within the political class, and the novel 2010 result raised questions about the role of the Governor-General in the event of a prolonged political impasse.

Few, however, expected that the family circumstances of the current incumbent, Quentin Bryce, would emerge as a mooted impediment to her exercising her constitutional functions. But on 23 August it was reported that, among others, 'a leading Australian ethicist', Dr Leslie Cannold (Tedmanson 2010), was arguing that Ms Bryce should play no part in the process of forming a new government because her daughter was married to Bill Shorten MP, a parliamentary secretary in the Gillard Government. 'It is important for the Governor General to recognise there is at least the appearance of a conflict and that she should excuse herself from deciding who forms the next government' (Cannold 2010; Tabakoff 2010).

Untroubled by the principle of the separation of powers, a prominent barrister, Peter Faris QC, suggested that the Chief Justice of the High Court could deputise for the Governor-General (Gibson and Welch 2010). The Chief Justice himself, Robert French, did not directly respond to Faris, but made it clear that, unlike in 1975, neither he nor the other High Court justices would be tendering advice to the Governor-General (Gordon et al 2010). Constitutional precedent, practice and convention provided little support to the Cannold/Faris contentions, but the Governor-General prudently sought the formal advice of the Solicitor-General as to whether her family circumstances created 'any constitutional or other legal impediment to the proper exercise of my functions' (Bryce 2010). His response was clear and unequivocal:

> The functions of the Governor-General are of the highest constitutional order. The circumstances in which the Governor-General might conceivably come to perform those functions in the exercise of the Governor-General's own deliberative judgment are, by definition, extraordinary...Yet the maintenance of the capacity of the Governor-General to act in such circumstances is critical. The notion that the Governor-General might in such circumstances be constitutionally inhibited in the performance of her functions by reason of a perception of bias or of a conflict of interest is one that, in my opinion, finds no foothold in the structure or text of the constitution. (Gageler 2010a, 2)

Consequently, he advised that the 'marriage of her daughter to Mr Shorten gives rise to no constitutional or other legal impediment to the proper discharge of her functions of office' (Gageler 2010a, 4).

The Negotiations Continue…

Meanwhile, the negotiations among the big parties and the crossbench MPs were proceeding in the expectation that they would involve a series of 'agreements' covering areas of parliamentary and electoral reform as well as policy commitments. The first of these—between Labor and the Greens—was somewhat peripheral to the actual task of forming government but did formalise Adam Bandt's commitment to Labor (Greens 2010). Its significance lay in the fact that from 1 July 2011 the Labor and Greens senators would constitute a majority in the upper house and have the capacity to influence (positively or negatively) the legislative agenda of a government of either party. The agreement contained a series of policy objectives, especially in the area of the environment, and proposed parliamentary and electoral reforms.

It was overshadowed, however, by the release, later on the same day (1 September), of the Treasury's economic analysis of the Coalition's election policies. Tony Abbott had initially resisted any such costing on the grounds that it could be subject to political interference by ministers, but relented when the Independents became insistent. The Coalition's economic creditability took a blow when Treasury identified a $3.5 billion shortfall in its costings. The next day, Andrew Wilkie controversially rejected a $1 billion offer from Tony Abbott to rebuild a hospital in his home State of Tasmania, describing it as 'reckless'. He also announced that he had entered a formal agreement to support Labor in supply and confidence votes (ABC 2010b). Labor could now count on 74 House of Representatives votes to the Coalition's 73, which meant that the decisions of Katter, Windsor and Oakeshott would determine who became prime minister.

The Decision

Needless to say, many of the exchanges among the three Independents, the parties and their advisers were and remain confidential. But a valuable snapshot into the deliberations of Katter, Windsor and Oakeshott was provided by ABC TV's *Four Corners* program, which was permitted to film some of their meetings. The program ('The deal': ABC 2010c), which aired on 4 October 2010, revealed the friendship and respect that had developed between the three and also the pressure they were under to come to a decision. Each was insistent that the needs of regional and rural Australia were paramount, but it remained uncertain whether they could maintain unity. The parliamentary arithmetic meant that Tony Abbott needed the votes of all three to become prime minister whereas Julia Gillard needed only two.

Katter was the first to announce his intention. While Katter's choice seemed to have been reached at the eleventh hour, there had been earlier indications of his final direction. During the negotiations Katter had described himself 'as the anti-Greens Member of Parliament' and was very uncomfortable with the agreement struck between the Greens and Labor on 1 September (ABC 2010c, 5). Significantly, he did not attend the briefings on climate change given to the other Independents by Lord Nicholas Stern and Professor Ross Garnaut. It was also reported that he had assembled a new team of advisers during the interregnum, some with Liberal Party connections, who convinced him to moderate his criticisms of the Coalition. Finally, he produced a 20-point negotiation list, which he put to Julia Gillard and Tony Abbott on 2 September on the basis that his support would go to whoever endorsed the bulk of it. Given that the document demanded there be no carbon or mining tax and no emissions trading scheme, it was not surprising that Labor rejected it. In fact, some accused Katter of structuring the document to achieve that very outcome (ABC 2010c, 10).

Katter's two Independent colleagues also made it clear to him that 'we're not going to make a decision based on your judgment of your 20-point plan' (ABC 2010c, 11). In a delayed, dramatic and lengthy media conference on the afternoon of 7 September, both declared that they would support a minority Labor administration on supply and confidence votes and treat ordinary legislation on its merits, thus ensuring that Julia Gillard would continue in the office of prime minister.

Given that it was the decision by Windsor and Oakeshott that ultimately determined who took government, it is important to examine their motives. They claimed that the three major policy issues that influenced them were regional education, the National Broadband Network (NBN) and climate change, and that in each case Labor's position was closer to their views than the Coalition's (ABC 2010c, 11). Policy was doubtless important, but so were political imperatives. As early as one day after the election, Rob Oakeshott publicly commented that the Independents 'would have to take into account the make-up of the Senate' (AAP 2010). Had the Independents installed a minority Coalition government it would have faced a Labor–Greens majority after 1 July 2011, which might well have curtailed or amended its legislation—including items negotiated with the Independents. Of greater significance was the strong desire of the Independents to avoid an early election and the likelihood of a return to majority government. Not only might this endanger the various policy and parliamentary reform agreements the Independents had negotiated with the big parties, but also their 'balance of power' influence would evaporate. Given the relative performances of the big parties at the 2010 poll, the Independents reckoned that a Coalition minority government would be more inclined to call an early election than a Labor one.

Tony Windsor and Rob Oakeshott then signed formal agreements with the Prime Minister and her deputy, Wayne Swan. These comprised four parts: a covering letter detailing proposed initiatives in each one's electorate; the 'agreement' proper, which related to supply and confidence and access of the Independents to the Prime Minister and other ministers; Annex A, which contained detail of proposed reforms to parliamentary and governmental procedures; and Annex B, which committed the government to a broad range of regional policy initiatives. The covering letters contained some remarkably local and specific commitments; Oakeshott, for example, was promised the 'upgrade of the Bucketts Way at Krambach—the main regional road between Gloucester and Taree' (Gillard 2010). The agreement signed, the second Gillard Government was sworn into office by the Governor-General on 14 September 2010.

Parliament and Pairs

It would be wrong, however, to suggest that the issue of parliamentary reform was altogether drowned in a sea of last-minute pork-barrelling. Annex A of the Prime Minister's agreement with the Independents, which dealt with parliamentary reform, had been negotiated by Rob Oakeshott and agreed to by both Labor and the Coalition earlier in the 17-day period. While it contained many important changes to the working of the House of Representatives, it was not particularly far-reaching and largely mirrored procedures that had operated in the Senate for many years. One of the perennial issues it addressed was the question of how to increase the 'independence' from party influence of the Speaker of the House. One clause required that 'both the Speaker and Deputy Speaker will, when in the Chair, be paired' (Gillard 2010, Annex A, 2.1). Even before the new Parliament sat, a controversy arose as to whether such an unusual arrangement was constitutionally permissible. In a parliament in which the majority is wafer thin, the granting of permanent pairs can provide the government with an additional buffer against defeat. Soon after the government was sworn in, Opposition Leader, Tony Abbott, began to express concerns over his earlier offer to pair the Speaker—especially as rumours persisted that Rob Oakeshott might take up the post (Massola 2010).

The pertinent section of the Constitution was Section 40, which states: 'Questions arising in the House of Representatives shall be determined by a majority of votes other than that of the Speaker. The Speaker shall not vote unless the numbers are equal, and then he shall have a casting vote.'

Pettifer's *House of Representatives Practice* explains that

> the pairs system…is an *unofficial* [his emphasis] arrangement…which enables a Member from one side of the House to be absent for any votes when a Member from the other side is to be absent at the same time or when…a member abstains from voting. By this arrangement…the relative voting strengths are maintained. (Harris 2005, 278)

Hitherto, the Australian Parliament had no experience of the granting of pairs to presiding officers. To clarify the matter, the government asked the Solicitor-General to provide advice on whether there was a constitutional impediment to a pairing arrangement involving the Speaker. The short answer was 'no', but the provisos and qualifications contained in the detail of his advice effectively nullified any numerical advantage the government might have been seeking. He advised that no arrangement could confer on the Speaker a deliberative vote, nor could it deprive him of a casting vote. He also agreed that the entire arrangement 'could only be voluntary'—meaning, of course, that it could be vetoed by the Opposition (Gageler 2010b).

Shadow Attorney-General, Senator George Brandis, went further and advised Tony Abbott that 'to extend pairing arrangements to the speaker would, in effect, be to treat the speaker's vote, proleptically, as if it were a deliberative vote, which is a plain violation of the prohibition section 40' (Brandis quoted in Drape 2010). Whether for constitutional or political reasons, the Opposition confirmed it would not grant a pair to the Speaker. When the Parliament met on 28 September, Labor's Harry Jenkins was elected to serve a second term, the only minor controversy being that Labor and some of the crossbenchers elected Liberal MP Peter Slipper as his deputy over the Opposition's official nominee, Bruce Scott, who was chosen as Second Deputy Speaker (Australian Parliamentary Debates 2010, 29).

Minority Government and the Future

The first session of the 43rd Parliament met on 28 September and rose for the Christmas recess on 25 November. Given the dramas of the election and the post-election period, it was a relatively mundane affair. Fifty-six bills passed the House of Representatives and the government lost only three divisions—none of them on legislation. An early indication that there had occurred at least some changes to the rules of the parliamentary game was the passage of the Evidence Amendment (Journalists' Privilege) Bill 2010, which strengthened the law permitting journalists to protect the identity of their source. Its significance lay in the fact that it was sponsored by Independent MP Andrew Wilkie and became the first Private Member's Bill to pass the House since 1996. The voting patterns of the six crossbenchers were unremarkable, save for one exception. Windsor, Oakeshott, Wilkie and Bandt were government loyalists whereas Crook gave 28 votes to the Coalition and only eight to the government. The surprise was Bob Katter who, despite his endorsement of a minority Coalition administration, voted with Labor in 22 of 33 divisions (Horne 2010, 7). Veteran press gallery correspondent Laura Tingle was positive in her end-of-year assessment of the performance of the new-look Parliament:

> Despite all the dire predictions [and]…despite the disappointment of newspaper editors determined to see it as an unmitigated disaster, the end-of-term report on how the hung parliament has been working must be that it has been operating effectively, whether at the level of a clearing house of ideas or as a legislative workhorse. (Tingle 2010)

Sceptics might respond that these are very early days and that the government's 'majority' is so precarious that its collapse and a consequential early election are inevitable. History does not support such a prediction: the 1940–43 hung Parliament ran its term despite experiencing a change of government, and so have the post-1989 State and Territory minority Parliaments. It is true that the loss by Labor of just one of its seats to a Coalition candidate in a by-election[5] would imperil its position, but even then an election would not be likely. Assuming big-party loyalty and a split of the crossbenchers four to two for Labor, the government would be left with 74 deliberative votes (exclusive of the Speaker) to the Coalition's 75, paving the way for the moving of a constructive vote of no-confidence. If such a vote were carried, convention and precedent would require Julia Gillard to resign as prime minister and advise the Governor-General to commission Tony Abbott. In the unlikely event that Gillard advised a dissolution of the House, it would quite properly be refused.

The only politically plausible path to an early election would be if Prime Minister Gillard, with her House 'majority' intact and emboldened by positive opinion polls, advised a dissolution to attempt to gain a party majority. As well as being a breach of an agreement with Tony Windsor and Rob Oakeshott that the next election will be held in September or October 2013, any election held before August of that year would be for the House of Representatives only, with a separate half-Senate election required to be held later for those senators set to retire in mid-2014. Even if the preconditions for a double-dissolution election were in place, Section 57 of the Constitution dictates that it could not be held

---

5   While there have been 37 by-elections for the House of Representatives since 1980, only three have been occasioned by death (one a suicide). It is an actuarial fact that members in the twenty-first century are much younger, fitter and healthier than those in earlier parliaments.

after April 2013. It is possible that Australia will have a different government before the end of 2013, but it is improbable that an election will occur before then.

References

Australian Associated Press (AAP). 2010. 'Independents to back "stable government"'. *Australian Associated Press*, 22 August.

Australian Broadcasting Corporation (ABC). 2010a. 'Labor back in front as election lead see-saws'. *ABC News*, 31 August, <http://www.abc.net.au/news/stories/2010/08/31/2998169.htm>

Australian Broadcasting Corporation (ABC). 2010b. 'Wilkie announces support for Labor'. *7.30 Report*, 2 September, ABC TV, <www.abc.net.au/7.30/content/2010/s30001110.htm>

Australian Broadcasting Corporation (ABC). 2010c. 'The deal'. [Program transcript]. *Four Corners*, 4 October, <www.abc.net.au/4corners/content/2010/s3029262.htm>

Australian Parliamentary Debates. 2010. House of Representatives, 28 September, *Australian Parliamentary Debates*.

Ashdown, Neil. 2010. 'Election 2010: independents hold balance of power in Australian coalition negotiations'. *Global Insight*, 26 August.

Asiamoney.com. 2010. 'Australia's politics takes on a Green hue'. *Asiamoney.com*, 1 September.

Bouris, Mark. 2010. 'Hazards lurk in minority rule'. *The Sunday Telegraph*, 29 August.

Brent, Peter. 2010. 'Who won the national vote?'. *The Australian Online*, 24 August, <http://blogs.theaustralian.news.com.au/mumble/index.php/theaustralian/comments/who_won_the_national_vote/>

Bryce, Quentin. 2010. Letter to Gageler, S., Solicitor-General, 23 August, Government House, Canberra.

Cannold, Leslie. 2010. 'How some manipulators have hijacked GG's moves'. *The Sun-Herald*, 29 August.

Cavalier, Rodney. 2010. 'Hung parliament in wartime was one of our best'. *The Australian*, 2 September.

Coorey, Phillip. 2010a. 'Liberal identified as making "Rambo-style" devil call'. *Sydney Morning Herald*, 30 August.

Coorey, Phillip. 2010b. 'The seven steps to power'. *Sydney Morning Herald*, 26 August.

Drape, Julian. 2010. 'Pairing Speaker not on, says Brandis'. *Sydney Morning Herald*, 22 September.

Eslake, Saul. 2010. 'Where is the vision?'. *The Age*, 25 August.

Gageler, Stephen. 2010a. *In the Matter of the Governor-General: Opinion*, SG No. 33 of 2010, 26 August.

Gageler, Stephen. 2010b. *In the Matter of the Office of Speaker of the House of Representatives: Opinion*, SG No. 37 of 2010, 22 September.

Gibson, Joel and Welch, Dylan. 2010. 'G-G seeks advice over possible conflict of interest in family link'. *Sydney Morning Herald*, 24 August.

Gillard, Julia. 2010. Letters to T. Windsor and R. Oakeshott, 7 September, Prime Minister, Parliament House, Canberra.

Gordon, Michael, Gibson, Joel and Welch, Dylan. 2010. 'GG in bind over Labor ties'. *The Age*, 24 August.

Greens. 2010. *Greens–Labor Agreement. 2010*, <www.greens.org.au>

Griffith, Gareth. 2010. *Minority governments in Australia 1989–2009: accords, charters and agreements*. Background Paper No. 1/10. Sydney: NSW Parliamentary Library Research Service.

Harris, I. C. [Pettifer, J. A.]. 2005≥ *House of Representatives Practice*. [Fifth edn]. Canberra: Department of the House of Representatives.

Horne, Nicholas. 2010. *Hung Parliaments and Minority Governments*. Canberra: Parliamentary Library, Parliament of Australia.

Justice Committee. 2010. *Constitutional processes following a general election— fifth report*, 16 March. London: House of Commons, UK Parliament.

Katter, Bob. 2010. 'Bob Katter's 20-point wish list'. *Sydney Morning Herald*, 3 September.

Mannheim, Markus. 2010. 'Hung parliament may help openness'. *The Canberra Times*, 23 August.

Marks, Kathy. 2010. 'Now Australia gets a taste of hung parliaments'. *The Independent* [UK], 23 August.

Martin, A. W. 1993. *Robert Menzies: A life. Volume 1: 1894–1943*. Melbourne: Melbourne University Press.

Massola, James. 2010. 'Clear rules against independent speaker, says George Brandis'. *The Australian*, 22 September.

Murphy, Katharine and Arup, Tom. 2010. 'Independents use their power to get a good deal'. *The Age*, 26 August.

Shann, Ed. 2010. 'Transparency is the best policy'. *Australian Financial Review*, 26 August.

Smith, Rodney K. 2006. *Against the Machines: Minor parties and independents in New South Wales*. Sydney: Federation Press.

Smith, Tony. 2010. 'All MPs have independents envy'. *Eureka Street* 20(16) (27 August).

Stuchbury, Michael. 2010. 'The economic costs of a fractured parliament could break us'. *The Australian*, 28 August.

Tabakoff, Nick. 2010. 'Question of G-G's partiality—2010 nation in the balance'. *The Daily Telegraph*, 23 August.

Tedmanson, Sophie. 2010. 'Family politics are election decider dilemma for the Governor-General; Australia'. *The Times* [London], 24 August.

Tingle, Laura. 2010. 'Fears of chaos somewhat overblown'. *Australian Financial Review*, 26 November.

Twomey, Anne. 2010. *The Governor-General's role in the formation of government in a hung parliament*. Legal Studies Research Paper No. 10/85, August. Sydney: Sydney Law School.

White, Leslie. 2010. 'New seat of power for rural people'. *Weekly Times*, 25 August.

Wilkie, Andrew. 2010. *Axis of Deceit: The extraordinary story of an Australian whistleblower*. [Second edn]. Melbourne: Black Inc. Agenda.

Zumbo, Frank. 2010. 'Happy to be left hanging'. *Mercury*, 3 September.

www.ingramcontent.com/pod-product-compliance
Lightning Source LLC
Chambersburg PA
CBHW061217270326
41926CB00028B/4665

* 9 7 8 1 9 2 1 8 6 2 6 3 2 *